- CREDITS -

Design: Aaron Rosenberg

Additional Design: Robert J Schwalb (Cerberus, Legendary Animals, additional ~~~~~~~~~~~~~~~~), Scott Bennie (original Mass Combat and Piety rules from T*estament: Roleplaying in the Biblical Era*).

Editing: Christina Stiles

Development: Robert J Schwalb

Art Direction and Graphic Design: Hal Mangold

Cover Art: James Ryman

Interior Art: Caleb Cleveland, Kent Burles, Joe Wigfield, Lisa Wood, Jonathan Kirtz, Britt Martin, Drew Baker & Beth Trott

Cartography: Shawn Brown

Executive Producer: Chris Pramas

Green Ronin Staff: Steve Kenson, Nicole Lindroos, Hal Mangold, Chris Pramas, Evan Sass, and Robert J Schwalb

Printed in the U.S.A.

GREEN RONIN PUBLISHING

P.O. Box 1723
Renton, WA 98057-1723

Email: custserv@greenronin.com
Web Site: www.greenronin.com

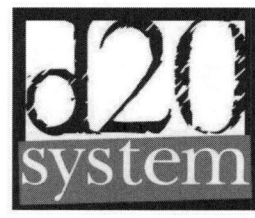

GREEN RONIN PUBLISHING

TABLE OF CONTENTS

TABLE OF CONTENTS

– INTRODUCTION –

INTRODUCTION: THE TROJAN WAR & THE HOMERIC AGE

Vast armies face each other across a broad plain, filling the field with a sea of spear tips, shields, and helmet plumes. Powerful warriors stalk about, marshaling their troops and confronting foes directly, their frames and features almost godlike in grace and strength. From a high tower within the walled city, a woman watches, her beauty the catalyst of all this bloodshed. The gods themselves observe, and frequently intervene. And on the battle rages, day after day, year after year.

Welcome to the *Trojan War*.

Immortalized in Homer's epic poem the *Iliad* and in dozens of lesser works, it is perhaps the most famous battle of all time. Few people in the modern world have not heard of Helen of Troy, whose face could launch a thousand ships, and of the Trojan Horse, settling the decade-long conflict. Most people who have read any literature have encountered references to Odysseus (also known as Ulysses) and Achilles. Adaptations of the epic can be found in plays, novels, movies, and television series.

And now, you can play a part in that epic struggle.

This book, the newest in the Mythic Vista series, details the Trojan War. It examines both sides of the conflict, and discusses the forces arrayed against Troy and those standing in its defense. More importantly, this book converts the battle into a campaign setting, offering new character classes, feats, skills, equipment, and other details based upon the war and its participants. Inside, you will find suggestions on how to enter that story, both as players and as GMs, so you can carve a space for your own adventures, yet still maintain the continuity of the original tale.

The most important thing to remember when playing the *Trojan War*, however, is that the battle was not among men alone. The gods took sides, and often stepped in to protect their favorites or target their enemies. Because all the combatants worshipped the same gods, this war was not a clash of ideologies. Both sides prayed to Zeus, Apollo, Athena, and others, and the gods quarreled amongst themselves as to which side should win. Some gods even switched sides during the war, or helped indiscriminately, even capriciously. Zeus, the king of the gods, switched sides more than did any of the other gods. One day, he defended an army, only to attack it the next. In many ways, though the Trojan War involved hundreds of thousands of men, it was really a battle among a handful of powerful warriors, a chess game where even those warriors proved mere pieces in the hands of their gods.

So, if you want to play in a world where the gods answer prayers directly, and where a man and his sword can win fame by sweeping through the enemy ranks, and where honor and wits are just as important as strength and size, start reading.

RUNNING A TROJAN WAR CAMPAIGN

The Trojan War is a perfect setting for a fantasy game. It was an era filled with heroes and gods and a time when many brave warriors rose to prominence and won immortal fame—usually by besting equally powerful warriors in the opposing army. Because the gods involved themselves directly, a *Trojan War* campaign can have as much magic as the GM wants, or as little. Monsters can appear, particularly in the hills or waters near the battlefield, and treasures may abound, or be totally absent. Moreover, the GM has a ready-made structure for events—he knows exactly when Achilles leaves the battle, that he dies before he comes back, and even how the conflict will end.

Of course, knowing all that does not mean the GM has to follow it. GMs should use Homer's work as a guideline rather than a boundary. Take whatever you like from *the Iliad* and *the Odyssey*, and then create your own stories using that as a framework. If your players want to play Achilles and Odysseus and the other Achaean leaders, you can start your game at any time during the war and let them alter events by their actions. If they decide to play Hector, Sarpedon, and the other Trojan heroes, perhaps they can actually save Troy from destruction. By playing in this setting, you are creating your own stories based upon the originals, and you are not required to follow them in every detail. The setting provides you with all the trappings you need to create a good story, but you and your players can then develop that story on your own, just as Homer developed his.

The most important elements to a *Trojan War* campaign are the constant conflict, the frequent intercession of the gods, the hunger for wealth and glory, and the sense that this was a moment when the greatest of men could shine. As long as your game includes these aspects, and the general feel of the era, it will be a proper *Trojan War* campaign. Do not build a story about merchants or common sailors—that is not the essence of the Homeric story. Focus upon the hero. It is how his choices and actions alter the course of an entire nation that makes a *Trojan War* campaign.

CHAPTER ONE: THE EPICS

This chapter summarizes the events described in the various epics, including the war, the events leading up to it, and the events following after.

BEFORE THE WAR

We have all heard how Paris' theft of the beautiful Helen started the Trojan War, but it really began with an apple.

Of course, the apple was no normal piece of fruit. The goddess Eris, or Discord, who had not been invited to the nuptials of Thetis, the water nymph daughter of Poseidon, and Peleus, chose to attend anyway. And as a sign of her displeasure at being slighted, she threw a golden apple among the guests at the reception banquet. The apple bore an inscription: "For the Fairest."

The mortal women present knew they could not compete with the beauty of the goddesses, so they simply ignored the stranger and her odd gift. But the goddesses, on the other hand, fell victim to their own vanity, and they argued about who most deserved the apple. Hera, Athena, and Aphrodite all claimed it, and their bickering filled the hall. Since they could not agree, and no one else present dared to displease the deities by choosing one of the others, the goddesses decided to select an impartial observer: the mortal Paris, a shepherd and prince of Troy.

The three goddesses approached Paris, and demanded he chose the most beautiful among them. Each goddess offered him a reward in turn. Hera promised him wealth and dominion over the world. Athena promised him wisdom and victory in war. Aphrodite, the goddess of love, promised him Helen, the most beautiful woman in the world. Naturally, Paris awarded Aphrodite the apple.

Aphrodite then led Paris to Sparta, and aided him in seducing Helen away from her husband, King Menelaus. For nine days, Menelaus entertained his royal guest, but then the King left for Crete to attend the funeral of his grandfather Catreus. After Menelaus' departure, Paris persuaded Helen to accompany him to Troy, and the two lovers fled into the night.

When the King returned home and discovered the betrayal, he swore to avenge himself and to retrieve Helen. As king of Sparta, a city of warriors, he marshaled his army, and prepared to set sail. But that was not the extent of the matter.

Everyone believed Helen, the daughter of Zeus and Leda, to be the most beautiful woman in the world. Because of this, many men sought her hand in marriage, including numerous kings. Helen's foster father, King Tyndareus, worried selecting one man among the suitors would cause war between all. But Odysseus, who had desired Tyndareus' niece Penelope, offered a solution: in exchange for Penelope, Odysseus instructed the king to demand all the suitors swear an oath, pledging to defend the marriage rites of the chosen man. The suitors agreed to this, and swore their oaths before the gods. Thus, when Paris abducted Helen, Menelaus and Agamemnon, his brother and king of Mycenae, gathered their troops. They rallied the former suitors, whose oaths bound them to support the venture against Troy, and their soldiers. This combined force is referred to collectively as the Achaeans—other names include the Danaans or the Argives, though, for simplicity's sake, this text uses Achaeans.

When the people of Troy saw this massive navy approach, Troy's King Priam ordered his people to prepare their defenses. The nine dynasties recognizing him as their overlord joined Priam's army.

Not everyone wanted to participate in the coming battle. Odysseus feigned insanity to avoid joining the Achaean army, but Agamemnon and Menelaus saw through the ruse, and forced him to leave his home and aid them in gathering their allies. The greatest challenge came in Thessaly, where the elderly King Peleus could not fight anymore. He had a son named Achilles, though, who all considered him the mightiest warrior alive. Thetis, Achilles' mother, knew from prophecies if her son went to war, he would not return, though he would win everlasting fame for his deeds. To prevent him from going, she disguised him as a woman and concealed him among the ladies of the household. The attempted deception did not fool the clever Odysseus, who easily discovered the youth's identity. Once recognized, Achilles gladly accepted the offer to fight with the other Achaeans, and took command of his father's Myrmidons.

A HOMERIC SETTING

Throughout this book, the Trojan War's era and the setting is referred to as Homeric. This is for three reasons. First, historians argue over when the Trojan War occurred (if it really happened at all), and so no fixed date can be offered. Second, this book focuses upon the Trojan War itself but also touches upon the events in the *Odyssey*, and to a lesser extent, Virgil's *Aeneid*, and the lands many of those invaders came from. Third, describing something as Trojan only covers the city of Troy and its neighboring lands, while calling something Achaean only applies to the invaders, yet the two forces had many common traits and features. The term Homeric, however, encompasses everyone involved in the battle, all of the lands associated with the story, and the plains before Troy and those distant kingdoms of the many Achaean leaders.

It took over two years for Menelaus to muster his forces for the trip to Troy, and many things happened along the way, nearly all involving the gods. At one point on the voyage, Athena becalmed the Achaeans' ships because Agamemnon had offended her. To appease her, he sacrificed his own daughter, Iphigenia, and though he appeased the goddess, the act offended many of the other captains, including Achilles,

and unrest between the two continued throughout the coming days. Achilles, however, was not free from blame, for later, at Tenedos, Achilles slew King Tenes, the son of Apollo. In response, the god sent a snake to bite the archer Philoctetes. Philoctetes' wound refused to heal, forcing his companions to leave him behind on an island, where he would survive for years by shooting birds from the sky.

THE WAR

When the Achaeans finally reached the Troad, the region around Troy, Odysseus and Menelaus went ahead as ambassadors to convince the Trojans to return Helen or face attack. Their mission failed, even though many Trojans wanted to send her back to avoid war. Failing to avert disaster, Odysseus and Menelaus returned to the fleet and sailed the rest of the way with their men to Troy, beaching their ships along the shore not far from the city itself. The Trojans flung heavy stones against the invaders to prevent their landing, but the Achaeans fought through. They leapt out upon the plain, and marched across, laying siege to the city.

The Achaeans had attacked many other lands on their way to Troy, including Thebes and Lyrnessus. Few could stand against them, and when they reached Troy, the captains had won many treasures. At Thebes, Agamemnon claimed the woman Chryseis as his prize, while Achilles chose the maiden Briseis at Lyrnessus.

These two women proved deadly to many of the Achaeans. Chryseis was the daughter of Chryses, a priest of Apollo, and after years of travel, he reached Troy seeking the Achaean captains. He begged them to return his daughter to him, and even offered handsome treasure as compensation. The men felt his request was reasonable and ought to be granted, since he was a priest, but Agamemnon refused, going so far as to threaten the man. Humiliated, Chryses left, praying to Apollo for revenge. The archer god, enraged at this treatment of his priest, set a plague upon the Achaeans. The contagion wreaked havoc among the Achaeans, killing many of them and jeopardizing their war effort, until finally, the seer Calchas explained the cause of the plague. He urged Agamemnon to return the girl and offer additional sacrifices as an apology to the god. Though this angered the arrogant king, Agamemnon finally agreed, but on one condition. If he had to give up the girl, he would take someone else's prize in return. Achilles denounced the king for his greed, and in reply, Agamemnon took Briseis as compensation. The mighty warrior did not stop him, but announced he would no longer fight in the war, and he and his men refused to take part in further conflict. This weakened the Achaeans, but heartened the Trojans. Odysseus, Nestor, and several others begged Achilles to reconsider, but the young warrior stubbornly refused to yield. To make matters worse, he complained to his mother Thetis, who then complained to Zeus. Owing Thetis his life, the king of the gods offered to repay her by making the Achaeans suffer until they had no choice but to appease Achilles fully.

The Achaeans continued to fight, even without their greatest champion, not realizing the gods had turned against them. Hector, a prince of Troy and the commander of their forces, proposed a truce, suggesting a duel be fought to settle the matter. Paris agreed to fight for the Trojans, since he had ultimately caused the war, and Menelaus insisted on fighting for the Achaeans. Menelaus would have killed his former guest had Aphrodite not rescued Paris and spirited him to safety. Then Athena encouraged the archer Pandarus to shoot at Menelaus, thus breaking the truce.

Despite Zeus' decree that the Achaeans suffer, Athena and Hera, the Achaeans' two greatest supporters, continued to aid them. Athena encouraged Diomedes to charge into battle. The warrior would have single-handedly routed the Trojans if Apollo had not intervened. Then Ajax and Hector faced one another in single combat, but neither could defeat the other. When night fell, they agreed to call the battle a draw, and exchanged gifts to show respect. The gifts, however, proved ill for both of them. Hector gave Ajax a sword, which Ajax later used to kill himself, and Ajax gave Hector a purple belt, with which Achilles later used to drag Hector's body behind him.

The conflict continued, and with Zeus' aid, the Trojans swept the battlefield and stormed the Achaean camp. Many of the mightiest Achaeans suffered wounds, and the Trojan Hector and his men burned many of their ships. Poseidon stepped in to aid the Achaeans—Zeus' attention had wandered—but the king of the gods soon noticed and helped the Trojans carry the day.

Agamemnon, seeing how desperate his situation had become, finally agreed to appease Achilles, and offered not only to return the girl but to give him a great amount of treasure as well. Achilles stood fast, refusing the gifts, even though his friends Odysseus and Ajax carried the message. Still, Achilles relented enough to allow his friend Patrocleus to put on his armor and lead the Myrmidons to the Achaeans' aid, believing that by wearing Achilles' armor, everyone would think he had returned to the battle, unnerving the Trojans and heartening the Achaeans. Achilles insisted his friend drive the Trojans back from the ships and nothing more, but Patrocleus let victory distract him, and pursued the Trojans across the battlefield, almost to Troy's walls. Again, the gods intervened. Apollo stunned the man and Euphorbus wounded him before Hector finally killed him and took Achilles' armor from his body.

When Achilles learned of his friend's death, anger swept through him, burning away his stubbornness. The greatest warrior swore revenge, and with new armor bestowed unto him by his mother, fashioned at the hands of the god Hephaestus, Achilles accepted Agamemnon's apology and gifts, and rejoined the battle. The Achaeans crushed the Trojans, while Achilles strove to face Hector. Zeus had decreed Hector's death, and so when the rest of the Trojans fled back to the city, Athena tricked Hector into remaining, so he faced Achilles alone. Though a mighty warrior himself, Hector was no match for Achilles, and soon fell to the man's wrath. Not content with this victory, Achilles desecrated his opponent's corpse, dragging the body behind his chariot all the way back to the boats. King Priam approached the Achaean camp alone and made a personal appeal to Achilles to take back Hector's body for proper burial. Achilles, always honorable, allowed the Trojan king his request, and so was Trojan's hero buried.

Achilles did not live long enough to savor his victory, though. Patrocleus' death had been the first in a series, and shortly after Hector's corpse returned to Troy, Paris shot Achilles with an arrow, piercing his ankle, the one place where Achilles was vulnerable. Apollo had guided the shaft, and thus avenged the death of his own son.

Following Achilles' death, the army presented his armor to the next best warrior in the camp. Ajax and Odysseus vied for the honor. When Odysseus won, Ajax went mad, and only Athena prevented him from slaughtering his own allies, turning his wrath mistakenly on the cattle, seeing them as soldiers. When he saw what he had done, shame overtook him, and he killed himself, falling upon the very sword Hector had bestowed to him. Thus, the Achaean army lost its two mightiest warriors in rapid succession.

The Achaeans then chose guile over force to win the day. They retrieved Philoctetes from his exile in Lemnos, his wound finally healed. Philoctetes shot and killed Paris, removing the war's catalyst.

Odysseus then stole into Troy, and removed the Palladium, a wooden statue sacred to Athena that protected the city from being sacked.

Finally, Odysseus suggested a new stratagem. The Achaeans constructed a massive hollow wooden horse, and engraved upon it the inscription: "For their return home, the Achaeans dedicate this thank-offering to Athena." Odysseus and several of the Achaeans' best warriors climbed inside the horse. The rest took their boats and other belongings and emptied the camp. The next day, finding the camp deserted and the horse standing in its midst, the Trojans assumed the Achaeans had finally fled. They dragged the horse into the city, and set it before Priam's palace, while they debated what to do with it. The seeress Cassandra saw the truth, but her curse was no one ever believed her visions. Laocoon, another seer, confirmed her words, but the gods sent serpents to kill him, and thus no one listened, and the Trojans spared the wooden horse.

That night, the Achaean Sinon lit a beacon lamp in the Achaean camp, guiding their ships back to shore, while Odysseus and his men crept out of the horse, overpowered the sentries, and opened the city's gates allowing their comrades into the city. The Achaeans swept through the sleeping Trojans, killing Priam and his remaining sons, and killing or taking the king's daughters as slaves. They even slew Hector's son Astyanax, a little boy. Of the royal family, only Aeneas, his father Anchises, and his son Ascanius escaped, and only with Aphrodite's aid. After killing everyone and dividing the spoils, the Achaeans set fire to the city. Victors, they gathered in their ships and set sail for their respective homes and waiting families.

AFTER THE WAR

Of the victors, not all returned to their former lives. Many had offended the gods, and now faced the consequences of divine wrath. Agamemnon returned to Mycenae, but his wife Clytemnestra had never forgiven him for the death of their daughter Iphigenia. When he returned, she and her lover poisoned and killed him, along with all of his other children. Only his son Orestes, who was away at the time, survived, and later revenged him, reclaiming the kingdom.

Lesser Aias, also known as Aias the Runner, offended Athena by violating her temple in Troy. As punishment, she asked Poseidon to send a violent storm to sink most of his departing fleet. Aias managed to live by clinging to a rock, but made the mistake of boasting that even the gods could not kill him. Outraged, Poseidon split the rock in two, and Aias fell into the sea and drowned.

Diomedes also suffered delays and difficulties. During the war, he wounded both Aphrodite and her lover Ares. The two gods caused a storm to maroon his ships along the Lycian coast, where King Lycus, an ally of Troy, captured them and intended to sacrifice them to Ares. Fortunately, the princess Callirrhoe helped Diomedes and some of his men escape. When Diomedes finally returned home, he discovered his wife Aegialeia cuckolded him with a local noble named Commetes; the two had ruled in his stead. With Athena's help, Diomedes defeated his wife's lover and he regained his kingdom.

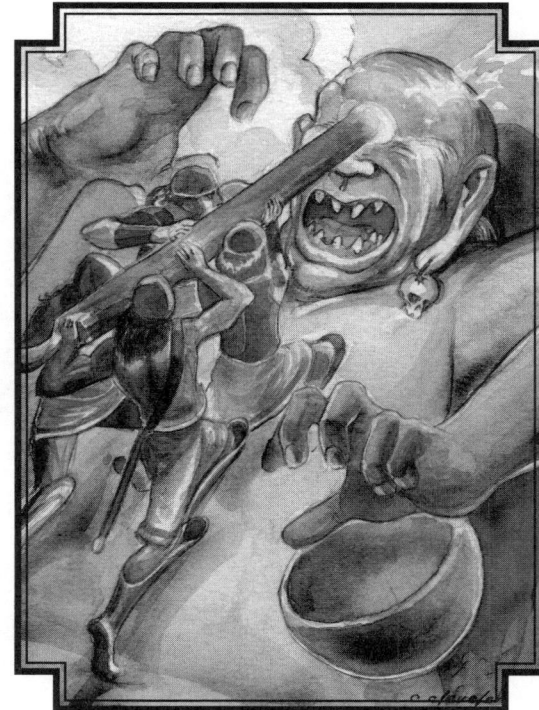

Menelaus also suffered the gods' ire. Angered it had taken so long to recover his wife and defeat the Trojans, he did not offer the gods sacrifices when he left Troy. As a result, the gods destroyed many of his ships and stranded the rest along the Egyptian coast. It took seven years before Menelaus and Helen found their way back to Sparta.

The most famous voyage home, however, belongs to Odysseus, the craftiest of all the Achaeans. After sailing from Troy, Odysseus and his men put in at an island, where they encountered the monstrous one-eyed Cyclopes. Odysseus blinded Polyphemus, the greatest of all Cyclopes, and escaped, but in his arrogance, he told the monster his name. Polyphemus prayed to his father Poseidon, and the great sea god capsized most of Odysseus' boats, killing nearly all of Odysseus' men. Though Odysseus survived, and eventually returned home to Ithaca, it took him ten long years. And when he arrived, he found his wife Penelope beset by suitors, who consumed all of his wealth. With the aid of his son Telemachus and the goddess Athena, who always protected Ithacan king, he killed the suitors and reclaimed his home.

As for the Trojans, Troy was destroyed but Aeneas and his father and son roamed the ocean. Aphrodite watched over them, and after many adventures, they settled along a distant shore, establishing a home there, a home that would one day become Rome.

CHAPTER TWO: CHARACTERS

Creating a *Trojan War* character is identical to creating characters in other d20 settings (see the *PHB* for details). In fact, creating a Homeric character may be somewhat easier. In this setting, everyone shares a common language, a common religion, and similar equipment. Additionally, players have only two race options: human or divine offspring. On the surface, this may suggest all Homeric characters are alike, but this is not true. Personalities, histories, and attitudes towards war, the gods, and their lives are all aspects separating one character from another. By focusing on these details, players create new and interesting characters who are well-suited members of the Achaean or Trojan armies, but who also stand out as individuals.

RACE

In the Trojan War, players may play standard humans or divine offspring. While there are other races, called monsters, in the Homeric world, they are not suited for player characters. In fact, anyone who does not look human is a monster. For more details on these types of characters, see **Chapter Eleven: Homeric Bestiary**.

HUMAN

Most characters in the Homeric world are human. They may originate from anywhere in the Mediterranean area, but the majority are either Achaean or Trojan. The two standard nationalities follow, and their racial statistics use those of humans in the *PHB*. At the GM's option, other nationalities may be available.

ACHAEAN

Those who fought under Agamemnon's command are collectively the Achaeans, Danaans, or Argives. The three names are interchangeable, though Achaean is most common.

The Achaeans originally came from Thessaly, in mainland Greece, and settled in Argos and Lacedaemon (southern Peloponnesus). Achaea, founded by Achaeus, lies in northern Peloponnesus.

Danus (or Danaus) fled Africa and Egypt and settled in Argolis. The reigning king, Gelanor, surrendered the kingdom to him, and Danaus named the people Danaans. His descendants mixed with the newcomers. The people are also known as Argives, as they came from Argolis, where the Achaeans and the Danaans met and mingled.

Homer often referred to the Achaeans as "long-haired," which suggests that they wore their hair long and loose. Most had fair skin, though tanned to bronze by the sun, and blond or light brown hair. Dark brown, black, and even red did appear, but were more rare—red was considered a mark of favor from the gods; dark brown and black were considered less pleasing to the eye.

TROJAN

The term "Trojan" refers to those who lived in the city of Troy and to anyone else that owed fealty to that city and its king (during the time of the war, King Priam). Priam ruled a large portion of Asia Minor, particularly along its west coast. Nine different dynasties acknowledged him as overlord.

The first dynasty was Troy itself, home of Priam and his 100 sons. Priam's son Hector led their forces and the army in general.

The second was Dardania, a region near Mount Ida. Its ruler, Anchises, was Priam's cousin. Anchises' son Aeneas commanded the Dardanian forces, and many considered him the second-in-command of the entire Trojan force.

The archer Pandarus led the third dynasty, the men of Zeleia.

The fourth was Lyrnessus, a city east of Mount Ida. King Mynes, whose daughter Briseis Achilles stole, ruled there.

Adrestus and Amphius, the sons of Merops, led the forces from the fifth dynasty, Adresteia.

Sixth were the men of Abydus and Percote, Practius, Sestos, and Arisbe, the region to the north of Troy. Asius, son of Hyrtacus, led them.

The seventh dynasty was the Lelegians. Priam's mother, Laothoe, was the daughter of the Lelegian king Altes.

The eighth dynasty was Thebes, home of King Eetion, whose daughter Andromache married Prince Hector of Troy. Thebes was also the home of Apollo's priest Chryses and his daughter Chryseis.

The island of Lesbos is sometimes considered the ninth dynasty, but other sources refer to the isle of Mysia, home of Heracles' grandson Eurypylus.

Homer refers to the Trojans as the horse-tamers or horse-lovers, and masters of charioteering. They have curlier hair than the Achaeans and a slightly darker complexion, with more almond-shaped eyes. Dark hair is common among them, and is a mark of beauty.

HUMAN ALLOWED CLASSES

Both the Achaeans and the Trojans are men of thought and action. They value physical prowess but also respect wit and wisdom. Human allowed classes include (new classes are in italics): barbarian (non-Achaeans and non-Trojans only—if the GM allows), bard, *charioteer*, *dedicated warrior*, druid, fighter, *magician*, *priest*, ranger, rogue, sorcerer.

Human allowed prestige classes include (new prestige classes are in italics): assassin (optional), loremaster, *orator*, *runner*, *seer*, and shadowdancer.

DIVINE OFFSPRING

In the Homeric world, the gods descend to Earth and interact with normal humans. Not only do these deities meddle in human affairs, many take lovers or permanent mates from humanity. Because of this, many of the more powerful mortal warriors are divine offspring. These individuals look like humans, but are more powerful.

Divine offspring are, literally, the children or descendents of gods. They fall into three categories: major, medium, and minor. Major divine offspring are the children of greater gods. Medium divine offspring are the children of lesser gods, or the grandchildren of greater gods. Minor divine offspring are the grandchildren of lesser gods or the great-grandchildren of greater gods. In other instances, the divine blood has been so diluted it no longer has any effect, and such characters are merely humans who can claim gods as ancestors.

PERSONALITY

Most divine offspring know their parentage, though their mortal parent may marry another mortal, who then raises the divine child as his or her own. In some cases, the parent is already married, and simply has an affair with a god and bears that god's child or children. Divine offspring quickly learn of their unusual lineage and of the powers inherited from that bloodline. As a result, divine offspring have generous doses of confidence… almost to the point of arrogance. They know their own strength and beauty, and they know their divine parent will help shield them from harm. Most divine offspring are outgoing, friendly, and courageous—they leap into danger, trusting their strength and their divine parent to save them.

Descending from a god is not always a boon, however. Other gods target the divine offspring of their enemies for they know by attacking them they upset the offspring's divine parent. Divine offspring seem to attract danger, and monsters often appear near their lands. Divine offspring experience a great pressure to excel. Being *as good as* a human is not enough for children of the gods—they aspire to be as great as their deity parents, and thus work harder and accept more risks. Wealth means little to divine offspring; honor and glory are everything.

PHYSICAL DESCRIPTION

Divine offspring are tall, taller than are their human kin. They range from six to seven feet tall for men and five and a half to six feet tall for women. Men are muscular, with broad shoulders and chests. Women have generous curves and softer skin. All divine offspring are lovely, with striking features and smooth complexions. Their hair can be golden blond, fiery red, jet-black, snow white, or startling silver. Their eyes can be any color, but are always rich, deep, and clear.

RELATIONS

Divine offspring spend their whole lives surrounded by humans, and normally get along well with them, despite their penchant for treating them as inferiors.

GENDER

The Homeric setting is male-centric. Kings rule most lands, and warriors are typically men. This does not mean, however, that women have no power, or even that they cannot be adventurers. Queens exert almost as much influence as their husbands, and when a husband dies or a king has only a daughter, a queen can rule alone. Goddesses may have priestesses instead of priests. Both Athena and Artemis encouraged women to be active, forceful, and trained in warfare. In fact, Queen Hippolyta ruled an entire nation of warlike women called Amazons. Female characters can be warriors from that land, but even if they hail from other nations, the Amazons' existence forces men to acknowledge that women can be powerful warriors. Circe also proves women can be effective magicians.

During the Trojan War, the only known female combatants were the Amazons. The Achaeans did not bring many women from home, though they captured many in their raids on nearby lands, and the Trojan women stayed in the city and continued their household duties. This does not mean that women were not among the warriors, merely Homer did not mention them. While the only female divine offspring in the *Iliad*, Helen, is not a fighter, she is physically more powerful than most of her human companions, and could be a formidable warrior if she chose.

ALIGNMENT

Divine offspring share at least one alignment trait with their divine parent. Thus, the child of a chaotic good god will be either chaotic or good, though not necessarily both.

DIVINE OFFSPRING LANDS

Divine offspring are typically the children of a god and a mortal king or queen. Thus, many of them rule their own lands. However, nowhere do divine offspring gather in large numbers, and so they have no homeland of their own. It is rare to find more than two divine offspring in a single city or nation, unless they are all close kin.

RELIGION

Divine offspring know the gods exist, and often speak with their divine parents directly. Some are very religious, since they can pray to their parent and receive an immediate and personal response. Others see no reason to pray, since their parent watches over them anyway, and so they do not bother to follow the proper observances.

LANGUAGE

Divine Offspring speak Greek and Olympian. They can also learn any other human language.

NAMES

Divine offspring have human names.

ADVENTURERS

Because divine offspring feel the need to prove their worth, many leave home upon reaching adulthood. They wander the world, looking for adventure and a chance to acquire glory. Divine offspring are good traveling companions since they go anywhere and try anything. Their strength makes them valuable allies in a fight. Divine offspring lack subtlety, however, and often fail to grasp the intricacies of diplomacy.

DIVINE OFFSPRING RACIAL TRAITS

- **Major Divine Offspring:** +2 Strength, +2 Dexterity, +2 Constitution, +2 Charisma, −2 Intelligence.
  Medium Divine Offspring: +2 Strength, +2 Dexterity, +2 Charisma, −2 Intelligence
  Minor Divine Offspring: +2 to Strength or Dexterity, +2 Charisma, −2 Intelligence
  Divine offspring are physically superior to standard humans. As they rely heavily on their physical prowess, they fail to develop their intellect, and so are less clever.

- **Medium:** As Medium creatures, divine offspring have no special bonuses or penalties due to their size.

- A divine offspring's base speed is 35 feet. Their divine heritage allows them to move slightly faster than humans.

- **Increased Piety:** Divine offspring have a higher initial Piety. The level of their starting Piety depends on their rank. Major divine offspring have an initial Piety score of 3, medium divine offspring have Piety of 2, and minor divine offspring have a piety of 1 (See **Piety, Chapter Eight: Religion and Piety**, page 91).

- Divine offspring receive a +2 racial bonus to Climb, Jump, and Swim checks. Divine offspring are all extremely athletic.

- Major divine offspring receive a +4 racial bonus to saves versus divine spells. Medium offspring receive a +2 racial bonus to saves against divine spells, and minor divine offspring receive a +1 bonus.

- Major divine offspring have a +3 natural armor bonus to AC. Medium divine offspring have a +2, and minor divine offspring receive a +1 natural armor bonus to AC.

- **Native Outsider:** As native outsiders, divine offspring may be raised, reincarnated, or resurrected, as any other living creature.

- **Automatic Languages:** Greek and Olympian. Bonus Languages: Any.

- **Favored class:** Dedicated warrior.

- **Level Adjustment:** Major divine offspring: +3; medium divine offspring: +2; minor divine offspring: +1.

- **Challenge Rating:** For NPCs, a major divine offspring's CR equals its character level +2. A medium divine offspring's CR is its character level +1. A minor divine offspring's CR is equal to its character level.

DIVINE OFFSPRING ALLOWED CLASSES

Because of their general arrogance, lack of subtlety, and lack of finesse, divine offspring are limited in their class selection. Members of this race favor more active and direct classes, where they can use their strength and size to advantage. Allowed classes include (new classes are in italics): barbarian, bard, *charioteer*, *dedicated warrior*, fighter, and ranger. Divine offspring can advance in either of these two prestige classes (the new class is in *italics*): *runner* and shadowdancer.

OCCUPATION

For those fighting in the war, the most common occupation is warrior. Other people stayed near the battlefield, however. Herdsmen tended cattle and other livestock. Shepherds handled sheep and goats. Farmers tilled fields and harvested crops. Blacksmiths forged and repaired armor and weapons, as well as any of the more mundane items like tools and cutlery. Other craftsmen shoed horses, built carts and chariots, constructed houses and battlements, assembled boats, and created a host of other items. Women cooked and cleaned, spun wool or other fibers into thread, wove upon looms, knitted, and sewed by hand.

Even in battle, people fall into different specialties. The fleet of foot functioned as lightly armored messengers and carried news between captains. Scouts worked alone, sneaking close to the enemy and reporting back on their position, numbers, and battle array. Infantrymen marched on foot, carrying spears and shields, while charioteers rode in small groups, using their speed and maneuverability to attack their enemies' flanks.

Most combatants in the war concentrated entirely on battle. Those only peripherally involved, or even the fighters before or after the war, found other ways to make a living. Most captains, of course, were kings, and when not off fighting, they spent their time protecting their borders and governing their lands.

PIETY

The gods are a major factor in the Homeric world. They are present in the lives of mortals more than in any other setting. This is both good and bad. On the one hand, the gods answer prayers quickly and may appear in person. On the other, the gods like to meddle in mortal affairs, and they can curse a man as easily as bless him.

To reflect the gods' influence, every *Trojan War* character has a Piety score. This score reflects a character's religious devotion tracking the quality and frequency of the character's religious observances. The gods favor characters with high Piety scores, allowing such characters to call upon them for special requests. Those with negative Piety scores have earned the enmity of the gods, who punish the mortals for their arrogance and their failure to show the proper respect. Divine offspring begin play as described under their entry, while humans begin with 0 piety. For more about Piety, see **Chapter Eight: Religion and Piety**, page 91.

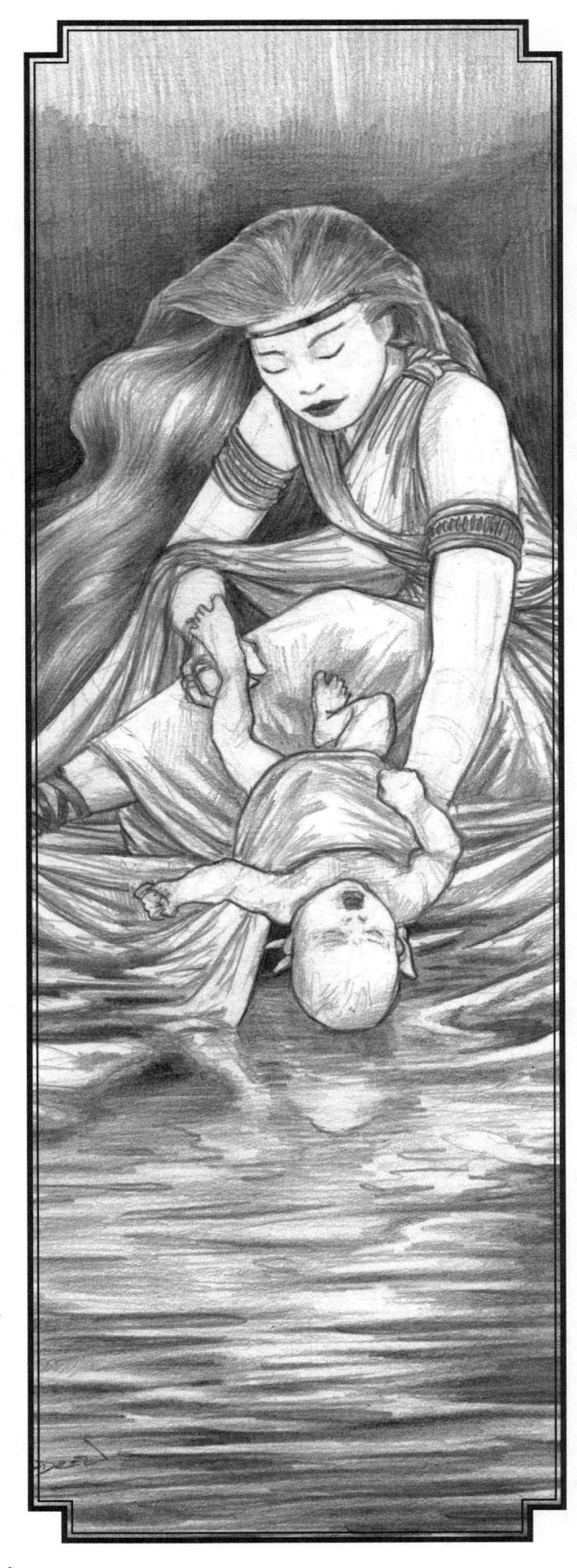

CHAPTER THREE: CHARACTER CLASSES

This section includes four new core classes: the charioteer, dedicated warrior, magician, and priest. It also introduces the orator, runner, and seer prestige classes. See **Chapter Four: Skills and Feats** for the new skills and feats mentioned in this chapter. In *Trojan War*, certain character classes are not used. The priest replaces the cleric, the dedicated warrior replaces the paladin, and the magician replaces the wizard. If you use other Green Ronin products, certain classes from the Master Class series are useful as well. The noble from the *Noble's Handbook* is an excellent choice for detailing the members of the Achaean and Trojan aristocracies. Likewise, you could expand the role of magic in your *Trojan War* campaign by incorporating the witch from the *Witch's Handbook*, serving as specialized priests and priestess of Hecate. Jason's wife Medea is an excellent example of a witch.

NEW CHARACTER CLASSES

The following classes are described in standard *PHB* format. Each class includes a section on participation, which describes how and why they might participate in the Trojan War, and the section on favored gods replaces the standard religion section. Although Homeric characters worship the Greek pantheon, individuals generally pray to one deity, and this section suggests an appropriate god for each character class.

CHARIOTEER

Most soldiers fight on foot, trudging slowly across battlefields with their weighty shields and spears. A handful of men, however, master the art of the horse and the chariot. From these small open cars, they can attack swiftly and race away. Charioteers (in Greek, "eqeta") are more than just warriors, however. They revel in the speed of their horses and in the ability to weave through crowds and race across open plains, delighting in the control they have over their steeds. For a charioteer, his horses are his closest companions, more trusted than any warrior, and lavished with more affection than any spouse.

Foot soldiers regard charioteers with awe, as well they should, for this elite group can sway the tide of battle, sweeping through foes like a starved lion might fall upon deer, scattering everyone in their path.

PARTICIPATION

Many of the great captains are charioteers, commanding troops from their chariots and rushing about the battlefield to aid beleaguered comrades. Everyone respects charioteers, and even foes remark upon their speed and mastery. When armies launch a full attack, they line their charioteers across the front of their force, letting them lead the charge and break the enemy line before the footmen arrive.

Diomedes and Nestor were two of the Achaeans' finest charioteers.

ADVENTURES

Charioteers search constantly for new challenges and new ways to test their speed and to demonstrate their control over their cars. During times of peace, many nations hold competitions, chariot races, and the victors can win both fame and fortune. Charioteers are also proud of their skills, and seek out worthy rivals to test themselves.

CHARACTERISTICS

Charioteers are strong warriors, fighting well while standing on solid ground. Their true talent, though, lies in driving chariots. While other warriors have difficulty balancing in the small, fast-moving car, or cannot control the horses well enough to navigate tight turns, the charioteers train until the chariot feels more comfortable than does the ground. Thereafter, they and their horses respond to obstacles and opponents almost as a single creature, reacting quickly, gracefully, and with awesome power. For a charioteer, the chariot is a weapon, a shield, a means of transport, and, sometimes, even a home.

ALIGNMENT

Charioteers are never lawful. They love the rush of speed and the sense of freedom too much to be tightly bound by laws. Charioteers are most often chaotic, responding to mood and whim. They can be good, neutral, or even evil. Evil charioteers become scourges trampling anyone in their path, and chaotic evil charioteers especially delight in the carnage they create.

FAVORED GODS

Charioteers most often pray to Poseidon, master of horses, and Athena, goddess of war and combat. Charioteers who are good archers may pray to Apollo. Chaotic evil charioteers likely worship Ares, though some may prefer Hermes.

BACKGROUND

Charioteers hail from cities or large towns. Smaller towns and villages have no access to the expensive chariots. Most charioteers are nobles who were given horses and a chariot in their youth, but some are commoners whose talents gained

them a noble's notice, then trained to serve as a charioteer in their lord's army. Others show them great respect, so they likewise expect charioteers to behave well, being gracious hosts and charming guests. Those who hate such niceties avoid them by staying with their chariots and only rarely frequenting the homes of other nobles.

RACES

Charioteers may be either human or divine offspring. Charioteers are generally of noble birth, as horses and chariots are costly for the common man.

OTHER CLASSES

Charioteers admire dedicated warriors for their zeal and close connection to their chosen god. They respect priests, particularly those who worship their favored god, and admire rangers for their wilderness skills. They appreciate the musical talents of bards, who sing of their exploits, thereby increasing their fame. They think druids odd but occasionally useful, while they see magicians as strange and dangerous. Rogues are untrustworthy, and fighters are useful, but ultimately limited in ability—charioteers often look down upon these warriors, both literally and figuratively.

GAME RULE INFORMATION

Charioteers have the following game statistics.

Abilities: Dexterity is the most important ability for a charioteer; it allows him to exert more control over his horses and maneuver his chariot more precisely. Strength is

also important both for manhandling the horses when necessary and for combat. Constitution allows the charioteer to ignore his wounds and continue fighting, while Wisdom helps him analyze a battlefield and find the best place to strike. Charisma can also be important, particularly for charioteers who lead others.

Alignment: Any nonlawful.
Hit Die: d10.
Starting Gold: 6d4 x 10 (150 gp).

CLASS SKILLS

The charioteer's class skills (and the key ability for each skill) are Appraise (Int), Balance (Dex), Bluff (Cha), Concentration (Con), Drive (Dex), Handle Animal (Cha), Intimidate (Cha), Jump (Str), Knowledge (tactics) (Int), Ride (Dex), and Spot (Int).

Skill Points at 1st Level: (2 + Int modifier) x 4.
Skill Points at Each Additional Level: 2 + Int modifier.

CLASS FEATURES

All of the following are class features of the charioteer.

WEAPON & ARMOR PROFICIENCY

The charioteer is proficient with all simple and martial weapons, with all armors and shields (except tower shields).

CHARIOT EXPERTISE (EX)

Charioteers train extensively with chariots, learning how to handle them under adverse conditions. Charioteers may take 10 on Drive checks in combat or while fighting.

TABLE 3-1: THE CHARIOTEER

Class Level	Base Attack Bonus	Fort Save	Ref Save	Will Save	Special
1st	+1	+0	+2	+0	Chariot expertise, Drive-by Attack
2nd	+2	+0	+3	+0	Gauge skill, sideswipe
3rd	+3	+1	+3	+1	
4th	+4	+1	+4	+1	Chariot Attack, trained steeds
5th	+5	+1	+4	+1	Skilled horseman
6th	+6/+1	+2	+5	+2	
7th	+7/+2	+2	+5	+2	Voice command
8th	+8/+3	+2	+6	+2	Capture
9th	+9/+4	+3	+6	+3	
10th	+10/+5	+3	+7	+3	Skillful maneuvering
11th	+11/+6/+1	+3	+7	+3	Wheeled attack
12th	+12/+7/+2	+4	+8	+4	
13th	+13/+8/+3	+4	+8	+4	Improved voice command
14th	+14/+9/+4	+4	+9	+4	Beyond Limits
15th	+15/+10/+5	+5	+9	+5	
16th	+16/+11/+6/+1	+5	+10	+5	Comforting Gait
17th	+17/+12/+7/+2	+5	+10	+5	Equine Command
18th	+18/+13/+8/+3	+6	+11	+6	
19th	+19/+14/+9/+4	+6	+11	+6	Equine Mastery
20th	+20/+15/+10/+5	+6	+12	+6	Prolonged Sideswipe

DRIVE-BY ATTACK

At 1st level, the charioteer gains Drive-By Attack as a bonus feat, even if he does not meet the prerequisites for this feat.

GAUGE SKILL (EX)

At 2nd level, a charioteer can assess another charioteer's skill. The charioteer must make an Appraise check (DC 10 + the opposing charioteer's charioteer level) to gauge an opponent's ability. If he succeeds, he knows what class abilities and chariot-related feats (like Chariot Shield) the opposing charioteer possesses. This does not reveal the exact level of the opposing character, only his abilities, though a player with this information can likely guess the charioteer's level. This ability only allows a charioteer to assess another charioteer; he cannot use it to gauge another character's abilities.

SIDESWIPE (EX)

At 2nd level, charioteers can sideswipe one target per round with their cab. The target must be within five feet of the chariot (anywhere along its route, not just as its starting point). The chariot makes a Drive check against the target's AC. On a successful check, the charioteer deals 1d6 points of damage. A sideswipe is a move action and may be used as part of a chariot's movement.

CHARIOT ATTACK

At 4th level, the charioteer gains Chariot Attack as a bonus feat, even if he does not meet the prerequisites for this feat.

TRAINED STEED (EX)

At 4th level, a charioteer can summon his horses and chariot. He must be within visual or audible range for them, but requires only a whistle or a nod. The horses run toward him at full speed, and halt right beside him so he can mount the chariot easily.

SKILLED HORSEMAN (EX)

At 5th level, the charioteer becomes so skilled with handling his animals, his steeds respond to his commands as if trained. The charioteer's team learns a new bonus trick starting at 5th level, learning one additional trick for every 5 levels attained thereafter. See **Chapter Four: Skills** in the *PHB* for details on tricks and the Handle Animal skill.

VOICE COMMAND (EX)

At 7th level, the charioteer can direct his horses by voice alone. He no longer needs reins to handle the chariot, though he takes a −2 penalty to AC, attack rolls, and Dexterity-based skill checks while doing so.

CAPTURE (EX)

Starting at 8th level, charioteers can leap into an unmanned and moving chariot to take control of it. This requires a DC 20 Ride check. The charioteer must be within five feet of the chariot to attempt this maneuver. If he succeeds, he not only leaps into the chariot, but he grabs the reins. Failing the check by 5 or less indicates the charioteer landed in the chariot but missed the reins. He must succeed a DC 15 Ride check to capture them as a move action.

Failing the roll by more than 5 but less than 15 indicates he missed the chariot completely, but managed to avoid being trampled by the horses. Failing by more than 15 or requires the charioteer to succeed a DC 15 Reflex save be run over by the horses and chariot, taking 2d6 points of damage as the horses and chariot roll over him.

SKILLFUL MANEUVERING (EX)

At 10th level, charioteers can add one-half their class level to Trample attacks and sideswipe attacks. Charioteers can only add this attack bonus when using reins to control the chariot.

WHEELED ATTACK (EX)

At 11th level, a charioteer can turn his chariot so quickly he can make a Trample attack a second time. Whenever the charioteer successfully hits a target with a Chariot Trample attack, the charioteer may make an additional Trample attack, albeit at a –5 penalty.

IMPROVED VOICE COMMAND (EX)

At 13th level, the charioteer no longer suffers a –2 penalty to AC, attack rolls, and Dexterity based skill checks while controlling his chariot without using the reins.

BEYOND LIMITS (EX)

At 14th level, a charioteer can push his horses beyond their normal limits. A horse can run at five times its normal movement, instead of four, can jump half again as far as normal, and gains +2 to Strength and Dexterity. The horses can only maintain this exertion for 1d6 + one-half the charioteer's class level in rounds before needing to stop. This exhausts the horses, however. The horses must rest 10 minutes for each round they exerted themselves. If the charioteer forces the horses to carry the chariot again before resting fully, they must make a DC 20 Fortitude check. If they succeed, they suffer 2d6 points of nonlethal damage and can only run at half their normal speed. A failed check, however, indicates the horses suffer 4d6 points of nonlethal damage, and collapse, useless for 1d4 days.

COMFORTING GAIT (EX)

At 16th level, a charioteer becomes more comfortable in the cab than he is on stationary ground. He gains a +2 circumstance bonus to all Reflex saves and Balance checks while in the chariot.

EQUINE COMMAND (EX)

At 17th level, the charioteer is a master horseman. Any horse the charioteer handles gains a bonus trick when ridden by the charioteer, or when pulling the charioteer's chariot. In addition, horses are always Friendly to charioteer. Finally, when the charioteer uses the Beyond Limits class feature, the horses may maintain exertion for 1d6 + the charioteer's class level in rounds, and the horse need rest only 1 minute for each round they exerted themselves.

EQUINE MASTERY (EX)

At 19th level, a charioteer can impose his will on other chariot teams. They must be able to see and hear him. If the other steeds have rider, or they pull an occupied chariot, the charioteer makes an opposed Handle Animal check against the other rider. If the charioteer succeeds, the horses obey his commands as if they were his own.

PROLONGED SIDESWIPE (EX)

As a full-round action, a 20th-level charioteer can direct his team and chariot to make a sideswipe attack against every enemy adjacent to the chariot's path.

EX-CHARIOTEERS

A charioteer who becomes lawful cannot gain new levels in charioteer, but retains all charioteer abilities.

DEDICATED WARRIOR

Most warriors accept the gods exist and some recognize these deities interfere in mortal affairs. Some warriors not only accept this notion, they embrace it. These warriors believe strongly in the gods, selecting one god as their personal favorite. They talk to this god, pray to him or her, and ask favors in return. The gods, pleased with this display of devotion, reward them with those favors, and delight in the warriors' victories. These are the dedicated warriors. They dedicate their every victory to the greater glory of their chosen god.

Normal fighters view dedicated warriors with awe because they have the blessing and protection of a particular god. The priests envy them because the warriors have both faith and military prowess. However, being a dedicated warrior is not always easy. By devoting themselves to a god, these warriors agree to accept that god's every dictate—whatever the dictate might be. Often dedicated warriors do not see their home for years, for their god's bidding forces them to wander the lands. Yet if they remain obedient, eventually the god rewards them with wealth and long life or a glorious death in battle, depending upon the god's caprice.

PARTICIPATION

Dedicated warriors flock to the Trojan War. The gods have taken an interest in the conflict, and so their warriors participate in

the war to win their favor. Interestingly, even if a god clearly supports one army, he still favors his dedicated warriors on the opposite side. For example, Apollo, who helped defend Troy, granted the Achaean archer Teucer signs of his divine favor.

Hector of Troy was a dedicated warrior of Apollo, and Odysseus was a dedicated warrior of Athena.

ADVENTURES

Dedicated warriors adventure for two reasons: to win glory for their god and to perform quests for their god. If a dedicated warrior sees a chance to impress people with his fighting skill and he is not already upon some other mission, he happily participates in the event at hand, so everyone will learn of his god's might.

CHARACTERISTICS

Dedicated warriors are powerful fighters who can call upon their gods for immediate aid in the form of increased strength, extra protection, healing, and certain other divine gifts. Dedicated warriors are the Homeric equivalent of the paladin, but they have a more immediate and personal relationship with their chosen god. They always possess deep and abiding faith, because they know their god exists and listens to their prayers.

ALIGNMENT

A dedicated warrior must have the same alignment as his chosen god.

FAVORED GODS

Most dedicated warriors select Athena, Ares, or Zeus as their personal deity. Apollo is also a popular choice, particularly for those who use bows. Someone who sails the sea and fights from a boat might choose Poseidon. The other gods are not considered warlike enough to support such displays of bravery and fighting skill. Each dedicated warrior must select one of god during character creation. This is the character's chosen god, and his sacrifices and libations must always be to this god first. He dedicates his victories to this god as well, and he must obey the god's commands. Breaking faith with his chosen god strips the dedicated warrior of his special abilities, and he cannot gain them back. Both gods immediately strike down a dedicated warrior who breaks away from one god and then prays to another, as the gods despise oath breakers. Dedicated warriors also must show respect to the priests of their god, and cannot fight priests or dedicated warriors who pray to the same deity.

BACKGROUND

Dedicated warriors are noble because they learned the arts of war and received a proper education. At some time during their training, they reached out to one of the gods, dedicating themselves to him in exchange for the god's favor. Each battle the dedicated warriors win strengthens this bond.

RACES

Dedicated warriors can be either human or divine offspring.

OTHER CLASSES

Dedicated warriors treat all priests with respect, viewing priests of their own god as spiritual leaders. They also respect other dedicated warriors, even if they follow other gods. Charioteers are worthy allies. Bards are useful and entertaining and the best means for spreading word of their own deeds, increasing the glory of their god. Rangers are almost a wilderness version of dedicated warriors, combining martial skills with divine spells. Consequently, dedicated warriors respect them, but rangers also confuse dedicated warriors because these wilderness champions rarely announce their god when fighting, and many are private about their prayers and sacrifices. Magicians are not to be trusted, and rogues have no honor because they sneak about lacking the courage to confront others openly.

GAME RULE INFORMATION

Dedicated warriors have the following game statistics.

Abilities: Strength is the most important ability for a dedicated warrior since he wins glory for his god through warfare. Constitution and Dexterity are also important, as is Charisma, encouraging others to like him and to believe him when he claims his god is the greatest member of the pantheon.

Alignment: The same as the chosen deity.

Hit Die: d10.

Starting Gold: 4d4 x 10 (100 gp).

TABLE 3-2: THE DEDICATED WARRIOR

Class Level	Base Attack Bonus	Fort Save	Ref Save	Will Save	Special
1st	+1	+2	+0	+0	Divine strength 1/day
2nd	+2	+3	+0	+0	Divine shield 1/day
3rd	+3	+3	+1	+1	Trap sense +1
4th	+4	+4	+1	+1	Divine celerity
5th	+5	+4	+1	+1	Divine strength 2/day
6th	+6/+1	+5	+2	+2	Trap sense +2
7th	+7/+2	+5	+2	+2	Divine shield 2/day
8th	+8/+3	+6	+2	+2	Improved strength
9th	+9/+4	+6	+3	+3	Damage reduction 1/–
10th	+10/+5	+7	+3	+3	Divine strength 3/day
11th	+11/+6/+1	+7	+3	+3	Divine blessing
12th	+12/+7/+2	+8	+4	+4	Divine shield 3/day
13th	+13/+8/+3	+8	+4	+4	Divine aid 1/day
14th	+14/+9/+4	+9	+4	+4	Damage reduction 2/–
15th	+15/+10/+5	+9	+5	+5	Divine strength 4/day
16th	+16/+11/+6/+1	+10	+5	+5	Favored sight
17th	+17/+12/+7/+2	+10	+5	+5	Divine shield 4/day
18th	+18/+13/+8/+3	+11	+6	+6	Divine aid 2/day
19th	+19/+14/+9/+4	+11	+6	+6	Damage reduction 3/–
20th	+20/+15/+10/+5	+12	+6	+6	Divine strength 5/day

CLASS SKILLS

The dedicated warrior's class skills (and the key ability for each skill) are Concentration (Con), Decipher Omen (Wis), Diplomacy (Cha), Drive (Dex), Handle Animal (Cha), Heal (Wis), Knowledge (nobility and royalty) (Int), Knowledge (religion) (Int), Knowledge (tactics) (Int), and Ride (Dex).

Skill Points at 1st Level: (2 + Int modifier) x 4.
Skill Points at Each Additional Level: 2 + Int modifier.

CLASS FEATURES

All of the following are class features of the dedicated warrior.

WEAPON & ARMOR PROFICIENCY

A dedicated warrior is proficient with all simple and martial weapons, but may only use weapons approved by his god. See sidebar for details. In addition, dedicated warriors are proficient with all armor and all shields (except tower shields).

PERMITTED WEAPONS BY DEITY

Deity	Permitted Weapons
Zeus	Sword (any) and throwing spear
Athena	Sword (any) and spear (any)
Ares	Axe (any), sword (any), and spear (any)
Apollo	Dagger and bow (any)
Poseidon	Sword and throwing spear
Hermes	Dagger, sling, and throwing spear
Artemis	Axe (any) and bow
Hephaestus	Hammer, mace (any), sword (any), and spear (any)
Hera	Mace (any)
Other gods	GMs choice

If the dedicated warrior uses a weapon not approved of by his god, he loses any current Piety points, and cannot access his special class abilities until he rids himself of the offending weapon. He must then offer sacrifices to the god for 1 day + 1 day per class level.

DIVINE STRENGTH (SU)

Once per day, a 1st-level dedicated warrior can call upon his favored god for additional strength. For a number of rounds equal to one-half his class levels (minimum 1 round), he gains a +2 bonus to Strength and Constitution. The dedicated warrior gains an additional instance of this ability at 5th level, and every 5 levels thereafter (3/day at 10th, 4/day at 15th, and so on).

DIVINE SHIELD (SU)

At 2nd level, dedicated warriors can ask his god for protection. Once per day, the dedicated warrior shines with a bright aura, granting him a +2 deflection bonus to AC and a +1 resistance bonus to all saves. These bonuses last for a number of rounds equal to one-half the dedicated warrior's class level. The dedicated warrior gains another use of this ability per day every 5 levels above 2nd-level (2/day at 7th, 3/day at 12th, and so on).

TRAP SENSE (EX)

Starting at 3rd level, a dedicated warrior gains a limited ability to sense danger before it occurs. He gains a +1 bonus on Reflex saves made to avoid traps and a +1 dodge bonus to AC against attacks made by traps. This bonus increases to +2 at 6th level. Trap sense bonuses gained from multiple classes stack.

DIVINE CELERITY

Filled with the energy of the gods, a 4th level dedicated warrior gains a +5 foot enhancement bonus to his base land speed. This benefit applies regardless of armor worn, and applies this benefit after armor and encumbrance modifiers are applied.

IMPROVED STRENGTH (SU)

Beginning at 8th level, the dedicated warrior's bonus to his Strength and Constitution scores from divine strength increase to +4.

DAMAGE REDUCTION (SU)

At 9th level, a dedicated warrior gains damage reduction. Subtract 1 from the damage the dedicated warrior takes each time he is dealt damage from a weapon or a natural attack. Every five dedicated warrior levels thereafter (14th and 19th level) this damage reduction rises by 1 point. Damage reduction can reduce damage to 0 but not below 0.

DIVINE BLESSING (SU)

The gods are not likely to let their champion die by accident. At 11th level, the dedicated warrior can heal a number of hit points of damage equal to twice his current dedicated warrior level each day, and can spread this healing out among several uses.

DIVINE AID (SU)

At 13th level, the dedicated warrior may ask his god to grant him an additional instance of any other class ability he possesses. Each day, the character can use any of his other special class abilities once more than normal and he does not have to decide until he uses it. The dedicated warrior gains an additional use of divine aid at 18th-level.

FAVORED SIGHT (SU)

Starting at 16th level, dedicated warriors can recognize their favored god, no matter how that god is disguised. No roll is required. This ability only works on the warrior's favored god, however-for other deities, he must make the normal Appraise check to denote status (if he has the Divine Sight feat, see Appraise (new use), **Chapter Four: Skills and Feats**, page 35).

MAGICIAN

In the Homeric world, most magic comes directly from the gods, received through prayers and sacrifices. Magicians, however, have learned to tap the power of the elements themselves, drawing upon emotions, thoughts, and other human elements for magic, while similar to the divine magic, actually comes from within.

Since the magician's power does not come from the gods, many fear them, particularly priests who consider their magic sacrilege of the worst sort. Magicians, however, exult in their non-god-given talents. While many magicians believe in the gods, and some even pray to them, they delight in knowing their own powers are not dependent on a god's whim. Priests who anger their gods receive no answer to their prayers, but magicians can summon their magic every day without fail even if the gods hate them. This also means magicians do not need to spend their time praying and sacrificing, so they can concentrate on other activities. Most magicians love to travel and see new sights, learning new spells along the way. They also enjoy meeting people, though some magicians make poor hosts and guests, earning the entire class a reputation for cruelty, arrogance, and mischief.

PARTICIPATION

Magicians are not formally invited to the Trojan War mainly because the kings do not trust arcane magic, but also because most magicians do not openly display their talents. Yet the chance to see Troy and mingle with so many nobles from so many different lands proves an irresistible call, so many magicians have joined the war, though they don disguises as simple warriors. They use their magic subtly to protect themselves and to bring victory to their comrades.

ADVENTURES

Magicians love travel and exploration. Circe, the most famous magician, lived alone on an island and enchanted anyone who dared approach, but she was an exception largely because she was not mortal. Most magicians hate being cooped up; they want to see the world. They enjoy using their magic, and like finding new opportunities. The most exciting thing for a magician is to meet another magician, or to discover some new creature, plant, or location possibly allowing them to learn new magic.

Magicians make good traveling companions, and can use their magic to aid their comrades.

CHARACTERISTICS

Magicians are the arcane spellcasting class for *Trojan War*. As this setting is combat-oriented, magicians here are somewhat hardier than their fantasy wizard counterparts, having been trained to withstand damage better than their counterparts. Standard sorcerers (but not wizards) do exist in the Homeric world, though most conceal their nature by claiming divine parentage. Magicians learn to use magic by tapping into the world around them and by channeling its energy through their wands. They can cast many different spells, though they work best when they have a connection to the subject. Magicians do not require books or material components (except for a few spells), and though not warriors, they can handle themselves in a fight.

ALIGNMENT

Magicians can be any alignment.

FAVORED GODS

Many magicians favor Hermes, the god of travelers, or Hecate, the goddess of night and magic. Few pray to Ares, whom most consider a brutish brawler.

BACKGROUND

Magicians generally have no school or formal organization, and most have never met another magician. They discover their abilities while growing up, and they hone them through practice and experimentation. Many pray to their favorite god for guidance, and the god teaches them how to channel energy into a wand. Others simply discover this by accident, or by thinking through the process. Magicians can be commoners or nobles, and can come from any nation or area, though most are from small towns and villages rather than large cities.

RACES

Only humans can be magicians. Divine offspring ties to divinity prevent them from learning magic of this sort.

OTHER CLASSES

Priests' ability to summon divine magic fascinates magicians. Dedicated warriors have their respect tinged with jealousy because these men are powerful fighters who can tap divine magic through direct pleas to a god without the concentration and discipline a magician requires. Magicians admire charioteers, fighters, and rangers for their martial skills, bards for their charisma and musical talent, and rogues for their stealth and knowledge. Druids intrigue magicians because these nature worshippers are most like them in attitude and practice, gaining power from the earth rather than from the gods.

The other classes are less enthusiastic about magicians, however. Priests despise magicians, considering arcane magic a blasphemy against the gods and a usurpation of their own gifts. Dedicated warriors see magicians as inferior versions of themselves with less combat skill and no ability to tap the gods directly. Many charioteers, rangers, and fighters view magicians as close to demons, since they have magic that does not come from the gods, and consider them useless in a fight. Only bards, druids, and rogues approach a magician openly; bards because the arcane casters intrigue them, rogues because they admire the magician's knowledge, and druids because they and magicians have so much in common.

GAME RULE INFORMATION

Magicians have the following game statistics.

Abilities: Intelligence is the most important ability for a magician, as it enables him to learn more about himself and the world around him, and because it lets him convert knowledge into learning new spells. Wisdom is also valuable since magicians require strong wills to focus their spells. Dexterity allows a magician to avoid danger more easily, while Constitution lets him stand his ground. Most magicians lack great strength or personal charm, and so most neglect Strength and Charisma.

Alignment: Any.

Hit Die: d6.

Starting Gold: 3d4 x 10 (75 gp).

CLASS SKILLS

The magician's class skills (and the key ability for each skill) are Concentration (Con), Craft (Int), Knowledge (all skills, taken individually) (Int), Profession (Wis), Spellcraft (Int), and Survival (Wis).

Skill Points at 1st Level: (2 + Int modifier) x 4.
Skill Points at Each Additional Level: 2 + Int modifier.

TABLE 3-3: THE MAGICIAN

Class Level	Base Attack Bonus	Fort Save	Ref Save	Will Save	Special	Spells per Day									
						0	1st	2nd	3rd	4th	5th	6th	7th	8th	9th
1st	+0	+0	+2	+2	Wand	3	1	—	—	—	—	—	—	—	—
2nd	+1	+0	+3	+3	Blood ties	4	2	—	—	—	—	—	—	—	—
3rd	+1	+1	+3	+3		4	3	1	—	—	—	—	—	—	—
4th	+2	+1	+4	+4		4	3	2	—	—	—	—	—	—	—
5th	+2	+1	+4	+4	Charge wine	4	3	2	1	—	—	—	—	—	—
6th	+3	+2	+5	+5		4	3	3	2	—	—	—	—	—	—
7th	+3	+2	+5	+5		4	4	3	2	1	—	—	—	—	—
8th	+4	+2	+6	+6	Enchanted gift	4	4	3	3	2	—	—	—	—	—
9th	+4	+3	+6	+6		4	4	4	3	2	1	—	—	—	—
10th	+5	+3	+7	+7		4	4	4	3	3	2	—	—	—	—
11th	+5	+3	+7	+7	Read wand	4	4	4	4	3	2	1	—	—	—
12th	+6/+1	+4	+8	+8		4	4	4	4	3	3	2	—	—	—
13th	+6/+1	+4	+8	+8		4	4	4	4	4	3	2	1	—	—
14th	+7/+2	+4	+9	+9	Recharge wand	4	4	4	4	4	3	3	2	—	—
15th	+7/+2	+5	+9	+9		4	4	4	4	4	4	3	2	1	—
16th	+8/+3	+5	+10	+10		4	4	4	4	4	4	3	3	2	—
17th	+8/+3	+5	+10	+10	Wand alternative	4	4	4	4	4	4	4	3	2	1
18th	+9/+4	+6	+11	+11		4	4	4	4	4	4	4	3	3	2
19th	+9/+4	+6	+11	+11		4	4	4	4	4	4	4	4	3	3
20th	+10/+5	+6	+12	+12	Absorb wand	4	4	4	4	4	4	4	4	4	4

CLASS FEATURES

All of the following are class features of the magician.

WEAPON & ARMOR PROFICIENCY

Magicians are proficient with all simple weapons. They are also proficient with any armor, but not with shields. Since the magicians channel their spells through wands and need not perform any intricate somatic gestures, they do not suffer arcane spell failure penalties for wearing armor.

SPELLS

A magician casts arcane spells, drawn from the magician's spell list (see **Chapter Five: Magic**, page 41). A magician chooses and prepares his spells ahead of time. He must use his wand to prepare them (see Wand below).

To learn or cast a spell, the magician must have an Intelligence score equal to at least 10 + spell level (Int 10 for 0-level spells, Int 11 for 1st-level spells, and so on). The Difficulty Class for a saving throw against a magician's spell is 10 + the spell level + the magician's Intelligence modifier.

Like other spellcasters, a magician can cast only a certain number of spells of each spell level per day. His base daily spell allotment is given on **Table 3-3: The Magician**. In addition, he receives bonus spells per day for high Intelligence score.

A magician's selection of spells is limited. He begins play knowing three 0-level spells and one 1st-level spell of your choice. At each new magician level, he gains one or more new spells, as indicated on **Table 3-4: Magician Spells Known**. Unlike spells per day, his Intelligence score does not affect the number of spells a magician knows; the numbers on **Table 3-4: Magician Spells Known** are fixed.

Upon reaching 4th level, and at every even-numbered magician level after that (6th, 8th, and so on), a magician can choose to learn a new spell in place of one he already knows. In effect, the magician "loses" the old spell in exchange for the new one. The new spell's level must be the same as that of the spell being exchanged, and it must be at least two levels lower than the highest-level magician spell the magician can cast. A magician may swap only a single spell at any given level, and must choose whether to swap the spell at the same time he gains new spells known for the level.

WAND (SU)

In the *Trojan War* campaign setting, wands are somewhat different. They are not used as charged devices capable of casting the same spell 50 times. They are instead the focus a magician uses to practice magic. Though a magician casts arcane spells, he cannot do so without his wand.

Newly created magicians are assumed to have already created his wand, but for characters multiclassing into magician, or those losing a wand, they must fashion a new one. Wands can be of any material, bronze, wood, or bone, but they all work the same. To create a wand, the magician must spend 8 hours carefully crafting the slender object, imbuing it with part of his essence, and attuning it to his mastery of the art. At the end of the day, the magician must succeed a DC 15 Craft check, using the appropriate skill for the medium of his work. Thus a magician crafting a wooden wand uses Craft (woodworking), while a bronze wand would require a Craft (metalworking) check.

Regardless of the material, a wand costs 100 gp per class level in materials, inks, and incense to properly attune, and an expenditure of 50 XP per class level. If the check fails, half of the materials are ruined, XP lost, and the magician must start again the next day.

Once crafted, a magician uses the wand to store his spells, much like a wizard stores spells in a spellbook. Better still, a magician's wand also serves the same function as a spell component pouch, fulfilling any material component requirements for the spell. A magician must still supply components for spells with material components listed with a gp price, or focuses, or any other unusual component.

At the start of each day, a magician must spend time in meditation, imbuing the spells he desires into the wand. It takes one half-hour per level of the highest spell the magician stores to prepare his spells. Thus, if a magician stores only 1st-, 2nd-, and 3rd-level spells, he needs only an hour and a half to prepare his wand.

Once the spells are stored, the magician cannot change them until the next day. For the rest of the day, the magician can call upon any of the wand's spells at a moment's notice, simply by raising the wand, waving it, and speaking the command words as a standard action. If the spell's casting time is longer than 1 standard action, the magician still uses the longer casting time. Once he recalls a spell from his wand, the spell is used for the day. Any unused spells fade after 24 hours, so the magician must recharge the wand the next morning. As magicians learn new spells, they may channel them into their wands as well; a wand has no limit to the number of spells they can contain.

For example, young Xanses is a 1st-level magician. He knows *daze*, *detect magic*, *flare*, and *resistance* as his cantrips, and *mage armor* and *magic missile* as his 1st-level spells. As he may only cast 3 0-level spells and 1 1st-level spell per day as a 1st-level wizard, he must select which spells he will imbue into his wand. He decides to imbue *daze*, *flare*, *resistance* for his 3rd-level slots, and *magic missile* for his first level slot.

BLOOD TIES (SU)

At 2nd level, magicians learn how to focus their spells upon a target through blood. By acquiring a sample of the target's blood and dipping the wand in the blood before casting (a free action), the magician's spell becomes more potent and more difficult to resist for that target. Subjects of blood ties suffer a –4 penalty to all saving throws against spells that magician casts for a number of minutes equal to the magician's Intelligence modifier. Thereafter the subject is immune to the effects of Blood Ties for 24-hours.

CHARGE WINE (SU)

At 5th level, the magician learns to impart some of his wand's power into wine. He cannot cast spells through the wine, but anyone drinking the charged wine the same day suffers a –4 penalty to saving throws against the magician's spells. The wine loses its magical potency after 24 hours, and the penalty fades in the same time. Charging wine requires one full-round action.

ENCHANTED GIFT (SU)

At 8th level, magicians can use gifts as links to their targets. The magician charges a gift, in much the same way he charges wine. He then presents the gift to his target. If the target accepts the gift and touches it, he suffers a –4 penalty to saving throws against the magician's spells for that day plus one day per caster level. Giving the gift back does not remove this connection, nor does destroying it. The connection can only be removed prematurely by a *remove curse* spell or similar magic.

TABLE 3-4: MAGICIAN SPELLS KNOWN

Level	\-	\-	\-	\-	\-	\-	\-	\-	\-	\-
	0	**1**	**2**	**3**	**4**	**5**	**6**	**7**	**8**	**9**
1st	4	2	—	—	—	—	—	—	—	—
2nd	5	3	—	—	—	—	—	—	—	—
3rd	5	3	2	—	—	—	—	—	—	—
4th	6	4	3	—	—	—	—	—	—	—
5th	6	4	3	2	—	—	—	—	—	—
6th	7	5	4	3	—	—	—	—	—	—
7th	7	5	4	3	2	—	—	—	—	—
8th	8	6	5	4	3	—	—	—	—	—
9th	8	6	5	4	3	2	—	—	—	—
10th	9	7	6	5	4	3	—	—	—	—
11th	9	7	6	5	4	3	2	—	—	—
12th	9	8	7	6	5	4	3	—	—	—
13th	9	8	7	6	5	4	3	2	—	—
14th	9	9	8	7	5	5	4	3	—	—
15th	9	9	8	7	6	5	4	3	2	—
16th	9	9	9	8	6	6	5	4	3	—
17th	9	9	9	8	7	6	5	4	3	2
18th	9	9	9	9	7	7	6	5	4	3
19th	9	9	9	9	8	7	6	5	4	3
20th	9	9	9	9	8	8	7	6	5	4

READ WAND (SU)

At 11th level, a magician can tap the energies in another magician's wand. He cannot cast spells with it, but he can see what spells it contains, and learn any spells he does not already know by succeeding at a Spellcraft check against a DC 15 + the spell level for each spell he would learn. These new spells may be learned immediately, but for a limited time, and he is limited in the number of extra spell levels he can learn by his Intelligence modifier per level. Thus, a magician with an 18 Intelligence can learn 4 spell levels worth of spells from another wand. For these purposes, a cantrip counts as a spell level of one-half. If the wand contains more spells he does not know, the magician can learn them upon gaining another level, just as he would learn any other new spell he encounters. Reading a wand requires one minute for every spell level the wand contains. Thus, reading a wand containing a 6th-level spell takes six minutes.

Spells learned from Read Wand do not remain with the magician long. When the magician prepares one of these learned spells, he unlearns the spell. He may cast this spell as he would any other spell he knows for the next day. At the end of the 24-hour period, he loses these spells unless he read the wand once more.

RECHARGE WAND (SU)

At 14th level, a magician can use the power of another wand to recharge his own. He must read the wand first. Then he can absorb the magical energy in the wand and can transfer it to his own. The energy transfers on a one-to-one basis, so if the wand contained four 1st-level spells, three 2nd-level spells, and one 3rd-level spell, the magician could recharge the same number of spells of those exact levels in his own wand. Wands only hold power for 24 hours, so he would have to use them within the 24 hours of the found wand's initial charging. A magician cannot overcharge his wand, so only his available spell slots can be replaced. Any remaining energy is lost.

WAND ALTERNATIVE

At 17th level, a magician no longer needs to use a wand to hold his spells. He still requires a focus, however, but he can use any crafted wood, metal, or stone item. The magician still has to craft this item by hand, just as he did with his wand, in order to imbue it, and he can only use one item at a time. To switch to a new item, he must destroy the previous one (whether it was a wand or another alternate object), causing 1d6+1 per class level points of nonlethal damage (maximum of 1d6+20) to the magician. Magicians often select amulets, rings, or some other type of jewelry as their alternate as these items are less conspicuous than carrying a wand.

ABSORB WAND

At 20th level, the magician learns how to tap another wand and keep its spells intact. He can cast spells from that wand as if it were his own, or he can take its charged spells and transfer them into his own wand. He must know the spell in order to cast it or transfer it, but the spells remain intact. Thus, if a magician finds a wand with four 5th-level spells in it, and he knows all four spells already, he can cast them from that wand or pull them into his own wand in addition to the spells he charged himself. Note that the magician must read the new wand before he can absorb its spells. This also means that, if he finds a spell he does not know he can attempt to learn it on the spot. The magician must make a Spellcraft roll (DC 10 + highest-level spell in the new wand) before he can use the new wand, however. This is only if he is casting spells from that wand directly, and does not apply if transferring the spells into his own wand. Transferring spells requires one minute per spell, regardless of spell level.

PRIEST

The gods exist and actively participate in mortal affairs. The gods actually take sides and many of them make personal appearances on the battlefield to aid their favored champions and turn the tide of battle. Most nobles, at least those with some form of divine heritage, have some gift at reading omens, and dedicated warriors can speak directly to the gods, but who speaks for the commoners? That is the role of the priest. These men and women mediate between gods and men, conveying their god's desires and moods to people and helping them to follow the path of respect and worship. Priests are advisors, counselors, and spiritual fathers, and they preach the virtues of their god even as they offer suggestions on mundane matters to improve a person's life.

PARTICIPATION

Priests are not combatants, so they do not fight in the Trojan War. Many of them stay on or near the battlefield, however, helping tend to the wounded and offer hope and guidance to the common soldiers. Priests decipher omens for commoners and help them understand the gods. Priests can interpret what it is the gods want; they can identify a god's moods, and teach how mortals can appease the deities. But they are more than just simple advisors and teachers; they are the favored servants of the deities. For example, during the war, Chryses, a priest of Apollo and father of the maiden Chryseis, asked the Achaeans to return his daughter. When Agamemnon refused, Apollo cast a plague upon the army.

ADVENTURES

Priests wander the land to bring their words and wisdom to the people. Some priests are fortunate enough to settle in temples or at shrines, but for most, the road is their home. They shepherd all the people of their nation, particularly those in rural areas who do not otherwise receive religious guidance. Priests make good traveling companions because they warn of supernatural dangers and of divine displeasure. Their prayers can help individuals overcome obstacles. Priests are not fighters themselves, but they can bless warriors and make them stronger.

CHARACTERISTICS

The priest is the Homeric equivalent to the cleric, but less combative and more spiritual. Priests speak directly to their chosen god, and pray to him or her for divine favors. The god grants these favors if the priest has been faithful and if the god is in a good mood. Priests are also guardians of truth. Judges and rulers often call upon priests to bear witness to a transaction or oath, for if they swear upon their god, priests cannot lie or dissemble. Finally, priests handle all religious rites such as presiding over funerals, functioning as emissaries to the dead, except for those performed by nobility. Finally, priests can see unquiet spirits and may speak with them, bridging the gulf between mortals and the dead.

ALIGNMENT

Priests must have an alignment within one step of their chosen god, and they cannot be neutral unless their god is likewise neutral.

FAVORED GODS

Priests must select one god as their favored god, and although they honor the entire pantheon, all of their petitions are for this god alone. Athena, Apollo, and Zeus are the most commonly selected, since Athena and Zeus favor wisdom and Apollo is the master of prophecy. Still, priests can select any of the gods as their patron.

BACKGROUND

Priests are of common birth, generally hailing from small towns, villages, and isolated farms. Many people encounter a wandering priest in their youth, who tutors them in the ways of the gods, showing them by example what it means to be a spiritual leader.

RACES

Divine offspring have little interest in commoners, and their conversations with their divine parents are private, hence all priests are human.

OTHER CLASSES

Fighters respect and honor priests, who are commoners like themselves but who have a special link to the gods. Rangers, who also have divine magic and who roam the wilderness, honor priests and admire their ability to advise people so wisely. Bards acknowledge priests as both spiritual leaders and likely sources of information. Rogues respect priests for their attempts to help people, but since most rogues are not religious, they may consider the priest's faith misplaced and misguided. Charioteers respect priests as the gods' messengers to the people, and while dedicated warriors acknowledge this, they consider priests inferior because they merely carry messages. Magicians find priests' ability to wield divine magic fascinating, while druids respect what priests can do but at the same time feel priests are misguided, for druids hold nature as the higher power.

Priests themselves admire warriors of all sorts, particularly the dedicated warriors who bear such a close relation to a god. They find rogues curious and many feel they need religious guidance, while rangers are good men and women who serve the gods in other ways. Bards spread tales of the gods, making them extremely welcome to any priest, even if the bards spread their tales for entertainment rather than instruction. Magicians, however, are not only fools but heretics, claiming they can do magic without the aid of the gods.

GAME RULE INFORMATION

Priests have the following game statistics.

Abilities: Wisdom is the most important attribute for a priest. It allows him to understand messages from his god and to offer good advice to his people. Charisma is also important, since priests spend much of their time consoling or counseling others. Intelligence is useful for deciphering events and for observing the world around them.

Alignment: The priest's alignment must be within one step of his god's, and he cannot be neutral unless his god is likewise neutral.

Hit Die: d8.
Starting Gold: 3d4 x 10 (75 gp).

CLASS SKILLS

The priest's class skills (and the key ability for each skill) are Appraise (Int), Concentration (Con), Craft (Int), Decipher Omen (Wis), Diplomacy (Cha), Heal (Wis), Knowledge (nobility and royalty) (Int), Knowledge (religion) (Int), Perform (Cha), Profession (Wis), and Spellcraft (Int).

Skill Points at 1st Level: (2 + Int modifier) x 4.
Skill Points at Each Additional Level: 2 + Int modifier.

CLASS FEATURES

All of the following are class features of the priest.

WEAPON & ARMOR PROFICIENCY

Priests are proficient with the quarterstaff, dagger, and the weapon approved by their god (see sidebar). Priests are not proficient with any form of armor or shield. If the priest

TABLE 3-5: THE PRIEST

Class Level	Base Attack Bonus	Fort Save	Ref Save	Will Save	Special	Petitions per Day	Max Spell Level
1st	+0	+0	+0	+2	Petition	3+1	1st
2nd	+1	+0	+0	+3	Divine protection 1/day	4+1	1st
3rd	+1	+1	+1	+3	Sense deception	5+2	2nd
4th	+2	+1	+1	+4		6+2	2nd
5th	+2	+1	+1	+4	Divine protection 2/day	7+3	3rd
6th	+3	+2	+2	+5		8+3	3rd
7th	+3	+2	+2	+5	Underworld awareness	9+4	4th
8th	+4	+2	+2	+6		10+4	4th
9th	+4	+3	+3	+6		11+5	5th
10th	+5	+3	+3	+7	Divine protection 3/day	12+5	5th
11th	+5	+3	+3	+7	Divine sight (god)	13+6	6th
12th	+6/+1	+4	+4	+8		14+6	6th
13th	+6/+1	+4	+4	+8	Divine sight (all gods)	15+7	7th
14th	+7/+2	+4	+4	+9		16+7	7th
15th	+7/+2	+5	+5	+9	Divine protection 4/day	17+8	8th
16th	+8/+3	+5	+5	+10		18+8	8th
17th	+8/+3	+5	+5	+10	Deity's favor	19+9	9th
18th	+9/+4	+6	+6	+11		20+9	9th
19th	+9/+4	+6	+6	+11		21+10	9th
20th	+10/+5	+6	+6	+12	Divine protection 5/day	22+10	9th

multiclasses into a class with a wider selection of weapon proficiencies, or takes a Martial Weapon Proficiency feat, he is still bound to use the weapon of his god. However, priests may pray for expanded weapon usage, such as through the spell *granted weapon*, which allows the priest to employ different types of weaponry. See **Chapter Five: Magic** for details on this spell.

PERMITTED WEAPONS BY DEITY

Deity	Weapon
Zeus	Throwing spear
Athena	Throwing spear
Ares	Throwing spear
Apollo	Bow (any)
Poseidon	Throwing spear
Hermes	Sling
Artemis	Bow (any)
Hephaestus	Warhammer
Hera	Mace (any)
Other gods	None (priests of other gods may only use the dagger and the quarterstaff).

PETITION

Priests summon divine magic. They do not cast spells themselves. Instead, a priest prays to his chosen god, and petitions for some divine effect. The effects function as spells. The priest can petition a certain number of times each day, based upon his level, and he can ask for any spell up to the highest one his level allows. Thus, a priest who can petition for a 9th-level spell could pray for 9th-level spells every time, if he so chose. Priests can also gain bonus petitions if they have a high Wisdom.

For each petition, the priest makes a caster level check against a DC 20 + the spell level. In this instance, a 1 is always a failure, and a 20 is always a success. If successful, the god acquiesces to the request, and casts the spell. A failure indicates the god chooses not to comply, either because he disapproves, or because he is not in a helpful mood.

Note priests do not need to prepare spells ahead of time, since they are not actually casting themselves. Thus, they can request any spell at any time, provided it is within their level range and they still have a petition left for the day. Furthermore, priests must have positive Piety points in order to make any request—otherwise their god not only refuses but also punishes them for lack of devotion. Thus, priests always offer prayers and libations at dawn, at dusk, and at other times preferred by their god. Finally, the priest must possess have a Wisdom score of 10 + the spell's level to be able to summon and wield the spell. The spell DC equals 10 + the priest's Wisdom modifier + the level of the spell.

While technically a god can do anything, each god has certain spheres of influence (these are not necessarily domains; see **Chapter 8: Religion and Piety** for each deity's specific domains). They will not cast a spell of a sphere they do not possess, no matter how well their priest rolls. Thus, Poseidon will never cast a fire spell nor will Hephaestus ever use a water spell. A brief list of the gods and the spheres follows. The GM should use his discretion when granting a priest character's request for spells from his deity.

The section on spells lists all the spells priests can petition, along with their spheres.

DOMAINS AND DOMAIN SPELLS

Each god has several domains (see the individual deity listings on page 81 in **Chapter Eight: Religion and Piety** for more

THE GODS' SPHERES OF INFLUENCE

Deity	Spheres of Influence
Zeus	Air, weather, knowledge, justice, diplomacy, creation, healing
Athena	War, knowledge, justice, diplomacy, healing
Ares	War, destruction, fire
Apollo	Knowledge, music, art, light, healing
Poseidon	Water, earth, horses
Hermes	Travel, stealth, trickery, diplomacy
Artemis	Hunting, night, moon, purity, healing
Hephaestus	Fire, creation, metal, earth, justice
Hades	Earth, death, darkness, cold
Hera	Knowledge, emotion, diplomacy, healing
Aphrodite	Emotion, diplomacy, trickery, water
Hecate	Night, darkness, air, knowledge, death

information). Domains represent the spheres the god is most comfortable with and has the most control over. Priests can petition for additional spells from those domains, known as domain spells, and these do not count against the normal limit for their petitions. Instead, priests have a separate number of domain spells they can petition each day, based upon their level. This is represented as the number after the plus sign, under Petitions per Day on Table **3–5: The Priest**. Petition checks for domain spells receive a +2 modifier to the check.

Priests, just as clerics in other settings, gain the benefits of Granted Powers without having to petition their gods for them.

DIVINE PROTECTION (SP)

At 2nd level, as a standard action, priests can call upon their gods for protection from harm. This gives the priest a +2 deflection bonus to AC and +2 resistance bonus to all saves. The protection appears as a faint glow around the priest, and lasts for 1 round per caster level. At 5th level, and every 5 levels thereafter, the priest can use this ability one additional time per day.

SENSE DECEPTION (SU)

Starting at 3rd level, priests can detect untruths as they are spoken. These priests have the permanent ability to sense lies as if under the effects of the *discern lies* spell.

UNDERWORLD AWARENESS (SU)

Priests of 7th-level or higher can always see and speak with spirits, as if always under the effect of the *deathly sight* spell. In addition, priests gain a +2 bonus to all Charisma-based skill checks made when interacting with spirits.

ORACLES

Apollo had normal priests, but he also had oracles. These individuals trained in prophecy to see glimpses of the future even without the aid of omens. Most oracles lived within Apollo's temples, like the oracle of Delphi. Worshippers could visit and, after making an offering to the archer god, ask questions of the oracle. The oracle would then tell them what he saw. Sometimes the vision was clear and straightforward. Other times, it was as vague as any normal omen. However, the oracle always spoke the truth, regardless of the consequences; as part of their religious observance, an oracle cannot lie.

Oracles can be created using the priest class or the seer prestige class, though neither is exactly right. If using the priest class, an oracle should place ranks in Perform (sing) and Perform (stringed instrument), to allow the character to sing and play the lyre, proper invocations to Apollo. Then the oracle should advance as a priest of Apollo until he can advance into the seer prestige class. As a special rule, the seer allows the priest of Apollo to retain Apollo as the chosen god, retaining all priestly abilities including the power to petition. Alternatively, if you use the *Psychic's Handbook*, you could create a multiclass priest/psychic who specializes in clairsentience and telepathy.

Oracles are extremely rare in the Homeric world. Apollo invests each with a tiny portion of his power and knowledge, and guards them jealously. He only has a handful of oracles at any given time, and only promotes a new one when an old one dies. Oracles do not retire; they retain their gifts until death. Apollo also prefers them to stay within the safety of his temples, so creating an adventuring oracle may require some explanation. Apollo could send an oracle on a mission, however, if it is something too important to entrust to any normal priest.

The other gods do not like oracles because they answer only to Apollo. The other deities, particularly Hera, Ares, and Poseidon, may throw obstacles in an oracle's path, or create false omens to discredit him.

Many oracles are born blind, or become blind when they gain the oracular sight. Others bind their eyes, to keep the mortal world from distracting them.

DIVINE SIGHT (SU)

Beginning at 11th level, priests can see through the disguise of their chosen god, recognizing him in any form. At 14th level, this ability extends to any god; the priest not only recognizes the divine being but also knows the deity's identity. This is a permanent ability, and does not require a roll.

DEITY'S FAVOR (SU)

As a full round action, a 17th-level priest may sacrifice one of his daily petitions to increase the benefits of divine protection. For the duration of the divine protection ability, he may also add his Wisdom bonus (if any) to his AC and saving throws.

NEW PRESTIGE CLASSES

The *Trojan War* setting places great emphasis on three things: combat skill, persuasiveness, and understanding the will of the gods. Each of these prestige classes deals with at least one of these elements. Although these classes are very much rooted in the *Iliad*, they translate into other d20 settings with little difficulty.

Humans can become any of these three prestige classes. Divine offspring can become runners, but are not eligible to become orators or seers. Their skills lie in the physical realms rather than in the verbal or divinatory spheres.

ORATOR

Among the Achaeans, two of the most respected leaders are Nestor and Odysseus. Both are warriors, but they are held in high regard more for their skill with words than combat. Their powers of persuasion win them the most acclaim, for both men are masters of rhetoric and oratory. They may convince cowards to fight, calm raging warriors, and incite emotions in their audiences. In short, both men are classic orators.

Orators are similar to bards in that they use sound to sway people. Where bards are entertainers, orators are inciters. They speak to crowds, not to delight and amuse them, but to convince them of some ideal or urge them onto some course of action. An orator uses his words as both weapon and whip, cutting down his enemies while goading his allies into action.

Oratory is more than the art of speaking well. It hinges upon listening as well. A good orator's words touch his audience partially because he has a gift for language but also because he studies the crowd and shapes his speech to suit them. If they show no signs of religious devotion, he does not call upon the gods for aid, but instead mentions the families they left back home. If the men jeer at comments about cowardice, he harps upon that theme, using it to sharpen his other arguments. A proper orator knows what his crowd wants, what they like and do not like, and uses those elements to strengthen his own case.

In the Homeric world, orators are the demagogues, the taskmasters, the generals, and the politicians. They either conceive strategies or endorse the plans of others, and then convince the armies to follow that tactic. Orators are often strong fighters themselves, and relate to their audience, using their ties as fuel for their lectures, but they are most dangerous when speaking because they can twist the truth any way they like, talking people into doing things they never intended.

Fighters are the most likely to become orators. They know war and combat, and they know enough strategy to see when something works and when it does not. They also learn to use their wits and their tongues instead of their swords. Dedicated warriors can become orators, gaining the gift of rhetoric from their god and swaying people to follow their god's preferred course of events. Magicians, who excel at study, make excellent orators, and some use this talent to distract others from their arcane interests. Rogues can also become orators, using their knowledge and agility to acquire information about their audience. Priests do not often become orators, unless ordered by their god, and druids, rangers, and barbarians prefer the quiet of the wilderness to amphitheaters full of men.

Kings keep orators on hand to endorse their plans and grow support from the people. In the army, commanders may employ orators to keep the other warriors focused upon battle and confident of victory.

ADAPTATION

Orators can become storytellers, dramatic bards who use words to entertain. They can also be more arcane, using rhetoric to hide verbal components and dramatic gestures to conceal the somatic ingredients. Alternatively, orators could become divine, channeling the will of their god to lead people along a particular path. No matter the nature of the character, orators focus upon the spoken word and upon public performance. They can be shy in private, but when faced with an audience an orator is fearless.

Hit Die: d6.

REQUIREMENTS

To become an orator, a character must meet the following criteria.

Race: Human
Base Attack Bonus: +4.
Skills: Bluff 2 ranks, Diplomacy 2 ranks, Intimidate 6 ranks, Perform (oratory) 4 ranks, and Sense Motive 4 ranks.
Feats: Distinctive, Persuasive.

CLASS SKILLS

The orator's class skills (and the key ability for each skill) are Appraise (Int), Bluff (Cha), Concentration (Con), Diplomacy (Cha), Gather Information (Cha), Intimidate (Cha), Knowledge (any) (Int), Listen (Wis), Perform (Cha), Sense Motive (Wis), and Spot (Wis).

Skill Points at Each Level: 4 + Int modifier.

CLASS FEATURES

All of the following are class features of the orator prestige class.

WEAPON & ARMOR PROFICIENCY

An orator gains no proficiency with any weapon or armor.

CAPTIVE AUDIENCE (EX)

Whenever a 1st-level or higher orator speaks to a gathered crowd or even a single individual, he may make a Perform (oratory) check against a DC determined by the crowd's general attitude. Attitudes reflect the general mood of the crowd. DCs are as follows.

CAPTIVE AUDIENCE

Attitude	DC
Hostile	50
Unfriendly	25
Indifferent	15
Friendly	10
Helpful	5
Fanatic	0

On a successful check, the orator holds the individual or group spellbound, as if under the effect of the *enthrall* spell. In addition, the orator gains a +4 circumstance bonus on any Charisma-based skill checks to improve their attitude. He can hold their attention for a number of hours equal to his Charisma modifier, or as long as he continues to speak, whichever is shorter. The effects of this ability only apply to those who can both see and hear the orator.

On a failed check, and if the crowd contains members who are Unfriendly or Hostile to the speaker, the orator takes a −4 penalty on Charisma-based skill checks to improve the crowd's attitude. Finally, if any member of the crowd is attacked, the effects end.

GLIB (EX)

Starting at 1st level, the orator may add his class levels in this prestige class to all Charisma-based skill checks made to affect an audience.

CHARMER (EX)

At 2nd level, the orator hones his skills as a speaker to invoke feelings of loyalty and trust in his audience. Once per day, per point of his Charisma bonus, an orator can add a +20 to a Charisma-based skill check to improve the attitude of an NPC in the audience. The improved attitude remains for a number of hours equal to the orator's class level.

At 6th level, the orator gains Improved Charmer and can apply this modifier to Charisma-based skill checks to improve the attitudes of one person per class level who listens in the audience. At 10th level, he gains Great Charmer and can improve the attitudes of two people per class level.

TAUNT (SU)

At 3rd level, the orator learns to use his language skills in combat. He can taunt his opponents, goading them into carelessness action and rage. To taunt an opponent, the orator must succeed a Bluff check opposed by the target's modified level check (1d20 + character level or Hit Dice + the target's Wisdom bonus [if any] + target's modifiers on saves against mind-affecting effects). If the orator wins, the target grows frustrated and takes a −2 penalty to hit for as long as the orator keeps talking. At 6th level, the orator can make general comments, taunting 1 opponent per orator level, though they all must be actively attacking him at the same time.

SUGGEST (EX)

Starting at 4th level, the orator can implant a suggestion in the mind of one of his listener, using his natural charisma, poise, and skill as a demagogue. To implant the suggestion, the orator must make a Bluff check opposed by the target's Sense Motive. If the orator wins, he implants a suggestion as per the *suggestion* spell. The effect of the suggestion lasts for 1 hour. The orator can use this ability a number of times per day equal to his Charisma modifier (minimum of 1/day).

TABLE 3-6: THE ORATOR

Class Level	Base Attack Bonus	Fort Save	Ref Save	Will Save	Special
1st	+0	+0	+0	+2	Captive audience, glib
2nd	+1	+0	+0	+3	Charmer
3rd	+1	+1	+1	+3	Taunt
4th	+2	+1	+1	+4	Suggest
5th	+2	+1	+1	+4	Lull
6th	+3	+2	+2	+5	Improved Charmer
7th	+3	+2	+2	+5	Awe
8th	+4	+2	+2	+6	Beast-tongue
9th	+4	+3	+3	+6	Assess audience
10th	+5	+3	+3	+7	Great Charmer

LULL (EX)

At 5th level, the orator can pitch his words to relax his audience, soothing them into a deep, restful sleep. He can target up to two people per class level. To relax the targets, the orator must make a successful Perform (oratory) check opposed by the target's Sense Motive check. If the orator wins, the subjects fall asleep for 1d4 rounds +1 round per class level. They may be awoken normally.

AWE (EX)

At 7th level, the orator is so skilled in delivering speeches he can overwhelm his audience. To awe an audience, the orator must make a successful Intimidate check against the audience's attitude (see Captive Audience above). If he succeeds, the audience is stunned for 1d4 rounds +1 round per class level.

BEAST-TONGUE (EX)

Beginning at 8th level, the orator can add his orator class levels to all Handle Animal checks and Wild Empathy checks (if he has this class feature from another class).

ASSESS AUDIENCE (EX)

At 9th level, an orator learns to read his audience. To do so, he must succeed a Sense Motive check opposed by the audience's Attitude (see Captive Audience above). If successful, the orator discerns what topics please his listeners the most and what angers them as well. The orator gains a +4 bonus to Charisma-based skills used on the audience from that point onward. In addition, the listener takes a –4 penalty to all opposed rolls against any of the orator's class abilities as the orator knows exactly how to affect him.

RUNNER

Homer describes Achilles, the central figure of *the Iliad*, as a runner. He chases Trojan warriors around the field, and no one can escape him. Even those on chariots have difficulty evading him. His attacks are swift and sudden, like a tornado or a lightning strike, appearing from nowhere and wreaking destruction before vanishing again. This is all because Achilles is a runner.

The runner is a warrior who specializes in speed. He learns to fight while moving quickly across the battlefield, giving his enemies little time to respond to his attacks. Runners learn agility as well, so they can weave between foes and around obstacles without slowing down. For a runner, combat is an obstacle course, and he selects a path taking him through the field as quickly as possible, coming close enough to strike before moving away again. The worst thing that can happen to a runner is to be trapped in a small space, forced to stand still and fight.

Some warriors jeer runners as cowards because they never stand still, but most know better. Runners have no fear of fighting. They know their greatest asset is their quickness.

Fighters and dedicated warriors are the most likely to become runners, adding speed to their already potent fighting skills. Barbarians are fearsome runners, combining their impressive speed and rage with a runner's celerity and momentum. Rogues are also dangerous runners, specializing in striking by surprise. Magicians, priests, druids, and bards rarely become runners because their interests lie in slower, more studied, activities. Charioteers never become runners, since doing so means stepping down from their prized chariots to fight on foot.

Armies possessing runners use them as advance troops, sending them crashing into the enemy to break their lines before the rest of the warriors arrive. Runners are also used to rescue vulnerable forces by distracting attackers until the force can retreat and regroup. Those runners who do possess stealth make excellent scouts, covering great distances quickly and quietly before dispatching any enemy sentries in their path.

NPC runners are usually attached to standard army forces, and provide them with information and support as necessary. Commanders may hold runners in reserve, using them only when their fearsome speed is needed. This is because runners are hard to train, so each one is valuable. Since a good runner can kill an enemy's leaders before battle really begins, a single strong runner can demoralize and destroy an army almost single-handedly, particularly if they have no runners of their own and no way to defend against such attacks. When both armies have runners, the speedy fighters can duel, racing across the field while fighting so quickly onlookers cannot tell who is winning.

TABLE 3-7: THE RUNNER

Class Level	Base Attack Bonus	Fort Save	Ref Save	Will Save	Special
1st	+1	+0	+2	+0	Fast movement +5 ft., momentum, steady
2nd	+2	+0	+3	+0	Skilled charge
3rd	+3	+1	+3	+1	Agile runner, fast movement +5 ft.
4th	+4	+1	+4	+1	Evasion
5th	+5	+1	+4	+1	Extended attack
6th	+6	+2	+5	+2	Fast entry, fast movement +5 ft.
7th	+7	+2	+5	+2	Quick defense
8th	+8	+2	+6	+2	Difficult target
9th	+9	+3	+6	+3	Fast movement +5 ft.
10th	+10	+3	+7	+3	Lightning strike

ADAPTATION

Runners can become a more spiritual class, calling upon a god for speed just as a dedicated warrior asks for strength. This would be particularly appropriate for anyone who worshipped either Hermes or Iris, since both are gods of speed. Running for them could become a form of prayer, a form of paying homage to the god.

As mentioned above, runners can also become masters of stealth, assassins who strike quickly and silently and then vanish into the night. Their speed allows them to attack with unusual force, while staying clear of responding attacks.

In the wilds, runners can focus on scouting and surveillance, moving through an area at high speed to check for signs of danger or damage. They could then circle back around to attack intruders. Runners can also keep pace with deer and other fast animals, bonding with the simple creatures over sheer enjoyment of the run.

Hit Die: d10.

REQUIREMENTS

To qualify to become a runner, a character must fulfill all the following criteria.

Race: Human or divine offspring
Base Attack Bonus: +6.
Skills: Knowledge (tactics) 4 ranks and Spot 4 ranks.
Feats: Cleave, Endurance, Power Attack, Run

CLASS SKILLS

The runner's class skills (and the key ability for each skill) are Balance (Dex), Climb (Str), Intimidate (Cha), Jump (Str), Knowledge (tactics) (Int), Listen (Wis), and Spot (Wis).

Skill Points at Each Level: 2 + Int modifier.

CLASS FEATURES

All of the following are class features of the runner prestige class.

WEAPON & ARMOR PROFICIENCY

A runner is proficient with all simple weapons, the throwing spear and short sword. He is also proficient with all armor and shields (except the tower shield). Runners are prohibited from using clubs, slings, longbows, composite longbows, greatswords, maces, or quarterstaffs, as they interfere with his movements. While using such weapons, he loses the fast movement ability.

FAST MOVEMENT (EX)

At 1st level, the runner's base movement is faster than the norm for his race by +5 feet. The runner gains additional +5 feet to his base speed at 3rd, 6th, and 9th levels. These bonuses apply when the runner is wearing no armor, light armor, or medium armor and not carrying a heavy load. Apply this bonus before modifying the runner's speed because of any load carried or armor worn. A barbarian's fast movement ability stacks with the runner's fast movement ability.

MOMENTUM (EX)

On a successful charge attack, a runner of 1st-level or higher adds one-half his class levels (to a maximum of +5) to his weapon damage roll.

STEADY (EX)

A 1st-level runner can speak normally while making a run action.

SKILLED CHARGE (EX)

Starting at 2nd level, a runner no longer takes a penalty to his Armor Class when making a normal charge attack. He still takes the normal –4 penalty when making an Extended Attack (see below)

AGILE RUNNER (EX)

Beginning at 3rd level, a runner may make a number of 90-degree turns during a charge attack equal to his Dexterity bonus (minimum of 1 turn). This ability allows the runner to charge around corners, avoid combatants, or other obstacles, while still building momentum for the inevitable clash of arms.

EVASION (EX)

At 4th level, a runner can avoid magical and unusual attacks with great agility. If he makes a successful Reflex saving throw against an attack normally dealing half damage on a successful save, he instead takes no damage. Evasion can be used only if the runner is wearing light armor or no armor. A helpless runner does not gain the benefit of evasion. If the runner already has Evasion from another class, he instead gains Improved Evasion.

EXTENDED ATTACK (EX)

At 5th level, the runner may quickly strike down his foes. A runner may make a special charge attack. He takes a –4 penalty to his AC for one round, but he can make a single melee attack against every foe he threatens along the path to his intended target. All these attacks suffer a –5 penalty.

FAST ENTRY (EX)

At 6th level, a runner learns to enter combat so quickly his opponents cannot react. Runners gain a +2 bonus to their Initiative checks. This stacks with Improved Initiative. In addition, when making a run action, he no longer provokes attacks of opportunity when moving through threatened squares.

QUICK DEFENSE (EX)

Starting at 7th level, the runner is so fast he can dodge blows before they hit him. Runners gain a +1 dodge bonus to their AC. In addition, in any round in which the runner moves twice his base land speed or more (such as a charge, overrun, or run action for example), he also gains a +2 bonus to his Reflex save. This last bonus lasts until the runner's next turn.

DIFFICULT TARGET (EX)

At 8th level, a runner is harder to target with ranged attacks. In any round in which the runner moves twice his base land speed or more, he gains a +4 bonus to AC against all ranged weapon attacks. This bonus lasts until the runner's next turn.

LIGHTNING STRIKE (EX)

At 10th level, a runner's charge is so deadly and surprising opponents have a hard time reacting to the attack. A runner's bonus to his attack roll when making a charge attack increases to +4 and he deals +1d6 points of damage on the attack. In addition, the subject of this attack must succeed a Will save against a DC 15 + the damage dealt or be shaken for 1d6 rounds.

SEER

The gods grant gifts to men, each according to their nature and their role in the heavenly plan. Some men receive great strength and skill at arms. Others acquire the gift of stirring speech, while others still learn to move quickly and quietly, to glide through the wilderness as a ghost. To a select few, the gods grant insight, both into the world and into their own minds and deeds. These rare men and women are the seers, and theirs is both a noble path, but a lonely one.

Most people assume that seers are highly religious, for they know the will of the gods. This is partially true. Seers interpret a god's mood and thoughts, but this means they know more than most how fickle, shallow, and random the gods can be. Seers also cannot have a chosen god. If they formerly had a chosen god, they have to cease worshiping that god and give up any powers or abilities gained from that singular devotion to become a seer (though some exceptions exist, namely Seers of Apollo). This is so to better serve and observe every member of the pantheon equally.

Seers spend much of their time pondering the gods and their actions, but this is not their only interest. They also watch people closely, studying men and women to read their thoughts and intentions. Seers have enough insight to make excellent advisors and counselors, except most lack diplomacy. Seers cannot lie about what they see—to do so would be to spurn their gift and possibly lose it forever. Thus, whenever asked, they must answer truthfully, no matter what the consequences.

Seers also cannot take payment for their services. Their insight is a divine gift, and selling it demeans both the gift and the giver. Most seers survive by accepting small gifts from the people they advise, since gifts are acceptable. Some live in nice homes but most spend their lives wandering the world, observing the gods' hands in different nations and upon different people.

Most people ask seers to interpret omens. Seers are experts at reading omens, in part because they understand the minds of the gods and because they know the minds of people as well. By knowing something about the intended recipient, a seer can better understand what an omen might mean, and thus translate it more easily and more accurately.

Kings keep a seer on hand to translate dreams and read other omens for them. Few have a seer permanently at court, however—the seer's tendency to speak the truth and inability to hold his tongue can cause embarrassment and sometimes

damage diplomatic meetings. Instead, seers may have a small home near the king's palace, so the king can summon them at a moment's notice.

When not translating omens, most seers spend their time watching the world around them. They enjoy seeing new things and discovering new ways in which the gods have touched people and objects. Seers also wander out of necessity. After telling kings unpopular interpretations, seers find themselves unwelcome there, and so they move on. Because of this, most seers have few personal possessions, learning to survive on what they find in the wild. Some seers solve this problem by settling in a remote area, making supplicants find them. They have less chance to interact with people this way, but gain more time to sit and reflect about life.

Seers can see not only omens and gods, but also ghosts. Even more than priests, they are the speakers for the dead, and the mediators between the dead and the living. When people think they have ghosts nearby, they summon a seer to find out what it is the ghosts want. Priests help appease the ghosts by performing rites and offering sacrifices, but the seers handle the actual discussions.

Some priests become seers, of course. These holy men and women realize their chosen god is just one aspect of the whole, and learn to look beyond that tiny portion. Depending upon the god, the former priest might retain his class abilities, like his ability to pray for divine aid. Athena, for example, allows her priests to become seers and still keep their priestly abilities because she is the goddess of knowledge and respects their desire to learn more and to understand the pantheon as a whole. Other gods are possessive, and strip priests of their abilities when the priest decides to listen to the other gods as well. A priest who wants to become a seer can volunteer for a quest demonstrating both his resolve and his natural powers of insight. If he succeeds in the quest, his former chosen god will grudgingly acknowledge that the priest's true calling is that of a seer, and allow him to retain his former class abilities, though now all the gods answer the seer's prayers. This does give seers one major advantage over regular priests: since seers worship all the gods equally, their petitions can request aid from any sphere.

Druids become seers and retain their abilities since their powers come from the earth rather than from a god. Those druids deciding the gods do play a role in life, and believe such interference should be studied, find themselves well suited to life as seers. Their previous interest in nature and earth serves as a starting point, and now they move on to watching people and gods, trying to see all of the elements involved.

Bards can also become seers. A bard travels from place to place, meeting different people and collecting all manner of stories. They use these stories for entertainment, but many are true or at least contain a hint of truth, and some bards become intrigued. They start looking for patterns to the stories, and for reasons behind them. Then they start wondering what the stories really mean and what purpose the gods' actions serve in them. From there it is a simple step to becoming a seer, and looking for answers to those questions. Bards make excellent seers; they are already talented observers, and they are familiar with mystic gifts. Furthermore, bardic seers are more diplomatic and more charismatic than are their brethren.

Barbarians and fighters can also become seers, though this is rare. These men of action may see something making them think about life beyond fighting and about the gods. Barbarians, because they keep their minds uncluttered, can interpret omens quickly and intuitively. They do not over-think matters, or let themselves be distracted by pleasantries and social constraints. Fighters have no special gift for seeing, but their combat skill does make them more formidable when someone dislikes the content of their vision or their interpretation of an omen. Rogues rarely become seers, since they focus so much on the here and now and are often masters of self-gratification. Magicians, who have little to do with the gods, usually do not become seers either, and charioteers are too focused upon their horses and chariots to see anything larger than their current environs. Dedicated warriors almost never become seers because doing so means renouncing their favored god, and dedicated warriors are *very* devoted to their deities.

Calchas was the most famous seer in the Trojan War. He risked Agamemnon's displeasure to reveal the reason behind Apollo's plague. On the Trojan side, both Cassandra and Laocoon had the gift of seeing, but Cassandra's was a double-edged sword: Apollo blessed her with phenomenal gifts of insight, but cursed her to have no one believe her pronouncements. The most famous seer of the Homeric era, however, was Teiresias, who could read the gods better than anyone, but often angered them with his tactlessness. Even after his death, Teiresias retained his gifts and Odysseus entered the land of the dead to consult with him, finding Teiresias more self-aware and intelligent than any other ghost.

ADAPTATION

Seers are more likely to be divine spellcasters, calling upon the pantheon as a whole to answer their prayers, but could be arcane spellcasters who use their own inner strength to steal glimpses of the gods' divine plans. Seers can also become more martial, focusing their abilities upon studying battlefield conditions and using their insight to give their army the advantage. Finally, seers could be bardic oriented, using performance, music, and drama to convey messages, and offering deliberately vague interpretations as a way to entice the audience, dragging them into the story. This last option is the most interesting variant because it allows seers to become more charismatic and more cunning, and it lets them become teachers rather than simple interpreters. In this version, seers actively force people to open their minds and consider other options by making them work to understand the omens and by subtly guiding them to the answer. A seer of this sort would actively seek out gatherings, and would use his knowledge of small and immediate events like

a parlor trick to captivate his audience. He would be a favorite of children, teaching them to look around, study events, and appreciate hidden truths by telling them stories about people and gods and the omens that connected them.

Hit Die: d6.

REQUIREMENTS

To become a seer, a character must meet the following criteria.

Race: Human.
Skills: Appraise and Sense Motive 4 ranks, Decipher Omen 8 ranks
Feats: Alertness
Special: The character must have successfully deciphered an omen important to the campaign, as determined by the GM.

CLASS SKILLS

The seer's class skills (and the key ability for each skill) are Appraise (Int), Concentration (Con), Decipher Omen (Wis), Heal (Wis), Knowledge (nobility and royalty) (Int), Knowledge (religion) (Int), Search (Int), Sense Motive (Wis), Spellcraft (Int), Spot (Wis), and Survival (Wis).

Skill Points at Each Level: 4 + Int modifier.

CLASS FEATURES

All of the following are class features of the seer prestige class.

WEAPON & ARMOR PROFICIENCY

A seer does gains no proficiency with any weapons or armor.

CLEAR SIGHT (EX)

Starting at 1st level, seers may add their class level to all Search and Spot checks made to notice a secret door or hidden compartment.

FUTURE GLIMPSE (SU)

A 1st-level seer may snatch a glimpse of the future a number of times per day equal to his Wisdom bonus (minimum of 1). To glimpse into the future, the seer must make a successful DC 15 Decipher Omen check. A successful check informs the seer what will happen in the immediate future, usually in general terms. For example, the seer might know that someone will betray the king, but not who or how. The seer gains a +2 insight bonus to his Initiative check, AC, all saving throws and ability checks for a number of rounds equal to one-half his class levels because he can adjust his actions respond to the sequence of upcoming events.

DIVINE GLIMPSE (SU)

At 2nd level, seers gain the Divine Sight feat. In addition, they may detect disguised gods with an Appraise check to denote status.

DEATHLY SIGHT (SU)

A 3rd level seer gains the ability to see ghosts and spirits at will, as per the *deathly sight* spell.

DIVINE ASSESSMENT (SU)

At 3rd level, seers can assess the mood of any gods nearby. The seer makes a DC 15 Decipher Omen check to do so. Success indicates he knows the god involved and that god's exact mood

TABLE 3-8: THE SEER

Class Level	Base Attack Bonus	Fort Save	Ref Save	Wil Save	Special
1st	+0	+0	+2	+2	Clear sight, future glimpse
2nd	+1	+0	+3	+3	Divine glimpse
3rd	+1	+1	+3	+3	Deathly sight, divine assessment
4th	+2	+1	+4	+4	Accurate sight, divine clarity
5th	+2	+1	+4	+4	Deathly speech
6th	+3	+2	+5	+5	Pious sight
7th	+3	+2	+5	+5	Divine understanding
8th	+4	+2	+6	+6	Divine scrutiny
9th	+4	+3	+6	+6	Divine vision
10th	+5	+3	+7	+7	Future sight

(see **Table 14–1: Divine Mood** in **Chapter Fourteen: Running a *Trojan War* Game**, page 142).

ACCURATE SIGHT (SU)

Seers of 4th level or higher can discern the race, nationality, class, and level of anyone they meet. This ability automatically penetrates disguises, spells, and any other means of concealing identity.

DIVINE CLARITY (SU)

At 4th level, a seer can see right through any god's disguise automatically. He no longer needs to make an Appraise check to denote status.

DEATHLY SPEECH (SU)

At 5th level, the seer can hear and speak to ghosts clearly at will, without any additional efforts (like the usual offerings), as per the deathly tongue spell. In addition, the seer gains a +2 insight

bonus on all Charisma-based skill checks when interacting with the dead.

PIOUS SIGHT (SU)

Starting at 6th level, seers automatically read an individual's Piety level. They cannot tell the subject's exact Piety score, but can tell if it is negative, positive, or zero, and if negative or positive they can tell if it is high or low (high being above 10, with low being below −10).

DIVINE UNDERSTANDING (SU)

Seers of 7th level or higher understand the messages and desires of the gods. They can tell which gods are involved, and, with a successful DC 18 Decipher Omen check, tell exactly what that god wants (death, sacrifices, apologies, quests, etc.) and from whom.

DIVINE SCRUTINY (SU)

At 8th level, a seer learns to see people's weaknesses. The seer must observe the target for 2 rounds, and thereafter, the seer understands the subject clearly. He cannot do anything else during this time but watch the person in question. For a number of days equal to the seer's class levels, the seer gains a +2 insight bonus on attack rolls against the subject of the seers scrutiny, a +2 insight bonus AC against all attacks made by the subject, and a +4 bonus to all Charisma-based skill checks made against that person.

DIVINE VISION (SU)

At 9th level, seers can see divine marks. The gods apply these marks to their children, their favorites, their protected animals, plants and locations, and their enemies. With a successful DC 20 Decipher Omen check, the seer can tell which god applied the mark and its meaning.

FUTURE SIGHT (SU)

Starting at 10th level, seers gain the power to look into the future. With a successful DC 25 Decipher Omen check, they can see the plans of the gods themselves. The seer gains a +4 bonus to all attack rolls, saving throws, skill checks, and ability checks made in circumstances involving that god and the god's spheres of influence, favorites, sacred places, and children for the one day per seer level. The seer may also grant a +2 bonus to others for that same duration by warning them of upcoming events.

CHAPTER FOUR: SKILLS AND FEATS

NEW SKILLS & SKILLS USES

The *Trojan War* employs all the skills as written in the *PHB*. This setting, however, focuses on social or military rank, proper presentation, and acquiescence to the will of the gods. New skills and new uses for existing skills follow. **Table 4–1: New Skills** uses the following abbreviations for the new classes presented in this book: Cht for charioteer, Ddw for dedicated warrior, Mag for magician, and Pri for priest.

APPRAISE (NEW USE)

Denote Status: In addition to appraising an item's value, you can use this skill to gauge a person's value in terms of social status, military rank, and Piety (if a priest).

Check: When meeting someone for the first time, or seeing him or her again after an absence, you can attempt an Appraise check. Appraising someone's status requires a successful check against a DC 15 (modifiers to this base DC are listed below). A successful check indicates you know if the target is of noble or divine birth and whether he is worthy of respect or of contempt. If you succeed the check by 5 or more, you learn the character's approximate rank (army commander, king, etc.). You also learn the severity of the target's sins (if they have negative Piety). Failure means you cannot estimate the person's status.

APPRAISE

Status	Appraise DC Modifier
Noble	–2
Royal	–4
Divine offspring, minor	–1
Divine offspring, medium	–2
Divine offspring, major	–3
Priest	–1
Positive Piety score	–1
Piety score below 0	–1
Piety score below –5	–2
Piety score below –10	–4
Character treated with contempt	–2
Character treated with severe contempt	–4

APPRAISE (CONTINUED)

Status	Appraise DC Modifier
Character is ostracized	–6
Character is in disguise	+2
*Character is a deity in disguise	+10
Character is disfigured or maimed	+2
Character is from a place with radically different ideas about rank	+2

All modifiers are cumulative.

*Requires the Divine Sight feat (see page 38) to correctly appraise.

Action: Appraising a person takes 1 minute (ten consecutive full-round actions).

Try Again: No.

Note: If the appraised target is a deity, this skill does not reveal his true nature unless you also have the Divine Sight feat. Otherwise, if you make a successful Appraise check on a disguised deity, you only learn the status of the individual the deity is imitating. A successful Appraise check does not reveal a subject's identity, only his rank; for instance, a target might be revealed as a king, but you would not learn his name or country of origin through use of this skill. Note racial bonuses and bonuses for using magnifying glasses or merchant's scales do not apply to Appraise checks made to denote a person's status.

Special: Priests can use this ability to gauge a character's exact Piety score.

Synergy: If you have 5 ranks in Knowledge (nobility and royalty), you gain a +2 bonus on Appraise checks to denote someone's status.

Untrained: Failure on an untrained check means no estimate.

BOAT (DEX)

You know the various parts of a boat. You also know how to handle them, from rowing oars to manning the tiller to trimming the sail.

Check: Routine tasks, such as ordinary boating, do not require a skill check. Make a check only when some unusual

TABLE 4-1: NEW SKILLS

Skill	Bbn	Brd	Cht	Ddw	Drd	Ftr	Mag	Pri	Rgr	Rog	Sor
Boat	C	C	cc	cc	C	cc	cc	cc	C	cc	cc
Decipher Omen	C	C	cc	C	C	cc	cc	C	cc	cc	C
Drive	cc	cc	C	C	cc	C	cc	cc	cc	C	cc
Knowledge (tactics)	cc	C	C	C	cc	C	C	C	C	cc	cc

BOAT

Special Circumstances	DC Modifier*	Consequences for failure
Calm water	—	No movement
Rough water	+5	No movement, DC 10 Balance check or DC 15 Strength check or go overboard.
Stormy water	+10	Movement in a random direction up to one-half boat's speed, DC 15 Balance check or DC 20 Strength check or go overboard.
Whirlpool	+15	Boat capsizes, everyone on board goes overboard.
Controlling a boat while under attack	+2	One-half speed
Boating without a full crew complement	+1 per missing member	One-half speed
Vessel damaged or boarded	+5	No movement

*All modifiers are cumulative.

circumstance exists (such as inclement weather or when you are attacked), or when boating during a dramatic situation (being under attack, for example, or trying to reach a destination in a limited amount of time). A boat check is a DC 10 modified by the following special conditions.

Action: A successful Boat check allows you to move the boat's speed as a move-action or double your boat's speed as a full-round action.

Try Again: Most boat checks have consequences for failure that make trying again impossible.

Special: A character can take 10 when boating, but cannot take 20.

Synergy: If you have 5 or more ranks in Profession (sailor), you gain a +2 bonus to Boat checks. If you have 5 or more ranks in Boat, you gain a +2 bonus to Balance checks while at sea.

Untrained: You may attempt a Boat check untrained, but at a −4 circumstance penalty.

DECIPHER OMEN (WIS)

You can read the desires and plans of the gods through various omens.

Check: Use this skill to interpret the meaning of omens. Upon seeing anything strange and unnatural, you can make a Decipher Omen check. The GM secretly makes this roll. The difficulty is based upon your knowledge of the god who sent the omen (if it is an omen) and the subtlety of the message.

DECIPHER OMEN

Condition	Decipher Omen DC
The omen could be completely natural	24
The omen looks slightly unusual, but is otherwise normal	20
The omen is clearly not normal, though it is possible	18
The omen is clearly not natural	15
The omen is blatantly supernatural	12

Situation Modifiers	Check Modifier
The god is the character's favored god	+2
The god is the rival of the character's favored god	-4
The character is waiting for an omen	+2
The omen was predicted beforehand and has certain distinct elements	+4

Action: Deciphering an omen is a full-round action.

Try Again: No. Once someone interprets an omen, they believe they translated the message correctly, even if they were completely wrong.

Special: See **Omens** on page 144 for more details on using these divine signs.

Synergy: If you have 5 or more ranks in Knowledge (arcana) you gain a +2 bonus to Decipher Omens checks.

DRIVE (DEX; TRAINED ONLY)

You can handle horse-drawn devices, such as chariots and carts.

Check: Routine tasks, such as ordinary driving, do not require a skill check. Make a check only when some unusual circumstance exists (such as inclement weather or an icy surface), or when driving during a dramatic situation (you are being chased or attacked, for example, or trying to reach a destination in a limited amount of time). In addition, any of the following tasks require checks.

DRIVE

Task	Drive DC
Driving a cart or chariot in combat	15
Driving while fighting	15
Guiding a cart through a narrow space	16
Guiding a chariot through a narrow space	15
Stopping a cart quickly	15
Stopping a chariot quickly	14
Tight turn in a cart	16
Tight turn in a chariot	15
Wide turn in a cart	12
Wide turn in a chariot	14

Situation Modifiers	Check Modifiers
Extra team of horses	+2
Fatigued horse	+5
Unfamiliar cart	+1
Unfamiliar chariot	+3
Unfamiliar team of horses	+3

All modifiers are cumulative.

Action: A Drive check is a Move action.
Try Again: Yes. A character who fails a driving check can try again after one round, but at a –2 penalty. The penalty increases by –2 each time the character fails the check.
Special: Charioteers train in driving chariots, and can ignore the penalties for driving in combat and driving while fighting.

KNOWLEDGE (INT; TRAINED ONLY)

Like the Craft and Profession skills, Knowledge actually encompasses a number of unrelated skills. Knowledge represents a study of some body of lore, possibly an academic or even scientific discipline. The fields of study as described in the *PHB* exist in the *Trojan War* setting.

In addition to the typical subjects covered by the standard fields of study, *Trojan War* adds these features to Knowledge (nobility and royalty) and introduces a new field of study: tactics.

• **Nobility and royalty:** *Dress*—You know how to properly carve and serve meat; *Recitation*—You know how to memorize and flawlessly repeat long speeches and other information.

• **Tactics:** Techniques and strategies for disposing and maneuvering forces in combat.

Action: Usually none. In most cases, making a Knowledge check does not take an action—you simply know the answer or you do not.
Synergy: In addition to the normal bonuses derived from skill synergy, you also gain a +2 bonus to Appraise checks involving an object related to your field of study. If you have 5 or more ranks in Knowledge (tactics) you gain a +2 bonus to Initiative checks.

NEW FEATS

Many of the feats found in the core rulebooks translate easily into the Homeric world. The exception, however, is the Item Creation feat. In the Homeric world, Hephaestus constructed the majority of magic items. Therefore, it is strongly recommended Item Creation feats either not be allowed in your campaign, or at least have increased entry requirements to remind everyone that in these myths the gods take their handiwork very seriously and magic items are extremely valuable and more than rare.

The following new feats fit the character of the *Iliad*.

BATTLEFIELD MAGIC (METAMAGIC)

Your leadership experience makes spellcasting easier.

Benefit: You can cast spells on a battlefield without needing to make a Concentration check.

BATTLEFIELD SEASONED

Your skill at fighting on the battlefield is renowned.

Benefit: You retain your Dexterity bonus to Armor Class when joining a Force. See **Chapter Seven: The Homeric Battlefield** for details.
Normal: Characters who join a Force as a soldier do not receive Dexterity bonuses to their AC unless they the Uncanny Dodge ability. Captains, however, retain their normal bonuses and Armor Class.

CHARIOT ATTACK (GENERAL)

You can use your chariot to trample opponents.

Prerequisite: Dex 15, Drive 7 ranks, Improved Overrun.
Benefit: You do not need to make a second Drive check to keep your chariot from toppling after making a Trample attack.
Normal: Chariots may be used for Trample attacks. The driver must make a Drive check against the target's AC to hit. On a successful hit, the driver must succeed a second Drive check (DC 15 + damage dealt) to keep the chariot from toppling. A fighter may choose Chariot Attack as one of his bonus fighter feats.

CHARIOT SHIELD (GENERAL)

You know how to use your chariot defensively, gaining more protection than normal.

Prerequisite: Dex 13, Drive 4 ranks.
Benefit: When mounted in a chariot, you automatically gain a +4 cover bonus to AC and a +2 cover bonus to Reflex saves, even without a shieldbearer. If you take the total defense action while in a chariot, or if you have a shield bearer, your cover bonus to AC increases to +8, and your bonus to Reflex saves increase to +4.

TABLE 4-2: FEATS

Feat	Prerequisites
Battlefield Seasoned	—
Chariot Attack[1]	Str 13, Dex 15, Drive 6 ranks
Chariot Shield[1]	Dex 13, Drive 4 ranks
Chariot Specialization[1]	Drive 6 ranks
Distinctive	Cha 15
Divine Sight	Wis 13, Sense Motive 2 ranks
Drive-by Attack[1]	Drive 4 ranks
Elusive	Hide 12 ranks
Favored	Must have a chosen god
Fierce	—
Lion of the Field	Base attack bonus +3
Noble	—
Pampered	Must have a chosen god
Pious	Piety 10, chosen god
Piteous	—
Quick Release[1]	Dex 17, Base attack bonus +6
Shield Swing	Str 13, shield proficiency
Step back	Dex 13, Base attack bonus +4
Stunning	Divine offspring, Cha 17
Thick skin	—
Unfazed	Iron Will
Valuable	Noble
Metamagic Feat	
Battlefield Magic	—
Targeted	Ability to cast 3rd-level spells

[1] A fighter may select this feat as one of his fighter bonus feats.

Normal: Chariots provide a +2 cover bonus to AC and a +1 cover bonus to Reflex saves.

Special: A fighter may choose Chariot Shield as one of his bonus fighter feats.

CHARIOT SPECIALIZATION (GENERAL)

When in a moving chariot, you can make devastating attacks.

Prerequisite: Drive 9 ranks.
Benefit: When in a moving chariot that moves at least its drawn speed, you may add +2 to weapon damage rolls from any melee weapon or thrown weapon you wield. If the chariot moves at twice its speed or faster, the bonus increases to +3.
Special: If you choose to add this bonus to weapon damage rolls, you take a –2 penalty to AC and you may not use the benefits of Chariot Shield. A fighter may choose Chariot Specialization as one of his bonus fighter feats.

DISTINCTIVE (GENERAL)

You stand out in a crowd. For leaders, this can be essential. It means your men can always find you, making it easier for you to give orders and hold your troops together.

Prerequisite: Cha 15.
Benefit: You have a striking appearance and are easily noticed. You gain a +2 bonus to your Leadership score and a +2 bonus to Diplomacy and Intimidate checks. If you are on a battlefield, your allies gain a +4 bonus to all Search and Spot checks made to locate you.

DIVINE SIGHT (GENERAL)

You are adept at spotting gods and goddesses.

Prerequisite: Wis 13, Sense Motive 2 ranks
Benefit: Whenever you meet someone, or see someone you have met, you can make an Appraise or Sense Motive check to determine his or her status. If the individual is actually a god in disguise, and you roll high enough to penetrate his disguise, you realize the target is actually a deity. In addition, you gain a +2 bonus to all Sense Motive checks.
Normal: The gods can appear as anyone and humans cannot see through their disguises.
Special: Additionally, dedicated warriors and priests with this feat gain a +2 bonus when encountering their favored god in disguise. Seers gain a +2 bonus to uncover any god.

DRIVE-BY ATTACK (GENERAL)

You can use the chariot's momentum to add power to your attack.

Prerequisite: Drive 4 ranks

Benefit: When in a chariot and using the charge action, you may move and attack as if with a standard charge and then move again (continuing the straight line of the charge). Your total movement for the round cannot exceed double your chariot's speed. You and your steeds do not provoke an attack of opportunity from the opponent you attack.

Special: A fighter may choose Drive-by Attack as one of his bonus fighter feats.

ELUSIVE (GENERAL)

You are difficult to pick out of a crowd. This is useful for anyone trying to sneak up on opponents, both assassins and those who want to get to a particular adversary without being stopped.

Prerequisite: Hide 8 ranks.

Benefit: You may use a crowd for concealment. In addition, while in a crowd, you may add your character level to your Hide check to blend in. If the crowd disperses, you lose this benefit.

EXTRA MUSIC (GENERAL)

Prerequisite: Bardic music.
Benefit: You can use your bardic music four extra times per day.
Normal: Bards without the Extra Music feat can use bardic music once per day per level.
Special: You can gain this feat multiple times, adding another four uses of bardic music each time.

FAVORED (GENERAL)

A god or goddess is partial to you. Once per week you may make a special request of that god, and if it is within his power and does not contradict the god's own plans or those of another deity, the god grants it. Note that these requests are for survival and honor, not for money. Asking a god for gold angers the god, but asking for help in surviving a storm or in being victorious in battle pleases him.

Prerequisite: Must have a chosen god.

Benefit: Once per week, you can ask for a boon as if your Piety was 10 (see **Piety, Chapter Eight: Religion and Piety**, page 91). Your actual Piety score does not matter at this time, as long as it is not negative, and this boon does not reduce your Piety modifier. This request is in addition to any allowable for positive Piety.

Special: You may only take this feat at 1st level. If your Piety score falls −20, you lose this feat permanently.

FIERCE (GENERAL)

Your primal nature is apparent to the creatures of the world. Thus, animals fear you.

Benefit: Whenever you come within 5 feet of an animal, you automatically force the animal to make a Will save against a DC equal to 10 + one-half your character level + your Charisma modifier. On a failed check, the animal becomes frightened for 1d4 minutes. If the animal succeeds, it is uneasy, but otherwise unaffected. Regardless of success or failure of the saving throw, an animal can only be affected by this feat once per 24-hour period.

Special: Because of your ferocity, you suffer a −4 penalty to Handle Animal checks and Wild Empathy checks.

LION OF THE FIELD (GENERAL)

You are a powerful force upon the battlefield and can wreak havoc among your foes.

Prerequisite: Base attack bonus +3

Benefit: When attacking a Force, you deal full damage to all members of that Force. Thus, if your attack does 12 points of damage, each member of that Force takes 12 points (See **Chapter Seven: The Homeric Battlefield** for more information on using this feat).

Normal: Damage against a Force is reduced by the same number as the Force's Damage Modifier (a Force with a x3 modifier takes only one-third the normal damage).

Special: You can take this feat twice, though taking it a second time requires you to have a base attack bonus of +6. If you take this feat a second time, you inflict double damage when attacking Forces. This does not apply when fighting individuals, even other Captains.

NOBLE (GENERAL)

Your noble blood lends you with an air of authority and command.

Benefit: You gain +4 bonus to any Charisma-based skill checks such as like Bluff, Diplomacy, or Intimidate when used against a subject of common blood. You also gain a masterwork short sword as part of your starting equipment.

Special: You may only take this feat at 1st level. Even if raised by commoners, you may select this feat provided your true parentage is noble.

PAMPERED (GENERAL)

The gods tolerate toward your flaws. Any sins earn you half the normal number of Piety points.

Prerequisite: You must have a chosen god.

Benefit: Sins cost half the normal number of Piety points.

Special: You may only take this feat at 1st level. If your Piety score falls −20, you lose this feat permanently.

PIOUS (GENERAL)

Your deity rewards your pious devotion.

Prerequisite: Piety 10, you must have a chosen god.

Benefit: Your character gains twice as many Piety points as normal for any good deed or religious observance.

Special: If your Piety ever falls to −6 or lower, you permanently lose access to this feat. You may select this feat at a future point, but only if your Piety returns to 10 or higher, and only if you make amends to your favored deity.

PITEOUS (GENERAL)

Enemies pity you, and pull back when striking.

Benefit: When attacked in combat, as a free action you may make a Bluff check opposed by an opponent's Sense Motive check. If you succeed, all nonmagical physical attacks from that opponent deal 1 point less damage than normal (to a minimum of 1 point of damage). This feat does not function against critical hits, attacks made with magical weaponry, spells, or spell-like abilities. Likewise, this feat offers no protection from attacks made by enraged opponents (such as a barbarian under the effects of rage).

Special: You may only take this feat at 1st level.

QUICK RELEASE (GENERAL)

You can use thrown weapons with amazing speed.

Prerequisite: Dex 17, Base attack bonus +6.

Benefit: When making a full attack with a thrown weapon, and when you have a second thrown weapon ready, you may make an additional attack at your highest base attack bonus, but each attack you make in that round (the extra one and the normal ones) takes a –2 penalty. You may use this feat in conjunction with Rapid Shot, but the penalties stack.

Special: A fighter may choose Quick Release as one of his bonus fighter feats.

SHIELD SWING (GENERAL)

You can ready a shield for use as a free action.

Prerequisite: Str 13, shield proficiency.

Benefit: You are adept at shield use, and can pull a shield from your back, swing it around, slip your arms through the straps, grip the hand strap, and be ready to use the shield immediately. You can don or remove a shield as a free action.

Normal: Readying a shield is a move action.

Special: You are still limited to one free action in a round, so you cannot don and remove a shield in the same round without expending a move action. A fighter may choose Shield Swing as one of his bonus fighter feats.

STEP-BACK (GENERAL)

You gain an additional 5-foot step at the end of your turn.

Prerequisite: Dex 13, Base attack bonus +4.

Benefit: When taking a full-round round action, you gain an additional 5-foot step at the end of your turn. This is in addition to the standard 5-foot step characters normally have. Movement granted by this additional 5-foot step does not provoke an attack of opportunity.

Normal: During a full-round action, you can take one 5-foot step before, during, or after the action.

STUNNING (GENERAL)

Your beauty stuns onlookers.

Prerequisite: Cha 17, divine offspring.

Benefit: Your appearance is so magnificent it can stun people. Anyone who looks at your naked face must succeed a Will save against a DC equal to 10 + one-half your level + your Charisma modifier or become stunned for 1d4 rounds.

TARGETED (METAMAGIC)

Your superior skills ensures the spell you cast strikes only your foes.

Prerequisite: Ability to cast 3rd-level spells.

Benefit: You may select a group consisting of a race, culture, or class to exclude from the effects of any spell you cast affecting an area, such as a burst, emanation, spread, line, cone, cylinder, sphere, or creatures at the time you cast the spell. For spells with durations longer than instantaneous or 1 round, the excluded group gains no special protection from the spell's effect beyond the first round. Only one group can be selected at a time. The selection may change with each spell (a magician could cast one spell and have it ignore Achaeans, and then cast another and have it ignore only the charioteers). For example, a spellcaster excludes a group of Achaeans from a *sleet storm* spell. Any Achaeans in the area are unaffected on the first round. However, on the following rounds, any Achaeans still in the area are subject to the spell's effects. A targeted spell uses up a spell slot two levels higher than their normal spell level.

Special: The caster must state a known group. Such a group cannot be based on relationships, except in instances of the same families. Thus, a magician could cast a spell that ignores everyone in the Atreides family, but he cannot cast a spell that ignores "my friends." The caster also cannot name individuals for this spell—they must fit within a specific group.

THICK SKIN (GENERAL)

Your hide is unusually tough and very resistant to physicial damage.

Benefit: Your natural armor bonus improves by +1.

Special: You may only take this feat at 1st level. Alternatively, if you immerse yourself in the River Styx while in the Underworld, you gain the benefits of this feat.

UNFAZED (GENERAL)

You have nerves of steel, and can perform non-combat actions in the midst of combat.

Prerequisite: Iron Will.

Benefit: You may take 10 on any class skill in which you have ranks while being threatened, though you may still not take 10 while otherwise distracted. Use of this feat does not avoid provoked attacks of opportunity for performing certain skill checks. In addition, you gain a +2 bonus on all Concentration checks. On the Battlefield, you do not take the –2 penalty to skill checks.

Normal: You may not take 10 when you are threatened or distracted. On the Battlefield, all skill checks are made at a –2 penalty.

VALUABLE (GENERAL)

Your social standing makes you more valuable to your opponents alive than dead.

Prerequisite: Noble.

Benefit: Your family is wealthy and willing to pay a handsome ransom to get you back alive. You gain +4 to Bluff and Diplomacy checks made when asking to be captured rather than be killed.

CHAPTER FIVE: MAGIC

People assume magic was everywhere during the Homeric age. After all, this was a time when gods walked the earth. But magic was actually quite rare, or at least it was not seen much in the epic tales. The gods had magic, of course, but their power resided in their sheer strength, their ability to become invisible, or to assume a mortal guise. Gods had the power to calm men, to heal them, to give them strength, or cloud their minds. They each mastered their realms; Poseidon had full control over the waves, Zeus the heavens, and Ares, the battlefields. Yet beyond these instances, we rarely see the deities do much most would consider magic.

Mortals using magic is even more rare. Circe, a magician in the *Odyssey*, used her magic to transform Odysseus' men into swine, then back again. She makes them younger and stronger when they become human again, but we do not see her perform any other spells. So where is all the magic?

One possibility is more magic occurs offstage. Human magicians may roam the earth, but are rarely religious and so tales about the gods do not involve them. The gods might encourage bards not to tell stories of such men and women in an effort to prevent, or at least deter others from forsaking religion in pursuit of magic. We do not see the gods or the priests acting on their behalf perform much in the way of spells, but perhaps this magic occurs offstage too. The gods take active roles in the Trojan War, but with other events, they watch from Mt. Olympus instead. In those cases, they might employ indirect tactics, answering prayers of their priests and sending aid in the form of divine spells.

A second possibility is we do see the magic but do not recognize it. When a warrior hurls his spear and hits a foe so hard, he knocks his enemy from his chariot, could that be the result of a spell? When Nestor speaks and manages to calm all the other Achaeans with only his words, perhaps this is magic as well. Homer shows us the results, but glosses over the causes so we may have priests praying and magicians casting along the sidelines, their spells affect the battles while they stay offstage. This could also account for some of the warriors having greater than normal strength, speed, and endurance, such as when Aias lifts a rock no two normal men could lift, and hurls it like a small stone. Perhaps he has magical aid as well.

The third possibility is this world has very little overt magic. The gods are magical beings, so everything they do is magic including the existence of their children, both human-like and monstrous. We may not see many magicians or spells because few exist here. Spells affect other creatures or objects. Perhaps, in the Homeric world, most of the magic is self-contained instead—people use magic to make themselves stronger, faster, or more charming, but have no idea how to cast spells on others. Circe may be a rarity, one of the few who have learned these other methods.

Any one of these interpretations work for the Trojan War, and you must decide which direction to take for your own game. Will you go with a more traditionally magical setting, with magicians and priests casting spells everywhere, or will you choose to have the magic more subtle and internal? The texts support any interpretation, so it is just a question of what you would prefer for your campaign.

This chapter, however, assumes you will employ the standard spell system for your game, and provides a selection of new spells in the format of the *PHB*. In addition, it provides a look at some changes required to fit within the texts, detailing changes to the standard assumptions of the core rulebooks. Finally, this chapter provides a revised spell list for both arcane and divine spellcasters, including new spells unique to the world of the *Trojan War*.

ARCANE MAGIC

All the standard schools of magic exist. Some of the schools have a different focus, however.

The Homeric world honors the dead, and though most treat ghosts with fear, they show respect. Hades does not allow the dead to walk again except as invisible, immaterial spirits. He does not tolerate the existence of undead, and so these creatures do not exist here. Because of these conceptual changes, necromancy taps life energy and death energy, allowing casters to interact with the dead, but there are no spells for dealing with undead as they do not exist.

Evocations are less common in the *Trojan War*, because they involve the most obvious display of magical power. Making a torch or a bonfire flare is one thing, but hurling a fireball is another. The gods do not approve of such overt magic. Most of the allowed evocation spells deal with manipulating existing forces such as tidal waves or bonfires rather than creating new ones.

Conjuration is also a bit different. The Homeric setting has only four known planes of existence—the Mortal World, Elysian Fields, Mt. Olympus, and the Underworld. Mt. Olympus is the home of the gods, the Elysian Fields is where great and blessed mortal heroes venture after death, while the Underworld houses all of the other dead. No outside planes exist, and so most summoning spells either summon natural creatures or do not function at all. Creation spells are also rare, because the gods frown upon creating something from nothing. They prefer men to modify existing objects, even if that means magically carving an object from raw rock or metal.

Abjurations, divinations, enchantments, illusions, and transmutations are all possible, and most of their spells are unchanged. Enchantment and transmutation are the most common, since Homeric characters commonly alter other people's emotions and thoughts, enhancing or diminishing a person or object's qualities.

The Homeric world readily accepts the notion of magic, since they know that the gods exist and work magic themselves. Arcane magic, though, does not come from the gods, a fact

ultimately cannot control. Others see them as blasphemers, usurping the powers of the gods. Reactions to arcane spellcasters ranges from discomfort to dislike to utter hatred. In some nations, people tolerate magicians, while in others people hunt and kill them without mercy. Magicians learn which lands are safe to inhabit, which are safe to visit, and which to avoid. Many also learn to conceal their gifts, masquerading as divine spellcasters.

DIVINE MAGIC

Divine magic is widely accepted in the Homeric setting, and highly respected. Everyone knows the gods are real, and that they grant the desires of their favorites. No one is surprised when a priest can heal a sick man, curse an enemy, or control the winds. Of course, the magic actually comes from the gods, and the priests merely call upon them for aid, but even so that gives a divine spellcaster authority and makes them too dangerous to offend lightly. Priests can use most of the spells presented in the *PHB* provided the spell fits within their god's portfolio. The only spells removed are those involving other planes, outsiders, the undead, and resurrection, since other planes do not exist, and Hades allows neither undead nor a continuation of life after the individual's time has ended.

Although divine spellcasters are accepted, people may still be uncomfortable around them. This is different from arcane casters, where people fear the gods may strike them down for their heresy. With divine spellcasters, people worry that they may cast divine disfavor on those they dislike. Thus, although priests are respected, many give them a wide berth just to be safe. To counter this, most priests pray for magic rarely, and do so in private whenever possible.

making many uncomfortable. Some view arcane spellcasters are heretics, dabbling in forces they cannot understand and

SPELL LISTS

ARCANE SPELLS

Below is a list of the arcane spells available in *Trojan War*. New spells are *italicized*.

0-LEVEL ARCANE SPELLS (CANTRIPS)

Abjur **Resistance:** Subject gains +1 on saving throws.
Div **Detect Poison:** Detects poison in one creature or small object.
Ench **Daze:** Creature loses next action.
Evoc **Dancing Lights:** Figment torches or other lights.
Flare: Dazzles one creature (-1 attack).
Light: Object shines like a torch.
Illus **Ghost Sound:** Figment sounds.
Trans **Mage Hand:** 5-pound telekinesis.
Mending: Makes minor repairs on an object.
Open/Close: Opens or closes small or light things.
Univ **Arcane Mark:** Inscribes a personal rune (visible or invisible).
Detect Magic: Detects spells and magic items within 60 ft.
Prestidigitation: Performs minor tricks.
Read Magic: Read scrolls and spellbooks.

1ST-LEVEL ARCANE SPELLS

Abjur **Alarm:** Wards an area for 2 hours/level.
Endure Elements: Exist comfortably in hot or cold environments.
Hold Portal: Holds door shut.
Protection from Chaos/Evil/Good/Law: +2 to AC and saves, counter mind control, hedge out elementals and outsiders.
Shield: Invisible disc gives +4 to AC, blocks *magic missiles*.
Conj **Grease:** Makes 10-ft. square or one object slippery.
Mage Armor: Gives subject +4 armor bonus.
Mount: Summons riding horse for 2 hours/level.
Obscuring Mist: Fog surrounds you.
Div **Comprehend Languages:** You understand all spoken and written languages.
Detect Secret Doors: Reveals hidden doors within 60 ft.
Identify ᴹ**:** Determines properties of magic item.
True Strike: +20 on your next attack roll.
Ench **Charm Person:** Makes one person your friend.
Hypnotism: Fascinates 2d4 HD of creatures.
Rampage: All nearby horses go mad.
Sleep: Puts 4 HD of creatures into magical slumber.
Evoc **Burning Hands:** 1d4/level fire damage (max 5d4).
Magic Missile: 1d4+1 damage; +1 missile per two levels above 1st (max 5).

Illus **Disguise Self:** Changes your appearance.
Magic Aura: Alters object's magic aura.
Silent Image: Creates minor illusion of your design.
Ventriloquism: Throws voice for 1 min./level.

Necro **Cause Fear:** One creature of 5 HD or less flees for 1d4 rounds.
Chill Touch: One touch/level deals 1d6 damage and possibly 1 Str damage.
Ray of Enfeeblement: Ray deals 1d6 +1 per two levels Str damage.

Trans *Adjust:* Armor resizes to fit wearer.
Animate Rope: Makes a rope move at your command.
Enlarge Person: Humanoid creature doubles in size.
Erase: Mundane or magical writing vanishes.
Expeditious Retreat: Your speed increases by 30 ft.
Feather Fall: Objects or creatures fall slowly.
Jump: Subject gets bonus on Jump checks.
Magic Weapon: Weapon gains +1 bonus.
Reduce Person: Humanoid creature halves in size.
Shear: The selected weapon cuts through weapons and armor, but half damage to opponent.
Shocking Grasp: Touch delivers 1d6/level electricity damage (max 5d6).
Trumpet: Everyone within range of the spell can hear the subject.

2ND-LEVEL ARCANE SPELLS

Abjur **Arcane Lock** ᴹ: Magically locks a portal or chest.
Obscure Object: Masks object against scrying.
Protection from Arrows: Subject immune to most ranged attacks.
Resist Energy: Ignores first 10 (or more) points of damage/attack from specified energy type.

Conj **Acid Arrow:** Ranged touch attack; 2d4 damage for 1 round +1 round/three levels.
Fog Cloud: Fog obscures vision.
Glitterdust: Blinds creatures, outlines invisible creatures.
Retrieve: A thrown weapon returns to the user's hand.
Summon Swarm: Summons swarm of bats, rats, or spiders.

Div **Detect Thoughts:** Allows "listening" to surface thoughts.
Locate Object: Senses direction toward object (specific or type).
See Invisibility: Reveals invisible creatures or objects.

Ench *Challenge:* Foes can only attack you one at a time.
Daze Monster: Living creature of 6 HD or less loses next action.
Hideous Laughter: Subject loses actions for 1 round/level.
Touch of Idiocy: Subject takes 1d6 points of Int, Wis, and Cha damage.

Evoc **Continual Flame** ᴹ: Makes a permanent, heatless torch.
Darkness: 20-ft. radius of supernatural shadow.
Flaming Sphere: Creates rolling ball of fire, 2d6 damage, lasts 1 round/level.
Gust of Wind: Blows away or knocks down smaller creatures.
Scorching Ray: Ranged touch attack deals 4d6 fire damage, +1 ray/four levels (max 3).
Shatter: Sonic vibration damages objects or crystalline creatures.

Illus **Blur:** Attacks miss subject 20% of the time.
Hidden Landmark: Sailors or charioteers do not notice existing landmarks and are thrown off course.
Hypnotic Pattern: Fascinates (2d4 + level) HD of creatures.
Invisibility: Subject is invisible for 1 min./level or until it attacks.
Magic Mouth ᴹ: Speaks once when triggered.
Minor Image: As *silent image*, plus some sound.
Mirror Image: Creates decoy duplicates of you (1d4 +1 per three levels, max 8).
Misdirection: Misleads divinations for one creature or object.
Phantom Trap ᴹ: Makes item seem trapped.

Necro **Blindness/Deafness:** Makes subject blinded or deafened.
Deathly Sight: You can see ghosts and spirits
False Life: Gain 1d10 temporary hp +1/level (max +10).
Ghoul Touch: Paralyzes one subject, which exudes stench that makes those nearby sickened.
Scare: Panics creatures of less than 6 HD.

Trans **Alter Self:** Assume form of a similar creature.
Bear's Endurance: Subject gains +4 to Con for 1 min./level.
Bull's Strength: Subject gains +4 to Str for 1 min./level.
Cat's Grace: Subject gains +4 to Dex for 1 min./level.
Control Current ꜰ: You redirect a water current.
Darkvision: See 60 ft. in total darkness.
Eagle's Splendor: Subject gains +4 to Cha for 1 min./level.
Fox's Cunning: Subject gains +4 Int for 1 min./level.
Knock: Opens locked or magically sealed door.
Levitate: Subject moves up and down at your direction.
Owl's Wisdom: Subject gains +4 to Wis for 1 min./level.
Pyrotechnics: Turns fire into blinding light or choking smoke.
Rope Trick: As many as eight creatures hide in extradimensional space.
Spider Climb: Grants ability to walk on walls and ceilings.
Stygian Armor: Subject's skin becomes thicker and extremely rough.
Tumult: The subject cannot be heard by anyone more than five feet away.
Whispering Wind: Sends a short message 1 mile/level.

3RD-LEVEL ARCANE SPELLS

Abjur **Dispel Magic:** Cancels magical spells and effects.
Explosive Runes: Deals 6d6 damage when read.
Magic Circle against Chaos/Evil/Good/Law: As *protection* spells, but 10-ft. radius and 10 min./level.
Nondetection ᴹ: Hides subject from divination, scrying.
Protection from Energy: Absorb 12 points/level of damage from one kind of energy.

Conj **Phantom Steed:** Magic horse appears for 1 hour/level.
Sepia Snake Sigil ᴹ: Creates text symbol that immobilizes reader.
Sleet Storm: Hampers vision and movement.
Stinking Cloud: Nauseating vapors, 1 round/level.

Div **Clairaudience/Clairvoyance:** Hear or see at a distance for 1 min./level.
Tongues: Speak any language.

Ench **Deep Slumber:** Puts 10 HD of creatures to sleep.

Heroism: Gives +2 bonus on attack rolls, saves, skill checks.

Hold Person: Paralyzes one humanoid for 1 round/level.

Misdirect: Target thinks he sees you elsewhere on the battlefield.

Rage: Subjects gains +2 to Str and Con, +1 on Will saves, −2 to AC.

Suggestion: Compels subject to follow stated course of action.

Evoc **Lightning Bolt:** Electricity deals 1d6/level damage.

Tiny Hut: Creates shelter for ten creatures.

Wind Wall: Deflects arrows, smaller creatures, and gases.

Illus **Displacement:** Attacks miss subject 50%.

False Omen: You create what appears to be a divine omen.

Illusory Script ᴹ: Only intended reader can decipher.

Invisibility Sphere: Makes everyone within 10 ft. invisible.

Major Image: As *silent image*, plus sound, smell and thermal effects.

Necro **Gentle Repose:** Preserves one corpse.

Ray of Exhaustion: Ray makes subject exhausted.

Vampiric Touch: Touch deals 1d6/two levels damage; caster gains damage as hp.

Trans **Blink:** You randomly vanish and reappear for 1 round/level.

Flame Arrow: Arrows deal +1d6 fire damage.

Fly: Subject flies at speed of 60 ft.

Gaseous Form: Subject becomes insubstantial and can fly slowly.

Haste: One creature/level moves faster, +1 on attack rolls, AC, and Reflex saves.

Keen Edge: Doubles normal weapon's threat range.

Magic Weapon, Greater: +1/four levels (max +5).

Secret Page: Changes one page to hide its real content.

Shrink Item: Object shrinks to one-sixteenth size.

Slow: One subject/level takes only one action/round, −2 to AC, −2 on attack rolls.

Water Breathing: Subjects can breathe underwater.

4TH-LEVEL ARCANE SPELLS

Abjur **Dimensional Anchor:** Bars extradimensional movement.

Fire Trap ᴹ: Opened object deals 1d4 damage +1/level.

Globe of Invulnerability, Lesser: Stops 1st- through 3rd-level spell effects.

Remove Curse: Frees object or person from curse.

Stoneskin ᴹ: Ignore 10 points of damage per attack.

Conj **Dimension Door:** Teleports you short distance.

Secure Shelter: Creates sturdy cottage.

Solid Fog: Blocks vision and slows movement.

Div **Arcane Eye:** Invisible floating eye moves 30 ft./round.

Detect Scrying: Alerts you of magical eavesdropping.

Locate Creature: Indicates direction to familiar creature.

Scrying ᶠ: Spies on subject from a distance.

Ench **Charm Monster:** Makes monster believe it is your ally.

Confusion: Subjects behave oddly for 1 round/level.

Crushing Despair: Subjects take −2 on attack rolls, damage rolls, saves, and checks.

Geas, Lesser: Commands subject of 7 HD or less.

Evoc **Shout:** Deafens all within cone and deals 5d6 sonic damage.

Illus **Hallucinatory Terrain:** Makes one type of terrain appear like another (field into forest, or the like).

Illusory Wall: Wall, floor, or ceiling looks real, but anything can pass through.

Invisibility, Greater: As *invisibility,* but subject can attack and stay invisible.

Phantasmal Killer: Fearsome illusion kills subject or deals 3d6 damage.

Rainbow Pattern: Lights fascinate 24 HD of creatures.

Shadow Conjuration: Mimics conjuration below 4th level, but only 20% real.

Necro **Bestow Curse:** −6 to an ability score; −4 on attack rolls, saves, and checks; or 50% chance of losing each action.

Contagion: Infects subject with chosen disease.

Deathly Tongue: You can speak with the dead.

Enervation: Subject gains 1d4 negative levels.

Fear: Subjects within cone flee for 1 round/level.

Trans **Enlarge Person, Mass:** Enlarges several creatures.

Hasty Defense ᶠ: Walls and other fortifications may be constructed in one-quarter their normal time.

Polymorph: Gives one willing subject a new form.

Reduce Person, Mass: Reduces several creatures.

Stone Shape: Sculpts stone into any shape.

5TH-LEVEL ARCANE SPELLS

Abjur **Break Enchantment:** Frees subjects from enchantments, alterations, curses, and petrification.

Dismissal: Forces a creature to return to native plane.

Conj **Cloudkill:** Kills 3 HD or less; 4–6 HD save or die, 6+ HD take Con damage.

Mage's Faithful Hound: Phantom dog can guard, attack.

Secret Chest ᶠ: Hides expensive chest on Ethereal Plane; you retrieve it at will.

Teleport: Instantly transports you as far as 100 miles/level.

Wall of Stone: Creates a stone wall that can be shaped.

Div **Prying Eyes:** 1d4 +1/level floating eyes scout for you.

Telepathic Bond: Link lets allies communicate.

Ench **Dominate Person:** Controls humanoid telepathically.

Feeblemind: Subject's Int and Cha drop to 1.

Hold Monster: As *hold person,* but any creature.

Mind Fog: Subjects in fog get −10 to Wis and Will checks.

Symbol of Sleep ᴹ: Triggered rune puts nearby creatures into catatonic slumber.

Evoc **Cone of Cold:** 1d6/level cold damage.

Sending: Delivers short message anywhere, instantly.

Illus **Dream:** Sends message to anyone sleeping.

False Vision ᴹ: Fools scrying with an illusion.

Magic Mist ᶠ: You create a concealing mist granting invisibility to those within.

Mass Disorder: Subjects think allies are enemies, and enemies allies.

Mirage Arcana: As *hallucinatory terrain,* plus structures.

Nightmare: Sends vision dealing 1d10 damage, fatigue.

Persistent Image: As *major image*, but no concentration required.

Seeming: Changes appearance of one person per two levels.

Shadow Evocation: Mimics evocation below 5th level, but only 20% real.

Necro **Blight:** Withers one plant or deals 1d6/level damage to plant creature.

Deathly Vision [F]: Anyone within range can see and speak with spirits.

Magic Jar [F]: Enables possession of another creature.

Symbol of Pain [M]: Triggered rune wracks nearby creatures with pain.

Waves of Fatigue: Several targets become fatigued.

Trans **Animal Growth:** One animal/two levels doubles in size.

Baleful Polymorph: Transforms subject into harmless animal.

Fabricate: Transforms raw materials into finished items.

Overland Flight: You fly at a speed of 40 ft. and can hustle over long distances.

Passwall: Creates passage through wood or stone wall.

Telekinesis: Moves object, attacks creature, or hurls object or creature.

Transmute Mud to Rock: Transforms two 10-ft. cubes per level.

Transmute Rock to Mud: Transforms two 10-ft. cubes per level.

Univ **Permanency** [X]: Makes certain spells permanent.

6TH-LEVEL ARCANE SPELLS

Abjur **Antimagic Field:** Negates magic within 10 ft.

Dispel Magic, Greater: As *dispel magic*, but +20 on check.

Globe of Invulnerability: As *lesser globe of invulnerability*, plus 4th-level spell effects.

Guards and Wards: Array of magic effects protects area.

Repulsion: Creatures cannot approach you.

Conj **Acid Fog:** Fog deals acid damage.

Deathly Guest: You may enter the Underworld and walk among the dead.

Div **Analyze Dweomer** [F]: Reveals magical aspects of subject.

Legend Lore [M F]: Lets you learn tales about a person, place, or thing.

True Seeing [M]: Lets you see all things as they really are.

Ench **Geas/Quest:** As *lesser geas*, plus it affects any creature.

Heroism, Greater: Gives +4 bonus on attack rolls, saves, skill checks; immunity to fear; temporary hp.

Suggestion, Mass: As *suggestion*, plus one subject/level.

Symbol of Persuasion [M]: Triggered rune charms nearby creatures.

Evoc **Chain Lightning:** 1d6/level damage; 1 secondary bolt/level each deals half damage.

Contingency [F]: Sets trigger condition for another spell.

Freezing Sphere: Freezes water or deals cold damage.

Illus **Mislead:** Turns you invisible and creates illusory double.

Permanent Image: Includes sight, sound, and smell.

Programmed Image [M]: As *major image*, plus triggered by event.

Shadow Walk: Step into shadow to travel rapidly.

Veil: Changes appearance of group of creatures.

Necro **Circle of Death** [M]: Kills 1d4/level HD of creatures.

Eyebite: Target becomes panicked, sickened, and comatose.

Symbol of Fear [M]: Triggered rune panics nearby creatures.

Trans **Bear's Endurance, Mass:** As *bear's endurance*, affects one subject/level.

Bull's Strength, Mass: As *bull's strength*, affects one subject/ level.

Cat's Grace, Mass: As *cat's grace*, affects one subject/ level.

Control Water: Raises or lowers bodies of water.

Disintegrate: Makes one creature or object vanish.

Eagle's Splendor, Mass: As *eagle's splendor*, affects one subject/level.

Flesh to Stone: Turns subject creature into statue.

Fox's Cunning, Mass: As *fox's cunning*, affects one subject/ level.

Move Earth: Digs trenches and build hills.

Owl's Wisdom, Mass: As *owl's wisdom*, affects one subject/ level.

Stone to Flesh: Restores petrified creature.

Transformation [M]: You gain combat bonuses.

Treasured Possession: You form a permanent bond with one item.

7TH-LEVEL ARCANE SPELLS

Abjur **Sequester:** Subject is invisible to sight and scrying; renders creature comatose.

Spell Turning: Reflect 1d4+6 spell levels back at caster.

Conj *Bloodsnake* [X]: Your blood transforms into a snake that dies your bidding.

Instant Summons [M]: Prepared object appears in your hand.

Mage's Magnificent Mansion [F]: Door leads to extradimensional mansion.

Phase Door: Creates an invisible passage through wood or stone.

Teleport, Greater: As *teleport*, but no range limit and no off-target arrival.

Teleport Object: As *teleport*, but affects a touched object.

Div **Scrying, Greater:** As *scrying*, but faster and longer.

Vision [M X]: As *legend lore*, but quicker and strenuous.

Ench **Hold Person, Mass:** As *hold person*, but all within 30 ft.

Insanity: Subject suffers continuous *confusion*.

Power Word Blind: Blinds creature with 200 hp or less.

Symbol of Stunning [M]: Triggered rune stuns nearby creatures.

Unman: Frightens creatures.

Evoc **Mage's Sword** [F]: Floating magic blade strikes opponents.

Illus **Invisibility, Mass:** As *invisibility*, but affects all in range.

Long Hour: You extend the length of day and night.

Project Image: Illusory double can talk and cast spells.

Shadow Conjuration, Greater: As *shadow conjuration*, but up to 6th level and 60% real.

Simulacrum [M X]: Creates partially real double of a creature.

Necro **Finger of Death:** Kills one subject.

Symbol of Weakness [M]: Triggered rune weakens nearby creatures.

Waves of Exhaustion: Several targets become exhausted.

Trans **Control Weather:** Changes weather in local area.

Reverse Gravity: Objects and creatures fall upward.

Statue: Subject can become a statue at will.

8TH-LEVEL ARCANE SPELLS

Abjur **Mind Blank:** Subject is immune to mental/emotional magic and scrying.

Protection from Spells [M] [F]: Confers +8 resistance bonus.

Conj **Incendiary Cloud:** Cloud deals 4d6 fire damage/round.

Maze: Traps subject in extradimensional maze.

Trap the Soul [M] [F]: Imprisons subject within gem.

Div **Discern Location:** Reveals exact location of creature or object.

Moment of Prescience: You gain insight bonus on single attack roll, check, or save.

Prying Eyes, Greater: As *prying eyes*, but eyes have *true seeing*.

Ench **Antipathy:** Object or location affected by spell repels certain creatures.

Binding [M]: Utilizes an array of techniques to imprison a creature.

Charm Monster, Mass: As *charm monster,* but all within 30 ft.

Demand: As *sending,* plus you can send *suggestion.*

Irresistible Dance: Forces subject to dance.

Power Word Stun: Stuns creature with 150 hp or less.

Symbol of Insanity [M]: Triggered rune renders nearby creatures insane.

Sympathy [F]: Object or location attracts certain creatures.

Evoc **Polar Ray:** Ranged touch attack deals 1d6/level cold damage.

Shout, Greater: Devastating yell deals 10d6 sonic damage; stuns creatures, damages objects.

Sunburst: Blinds all within 10 ft., deals 6d6 damage.

Telekinetic Sphere: As *resilient sphere,* but you move sphere telekinetically.

Illus **Scintillating Pattern:** Twisting colors *confuse,* stun, or render unconscious.

Screen: Illusion hides area from vision, scrying.

Shadow Evocation, Greater: As *shadow evocation,* but up to 7th level and 60% real.

Necro **Horrid Wilting:** Deals 1d6/level damage within 30 ft.

Symbol of Death [M]: Triggered rune slays nearby creatures.

Trans **Iron Body:** Your body becomes living iron.

Polymorph Any Object: Changes any subject into anything else.

Temporal Stasis [M]: Puts subject into suspended animation.

Restore Youth: The target grows younger.

9TH-LEVEL ARCANE SPELLS

Abjur **Freedom:** Releases creature from *imprisonment.*

Imprisonment: Entombs subject beneath the earth.

Mage's Disjunction: Dispels magic, disenchants magic items.

Conj **Refuge** [M]: Alters item to transport its possessor to you.

Teleportation Circle [M]: Circle teleports any creature inside to designated spot.

Div **Foresight:** "Sixth sense" warns of impending danger.

Ench **Dominate Monster:** As *dominate person,* but any creature.

Hold Monster, Mass: As *hold monster,* but all within 30 ft.

Power Word Kill: Kills one creature with 100 hp or less.

Evoc **Meteor Swarm:** Four exploding spheres each deal 6d6 fire damage.

Illus **Shades:** As *shadow conjuration,* but up to 8th level and 80% real.

Weird: As *phantasmal killer,* but affects all within 30 ft.

Necro **Energy Drain:** Subject gains 2d4 negative levels.

Soul Bind [F]: Traps newly dead soul to prevent *resurrection.*

Wail of the Banshee: Kills one creature/level.

Trans **Etherealness:** Travel to Ethereal Plane with companions.

Restore youth, Greater [X]: As the spell *Restore youth,* but permanent.

Shapechange [F]: Transforms you into any creature, and change forms once per round.

Time Stop: You act freely for 1d4+1 rounds.

DIVINE SPELLS

Below is a list of spells appropriate for the *Trojan War* setting. New spells are italicized.

0-LEVEL DIVINE SPELLS (ORISONS)

Create Water: Creates 2 gallons/level of pure water.

Cure Minor Wounds: Cures 1 point of damage.

Detect Magic: Detects spells and magic items within 60 ft.

Detect Poison: Detects poison in one creature or object.

Guidance: +1 on one attack roll, saving throw, or skill check.

Inflict Minor Wounds: Touch attack, 1 point of damage.

Light: Object shines like a torch.

Mending: Makes minor repairs on an object.

Purify Food and Drink: Purifies 1 cu. ft./level of food or water.

Read Magic: Read scrolls and spellbooks.

Resistance: Subject gains +1 on saving throws.

Virtue: Subject gains 1 temporary hp.

1ST-LEVEL DIVINE SPELLS

Bane: Enemies take −1 on attack rolls and saves against fear.

Bless: Allies gain +1 on attack rolls and saves against fear.

Bless Water [M]: Makes holy water.

Cause Fear: One creature of 5 HD or less flees for 1d4 rounds.

Command: One subject obeys selected command for 1 round.

Comprehend Languages: You understand all spoken and written languages.

Cure Light Wounds: Cures 1d8 damage +1/level (max +5).

Curse Water [M]: Makes unholy water.

Deathwatch: Reveals how near death subjects within 30 ft. are.

Detect Chaos/Evil/Good/Law: Reveals creatures, spells, or objects of selected alignment.

Detect Undead: Reveals undead within 60 ft.

Divine Favor: You gain +1 per three levels on attack and damage rolls.

Divine Mark: You can mark a person, object, creature, or place with divine writing.

Doom: One subject takes −2 on attack rolls, damage rolls, saves, and checks.

Endure Elements: Exist comfortably in hot or cold environments.

Entropic Shield: Ranged attacks against you have 20% miss chance.

Granted Weapon: You petition your god to use a weapon other than those you can already use.

Hide from Undead: Undead can't perceive one subject/level.

Inflict Light Wounds: Touch deals 1d8 damage +1/level (max +5).

Magic Stone: Three stones gain +1 on attack, deal 1d6 +1 damage.

Magic Weapon: Weapon gains +1 bonus.

Obscuring Mist: Fog surrounds you.

Protection from Chaos/Evil/Good/Law: +2 to AC and saves, counter mind control, hedge out elementals and outsiders.

Remove Fear: Suppresses fear or gives +4 on saves against fear for one subject + one per four levels.

Sanctuary: Opponents can't attack you, and you can't attack.

Shield of Faith: The spell's aura grants +2 or higher deflection bonus.

2ND-LEVEL DIVINE SPELLS

Aid: +1 on attack rolls and saves against fear, 1d8 temporary hp +1/level (max +10).

Align Weapon: Weapon becomes good, evil, lawful, or chaotic.

Augury [M F]**:** Learns whether an action will be good or bad.

Bear's Endurance: Subject gains +4 to Con for 1 min./level.

Bull's Strength: Subject gains +4 to Str for 1 min./level.

Calm Emotions: Calms creatures, negating emotion effects.

Consecrate [M]**:** Fills area with positive energy, making undead weaker.

Cure Moderate Wounds: Cures 2d8 damage +1/level (max +10).

Darkness: 20-ft. radius of supernatural shadow.

Death Knell: Kills dying creature; you gain 1d8 temporary hp, +2 to Str, and +1 level.

Delay Poison: Stops poison from harming subject for 1 hour/level.

Desecrate [M]**:** Fills area with negative energy, making undead stronger.

Eagle's Splendor: Subject gains +4 to Cha for 1 min./level.

Enthrall: Captivates all within 100 ft. + 10 ft./level.

Find Traps: Notice traps as a rogue does.

Gentle Repose: Preserves one corpse.

Hold Person: Paralyzes one humanoid for 1 round/level.

Inflict Moderate Wounds: Touch attack, 2d8 damage +1/level (max +10).

Make Whole: Repairs an object.

Owl's Wisdom: Subject gains +4 to Wis for 1 min./level.

Remove Paralysis: Frees one or more creatures from paralysis or *slow* effect.

Resist Energy: Ignores 10 (or more) points of damage/attack from specified energy type.

Restoration, Lesser: Dispels magical ability penalty or repairs 1d4 ability damage.

Shatter: Sonic vibration damages objects or crystalline creatures.

Shield Other [F]**:** You take half of subject's damage.

Silence: Negates sound in 15-ft. radius.

Sound Burst: Deals 1d8 sonic damage to subjects; may stun them.

Spiritual Weapon: Magic weapon attacks on its own.

Status: Monitors condition, position of allies.

Undetectable Alignment: Conceals alignment for 24 hours.

Zone of Truth: Subjects within range cannot lie.

3RD-LEVEL DIVINE SPELLS

Becalm: All wind in the area dies away, leaving the air perfectly quiet.

Bestow Curse: −6 to an ability score; −4 on attack rolls, saves, and checks; or 50% chance of losing each action.

Blindness/Deafness: Makes subject blinded or deafened.

Bounty: If the area contains any edible fruits or animals, the subjects will find it before the spell ends.

Contagion: Infects subject with chosen disease.

Continual Flame [M]**:** Makes a permanent, heatless torch.

Create Food and Water: Feeds three humans (or one horse)/level.

Cure Serious Wounds: Cures 3d8 damage +1/level (max +15).

Daylight: 60-ft. radius of bright light.

Deeper Darkness: Object sheds supernatural shadow in 60-ft. radius.

Dispel Magic: Cancels spells and magical effects.

Glyph of Warding [M]**:** Inscription harms those who pass it.

Helping Hand: Ghostly hand leads subject to you.

Inflict Serious Wounds: Touch attack, 3d8 damage +1/level (max +15).

Invisibility Purge: Dispels invisibility within 5 ft./level.

Locate Object: Senses direction toward object (specific or type).

Magic Circle against Chaos/Evil/Good/Law: As *protection* spells, but 10-ft. radius and 10 min./level.

Magic Vestment: Armor or shield gains +1 enhancement per four levels.

Mantle of Leadership: A blaze of light surrounds the target, making him seem noble and more commanding.

Meld into Stone: You and your gear merge with stone.

Obscure Object: Masks object against scrying.

Prayer: Allies +1 bonus on most rolls, enemies −1 penalty.

Protection from Energy: Absorb 12 points/level of damage from one kind of energy.

Remove Blindness/Deafness: Cures normal or magical conditions.

Remove Curse: Frees object or person from curse.

Remove Disease: Cures all diseases affecting subject.

Restorative Sleep: Everyone within spell range falls into a deep sleep and awakens refreshed.

Rough Seas: The water becomes choppy, and large waves buffet both boats and swimmers.

Searing Light: Ray deals 1d8/two levels damage, more against undead.

Speak with Dead: Corpse answers one question/two levels.

Stone Shape: Sculpts stone into any shape.

Water Breathing: Subjects can breathe underwater.

Water Walk: Subject treads on water as if solid.

Wind Wall: Deflects arrows, smaller creatures, and gases.

4TH-LEVEL DIVINE SPELLS

Air Walk: Subject treads on air as if solid (climb at 45-degree angle).

Bulwark: Allies gain 1d4 hit points and a +1 bonus to attack and weapon damage rolls.

Control Water: Raises or lowers bodies of water.

Cure Critical Wounds: Cures 4d8 damage +1/level (max +20).

Death Ward: Grants immunity to death spells and negative energy effects.

Dimensional Anchor: Bars extradimensional movement.

Discern Lies: Reveals deliberate falsehoods.

Dismissal: Forces a creature to return to native plane.

Divination [M]**:** Provides useful advice for specific proposed actions.

Divine Anger: Reduce target's Piety score.

Divine Blessing: Increase target's Piety score.

Divine Glow: Glow with a holy light.

Divine Mark, Greater [X]**:** As *Divine Mark*, but the marks are permanent.

Divine Power: You gain attack bonus, +6 to Str, and 1 hp/level.

Freedom of Movement: Subject moves normally despite impediments.

Giant Vermin: Turns centipedes, scorpions, or spiders into giant vermin.

Imbue with Spell Ability: Transfer spells to subject.

Inflict Critical Wounds: Touch attack, 4d8 damage +1/level (max +20).

Magic Weapon, Greater: +1 bonus/four levels (max +5).

Neutralize Poison: Immunizes subject against poison, detoxifies venom in or on subject.

Poison: Touch deals 1d10 Con damage, repeats in 1 min.

Rally: Magically transport allies to you.

Repel Vermin: Insects, spiders, and other vermin stay 10 ft. away.

Restoration [M]**:** Restores level and ability score drains.

Sending: Delivers short message anywhere, instantly.

Spell Immunity: Subject is immune to one spell per four levels.

Tongues: Speak any language.

5TH-LEVEL DIVINE SPELLS

Ally's Shield: Large-scale natural or magical attacks do no harm to your allies.

Atonement [F X]**:** Removes burden of misdeeds from subject.

Break Enchantment: Frees subjects from enchantments, alterations, curses, and petrification.

Cleanse: You can remove any taint of illness or poison, including magical effects.

Command, Greater: As *command*, but affects one subject/level.

Commune [X]**:** Deity answers one yes-or-no question/level.

Cure Light Wounds, Mass: Cures 1d8 damage +1/level for many creatures.

Dispel Chaos/Evil/Good/Law: +4 bonus against attacks.

Disrupting Weapon: Melee weapon destroys undead.

Fester: A targeted wound does not heal without magical means, and inflicts an additional 1d4 points of damage per hour.

Flame Strike: Smite foes with divine fire (1d6/level damage).

Glass Wave: All waves in the area fade away, leaving the water smooth as glass.

Hallow [M]**:** Designates location as holy.

Inflict Light Wounds, Mass: Deals 1d8 damage +1/level to many creatures.

Insect Plague: Locust swarms attack creatures.

Mark of Justice: Designates action that will trigger *curse* on subject.

Plane Shift [F]**:** As many as eight subjects travel to another plane.

Righteous Might: Your size increases, and you gain combat bonuses.

Scrying [F]**:** Spies on subject from a distance.

Slay Living: Touch attack kills subject.

Spell Resistance: Subject gains SR 12 + level.

Symbol of Pain[M]: Triggered rune wracks nearby creatures with pain.

Symbol of Sleep[M]: Triggered rune puts nearby creatures into catatonic slumber.

Tremor: The ground shudders, tossing people and items off-balance.

True Seeing[M]: Lets you see all things as they really are.

Unhallow[M]: Designates location as unholy.

Wall of Stone: Creates a stone wall that can be shaped.

6TH-LEVEL DIVINE SPELLS

Anoint[M]: You transform the subject into a dedicated warrior of your god for a limited time.

Animate Objects: Objects attack your foes.

Antilife Shell: 10-ft. field hedges out living creatures.

Banishment: Banishes 2 HD/level of extraplanar creatures.

Bear's Endurance, Mass: As *bear's endurance,* affects one subject/ level.

Blade Barrier: Wall of blades deals 1d6/level damage.

Bull's Strength, Mass: As *bull's strength,* affects one subject/ level.

Create Undead: Create ghouls, ghasts, mummies, or mohrgs.

Cure Moderate Wounds, Mass: Cures 2d8 damage +1/level for many creatures.

Dispel Magic, Greater: As *dispel magic,* but up to +20 on check.

Eagle's Splendor, Mass: As *eagle's splendor,* affects one subject/ level.

Earth Swallowed: The earth opens and swallows the target.

Find the Path: Shows most direct way to a location.

Forbiddance[M]: Blocks planar travel, damages creatures of different alignment.

Geas/Quest: As *lesser geas,* plus it affects any creature.

Glyph of Warding, Greater: As *glyph of warding,* but up to 10d8 damage or 6th-level spell.

Harm: Deals 10 points/level damage to target.

Heal: Cures 10 points/level of damage, all diseases and mental conditions.

Heroes' Feast: Food for one creature/level cures and grants combat bonuses.

Heroic Aura[M]: No one under 4HD can attack the subject, not even in a group.

Inflict Moderate Wounds, Mass: Deals 2d8 damage +1/level to many creatures.

Owl's Wisdom, Mass: As *owl's wisdom,* affects one subject/level.

Plague: You can cast a plague upon your enemies.

Symbol of Fear[M]: Triggered rune panics nearby creatures.

Symbol of Persuasion[M]: Triggered rune charms nearby creatures.

Vengeful Wave: Water rises up as a wave, and washes over the target.

Wind Walk: You and your allies turn vaporous and travel fast.

Word of Recall: Teleports you back to designated place.

7TH-LEVEL DIVINE SPELLS

Blasphemy: Kills, paralyzes, weakens, or dazes nonevil subjects.

Control Weather: Changes weather in local area.

Cure Serious Wounds, Mass: Cures 3d8 damage +1/level for many creatures.

Destruction[F]: Kills subject and destroys remains.

Dictum: Kills, paralyzes, slows, or deafens nonlawful subjects.

Holy Word: Kills, paralyzes, blinds, or deafens nongood subjects.

Inflict Serious Wounds, Mass: Deals 3d8 damage +1/level to many creatures.

Refuge[M]: Alters item to transport its possessor to you.

Regenerate: Subject's severed limbs grow back, cures 4d8 damage +1/level (max +35).

Repulsion: Creatures can't approach you.

Restoration, Greater[X]: As *restoration,* plus restores all levels and ability scores.

Resurrection[M]: Fully restore dead subject.

Scrying, Greater: As *scrying,* but faster and longer.

Spirit Away[M]: If the subject fall to 1 hp or less during the spell's duration he is instantly teleported to safety.

Summon Monster VII: Calls extraplanar creature to fight for you.

Symbol of Stunning[M]: Triggered rune stuns nearby creatures.

Symbol of Weakness[M]: Triggered rune weakens nearby creatures.

Word of Chaos: Kills, *confuses,* stuns, or deafens nonchaotic subjects.

8TH-LEVEL DIVINE SPELLS

Antimagic Field: Negates magic within 10 ft.

Breathe Life[X]: You transform inanimate objects into living creatures that do your bidding.

Cloak of Chaos[F]: +4 to AC, +4 resistance, and SR 25 against lawful spells.

Create Greater Undead[M]: Create shadows, wraiths, spectres, or devourers.

Cure Critical Wounds, Mass: Cures 4d8 damage +1/level for many creatures.

Dimensional Lock: Teleportation and interplanar travel blocked for one day/level.

Discern Location: Reveals exact location of creature or object.

Earthquake: Intense tremor shakes 5-ft./level radius.

Earth Swallowed, Greater[X]: Same as *Earth Swallowed,* except that the earth closes up again afterward, trapping the victim inside.

Fire Storm: Deals 1d6/level fire damage.

Holy Aura[F]: +4 to AC, +4 resistance, and SR 25 against evil spells.

Inflict Critical Wounds, Mass: Deals 4d8 damage +1/level to many creatures.

Shield of Law[F]: +4 to AC, +4 resistance, and SR 25 against chaotic spells.

Spell Immunity, Greater: As *spell immunity,* but up to 8th-level spells.

Symbol of Death[M]: Triggered rune slays nearby creatures.

Symbol of Insanity[M]: Triggered rune renders nearby creatures insane.

Unholy Aura[F]: +4 to AC, +4 resistance, and SR 25 against good spells.

9TH-LEVEL DIVINE SPELLS

Breathe Life, Greater[X]: Same as *Breathe Life,* but the spell creates humans.

Energy Drain: Subject gains 2d4 negative levels.

Heal, Mass: As *heal,* but with several subjects.

Implosion: Kills one creature/round.

Occlude: Your god blocks other gods from interfering.

Soul Bind[F]: Traps newly dead soul to prevent *resurrection.*

Storm of Vengeance: Storm rains acid, lightning, and hail.

Summon Monster IX: Calls extraplanar creature to fight for you.

NEW SPELLS

ADJUST

Transmutation

Level: Mag 1
Components: V, S
Casting Time: 1 standard action
Range: Touch
Target: One unattended piece of armor or clothing
Duration: Instantaneous
Saving Throw: None
Spell Resistance: No

Adjust instantly resizes a piece of unattended clothing or armor to fit you perfectly. This spell affects magic clothing and armor as well as mundane items.

ALLY'S SHIELD

Abjuration

Level: Pri 5
Components: V, S, DF
Casting Time: 1 standard action
Range: Close (25 ft. + 5 ft./level)
Target: Up to two creatures/level within spell range
Duration: 1 round/level (D)
Saving Throw: None
Spell Resistance: No

All creatures affected by ally's shield gain immunity to the damage dealt by any large-scale disaster, such as an earthquake, falling tree, or tidal wave, occurring during the spell's duration. Just the warded creatures and their personal equipment are unaffected for the duration. Creatures so protected are no immune to the incidental dangers of the disaster, such as drowning or suffocation. They merely ignore damage.

This spell also protects the caster's allies from any spell replicating a large-scale natural occurrence, such as *earthquake* and *whirlwind*.

ANOINT

Transmutation

Level: Pri 6
Components: V, S, M, DF
Casting Time: 1 standard action
Range: Touch
Target: One humanoid
Duration: 1 round/level
Saving Throw: Will negates (harmless)
Spell Resistance: No

For a limited time, *anoint* transforms a subject into a dedicated warrior of your god. For the duration of the spell, the subject gains a +1 insight bonus to attacks and weapon damage rolls per six caster levels (+2 at 12th level, +3 at 18th level, and so on to a maximum of +5). In addition, the subject gains the class featured of a dedicated warrior whose level equals one-half your caster level.

Material Component: a small wooden icon of your god worth 100 gp.

BECALM

Transmutation [Air]

Level: Pri 3
Components: V, S, M, DF
Casting Time: 1 standard action
Range: Long (400 ft. + 40 ft./level)
Area: 80-ft.-radius emanation, +5 ft./2 levels
Duration: 1 hour/level
Saving Throw: None
Spell Resistance: No

You create a magical barrier that blocks all air currents, leaving the air perfectly calm.

Material Component: a scrap of sailcloth

BLOODSNAKE

Conjuration (Creation)

Level: Mag 7
Components: V, S, XP
Casting Time: 1 standard action
Range: Close (25 ft. + 5 ft./2 levels)
Effect: One small-sized serpent
Duration: 1 hour/level (D)

To cast *bloodsnake*, you must spill your blood, dealing at least 1 point of damage to yourself. The blood then forms into a crimson snake, called a bloodsnake. The created serpent has the following statistics.

Bloodsnake; CR —; Small magical beast; HD (equal to caster level); hp (one-half the caster's); Init +3; Spd 20 ft., climb 20 ft., swim 20 ft.; AC 17, touch 14, flat-footed 14; Base Atk +0; Grp –6; Atk +4 melee (1d2–2 plus poison, bite); Full Atk +4 melee (1d2–2 plus poison, bite); SA poison; SQ scent; AL as caster; SV Fort +2, Ref +5, Will +1; Str 6, Dex 17, Con 11, Int (as caster), Wis 12, Cha 2.

Skills and Feats: Balance +11, Climb +11, Hide +11, Listen +7, Spot +7, Swim +6; Weapon Finesse

Poison (Ex): Injury, Fortitude (DC 10 + one-half the caster's HD + the caster's Charisma modifier), initial damage 2d4 points of damage, secondary damage death.

The created snake is completely loyal to its creator, and obeys any of your commands to the best of its ability. You always know where the bloodsnake is, and can scry on it as if it were a familiar. When the spell ends, the snake breaks apart into a mess of partially coagulated blood.

XP Cost: 100.

BOUNTY

Conjuration (Summoning)

Level: Pri 3
Components: V, S, M, DF
Casting Time: 1 standard action
Range: Long (400 ft. + 40 ft./level)
Area: Circle, centered on you, with a radius of 400 ft. + 40 ft./level
Duration: 1 min./level (D)

You sense the direction of a supply of nourishing food and beverage within range of the spell. This spell does not determine the type of food found, or its ownership. The spell is blocked by even a thin sheet of lead. Only animals typically consumed by people of your race can be found by means of this spell. Creatures cannot be found by this spell.

Material Component: an olive pit and a boar bristle

BREATHE LIFE

Transmutation

Level: Pri 8
Components: V, S, M, DF, XP
Casting Time: 1 standard action
Range: Close (25 ft. + 5 ft./level)
Target: One nonmagical unattended object of up to 10 cu. ft./level
Duration: Instantaneous
Saving Throw: None
Spell Resistance: No

You transform inanimate objects into living creatures that do your bidding. You can select the type of creature, though it must be an animal, and appropriate for the object's size. The size of the object determines the size creature you can choose—tiny objects can become small creatures, small objects can become medium creatures, medium and larger objects can become large creatures. An object can always become a creature its own size or one size smaller. Once you determine the creature and cast the spell, the object instantly transforms into the desired animal. The object gains all the characteristics of an animal of its kind. The creature also retains its hardness that it had as an object. This creature is not natural and does not need to eat, drink, sleep, or breathe. It is friendly toward the caster, though not bound to him.

Material Component: a piece of the same material as the selected object(s)

XP Cost: 50 per 10 cu. ft. transmuted.

BREATHE LIFE, GREATER

Conjuration (creation)

Level: Pri 9
Target: A number of Medium-size and unattended objects equal to one-half your caster level.

This spell functions like *breathe life*, except it creates humans from unattended objects instead of animals. The transmuted human has average statistics. Determine its class from the following list: commoner, expert, warrior. In addition, the transmuted humans retain the hardness value they had as objects. The transmuted human is friendly toward you, but not bound to you. If you have empty follower slots from the Leadership feat, you may fill those slots with these transmuted humans.

XP Cost: 5000 XP.

BULWARK

Enchantment (Compulsion) [Mind-Affecting]

Level: Pri 4
Components: V, S, DF
Casting Time: 1 standard action
Range: Close (25 ft. + 5 ft./level)
Target: One creature/level, no two of which can be more than 30 ft. apart
Duration: 1 round/level (D)
Saving Throw: None
Spell Resistance: Yes (harmless)

You can augment your allies combat abilities. All affected allies gain a +1 morale bonus to attack and weapon damage rolls per four caster levels beyond 7th (+2 at 11th, +3 at 15th) to a maximum of +5. In addition, these characters gain 1d4 temporary hit points +1 per caster level (to a maximum of +15). These benefits remain as long as the affected creatures do not move more than 5-feet from the space at which they gained these benefits. Moving beyond the permitted distance ends the effects of this spell for that character.

CHALLENGE

Enchantment (Compulsion) [Mind-Affecting]

Level: Mag 2
Components: V, S
Casting Time: 1 standard action
Range: 10 ft.
Area: All living creatures within a 10 ft. burst.
Duration: 1 round/level (D)
Saving Throw: Will negates
Spell Resistance: Yes

All living creatures who are Hostile towards you and fail their save feel compelled to fight you in single combat. Only one such foe may face you at a time. The remaining opponents are free to act normally, such as fighting other combatants, but they may not attack you in any way (including spells).

CLEANSE

Conjuration (Healing)

Level: Pri 5
Components: V, S, M, DF
Casting Time: 1 standard action
Range: Touch
Target: One living creature
Duration: Instantaneous
Saving Throw: Fortitude negates (harmless)
Spell Resistance: No

Cleanse removes any taint of illness or poison. A poisoned creature suffers no additional effects from the poison, and any temporary effects are ended, but the spell does not reverse instantaneous effects, such as hit point damage, temporary ability damage, or effects that do not go away on their own.

Cleanse also cures all diseases that the subject is suffering from. The spell kills parasites, including green slime and others. Certain special diseases may not be countered by this spell or may be countered only by a caster of a certain level or higher. Since the spell's duration is instantaneous, it does not prevent reinfection after a new exposure to the same disease. Any damage already sustained from illness or poison remains and must be healed normally or magically.

Finally, *cleanse* also grants the subject 1 Piety point per your level if they have a negative Piety score, though it does not raise them above 0.

Material Component: a moly leaf.

CONTROL CURRENT

Transmutation [Water]

Level: Mag 2
Components: V, S, F
Casting Time: 1 standard action
Range: Medium (100 ft. + 10 ft./level)
Target: One water current within range
Duration: 1 minute/level (D)
Saving Throw: None
Spell Resistance: No

You may redirect a water current, thus altering the course of a ship. This does not create a new current, but pulls an existing one into an unfamiliar path. This can affect other currents in its path, and can have unintended effects throughout the immediate area.

Focus: A lodestone.

DEATHLY GUEST

Conjuration (Teleportation)

Level: Mag 6
Components: V, S, M
Casting Time: 1 standard action
Range: Personal
Target: You
Duration: 10 minutes/level

You open a temporary conduit to the Underworld, allowing you passage to the realm of the dead. In addition, while in the Underworld, you are not at risk from attack by the spirits of the dead, nor do they plead for aid. You may leave the Underworld at any time, without harm or constraint. However, if you eat or drink anything while in the Underworld, you may never leave.

Material Component: Drops of milk and honey, blood, wine, and water

DEATHLY SIGHT

Necromancy

Level: Mag 2
Components: V, S, M, F
Casting Time: 1 standard action
Range: Personal
Target: You
Duration: 1 minute/level (D)

You see any ghosts or spirits within your visual range.

Material Component: A drop of blood.

Focus: Two copper pieces (placed over the eyes)

DEATHLY TONGUE

Necromancy

Level: Mag 4
Components: V, S, M
Casting Time: 1 standard action
Range: Personal
Target: You
Duration: 1 minute/level (D)

You gain the ability to speak and understand the language of any dead creature, whether it is a racial tongue or a regional dialect. You may speak only one language at a time, although you may be able to understand several languages. You can make yourself understood as far as your voice carries. This spell does not predispose any creature addressed toward you in any way.

Deathly tongue can be made permanent with a *permanency* spell.

Material Component: a drop of blood.

Focus: one copper piece placed on the tongue.

DEATHLY VISION

Necromancy

Level: Mag 5
Components: V, S, M, F
Casting Time: 1 standard action
Range: Close (25 ft. + 5 ft./level)
Target: One creature/level, no two of which can be more than 30 ft. apart
Duration: 1 minute/level
Saving Throw: Will negates (harmless)
Spell Resistance: Yes (harmless)

This spell grants the effects of *deathly sight* and *deathly tongue* to all affected creatures within range of the spell.

Material Component: a drop of blood, two copper pieces (placed over your own eyes).

Focus: small onyx statuette of a ram.

DIVINE ANGER

Evocation

Level: Pri 4
Components: V, S, M, DF
Casting Time: 1 standard action
Range: Close (25 ft. + 5 ft./level)
Target: One humanoid
Duration: Instantaneous
Saving Throw: Will negates
Spell Resistance: Yes

You invoke the wrath of your god, instantly reducing the target's piety by 1 point per caster level. Any penalties for low or negative Piety scores apply. The target may remove these penalties through normal means.

Material Component: A pinch of ash.

DIVINE BLESSING

Evocation

Level: Pri 4
Components: V, S, M, DF
Casting Time: 1 standard action
Range: Close (25 ft. + 5 ft./level)
Target: One living humanoid
Duration: Instantaneous
Saving Throw: Will negates (harmless)
Spell Resistance: Yes (harmless)

You bestow divine favor upon someone, instantly increasing the target's piety by 1 point per caster level. Any benefits for positive or high Piety scores apply.

Material Component: a drop of wine.

DIVINE GLOW

Enchantment (Compulsion) [Mind-Affecting]

Level: Pri 4
Components: V, S, M, DF
Casting Time: 1 standard action
Range: Close (25 ft. + 5 ft./level)
Target: One humanoid
Duration: 1 minute/level (D)
Saving Throw: Will special (see text)
Spell Resistance: Yes (see text)

You suffuse a target with a bright holy light. All foes within 60 feet must succeed a Will save against the spell's DC or be dazed for 1 round. Creatures of 10 or more HD are not affected.

Material Component: A small, highly polished metal disc, such as a coin.

DIVINE MARK

Universal

Level: Pri 1
Components: V, S, M, DF
Casting Time: 1 round
Range: Touch
Target : One creature or object
Duration: 1 day/level (D)
Saving Throw: None
Spell Resistance: Yes

You can mark a creature or object with divine writing. These marks are invisible to anyone except the gods, other divine casters, and seers. You may select from any of the following marks:

Disliked: This mark indicates the creature or object is an enemy of the god. If a creature, it takes a −1 insight penalty to skills related to the god's spheres and a −1 penalty to saves against spells or effect within that god's sphere.

Favored: This mark shows a person or object is a favorite of the deity. If a creature, the target gains a +1 insight bonus to skills related to the god's spheres (for example, Craft for Hephaestus, Diplomacy for Athena), and a +1 insight bonus to saving throws against spells or effects within that god's sphere (fire for Hephaestus, water for Poseidon).

Profane: This mark reveals the creature or object as something offensive to your god. If a creature, it loses 1 Piety point. Anyone who attacks this person or object earns an additional Piety point for removing the offense from the god's sight.

Sacred: This mark designates the creature or object as sacred to your god. If a creature, it gains +1 piety. Anyone attacking this person or object commits the sin of attacking a sacred object, and receives the appropriate piety point penalty.

Material Component: a drop of wine and a piece of chalk.

DIVINE MARK, GREATER

Universal

Level: Pri 4
Components: V, S, M, DF, XP
Duration: Permanent

This spell functions exactly like *divine mark*, except for above.

XP Cost: 500.

EARTH SWALLOWED

Evocation [Earth]

Level: Pri 6
Components: V, S, M, DF
Casting Time: 1 standard action
Range: Medium (100 ft. + 10 ft./level)
Targets: One creature/2 levels
Duration: Instantaneous
Saving Throw: Reflex negates
Spell Resistance: No

You cause the earth to split wide and swallow the targets. Affected creatures who fail their saving throw fall into the hole to a depth of 10 feet per caster level, taking the appropriate falling damage. The hole does not close and remains open indefinitely. Subjects can climb out of the hole by succeeding a DC 20 Climb check.

Material Component: A pinch of dirt.

EARTH SWALLOWED, GREATER

Evocation [Earth]

Level: Pri 8
Components: V, S, M, DF, XP

This spell functions exactly as *earth swallowed*, except the earth closes up afterwards, trapping the victim inside, buried alive. See

Cave-ins and Collapses in **Chapter Three: Adventures** in the *DMG* for details.

XP Cost: 300 per target.

FALSE OMEN

Illusion (Phantasm) [Mind-Affecting]

Level: Mag 3
Components: V, S
Casting Time: 1 standard action
Range: Medium (100 ft. + 10 ft./level)
Target: One creature/level
Duration: 1 round/level
Saving Throw: Will disbelief
Spell Resistance: No

You create what appears to be a divine omen. You determine the appearance of the omen when casting. Anyone who fails the saving throw tries to interpret the image as if it were real, and with a successful check they decipher the message you intended the omen to convey.

FESTER

Necromancy

Level: Pri 5
Components: V, S, DF
Casting Time: 1 standard action
Range: Medium (100 ft. + 10 ft./level)
Target: One living creature
Duration: Instantaneous
Saving Throw: Fortitude negates
Spell Resistance: Yes

The subject of this vile spell cannot heal damage naturally. He can only recover lost hit points through magical healing. In addition, he takes 1d4 points of damage per hour. Finally, the victim takes a –4 penalty to all Charisma based checks as his body reeks of putrescence. A target fully healed by magical means removes the effects of this spell. *Remove curse* also counters *fester*.

GLASS WAVE

Transmutation [Water]

Level: Pri 5
Components: V, S, DF
Casting Time: 1 standard action
Range: Close (25 ft. + 5 ft./level)
Area: 50 ft. +5 ft./level-radius emanation
Duration: 1 round/level (D)
Saving Throw: None
Spell Resistance: No

You cause the waters to grow still, making the water in the affected area smooth as glass.

GRANTED WEAPON

Transmutation

Level: Pri 1
Components: V, DF
Casting Time: 1 standard action
Range: Personal

Target: You
Duration: 1 round/level

You petition your god to grant you use of weapons of war. You gain use of Martial Weapon Proficiency or Exotic Weapon Proficiency in the desired weapon for the duration of the spell.

Material Component: a drop of wine and a drop of blood

HASTY DEFENSE

Transmutation

Level: Mag 4
Components: V, S, M
Casting Time: 1 standard action
Range: Medium (100 ft. + 10 ft./level)
Area: All creatures within a 400 ft. burst.
Duration: 1 hr/level (D)
Saving Throw: None
Spell Resistance: No

This spell hastens the construction of walls and other fortifications, such that they only take one-quarter of the normal time to erect by enhancing the abilities of those building them. It increases their building speed to supernatural levels by granting a +20 bonus to their Craft checks, but only for building fortifications.

Material Component: a sliver of wood and a chip of stone.

HEROIC AURA

Abjuration

Level: Pri 6
Components: V, S, M, DF
Casting Time: 1 standard action
Range: Close (25 ft. + 5 ft./level)
Target: One creature/level
Duration: 1 round/level
Saving Throw: Will negates (harmless)
Spell Resistance: Yes (harmless)

Opponents of 4 HD or less cannot attack the creature (or creatures) protected with the *heroic aura*. This protection even extends to spells as well as physical attacks.

Material Component: A pinch of gold dust worth 50 gp.

HIDDEN LANDMARK

Illusion (Glamer)

Level: Mag 2
Components: V, S
Casting Time: 1 standard action
Range: Long (400 ft. + 40 ft./level)
Area: 25 ft. +5 ft./level-radius circle
Duration: 1 minute/level
Saving Throw: Will disbelieves (if interacted with)
Spell Resistance: No

You make the ground and waters within range look nondescript by hiding any distinctive features like unusual rock formations or odd trees. Anyone who fails their saving throw cannot find any landmarks in the area, and so cannot orient themselves properly, taking a –10 penalty to Survival checks or untrained Wisdom checks to avoid natural hazards or from getting lost.

LONG HOUR

Illusion (Glamer)

Level: Mag 7
Components: V, S
Casting Time: 1 standard action
Range: Medium (100 ft. + 10 ft./level)
Area: Creatures in a 50-ft.+5 ft./level-radius spread centered on the character
Duration: 10 min./level
Saving Throw: Will disbelieves
Spell Resistance: Yes

The day or night seems to last longer than it should, and dusk or dawn does not appear. When the spell finally ends, it ends abruptly, so if the illusion hid the dawn it suddenly changes from deep night to bright day, or if it masked the dusk the day suddenly plunges into darkness.

MAGIC MIST

Illusion (Glamer) [Mind-Affecting]

Level: Mag 5
Components: V, S, F
Casting Time: 1 standard action
Range: Close (25 ft. + 5 ft./level)
Area: 20-ft.-radius emanation centered on the character
Duration: 1 round/level (D)
Saving Throw: Will negates (harmless)
Spell Resistance: Yes (harmless)

You create a fog of magical mist. All creatures become invisible, as per *greater invisibility*. In addition, those outside of the spell's area subconsciously swerve to avoid the mists. If these creatures succeed a Will save against the spell's DC, they notice their unusual behavior, though not necessarily the cause.

Focus: A silver pendant with a cloud engraved on one side

MANTLE OF LEADERSHIP

Enchantment [Fear, Mind-Affecting]

Level: Pri 3
Components: V, S, M, DF
Casting Time: 1 standard action
Range: Close (25 ft. + 5 ft./level)
Target: One creature
Duration: 1 minute/level (D)
Saving Throw: Will negates (see text)
Spell Resistance: Yes (see text)

Mantle of leadership enhances the targets natural qualities, making him appear more noble and commanding. The subject gains a +2 bonus to all Charisma-based skill checks and all Morale checks of attached the attached Force. All foes within 30 feet of the subject must succeed a Will save against the spell or become frightened. In addition, all allies within 30 feet gain a +4 morale bonus to Will saves.

Material Component: a sun-shaped metal disc

MASS DISORDER

Illusion (Glamer)

Level: Mag 5
Components: V, S, M

Casting Time: 1 standard action
Range: Medium (100 ft. + 10 ft./level)
Target: One creature/level
Duration: 1 round/level (D)
Saving Throw: Will negates
Spell Resistance: Yes

Affected creatures who fail their saving throw perceive their allies as enemies and their enemies as allies. They hear the shouts of their friends as threats by an opponent, and the jeers of their enemies and encouragement from their allies. The subject attacks his perceived enemies to the best of his ability.

Material Component: scraps of cloth from the uniforms or clothing of men from both sides

MISDIRECT

Enchantment (Compulsion)

Level: Mag 3
Components: V, S, M
Casting Time: 1 standard action
Range: Close (25 ft. + 5 ft./level)
Target: One creature
Duration: 1 round/level (D)
Saving Throw: Will disbelief
Spell Resistance: Yes

You force a target to think he sees you elsewhere on the battlefield. He pursues you to the best of his ability, but can never quite catch you. The subject of the spell may attempt a new saving throw each round on his turn as a free action.

Material Component: A bit of wool.

OCCLUDE

Abjuration

Level: Pri 9
Components: V, S, DF
Casting Time: 1 standard action
Range: 30 ft.
Area: All creatures within a 30-ft.-radius spread centered on the character
Duration: 1 round/level (D)
Saving Throw: Will negates
Spell Resistance: Yes

You channel the power of your deity to suppress the influence of other gods in the spell's area. All creatures who fail their save are temporarily blocked from access to their god. They cannot cast divine spells in the area, not may they secure divine aid. In effect, no gods exist, aside from your, within the spell's area. Characters worshipping your deity are not affected by this spell.

PLAGUE

Necromancy

Level: Pri 6
Components: V, S, M, DF
Casting Time: 1 standard action
Range: 120 ft.
Target: All living creatures within a 120 ft. burst centered on you.
Duration: Instantaneous

Saving Throw: Fortitude negates
Spell Resistance: Yes

You unleash a terrible plague among your enemies. All creatures who fail the save take 2d8 points of damage and gain a disease as per *contagion*.

Material Component: A miniature bow and arrow

RALLY

Conjuration (Summoning)

Level: Pri 4
Components: V, S, M, DF
Casting Time: 1 standard action
Range: 100 ft.
Target: All allies within a 100 ft. burst.
Duration: 1 round/level (D)
Saving Throw: Will negates (harmless)
Spell Resistance: Yes (harmless)

This spell magically transports all allies within 100 feet to vacant spaces near you. Allies remain for the spell's duration, before returning to their location prior to the casting of this spell. If there are not enough available spaces for your allies to appear, then they do not arrive.

Material Component: a miniature war horn

RAMPAGE

Enchantment (Compulsion) [Mind-Affecting]

Level: Mag 1
Components: V, S
Casting Time: 1 standard action
Range: Close (25 ft. + 5 ft./level)
Target: One horse/level
Duration: 1 round/level
Saving Throw: Will negates
Spell Resistance: Yes

You cause a target horse to enter a rage, gaining a +2 bonus to Strength and Constitution, a +1 bonus to Will saves, and a −2 penalty to AC. The horse tries to throw its riders or break free from its yoke. The rider may attempt a Ride check against the DC of the spell as a full round action to control the steed for that round. On a failed check, the horse throws the rider and runs in a random direction.

RESTORATIVE SLEEP

Conjuration (Healing)

Level: Pri 3
Components: V, S, DF
Casting Time: 1 standard action
Range: Touch
Target: One creature per level touched.
Duration: 1 day
Saving Throw: Fort negates
Spell Resistance: Yes

Morpheus' visits can have healing powers. Subjects of *restorative sleep* heal double the normal rate, recovering 2 hit points per character level after a full night's sleep. If the subject undergoes complete bed rest for an entire day and night, he recovers 4 hit points per character level.

RESTORE YOUTH

Transmutation

Level: Mag 8
Components: V, S
Casting Time: 1 standard action
Range: Touch
Target: One person/5 levels touched
Duration: 1 day/level
Saving Throw: None
Spell Resistance: No

The subject of this spells becomes 1d4 + 1 year per 2 caster levels younger (to a maximum of 1d4+10 years). The subject retains all current knowledge, skills, and abilities, but if his physical abilities were reduced by the decrease in years, he returns to his youthful levels.

RESTORE YOUTH, GREATER

Transmutation

Level: Mag 9
Components: V, S, M, XP
Duration: Instantaneous

This spell functions exactly like *restore youth*, except for above.

XP Cost: 1000.

RETRIEVE

Conjuration (Teleportation)

Level: Mag 2
Components: V, S
Casting Time: 1 standard action
Range: Touch
Target: Weapon touched
Duration: 1 round/level
Saving Throw: None
Spell Resistance: No

Retrieve automatically returns the affected weapon to the wielder who threw it, regardless of whether the weapon struck the target or not. A character may throw this weapon at his full normal rate of attacks (much like a character with a bow).

ROUGH SEAS

Transmutation

Level: Pri 3
Components: V, S, DF
Casting Time: 1 standard action
Range: Close (25 ft. + 5 ft./level)
Area: 50 ft. +5 ft./level-radius emanation
Duration: 1 round/level (D)
Saving Throw: None
Spell Resistance: No

This spell changes the water conditions to Stormy waters. Swimming characters must succeed a DC 20 Swim check to stay above the water, and they may not take 10, even if they are not otherwise distracted or threatened. In addition, all Boat check DCs are at +10.

SHEAR

Transmutation

Level: Mag 1
Components: V, S
Casting Time: 1 standard action
Range: Touch
Target: Masterwork weapon touched
Duration: 1 round/level (D)
Saving Throw: None
Spell Resistance: No

This spell makes a masterwork melee slashing or piercing weapon razor sharp, allowing the wielder to make all attacks with that weapon as melee touch attacks. However, the weapon deals only half damage on a successful hit.

SPIRIT AWAY

Conjuration (Teleportation)

Level: Pri 7
Components: V, S, M
Casting Time: 1 hour
Range: Touch
Target: Creature touched
Duration: 1 day/level
Saving Throw: Fortitude negates (harmless)
Spell Resistance: Yes (harmless)

Whenever the target creature falls to 1 hit point or less, the individual and all objects it is wearing and carrying (to a maximum of the character's heavy load) are instantly transported to a location as determined by you at the time of the casting. No other creatures are affected (aside from a familiar that is touching the subject). Once the location is determined, you cannot change it. The destination must be a location familiar to the caster.

Material Component: Ointments, incenses, and rare herbs worth 1,500 gp.

STYGIAN ARMOR

Transmutation

Level: Mag 2
Components: V, S, M
Casting Time: 1 standard action
Range: Touch
Target: Creature touched
Duration: 1 round/level
Saving Throw: Fortitude negates (harmless)
Spell Resistance: Yes

Stygian armor toughens a creature's skin. The effect grants a +4 enhancement bonus to the creature's existing natural armor bonus. The enhancement bonus provided by Stygian armor stacks with the target's natural armor bonus, but not with other enhancement bonuses to natural armor. A creature without natural armor has an effective natural armor bonus of +0, much as a character wearing only normal clothing has an armor bonus of +0.

In addition, the subject takes a –4 penalty to all Charisma-based skill checks and ability checks due to the grotesque changes to his appearance.

Material Component: A drop of water from the River Styx

TREASURED POSSESSION

Transmutation

Level: Mag 6
Components: V, S, M
Casting Time: 1 hour
Range: Touch
Target: Object touched
Duration: Permanent
Saving Throw: Fortitude negates (harmless)
Spell Resistance: No

You cast *treasured possession* on an object you possess valued at 50 gp or more. You form a permanent bond with the item. You cannot accidentally lose or misplace the item, and it remains at hand at all times. Attempting to steal the object from you is difficult, and requires the thief to succeed a DC 20 Strength check to move it. If the thief succeeds the check, he may drag it, as if he were moving a weight equal to 5 times his maximum load.

You may only bond with one item at a time. If you chose to release the bond with your current item in order to bond with a new item, you lose 500 XP, and take 1d4 points of damage per level.

Material Component: Undiluted wine and olive oil, which you rubbed onto the item.

TREMOR

Evocation [Earth]

Level: Pri 5
Components: V, S, DF
Casting Time: 1 standard action
Range: 120 ft.
Area: 120-ft.-radius emanation centered on you.
Duration: 1 round
Saving Throw: See text
Spell Resistance: No

When you cast *tremor*, the ground shudders as if affected by a mild earthquake. The knocks people off-balance, and tips objects, and more. The effect lasts for 1 round, during which time creatures on the ground may only move or attack if they succeed a DC 15 Balance check or fall prone. A spellcaster on the ground must succeed a Concentration check against a DC 15 + spell level or lose any spell he or she tries to cast.

The tremor is not powerful enough to affect structures or terrain features in any sort of meaningful way. However, unattended objects that fall take 1d4 points of damage, enough to break small and fragile items.

TRUMPET

Transmutation [Language-Dependant, Sonic]

Level: Mag 1
Components: V
Casting Time: 1 standard action
Range: Touch
Target: Creature touched
Duration: 1 round/level (D)
Saving Throw: Fortitude negates (harmless)
Spell Resistance: Yes (harmless)

The subject's voice carries impossible distances. All creatures who can see the subject can likewise hear the subject, regardless of distance. This spell does not grant understanding, merely the ability hear the subject.

TUMULT

Transmutation [Language-Dependant, Sonic]

Level: Mag 2
Components: V
Casting Time: 1 standard action
Range: Close (25 ft. + 5 ft./level)
Target: One living creature
Duration: 1 round/level (D)
Saving Throw: Will negates
Spell Resistance: Yes

You mute the subject's words so that he cannot be heard by anyone farther than 5 feet away. Other creatures within 30 feet of the subject may attempt to Read Lips by making a successful Spot check as normal.

UNMAN

Enchantment (Compulsion) [Fear, Mind-Affecting]

Level: Mag 6
Components: V
Casting Time: 1 standard action
Range: 60 ft.
Targets: All living creatures in a 60-ft.-radius burst
Duration: 1 round/level (D)
Saving Throw: Will negates
Spell Resistance: Yes

You fill your enemies with an unnatural dread. Subjects who succeed their saves against the spell become shaken for 1 round. Those who fail become panicked for 1d4 rounds +1 round per level. If cornered, a panicked creature begins cowering, (see **Chapter Eight: Glossary** in the *DMG* for details on fear).

VENGEFUL WAVE

Evocation [Water]

Level: Pri 6
Components: V, S, DF
Casting Time: 1 round
Range: Long (400 ft. + 40 ft./level)
Area: One 10-ft. wave of water
Duration: 1 minute/level (D)
Saving Throw: Reflex half
Spell Resistance: No

You cause an area of water, such as that along a coastline, to rise up as a wave and crash down onto a target each round for the duration of the spell. The wave attacks once per round, and its attack bonus equals your caster level + your Wisdom modifier, +11 for the wave's Strength score (33), and −1 for being Large.

The wave deals 1d8+11 points of damage on each attack, and any creature struck must succeed a Reflex save or be knocked prone and dragged back into the water. He must succeed a Swim check to keep above the water as if swimming in Stormy waters.

CHAPTER SIX: EQUIPMENT

The Homeric setting has a very specific feel to it. To maintain this flavor, certain equipment necessarily cannot appear. Other items are restricted, while others that have faded from the medieval world are still in common use.

THE AGE OF BRONZE

Archaeologists and scholars debate exactly when the Trojan War occurred, if it occurred at all. Troy itself has been located, and though the city was destroyed and rebuilt many times, its seventh incarnation closely matches Homer's description and fits the right era. Scholars currently believe the Trojan War began between 1280 and 1175 BCE. The most popular claim holds that it began in 1218 BCE, which means it ended in 1209. Others argue for 1184 or 1179 BCE as the starting date.

All of these dates place the war in the historical Bronze Age and the Late Mycenaean Period. What does that mean? First, it means bronze was the metal of choice. Bronze was an alloy, usually 90 percent copper and 10 percent tin, and tin had to be imported from the Middle East or from Britain. However, processing and smelting iron ore was still at an early stage. Iron could not yet be carburized in a kiln (a complicated process of melting the iron completely, then plunging it into cold water, and then tempering it with additional heat treatments at different temperatures), and so was melted and then hammered to produce wrought iron. Wrought iron was heavy, dull, and more brittle than bronze. Iron had the added difficulty of a higher melting point than bronze, requiring much hotter forges (iron's melting point is 1530 degrees Celsius versus 1100 degrees for bronze) to melt the iron completely. The people of this period most commonly used iron for simple farm equipment and other household tools. They cast anything requiring sharp detail or high endurance into bronze instead. Thus, a pot or cauldron might be made of iron, but armor and weapons, which needed balance and careful molding, were more often made from bronze. Bronze weapons held a better edge than iron, and they required less sharpening. They were also less likely to rust.

While bronze was not as hard as wrought iron or steel—it dented or bent more easily—it was stronger and more durable than regular iron. A bronze sword would not cut through bone easily, but it could carve flesh without difficulty, and a bronze-headed spear could pierce bronze armor without a problem. Bronze also proved more malleable than iron, which made it easier to work and less likely to break—a bronze spearhead would bend before it broke, which meant it the warrior could heat it and pound it back into shape with ease. Bronze swords could shatter when struck a heavy blow, of course, but that was uncommon. Because bronze had a lower melting point, blacksmiths could set up portable forges easily and thus repair and even forge armor and weapons close to the battlefield.

Bronze armor was better than iron in several other ways. Bronze was lighter, so armor weighed less. Since it resisted rust longer, it did not leave stains on clothing as much. Bronze also trapped less heat, making it less effective for cooking but better for armor, where warriors overheated from wearing so much metal on a sunny day. Finally, because of its lighter weight, bronze armor did not provide as much hindrance to activities like jumping, climbing, and even swimming.

Unfortunately, because it had so many uses, bronze was very valuable. Most commoners could not afford items made of bronze. Tools were made of wood, stone, or even baked clay when possible. Metal was a treasured commodity and only nobles could afford large amounts of it.

IRON AND TESTAMENT

In *Testament*, iron weapons are described as superior to bronze weapons. *Testament* refers to the carburized iron available in the Iron Age, not the wrought iron available in the Homeric era.

CURRENCY

According to historians, the first coinage system started in Argos in the 7th century BCE, at least four centuries after the Trojan War. Thus, strictly speaking, coins do not belong in this game. Yet this does not mean money did not exist, only that it had not been standardized.

People certainly used precious metals for purchases during this period, but as no standard coin existed, most men simply bartered an amount: "I will give you this lump of gold, as large as my thumb, in exchange for that fine tunic and that good woolen cloak." We do know of one set amount, the talent, but this was not something that could be used in everyday purchases. Talents were large bars of gold used by nobles to more tally and store their wealth. They could be bronze, silver, or gold, though silver was the most common. The term "talent" was used in several places, including both Greece and Israel, and though they all meant large bars or bricks of precious metal, the exact size and weight varied. The easiest standard is from Biblical Israel, where a talent of silver weighed 100 pounds, while a talent of gold weighed 200 pounds. Since coins are supposed to weigh roughly one third of an ounce, or 50 to a pound, that suggests that a talent of silver roughly equaled 5,000 silver pieces. Even if we assume that gold talents were the same size but twice as heavy (because gold is a heavier metal), a talent of gold would contain 5,000 gold pieces. Thus, when Alcinous the king of the Phaeacians declares that each of the thirteen nobles in the land will give Odysseus a talent of gold, in game terms they are awarding him a grand total of 65,000gp!

Obviously, talents are not going to be carried in backpacks or a belt pouches. Adventurers could use smaller lumps of metal as payment, however, and the easiest way to handle these is to use the copper piece, silver piece, and gold piece standards, with the understanding these standards apply to approximate weights of the metals in question. If a lump of silver weighed roughly one third of an ounce, it counts as a silver piece. Most commoners would see only copper pieces, however, or occasionally a bit of silver. Gold remained in the hands of the nobility—or in the hands of warriors who sacked rich cities.

Of course, barter proved far more common than the use of money, even among men of substance. Beggars received bread and meat rather than money, and craftsmen traded services for food, shelter, or clothing. Farmers sold their produce and livestock in exchange for clothing, tools, and anything else they needed.

Items did not have a standard price. If two men met, and one had cloth but needed meat and the other had hogs but wanted linen, they would work out a trade that seemed fair to both of them. It did not matter that the same number of hogs had bought double the linen the month before, because they could just as easily be worth half as much the following month, depending upon how much linen the first man had and how much meat he needed.

Gems are also viable currency—amber and pearls were particularly common—as could horses, crafted goods, and even people in areas where slavery was acceptable. In short, anything someone else wanted could be counted as money.

BARTERING

While not historically accurate, for game purposes, we recommend you use the standard coinage rates and the included item prices for ease. However, you may wish to use a bartering system to achieve a more accurate setting. Use the following rules, adapted from *Testament*, to facilitate bartering in *Trojan War*.

Handle trivial purchases by simply exchanging valuables at the listed price, either in this book, or in the *PHB*. For large, urgent, or uncommon purchases, have the buyer make an Appraise check and the seller a Bluff check. The GM makes both checks in secret, with the result of the Bluff check used as a modifier on the Appraise check.

The scarcity of the items haggled determines the DC of the seller's Bluff check. If the seller succeeds the Bluff check, the amount by which his roll exceeds the DC is applied as a penalty to buyers the Appraise check. See **Table 6–1: Barter Bluff Checks** for details on Bluff DCs.

If the buyer makes a successfully Appraise check (see **Table 6–2: Appraise Checks**), he appraises the item within 91 to 110% (90 + 1d20) of the actual value, and is able to close a deal at that price—the actual haggling to arrive at that final price can be skipped in the interest of speeding play.

If the buyer fails the Appraise check, he estimates the item's value at 50% to 140% (40 + 1d10 x 10) its actual worth.

TABLE 6–1: BARTER BLUFF CHECKS

Item Availability	Example	DC
Abundant	Everybody has one	30
Plentiful	All but the poorest have one	25
Common	Available in most markets	20
Uncommon	Few dealers have one	15
Scarce	Nearly impossible to find	10

TABLE 6–2: APPRAISE CHECKS

Scarcity	DC
Abundant	12
Plentiful	14
Common	16
Uncommon	18
Scarce	20

The seller, of course, accepts any sale at more than the actual value, and refuses any offer of less than par.

If the buyer pays with goods instead of coin, the process then has to be reversed to determine the value of whatever the buyer offers in trade. Once both parties are satisfied as to the value of the items under consideration, then deciding whether to make an exchange is straightforward.

Buyers and sellers may gain bonuses or penalties to their checks depending on outside factors as determined by the GM.

WEAPONS

The common weapon of the Homeric age was the footman's spear. These impressive polearms extended twelve feet, and had strong wooden shafts with foot-long bronze blades at the front and a heavy bronze spike at the butt. Footmen stabbed their foes from behind the safety of a shield wall, planting the butt of their spear in the ground and then inserting the shaft and head through the gaps between their shields.

Throwing spears were also common. This six-foot-long spear had a head of double-edged bronze. Charioteers favored these spears, and hurled them from their chariots as they charged through the enemy ranks. Throwing spears were long enough and heavy enough they could be used in combat, and warriors often stabbed nearby enemies with them before finally throwing them at distant targets.

Nobles and captains wore swords, but common soldiers rarely owned such costly weapons. Swords typically had a leaf-shaped double-edged blade and a wooden handle covered with studs of silver or bronze. Most swords were short swords, but renowned

TABLE 6-3: WEAPONS

	Cost	Dmg (S)	Dmg (M)	Critical	Range Increment	Weight[1]	Type
Simple Weapons							
Unarmed Attacks							
Unarmed Strike	—	1d2[2]	1d3[2]	x2	—	—	Bludgeoning
Light Melee Weapons							
Dagger	2 gp	1d3	1d4	19–20/x2	10 ft.	1 lb.	Piercing or slashing
Mace, light	5 gp	1d4	1d6	x2	—	4 lb.	Bludgeoning
Sickle	6 gp	1d4	1d6	x2	—	2 lb.	Slashing
One-Handed Melee Weapons							
Club	—	1d4	1d6	x2	10 ft.	3 lb.	Bludgeoning
Mace, heavy	12 gp	1d6	1d8	x2	—	8 lb.	Bludgeoning
Two-Handed Melee Weapons							
Quarterstaff[3]	—	1d4/1d4	1d6/1d6	x2	—	4 lb.	Bludgeoning
Ranged Weapons							
Sling	—	1d3	1d4	x2	50 ft.	0 lb.	Bludgeoning
Bullets, sling (10)	1 sp	—	—	—	—	5 lb.	—
Martial Weapons							
Light Melee Weapons							
Axe, throwing	8 gp	1d4	1d6	x2	10 ft.	2 lb.	Slashing
Shield, any	Special	1d2	1d3	x2	—	Special	Bludgeoning
Sword, short	10 gp	1d4	1d6	19–20/x2	—	2 lb.	Piercing
One-Handed Melee Weapons							
Throwing spear	2 gp	1d6	1d8	x2	40 ft.	4 lb.	Piercing
Battleaxe	10 gp	1d6	1d8	x3	—	6 lb.	Slashing
Longsword	15 gp	1d6	1d8	19–20/x2	—	4 lb.	Slashing
Trident	15 gp	1d6	1d8	x2	10 ft.	4 lb.	Piercing
Warhammer	3 sp	1d6	1d8	x3	—	5 lb.	Bludgeoning
Two-Handed Melee Weapons							
Footman's Spear[4]	5 gp	1d6	1d8	x3	20 ft.	6 lb.	Piercing
Greatsword	50 gp	1d10	2d6	19–20	—	8 lb.	Slashing
Ranged Weapons							
Longbow	75 gp	1d6	1d8	x3	100 ft.	3 lb.	Piercing
Arrows (20)	1 gp	—	—	—	—	3 lb.	—
Longbow, composite	100 gp	1d6	1d8	x3	110 ft.	3 lb.	Piercing
Arrows (20)	1 gp	—	—	—	—	3 lb.	—
Shortbow	30 gp	1d4	1d6	x3	60 ft.	2 lb.	Piercing
Arrows (20)	1 gp	—	—	—	—	1 lb.	—
Shortbow, composite	15 gp	1d4	1d6	x3	70 ft.	2 lb.	Piercing
Arrows (20)	1 sp	—	—	—	—	1 lb.	—

[1] Weight figures are for Medium creatures. A Small weapon weighs half as much.
[2] This weapon deals nonlethal damage [3] Double weapon [4] Reach weapon

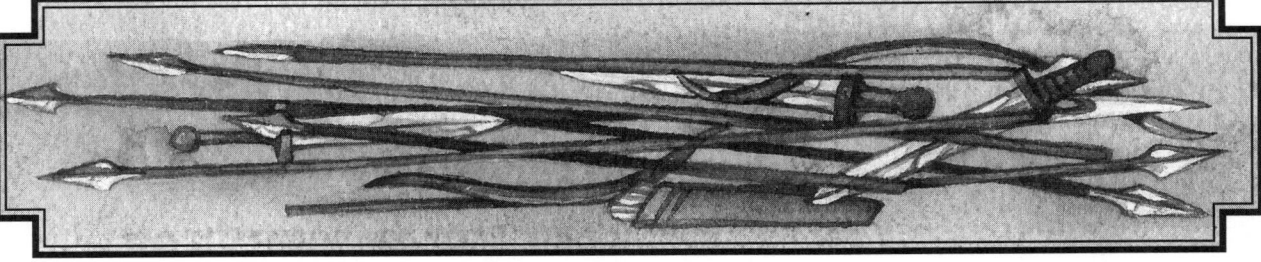

or wealthy warriors might own longswords or even greatswords.

Some warriors also used axes. Though far less expensive than swords, axes are not as agile. Most axes had a long polished wooden haft and a bronze head that curved down into a single blade.

Composite bows were common for hunters but rare in battle. The weapons could be devastating in the right hands, but took too long to draw, and so only expert archers dared to fight with them, and then only from behind the protection of a comrade.

Maces and clubs could also be used particularly by anyone who could not afford a sword or an axe. Quarterstaffs appeared from time to time, usually in the hands of travelers or old men, and individuals used them as often for walking as for self-defense. Children typically played with slings, and youths still used them for hunting and for antagonizing opponents.

Table 6–3: Weapons details weapons available in the Homeric setting. While bronze is traditionally lighter than iron, depending on the amount of tin in the alloy, bronze can sometimes weigh more than iron, and more than cast iron. The following tables reflect approximate weights of weapons, given the variations of quality. Use prices for comparative value for bartering.

ARMOR

Because bronze was so expensive, most common fighters wore armor made of leather, linen, or canvas. These materials were very lightweight, and did offer some protection, particularly when layered, the most common armor technique of this period. Armorers would hammer out thin sheets of bronze, tin, or even silver, or take sheets of canvas, linen, and leather. They would tack these together, cut to size, mold to form, and then seal with wax along the edges. All-metal armor usually had a thin rim of metal to hold it together, while the cloth and leather versions used wax. By using so many thin layers, the armor stayed light and flexible, but offered a good deal more protection. It was also much easier to repair. If a weapon pierced the outermost layer, an armorer could remove and replace that layer. In the meantime, if a breastplate had four layers, and the first two had been pierced, it still had two layers left intact.

Because of the warm, sunny climate, warriors did not use heavy, all-encompassing armor. Speed, mobility, and keeping cool were more important than full-body protection. In addition, warriors assembled armor piecemeal rather than purchasing it all at once. The available armor pieces for this setting are as follows.

CUIRASS OR BREASTPLATE

This armor covers the torso, molded to the individual. A second matching piece covers the back, with leather straps holding the two together along the sides. The breastplate could be made of linen, canvas, leather, or metal, and layered or not. Donning a cuirass or breastplate takes 2 minutes or 1 minute donned hastily, and may be removed in 1 minute or half this time with help.

GREAVES

These molded pieces cover the legs from just below the knee down to just above the foot. They have no backs, and straps around the back and with clips attaching to the bottom to the sandals secure them. Greaves could be made of linen, canvas, leather, or metal, and layered or not. Donning a greaves takes 1 minutes or 5 rounds donned hastily, and may be removed in 1 minute or half this time with help.

PETURGIS OR BELT

This is essentially an apron, fastening to the belt and covering the groin. Some peturgis are solid fabric or leather, but most are strips of leather hanging loose from the belt, offering some protection while not limiting movement. Some warriors wear a wide, thick belt wrapping around their pelvis, serving the same purpose as the peturgis. Donning a peturgis or belt takes 1 full-round action or a move action if donned hastily, and may be removed in one move action.

HELMET OR CAP

Helmets come in a variety of shapes, but cover the top and back of the head completely. Most Homeric helmets cover the sides as well, and curve down over the brow, leaving an open area in front for eyes, nose, and mouth. Helmets are usually made of bronze or hardened leather, and often sport tusks, horns, or plumes. An old-fashioned helmet—still seen occasionally during the Trojan War—was made from boar tusks that had been split down their length and then fastened to a leather framework with thongs.

Common soldiers often wear simple caps instead of helmets. These caps are made from thick hide, and fit closely to the top of the head, but do not cover the back or sides at all.

Donning a cap or help takes the same amount of time as donning a shield.

PANOPLY

A full suit of armor for this period, called a panoply, consists of four pieces: cuirass, greaves, peturgis, and a helmet. Even with panoplies, the components rarely match. Not everyone could afford a full panoply, of course—not even if made from canvas and linen rather than bronze. Donning a full suit of armor requires 4 minutes, donning hastily 1 minute, and removing armor 1 minute or half this time with help.

ARMOR STANDARDS FOR HOMERIC SOLDIERS

Homeric warriors do not wear boots—sandals being more practical in the warmer climate—or gauntlets. Some wear arm bracers, but they generally keep their hands bare to grasp their weapons with ease. Belts are used for protection, not for holding anything. Swords hang from baldrics and down at the side rather than being fastened to the waist.

Common soldiers usually have only a cap and a shield for protection. More experienced warriors carry a breastplate, which they earned in battle, to add to their protection. Distinguished warriors have a peturgis or a wide belt. They also wear helmets, but only the finest warriors or wealthy nobles own greaves.

Some soldiers wear armor from animal skins. Those who do where hides, toss them over one shoulder and fastened it around the middle with a belt. The skins of big cats are particularly favored, both for their protective fur and for their distinctive coloring.

SHIELDS

In the Homeric setting, many warriors have only their shields and their helmets for defense. Large and strong men still use tower shields, but the general shield shape evolved to become more streamlined. Because warriors fight primarily on foot, their shields are shaped to allow for freedom of movement. Round shields and the more recent crescent and dyplon designs are the favorites.

Shields are typically made from hide or metal. Hide shields have wooden frames. Armorers add bosses and rivets, both for decoration and for added protection. The wealthy layer their shields in the same way as their armor, usually with several layers of hide and then a layer of tin or bronze for the surface.

The available shields for this setting are as follows.

CRESCENT SHIELD

Runners use these shields. They are round with a section cut out of the bottom, so that the crescent's horns point downward. Their wielders can sling them on their backs back, allowing them to run without bumping against the shield's lower edge.

DYPLON SHIELD

The most common style of shield, it has curved edges and cut-outs on each side. Its figure-eight shape lets it provides full protection but, when slung on the back, does not block the runner's elbows or feet. The side-notches also allow spears to thrust between a pair of interlocking shields.

ROUND SHIELD

An older shield style, the round shield provides more side cover than does the dyplon. Its shape means it has no edges to catch on anything while running, and a warrior can easily thrust around it with a sword or a spear.

TOWER SHIELD

This massive shield serves as a portable wall. Only men strong enough to carry them easily use it.

ARMORING UP

Characters, as mentioned above, assemble armor from various pieces. They do not purchase entire suits at a time. **Table 6–4: Armor and Shields** presents the available armor and shields in the Trojan War. A character can wear all of the following items together or separate: belt or peturgis, cuirass or breastplate, greaves, and a helmet or cap, forming panoply when fully assembled. Simply add the armor bonuses derived from each component. The sum of these bonuses equals your armor bonus. Finally, recall *Trojan War* does not use Arcane Spell Failure (ASF) as a factor in armor, given the common construction. If you plan to use these armors in other settings, assume each linen and canvas component confers a 3% chance for ASF, tin 5% chance for ASF, and 10% for bronze, such that a linen and canvas panoply would have an ASF of 12%, tin 20%, and bronze 40%. For Maximum Dexterity Bonus, assume any armor starts by allowing a +8 Max Dex bonus. Each armor component reduces the Maximum Dexterity Bonus by the indicated amount. Likewise, sum the Armor Check Penalty, and Weight of all of the components.

TABLE 6-4: ARMOR AND SHIELDS

Armor	Cost	Armor/Shield Bonus	Maximum Dex Bonus	Armor Check Penalty	—Speed— (30 ft.)	(20 ft.)	Weight
Belt	2 gp	+1	—	0	30 ft.	20 ft.	1 lb.
Cuirass							
Linen	10 gp	+1	–2	0	30 ft.	20 ft.	5 lb.
Canvas	10 gp	+1	–2	0	30 ft.	20 ft.	8 lb.
Leather	20 gp	+2	–3	–1	30 ft.	20 ft.	10 lb.
Tin	100 gp	+2	–3	–1	30 ft.	20 ft.	15 lb.
Bronze	150 gp	+3	–3	–1	20 ft.	15 ft.	15 lb.
Greaves							
Linen	8 sp	+1	—	0	30 ft.	20 ft.	1 lb.
Canvas	5 sp	+1	—	0	30 ft.	20 ft.	1 lb.
Leather	1 gp	+1	—	0	30 ft.	20 ft.	3 lb.
Tin	10 gp	+2	—	0	30 ft.	20 ft.	5 lb.
Bronze	20 gp	+2	—	0	30 ft.	20 ft.	5 lb.
Helmet							
Cap	5 sp	+1	—	0	30 ft.	20 ft.	1 lb.
Leather	2 gp	+1	—	0	30 ft.	20 ft.	3 lb.
Bronze	10 gp	+2	—	0	30 ft.	20 ft.	5 lb.
Peturgis							
Linen	8 sp	+1	—	0	30 ft.	20 ft.	1 lb.
Canvas	5 sp	+1	—	0	30 ft.	20 ft.	1 lb.
Leather	1 gp	+1	—	0	30 ft.	20 ft.	3 lb.
Leather Strips	2 gp	+1	—	0	30 ft.	20 ft.	2 lb.
Crescent Shields							
Leather	7 gp	+1	—	–3	30 ft.	20 ft.	15 lb.
Bronze	20 gp	+2	—	–3	30 ft.	20 ft.	20 lb.
Dyplon Shields							
Leather	10 gp	+1	—	–2	30 ft.	20 ft.	15 lb.
Bronze	30 gp	+2	—	–3	30 ft.	20 ft.	20 lb.
Round Shields							
Leather	7 gp	+1	—	–5	25 ft.	20 ft.	10 lb.
Bronze	20 gp	+2	—	–5	25 ft.	20 ft.	15 lb.
Tower Shields							
Leather	10 gp	+2	—	–10	20 ft.	15 ft.	20 lb.
Bronze	30 gp	+3	—	–10	20 ft.	15 ft.	45 lb.

ARMOR PROPERTIES

Armor Property	Cost Modifier
Breathable	x2 total price
Burnished	+200 gp
Chased	x2 total price
Doubled	x2 total price
Fitted	x2 total price

LAYERING

Each entry refers to just a single layer of armor. Each additional layer costs half the normal value of a regular armor or shield and adds half the normal weight, but likewise increases the Armor Check Penalty and AC by half the normal value rounded down. Thus, a layered tower shield with two layers of leather and one of bronze would cost 50 gp and have an AC of +6. It would also weigh 53 lbs.

ARMOR PROPERTIES

The following properties are nonmagical modifications enhancing the usefulness of armor. Crafting armor with this properties requires a DC 20 Craft check, just as if the armorer fashioned a masterwork suit of armor.

BREATHABLE

The armor is cunningly constructed, with slots or vents for air. No one wearing this armor can overheat in it, regardless of the ambient temperature.

BURNISHED

The armor has been finished with an unusually high gloss. When the sun strikes its polished surface, opponents are dazzled by the glare. Anyone looking at the armor in sunlight must make a DC 10 Fortitude save to avoid being dazzled for 1 round. This quality applies only to metal armors or shields.

CHASED

Gold detail work enhances the armor. The wearer gains a +1 bonus to all Intimidate checks.

DOUBLED

One of the armor's layers was doubled over, making it stronger than normal. The armor bonus provided by the piece is provides an armor bonus +1 greater than normal.

FITTED

The armor is tailored to a specific individual. The armor's maximum Dexterity bonus increase by +1, and reduces the armor check penalty by 1.

TEMPERED

The armorer heated and refolded the armor to make it stronger. The piece confers an armor bonus +1 higher than normal.

GOODS

Commoners in the Homeric age had few possessions, in part because they needed very little. The weather was usually temperate, growing cold enough at night to require a light blanket and a dying fire, but warm enough during the day that people wore as little as possible. Homes were simple, with large stone hearths providing both warmth and a place to cook. Furniture was wooden and rough-hewn, fashioned by its owners. Chairs were simple backless stools or benches with furs thrown atop them for cushioning, and smaller stools were set nearby to rest one's feet. Mugs and tankards were either wooden or stone, or crafted out of leather and sealed with heated pitch. They used wooden serving platters to hold meat and bread, and shallow bowls for mixed wine. Most commoners did not have beds at all, but used piles of furs and rugs as a mattress with cloaks and blankets pulled over them for warmth.

Clothing was simple. Men wore loincloths or kilts, and short-sleeved tunics, with cloaks for when it grew cold. Women wore lightweight shifts (thin, short, sleeveless dresses) or light dresses, or loose tops and skirts. Nobles, priests, and orators sometimes wore long, loose robes—these could be worn open over other clothing, or worn closed (either belted at the waist, or fastened by clasps down its front edges) over nothing but a loincloth or a shift. People went barefoot at home, but wore sandals outside—boots were reserved for the mountains, which were far colder.

Those with money, both nobles and successful merchants, had fancier belongings. Chairs had backs, and made from wood or metal. Bowls, plates, and cups were usually metal as well. Instead of a single large table, they used smaller tables, and could be set beside a chair so that a guest could eat easily. Beds were still uncommon, though the richest might have actual bed frames, but nobles had piles of rugs and furs, and could provide bedding for several guests on short notice.

GOODS DESCRIPTIONS

Cauldron: Most travelers have one of these large, heavy cooking pots. Cauldrons have wide mouths and handles on either side for lifting. They are most often copper, though some are of bronze or iron. Gold is too soft for these items, which sit above fires for hours on end.

Chair, backed: This fancy seat has an actual carved back.

Chair, backless: This simple seat is little more than a stool or bench with a fur thrown across it.

Footstool: These small, low stools are placed in front of a chair, so that the person sitting can rest his feet.

Goblet: A heavy drinking cup with a long stem, a wide base below that, and no handle.

Kilt: A piece of cloth wrapped around the waist and pelvis, creating a loose skirt. Belts and pins hold the kilt in place.

TABLE 6-5: GOODS

Item	Cost	Weight	Item	Cost	Weight
Backpack (empty)	2 gp	2 lb.	Loincloth	1 cp	*
Barrel (empty)	2 gp	30 lb.	Mug		
Basket (empty)	4 cp	1 lb.	Leather	4 cp	1 lb.
Bedroll	1 sp	5 lb.	Wooden	2 cp	1 lb.
Blanket, winter	5 sp	3 lb.	Stone	2 cp	2 lb.
Bowl, mixing			Pitcher, clay	2 cp	5 lb.
Wood	5 cp	1 lb.	Platter		
Silver	25 gp	1 lb.	Wood	3 cp	2 lb.
Gold	250 gp	2 lb.	Silver	10 sp	4 lb.
Bucket (empty)	5 sp	2 lb.	Gold	40 gp	10 lb.
Candle	1 cp	*	Pot, iron	5 sp	10 lb.
Canvas (sq. yd.)	1 sp	1 lb.	Pouch, belt	1 sp	3 lb.
Cauldron			Robe		
Copper	1 gp	10 lb.	Simple	1 sp	10 lb.
Bronze	10 gp	10 lb.	Formal	5 sp	10 lb.
Iron	5 gp	20 lb.	Expensive	15 gp	12 lb.
Chair, backless			Clasped	20 gp	14 lb.
Wooden	1 sp	4 lb.	Rope, hemp (50 ft.)	1 sp	10 lb.
Bronze	6 gp	6 lb.	Sack (empty)	1 cp	1/2 lb.
Gold	250 gp	10 lb.	Shift	1 cp	1 lb.
Chair, backed			Stool, folding	3 sp	2 lb.
Wooden	3 sp	8 lb.	Table		
Bronze	15 gp	10 lb.	Large	4 cp	40 lb.
Gold	300 gp	18 lb.	Small, plain	3 cp	10 lb.
Chest (empty)	8 sp	15 lb.	Small, fancy	9 sp	12 lb.
Fishhook	1 cp	*	Tent	1 gp	20 lb.
Fishing net, 25 sq. ft.	4 sp	5 lb.	Thread, colored	varies	*
Footstool			Torch	1 cp	1 lb.
Wood	2 cp	1 lb.	Tripod		
Stone	5 cp	4 lb.	Copper	2 sp	5 lb.
Bronze	2 gp	2 lb.	Bronze	5 sp	5 lb.
Gold	60 gp	4 lb.	Iron	3 sp	10 lb.
Goblet			Tunic		
Bronze	2 gp	2 lb.	Plain	3 cp	1 lb.
Silver	6 gp	2 lb.	Formal	2 sp	2 lb.
Gold	18 gp	3 lb.	Expensive	5 gp	3 lb.
Jug, clay	3 cp	9 lb.	Waterskin	4 cp	4 lb.
Kilt	1 cp	1 lb.	Whetstone	1 cp	1 lb.

Loincloth: A simple cloth wrapped several times around the pelvis to protect the groin.

Mixing bowl: Everyone in the Homeric age has one of these shallow bowls. Mixing bowls are used for drinking wine (see **Food and Drink**, page 69), but they can also be used to hold food. Beggars often carry mixing bowls, and eat any food they receive in the same bowl. Simpler mixing bowls are made of wood, while fancier ones are bronze, silver, or even gold, but even the wooden bowls are carefully sanded smooth, because people also use the bowls to offer libations to the gods.

Mug: A solid cup, often with a handle.

Platter, serving: This long platter is flat or has a very shallow curve, with a raised lip all around and handles at either end. Food, usually bread or meat, is set in the center.

Robe: This is a loose garment that hangs down to the feet. Some robes have sleeves, but others are simply a piece of fabric slit down the middle and then cut along either side to make space for the arms to poke out.

Sandals: These open-toed shoes are little more than thick leather soles and straps to bind it to the feet. Because of the warm weather, most people wear these unless walking through brambles or harsh terrain.

Shift: A thin, loose, sleeveless garment for women that extends just past the groin.

Stool, folding: Simple hinged wooden frames with a piece of canvas stretched across them. These stools are small enough that a traveler can carry them in a bag slung over his shoulder, or hanging from a cord across his back.

Tripod: A common item for travelers, this three-legged stand has no top but a thick metal band linking its legs at top. The tripod is set over a fire, so that a cauldron can be set atop it, held securely by the band, for cooking. Tripods are usually made of metal, bronze, copper, or sometimes iron.

Tunic: A simple garment, similar to a short dress for a man. Most tunics hang to just below the groin, and are often slit on the sides for easier movement.

COLOR

Clothing in the Homeric setting is most often buff-colored, the natural appearance of the fabric or leather. Cloth can be set out to bleach under the hot sun, and so white items are common though these not used as work garments. Dyes are available but expensive, and only the rich can afford them.

Black was the most easily produced color, since it could be created by burning wood (which produced black with a blue tinge) or by slowly burning ivory or bone in a hot fire (bone black, a slightly warmer color). Most dyes, however, come from minerals or plants, crushed into powder and then mixed with water. The most common pigments were yellow and green, derived from a mixture of juice from parsley, flowers, sap, and berries. Sap green was the most common of these though, but because of the time involved in mixing ingredients, even it was expensive. Deposits of peat or brown coal yielded shades of brown, and iron oxide produced muted reds, yellows, and browns. Verdigris (French for "green of Greece") is a blue-green produced by letting copper sit beneath grape skins in the sun. The copper darkens from the combination of sun and minerals, and develops a green-blue crust, its equivalent to rust. Dyers scrape this off, ground it, and mix it with wine or vinegar.

Deep red carmine came from the dried and crushed bodies of a particular variety of female wingless insect. Rose and pale crimson dyes were crushed madder root. Reddish orange came from the bodies of certain red insects or worms. Blues could be produced from certain plants, including dark blue indigo, which comes from the fermented leaves and flowering stalks of the indigo shrub. Other blues came from crushed stones like lapis, or from other minerals. Purple, made from the crushed bodies of certain sea snails, was a royal color because it was so rare only kings could afford it. Deep, crimson purple was often referred to as Tyrian purple because Tyre was the only land with enough of those sea snails to create the color in its full intensity (each snail produced only a tiny drop of color, so millions were required to dye an entire garment). Sky-blue

and deep blue (often called Egyptian blue) were also produced from these snails, making Tyre the dye capital of the world, and an extremely wealthy nation.

When dyers dyed clothing, they did just enough to lend a hint of the color, so most garments looked washed-out. People often purchased colored threads and embroidered their clothing, stitching borders around cuffs and collars or even designs across the torso, as ways to enliven their appearance. Rich, vivid hues required the cloth to be saturated with dye, and so these were extremely costly. After their duel, Hector gave Ajax an excellent bronze sword with silver studs, but Ajax gave Hector a belt of rich violet in return. The two items were both handsome gifts, and of equivalent value.

Because of its cost, dyed cloth of any sort was a worthy gift. Vials of dye, whether in powder form or as liquid, were worth more than gold. The wealthy merchants who purchased them carefully guarded these items, and dyers often worked for a merchant, trader, or clothier on their premises, so the dye never left the owner's sight.

CHARIOTS

Chariots were the battleships of the ancient battlefield, used to quickly transport firepower into range of the enemy while providing some measure of protection to the warriors inside that was not afforded to archers on horseback. The chariot first appeared in Greece around 1600 BCE, and rapidly became a major facet in land battles. The Egyptians and Syrians also had chariots at this time, but the Greek version, known as an "eqeta" (or "follower"), was stronger and heavier, with leather and wooden construction rather than the wicker basket approach the Egyptians favored. A team of two horses (often called a "span") pulled the Greek chariots, and the chariot's crew consisted of a charioteer and a warrior. In battle, the chariots would mass along the front line of the army and race into the fray, followed by the slower footmen with their tower shields and long spears.

By the Trojan War, however, this had changed. Footmen had become faster, and many used shorter throwing spears and the

TABLE 6-6: DYES

Dye	Source	Cost per 1 oz. vial
Black	Ground coal or burnt wood	10 gp
Light green (sap green)	Crushed parsley, grass, and leaves	10 gp
Yellow-green	Crushed seeds and grass	10 gp
Dull yellow	Iron oxide	10 gp
Brown	Peat	10 gp
Dark green	Plant sap	15 gp
Blue-green	Verdigris	25 gp
Bright yellow	Ground sulfur	25 gp
Rose red	Crushed madder root	25 gp
Rust red	Iron powder	25 gp
Carmine	Crushed insects	30 gp
Orange	Crushed red worms ("bloodworms")	35 gp
Indigo Blue	Indigo shrub	35 gp
Sky blue	Ground snails	40 gp
Bright blue (Egyptian blue)	Ground snails	50 gp
Tyrian purple	Crushed sea-snails	100 gp

bonus to Reflex saves. A shieldbearer grants cover from attacks originating on his side of the chariot, increasing the cover bonus to +4 to AC and +2 to Reflex saves.

If a chariot driver dies, the charioteer or shieldbearer may perform a move action to grab the reins and attempt to control the vehicle. It requires a DC 15 Ride check to take control of a runaway chariot; failure results in the chariot toppling, dealing 1d10 damage to all occupants.

Chariots may be used for Trample attacks. The driver must make a Drive check against the target's AC to hit. On a successful hit, the driver must succeed a second Drive check (DC 15 + damage dealt) to keep the chariot from toppling.

GREEK CHARIOT

A standard Greek chariot has a solid wooden frame with thick hide stretched over that to form the cab. The front of the cab rises to chest-height, while the sides slope down slightly—charioteers can hurl spears from the front, but are more likely to strike from the side with sword or axe. Some chariots have fronts that rear as high as a man's head, but dip down in the center to allow space for throwing spears. The back of the chariot is open, allowing the charioteer to mount or dismount quickly. Racks along the sides hold spears, javelins, and other weapons. Often a box is built into the floor in front to hold other items, like spare whips, torches, and rope. Though a single span, a matched pair of horses, usually pulls the chariot, additional horses can be attached to increase speed. The large wheels on either side are wooden, though often they have metal rims to reinforce them, and to cause more damage when they roll over enemy soldiers. Expensive chariots have inlays of metal, ivory, ebony, or horn on the wheels and the cab.

A handful of chariots actually had metal cabs, made of beaten bronze rather than leather. These were so rare, because of additional cost involved, only major kings, or the leaders of great armies, could afford such vehicles.

MASTERWORK CHARIOTS

Masterwork chariots provide a +1 bonus to their driver Drive check modifier, a +1 to the chariot's Hardness, and they cost an additional 700 gp.

BOATS

To reach Troy, the Achaean army sailed over the sea in a fleet of ships. Homer describes these as black-hulled boats, but says little else about them. The Homeric boats were actually biremes. The only people who owned their own biremes were kings, wealthy nobles, and rich traders who sailed the sea. Fishermen

less cumbersome dyplon shields. Chariots did not have to hold the front line alone and could range about the battle, targeting other chariots and any other enemy commanders.

This change meant fewer chariots appeared in battles, but at the same time, it freed the chariots from the responsibility of the deciding first charge, allowing them to act as individuals. Charioteers became warriors in their own rights; they could control their chariots with one hand, allowing them to attack enemies with a weapon held in the other. Chariots became the preferred platform for army commanders; the chariots allowed them to reach any place on the battlefield quickly, and they allowed them to see above the heads of the foot soldiers, so they could better assess the battle.

Chariots have two or three riders: a driver and a charioteer (a position in the chariot that should not to be confused with the charioteer character class), armed with javelins or a bow, and sometimes a shieldbearer. They provide partial cover for the occupants, granting a +2 bonus to AC, and a +1 cover

TABLE 6-7: HOMERIC CHARIOTS

Chariot	Hp	Hardness	Drive Check Modifier	Maximum Speed	Trample Damage	Weight	Cost
Standard	125	12	–3	60 ft.	2d6	350 lb.	650 gp
Masterwork	125	13	–2	60 ft.	2d6	350 lb.	1,350 gp
Metal Cab	150	15	–3	60 ft.	2d6+3	500 lb.	1,000 gp
Masterwork Metal Cab	150	16	–2	60 ft,	2d6+3	500 lb.	1,350 gp

THE BIREME

Ship	Hp	Hardness	Speed	Ram Damage	Weight	Cost
Bireme	500	12	120 (oars), 240 (sails)	15d20+25	5,000 lbs.	21,000 gp

and regular traders used smaller, less warlike boats, usually equipped with a fixed mast and a single set of oars.

Biremes: These warships have broad bottoms, allowing them to sail in shallower waters. They have outriggers and two banks of oars—the upper row of oarsmen sit on benches farther out to the side, so that their oars do not interfere with those of the men below them. A standard bireme has 100 oarsmen, 50 to a side.

In addition to the oars, biremes have tall masts capable of disassembly when not in use—a long furrow runs down the center of the deck, where the mast lays when not used. The crew covers it with a tarp to protect it from rain. When the winds are favorable, the crew lifts the mast from its furrow and sets its base into a stout wooden box at the center of the ship, which has a hole cut in it to fit the mast. They lash the mast into place, and ring up the sails to catch the wind.

Biremes also have long, sharp bows that protrude above the water, used to ram enemy ships.

FOOD AND DRINK

People in the Homeric age rarely ate vegetables. Pears, apples, and grapes were all common. Olives were very popular, and great groves of olive trees stood in many lands. Grains were also common, particularly barley, which could be used to make bread. Nevertheless, the single most popular item on any menu was meat. Hogs, oxen, cattle, sheep, and goats all provided meat; the terrain determined the availability of a particular animal meat.

When invading, an army actually brought animals with it, and herdsmen tended them during the day, while the warriors fought, so fresh meat would be available each night. A typical meal consisted of meat, bread, and olives. Wine was the most common drink, though during the day men often refreshed themselves with cool water from a stream or well.

WINE

Homeric wine was extremely potent and had a very strong flavor. To make the wine last longer, and to mellow its taste, a small portion was poured into a mixing bowl, and was then mixed with water, right before serving it.

Diluting the wine is an important part of the ritual of welcoming a guest. Mixing bowls tended to be of high quality as they were handed to guests upon entering a house, so they were the first thing a guest would see and the first indication of their host's wealth. For particularly honored guests, a host might use slightly less water, making the wine stronger. Odysseus, when he encountered the Cyclopes Polyphemus, gets the one-eyed giant drunk with a single wineskin of pure and potent unmixed wine.

A normal mixture was one part wine to 12 parts water, which meant that a spoonful of wine would be enough for a mixing bowl that served eight to 10 cups of wine.

CHAPTER SEVEN: HOMERIC BATTLEFIELDS

Homeric army battles are much more spectacular and heroic than real world battles; those who sneer at the idea of one man slaying hundreds of men in a single fight may be taken aback by Homer's scriptural accounts.

Testament presented a Biblical Battlefield Resolution System to handle epic combat. That system has been modified slightly to create the Homeric Battlefield Resolution System. The major difference is in the Biblical system, the armies rarely move from their initial position. In the Homeric system, both sides advance and retreat, gaining or losing ground depending upon their fortunes.

THE BASICS

These mass combat rules assume that there are two opposing armies facing each other on the field, each trying to force the other back. Thus, the battle is a constant struggle to advance, and the army finally reaching the enemy's stronghold is the victor.

All armies are composed of Forces. A Force is a group of fighters who answer to the same Captain, whether they are his kinsmen, or simply men who chose to follow him into battle. A Force can be as small as 10 men or as large as 500. Its warriors can all use the same weapons and armor, or it can have a variety within it. For example, a charioteer and four infantrymen could be a Force. Each army can have any number of Forces, from one to 20. A single figure represents a Force on the battlefield, and the entire Force moves as one.

Each army also has individuals (including the PCs) known as Captains. Captains are powerful warriors who have authority over one or more Forces. Captains can act with their Force, or they can act individually.

Every round, each Force and each Captain gets an action. These actions can target another Force or another Captain, or both if the opposing Captain stays within his Force. These actions can inflict damage upon the target. If a Force takes enough damage, or suffers certain other conditions described below, it must make a Morale check. If the Force fails this check, it flees the battle. A battle ends when every Force and Captain of one army has been either killed, captured, or driven away, or when one side calls an end to the day's hostilities.

To simulate Homer's epic battle scenes, where a single hero can devastate several Forces single-handedly, each Force is assigned characteristics as if it were a single character. This allows Captains to target Forces directly, and even to vanquish them in combat.

One of the reasons the Trojan War lasted 10 years was because so many different armies participated. At any given time, half of the forces on each side might be sitting out the battle, resting and recovering from wounds or repairing armor and weapons, yet fighting still covered the field between the two camps. Thus, even if one Force retreated or fell, only a small portion of the army is weakened.

TIME AND INITIATIVE

Rounds in mass combat are battlefield rounds. They have no set duration, but for the purposes of determining the duration of spells, one battlefield round equals 20 minutes.

At the beginning of the round, each Captain rolls initiative. On a Captain's initiative, he can select from a number of possible actions. If he currently leads a Force and his action includes them, they act on his initiative. If the Force acts on its own, its initiative is one lower than the Captain's—if the Captain dies, until someone else takes control that Force, it still operates on its same initiative.

Traditionally, Homeric forces do not fight at night. Once the sun goes down, warriors can no longer see their opponents clearly so they retreat to their camps, clean their wounds, eat, and plan for the next day.

HOW FIGHTING WORKS

At the start of the battle, the armies line up facing each other, Force to Force. The battlefield is divided into squares, similar to the 5-foot squares used for individual combat, but these squares are 30 feet to a side. Each square can hold one Force and up to four Captains. Traditionally, the armies array themselves in straight lines facing one another. Additional Forces create second and even third rows, or wait in reserve at the army's stronghold. On its initiative, a Force can attack any Force or

> *When they were got together in one place shield clashed with shield and spear with spear in the rage of battle. The bossed shields beat one upon another, and there was a tramp as of a great multitude--death-cry and shout of triumph of slain and slayers, and the earth ran red with blood. As torrents swollen with rain course madly down their deep channels till the angry floods meet in some gorge, and the shepherd on the hillside hears their roaring from afar--even such was the toil and uproar of the hosts as they joined in battle.*
>
> —Homer, *The Iliad*, Book II

FORCES IN THE TROJAN WAR

The Achaeans launched a full-scale war against the Trojans, meaning every nation of Achaea was asked to send troops. The Trojans responded by rallying their own allies. Homer remarks, when discussing the Achaean troops, he could not name every man in that army even if he had 10 mouths. He does list, however, the forces involved, each of them an army in its own right. Here is a partial listing of the armies on both sides.

Achaeans: Boeotians, Phocians, Locrians, Abantes, Athenians, Argosians, Myceneans, Arcadians, Cephallenians, Aetolians, Cretans, Rhodians, Myrmidons, Magnetes

Trojans: Trojans, Dardanians, Pelasgians, Thracians, Paeonians, Paphlagonians, Alizones, Mysians, Phrygians, Carians, Lycians

Captain in an adjacent square. If no one occupies an adjacent square, the Force can move into that square itself. The attacking Force compares its attack roll to the defender's Armor Class. If the attack hits, it inflicts an equal amount of damage on every member of the opposing Force. Apply the damage rolled to each defender, instead of dividing it among them. Captains, however, may have a higher Armor Class than their warriors, and so they may escape being hit by the attack.

If the tide of battle turns against a Force, it can make a DC 13 Morale check (see **Morale** on page 73). The force makes this check whenever its forces face any of the following conditions. Each condition beyond the first increases the Morale check DC by +1.

- The Force is exposed to spells (see **Spell Effects**, page 74-75).
- One or more of its Captains has been killed, captured, or driven off.
- The Force's commanding Captain abandons it for another Force, or to fight solo.
- The leader of the Force's army is killed, captured, or driven off—note the leader can be anywhere on the battlefield, but the Force must see his defeat.
- It is surrounded by enemy Forces.
- The Force loses at least half its original hit points.
- The Force's Captain loses at least half his original hit points.

If the Force fails the Morale check, it flees the field, taking the shortest route back to its stronghold. Any Captains attached to that Force can retreat, attach themselves to a different Force (see the section on **Changing Position**, below), or fight alone.

Because each army has so many Forces, the battle rarely has a clear winner. Most days the fighting ends because night has fallen, and the warriors all break until dawn the next day.

TERRAIN

The plain before the city of Troy, where the war occurs, is level and has no major obstructions. Because of this, terrain is not a major element of the combat system.

If you apply this system to other locations (like the rocky island of Ithaca, too small and uneven for chariots), you may want to make some adjustments. For example, certain troop types or equipment pieces are unsuitable. Forces may also have penalties to AC or to attack if their armor and weapons are ill suited to the terrain. Anyone fighting on unfamiliar terrain suffers a −1 penalty to all Morale checks.

PURSUIT

If a Force fails its Morale check and leaves the battlefield, the Force attacking it can pursue. The pursuer takes an attack of opportunity from any enemy Forces in adjacent squares, but gains a +4 bonus to attack the retreating Force. Once attacked again, the fleeing Force can attempt another Morale check to turn and fight. Fleeing Forces can pass through allied forces' squares without penalty or hindrance. Pursuers, however, may find themselves facing a fresh enemy.

FORCES

Each Force has the following statistics.

- Troop Quality
- Hit Points
- Armor Class
- Initiative Modifier
- Base Attack Bonus
- Base Damage
- Damage Multiplier
- Base Morale
- Battlefield Feats

A Force may also have one or more Captains (PCs, NPCs, or both). Captains are detailed separately.

TROOP QUALITY

There are four troop qualities: Green, Trained, Veteran, and Legendary. The GM picks a quality for each Force. A player may take Battlefield feats to increase the quality of some or all of his Forces (see **Battlefield Feats**, page 76).

Green units consist of untrained and untested troops, or troops from a society where military combat is rare. The baseline Green unit is composed of 1st-level warriors.

Trained units are a mix of green and seasoned troops, or average troops from a society where war is frequent. The baseline Trained unit is composed of 2nd-level warriors.

Veteran units consist of troops who have fought together for several consecutive campaigns, and have few (if any) green troops to hinder them. The baseline Veteran unit is composed of 5th-level warriors.

Legendary troops are people of heroic bent who work well together and who have extensive military experience. The baseline Legendary unit is composed of 8th-level warriors.

An army can have different quality units for each of its Forces; the Trojan army, for instance, consisted of Green footmen, Veteran charioteers, and Legendary archers.

HIT POINTS

The term "hit point" denotes the *size* of a Force. The correlation between hit points and the number of figures on each Force varies. The three scales of man-to-Force composition used in *Trojan War* are:

Realistic: 1 hit point = 1 person
Heroic: 1 hit point = 50 people
Mythic: 1 hit point = 1,000 people

A **Realistic** ratio provides a much stronger army and a more believable result.

A **Heroic** ratio allows PC-level characters to dominate the battlefield.

A **Mythic** ratio produces casualty figures that belong in myths about godlike heroes and their martial prowess.

Once the scale is established, determine the number of combatants, and then multiply it by the Force's army quality Hit Point Modifier. For example, a Heroic scale 1,000-man Veteran Force would have (1,000 ÷ 50 x 5) 100 hit points.

After a battle is over, multiply the number of hit points of damage suffered by each of the Forces of the defeated army against the hp-to-man ratio. This determines how many dead bodies are left lying on the field, and thus how much treasure the victors can carry home with them. Keep in mind, however, only Captains have quality armor and weapons, and Captains are never included as part of the Force's casualties—Captains must be targeted directly before they can be killed, and their gear stripped from their corpses.

ARMOR CLASS

Armor on the battlefield is determined by armor type worn, natural toughness, and magical deflection bonuses. Because of the nature of mass battles, individuals cannot use Dexterity to protect themselves, so they receive no Dexterity modifiers to AC.

INITIATIVE MODIFIER

Initiative modifiers are equal to the best Charisma modifier among the Captains (including PCs) attached to the Force. A Force wearing light or no armor receives a +1 bonus to Initiative checks. A Force wearing full panoply receives a –1 penalty to Initiative checks.

TABLE 7-1: TROOP STATS

Quality	Hit Point Multiplier	Base Attack Bonus	Base Morale	Damage Multiplier	Feats
Green	x1	+0	–3	x2	2
Trained	x2	+2	+0	x3	4
Veteran	x5	+5	+3	x4	6
Legendary	x8	+8	+6	x5	8

BASE ATTACK BONUS

The Base Attack Bonus is the bonus on the Force's attack roll, based on troop quality.

BASE DAMAGE

This is the Force's damage roll for its usual attack. Typically, it is the damage done by the weapon used by the majority of the Force, plus any bonuses for Battlefield Feats.

Apply damage first to all Captains hit on the enemy Force, then multiply it by the Damage Multiplier and apply it to the hit points of the troops on the enemy Force.

DAMAGE MULTIPLIER

On a successful attack, after applying the base damage to the Captains, multiply the same number by the Damage Multiplier and then apply the sum to the hit point total of the Force.

BASE MORALE

If a Force has to make a Morale check, it has a base morale depending on its troop quality. The commanding Captain's Charisma modifier modifies this. A Force wearing light no armor receives a –1 penalty to Morale checks. One wearing full panoply receives a +1 bonus to Morale checks.

BATTLEFIELD OMENS

Omens occurring on the battlefield may increase the morale of an army or Force. Most omens require interpretation, but certain signs need no explanation, and these encourage whichever army the omen favors. If such a widespread omen occurs, every Force on that side gains +1 bonus to Morale checks. Forces on the opposing side suffer a –1 penalty to Morale checks, knowing the gods turned against them. For omens requiring interpretation, a Force who succeeds a Listen check against a DC 12 +2 for every square between the Force and the seer gains a +1 bonus to its Morale check if the omen favors them, and a –1 penalty if it goes against them.

CHARACTERS ATTACHED TO UNITS

In addition to regular troops, every Force may have player characters and NPCs attached to it. Any character with a base attack bonus greater than the force counts as a Captain. Captains have freedom of movement on the field (see below). A character whose base attack bonus is equal to or lower than the Force's base attack bonus becomes another soldier in that force. Once attached to a Force, these soldiers may not move, except when the Force splits or moves as a whole.

BATTLEFIELD FEATS

Every Force can choose a number of Battlefield Feats representing special abilities, training, tricks, and traits (see page 76). Each Green Force can have two Battlefield Feats. Trained Forces have four feats. Veteran Forces have six, while Legendary Forces have eight Battlefield Feats.

Fighting on a battlefield is very different than fighting one-on-one, and Armor Class adjusts accordingly. Characters who join a Force as a soldier do not receive Dexterity bonuses unless they have the Battlefield Seasoned feat or the Uncanny Dodge ability. Captains retain their normal bonuses and Armor Class.

Characters attached to units act as they normally do.

BATTLEFIELD ACTIONS

Each round, every Captain attached to a Force gets to choose a single battlefield action. The actions available are as follows.

- Cast a spell or use a magic item
- Attack an enemy Force
- Support the Force
- Command the Force
- Use a skill
- Change position or withdraw from battle (Captain)
- Withdraw from or enter battle (Force)
- Challenge an enemy Captain

A Force held in reserve cannot participate in the battle. If it has the Combat Healing feat, it can use that feat as its action in a round, but the only other action it can opt to take is to enter the battle line, replacing a withdrawn or routed Force.

CAST A SPELL

Battlefield use of spells is tricky to adjudicate. Change the following general guidelines as the situation warrants. Spells cast directly against Captains should be handled through Captain vs.

Captain combat (see **Challenging an Enemy Captain**, page 76).

Because of the constraining conditions on the battlefield, a spellcaster can cast the same number of spells in a battlefield round as he would in a round of normal combat.

A spellcaster must make a Concentration check against a DC 15 + spell level + any damage sustained to successfully cast his spell, unless he has the Battlefield Magic character feat (see **Chapter Four: Skills and Feats**, page 37).

Using supernatural abilities does not require a Concentration check, but they follow all other rules of battlefield spellcasting.

Spellcasting at a Force whose members have Spell Resistance requires the appropriate Resistance check be made. If only Captains have Spell Resistance, their checks are rolled individually.

If a spell allows a saving throw, make a single roll is made for the entire Force using the save bonus appropriate for a warrior of the Force's troop quality; Captains (including player characters) roll their own saves as per normal.

SPELL EFFECTS

In general, non-damaging spells that have a 20-minute duration or less or affect less than a 20-ft. radius have no appreciable effect on the battlefield. **Table 7-2: Spell Effects** shows exceptions to that rule and the specifics of some spells. Other effects can be extrapolated from these: *soften earth and stone* (or even a heavy rain) has effects similar to *slow*, *fog cloud* duplicates *invisibility* and so on.

ATTACK AN ENEMY FORCE

Captains can attack opposing Forces directly, instead of lending their strength to whatever Force they command. The Captain must have a base attack bonus equal to or greater than that of the targeted Force. He gets the same number of attacks per battlefield round as he would in a round of normal combat. His damage is reduced, however. Take the targeted Force's Damage Multiplier, and divide the Captain's damage by that number. Thus, a Captain attacking a Green Force would only do half his damage, because their Damage Multiplier is x2. He would only do one-fifth his normal damage to a Legendary Force. The feat Lion of the Field (see **Chapter Four: Skills and Feats**, page 39) allows him to increase this damage ratio.

SUPPORT THE FORCE

A Captain can lend aid to his men instead of taking an attack. He does not get a separate first attack, but the Force gains half his BAB as a bonus to their attack. If the Captain has more attacks than his Force, he may make those additional attacks, but after the Force has struck. Thus, a Captain with a BAB of +8/+3 aiding a Force with a BAB of +4 grants the Force a +4 bonus to its attack, and then gets to make his second attack at +3, normally.

COMMAND THE FORCE

Unless the troops have the Independent Battlefield Feat, they need guidance. Only one Captain may act as commander for each Force, forgoing all other combat options to give commands, such as choosing between targets if the Force has a targeting option or ordering the use of a battlefield maneuver to be carried out that round. The Force uses that commander's Charisma modifier for Morale and initiative rolls.

Note supporting the Force and commanding it are very different. When providing support, a Captain does not give any commands, but bolsters his troops with his presence and his own martial prowess. Command means he is not attacking (though the Force can still attack, just without any bonus from him) but issuing orders. If the Force's last order still fits the situation (like "kill them all!"), no new commands are necessary.

USE A SKILL

Skill use in the middle of battle incurs a –2 circumstance penalty. The Unfazed character feat (see **Chapter Four: Skills and Feats**, page 40) negates this penalty.

CHANGE POSITION/ WITHDRAW FROM BATTLE (CAPTAIN)

Captains can move about the battlefield at will. They do not need a roll to detach from their current Force, though any Force without the Independent feat needs to succeed a Morale check to maintain order if its leader departs.

If a Captain attaches himself to a new Force, and that Force has enemies in an adjacent square, he must succeed a DC 13 Reflex save. If successful, he moves to the new Force without incident. If he fails the save, he provokes an attack of opportunity (against him, not the Force) from the opposing Force before he can make his move.

PCs attached to a Force as a soldier can make the same Reflex save if their Force is routed. If they succeed, they can attach themselves to a different Force instead of fleeing the battle.

Captains who wish to withdraw from the field (personally, rather than with their Force) must make a Reflex save against a DC 10 + 2 per Force Quality above Green. On a failed check, they incur attacks of opportunity from any adjacent enemies. A successful save means they do not provoke attack of opportunity, but are still at risk from enemies along the path of retreat as normal.

WITHDRAW FROM BATTLE/ ENTER BATTLE (FORCE)

A Captain can order his Force to leave the battlefield at any time. Doing so incurs an attack of opportunity from any adjacent opposing Forces, followed by a Morale check. If any attack of opportunity is successful, the Morale check suffers a penalty equal to the base damage of the attack, before application of the Damage Multiplier. If more than one attack of opportunity hits, the penalty is the sum of those base damages. If the Force succeeds the Morale check succeeds, it escapes and can reform itself as reserves. On a failed check, the Force routs (see below).

A Captain commanding a reserve Force can deploy his troops if any opposing Force has an empty adjacent square. A Force attempting to march onto the battlefield after the battle has started provokes an attack of opportunity and must make a Morale check. If the attack of opportunity is successful, the Morale check suffers a penalty equal to the base damage of the attack (before application of the Damage Multiplier). If the Morale check is successful, the Force ignores the attack and

moves into position. On a failed check, the Force returns to the position it held before the attempt to join the battle.

ROUTS

Forces retreat from the field in an orderly fashion maintaining their ranks and keeping their shields and weapons at the ready—such a Force can fight while retreating. Sometimes, however, a Force looks at its opposition and quakes in terror. The men back away, trembling, weapons falling from limp hands. They break ranks and run toward the nearest allied stronghold, ignoring their Captain's orders. This is a rout.

TABLE 7-2: SPELL EFFECTS

Spell	Effect
"Mass" spell	Affects entire Force as written
Any *death* spell or *power word kill*	2 points damage/caster level
Instantaneous damage spell (*e.g.*, *fireball*)	1/10 damage to a Force
Charm effect, 20 ft + radius	Morale check or Damage Multiplier reduced by –1
Courage effect, 20 ft.+ radius	Bonus on all Morale checks
Curse effect, 20 ft.+ radius	Penalty to Armor Class
Deafen effect, 20 ft.+ radius	Morale check or negate maneuver
Enervation/poison effect, 20 ft.+ radius	Penalty to damage roll
Entangle/paralysis effect, 20 ft.+ radius	Morale check or penalty to attack bonus
Fear effect, 20 ft.+ radius	Morale check or rout
Fly	+2 Armor Class bonus to target vs. ground-based opponents
Haste	+2 to Force's initiative checks
Illusion effect, 20 ft.+ radius	
Demoralizing illusion (*e.g.*, show many people dying)	Morale check or rout
Reposition Illusion (*e.g.*, enemy is somewhere they're not)	Penalty to attack bonus
Summon illusory opponent	Morale check or lose next attack
Invisibility	+2 Armor Class bonus
Invisibility, 20 ft.+ radius	bonus to Force Armor Class, bonus to base damage
Silence, 20 ft.+ radius	Morale check or negate maneuver
Sleep effect, 20 ft.+ radius	Morale check or penalty to attack bonus
Slow, 20 ft.+ radius	–2 to a Force's initiative checks
Stun effects, 20 ft.+ radius	Morale check or lose next attack
Wall of force/iron/etc.	
positioned to isolate a commander	Reflex save or Captain is isolated until barrier is gone
positioned to block charge, missile hurling	Negate maneuver
positioned as a general barrier	Penalty to Force's attack bonus

Spell Type	Morale Check Penalties
Spell is 1st-2nd level	–0 to enemy Morale check
Spell is 3rd-4th level	–2 to enemy Morale check
Spell is 5th-6th level	–4 to enemy Morale check
Spell is 7th-8th level	–6 to enemy Morale check
Spell is 9th+ level	–8 to enemy Morale check
Power word	–1 additional Morale

Bonus/Penalty: If a spell gives a bonus or penalty to one or more of a Force's statistics, a 1st-2nd-level spell gives a +/-1 bonus/penalty, 3rd-4th-level spells give +/-2, 5th-6th level spells give +/-3, 7th-8th-level spells give +/-4, and 9th (or higher) level spells give +/-5. If the effect comes from a supernatural or spell-like ability that does not have an equivalent spell, divide the caster's Hit Dice by 2 to get the equivalent spell level. If a spell affects multiple statistics, split the bonus or penalty between the statistics; *e.g.*, a 9th-level spell could adjust five statistics by +/-1 each, or one by +/-5.

Negate Maneuver: This means that no battlefield maneuver may be deployed that round.

A routed Force cannot fight or defend itself. It loses all cohesion, shifting from a troop of warriors to a scattered collection of frightened men. Any opposed Force in an adjacent square gains an attack of opportunity, and the routed Force is flat-footed. After one round, however, the routed Force is spread to thin for anyone to attack. That Force is effectively gone, though any survivors regroup 1d4 hours later.

CHALLENGE AN ENEMY CAPTAIN

A Captain can challenge any single enemy Captain to single or small-group combat. This is resolved separately from the main combat using normal combat rules. Because of the differing time scales between battlefield and normal combat, the entire challenge takes place in the space of one battlefield round. The two opponents begin combat 20-120 ft. (2d6x10) apart.

The first round of any single combat is used to declare. Each Captain announces his name and lineage, so if defeated, his opponent can say whom it was that he conquered. This also lets Captains find out if their opponent is worth ransoming if defeated.

At the beginning of the fight, multiple Captains may team up to challenge an enemy Captain (or Captains). If a Captain wishes to join a challenge already in progress, he must make a DC 18 Reflex save. If he succeeds, he arrives 1d6 normal rounds later.

A Captain may choose to flee the battle rather than accept the challenge. He must make a Reflex save against a DC 10 + the level or Hit Dice of the most powerful challenger (typically the character with the highest level) to blend in with his Force or otherwise avoid the challenger.

A Captain may not take part in more than one combat in a battlefield turn.

BATTLEFIELD FEATS

Battlefield feats are divided into Qualities, Maneuvers, and Specials. Qualities affect a Force at all times. To perform a Maneuver, the Force must have a Captain who spends his entire battlefield action directing them or it must have the Independent battlefield feat. If no Captain is present, the Force may not employ any of its Maneuvers. A Force can only perform one Maneuver in a round. Finally, consult individual entries for details on each Special feat. Note a feat with a Force Quality prerequisite is available to Forces of the troop quality or better.

ALLIED FORCE (QUALITY)

Your Force has close ties with another and can look to them for support.

Benefit: If a Force loses their Captains and has an allied Force in any adjacent square, it can look to that Force's Captain for leadership. The Force does not have to make a Morale check. Any Morale checks made are at +2 as long as the allied Force is in an adjacent square.

BATTLEFIELD DOMINANCE (QUALITY)

Your Force exploits the weakness of inferior opponents.

Prerequisite: Veteran.
Benefit: The Force gains a +2 bonus on attack and damage rolls (not Damage Multiplier) on all attacks against units with a lower quality rating, such as a Legendary Force against a Green, Trained, and Veteran sides, while a Veteran Force gains this bonus against a Green and Trained Force.

BATTLE-HARDENED (QUALITY)

Your Force is hardier on the battlefield than most units.

Benefit: The Force has 10% more hit points that it normally should have based on quality and size. When the Force suffers damage, the number of soldiers actually slain is proportional to the unit's original hit points. A unit with one level of Battle-Hardened that suffers 22 points of damage loses that many hit points from its total, but only 20 hit points worth of troops (see Hit Points, page 72, for man-to-Force ratios) actually die.
Special: You may select this feat multiple times.

BLINDING SPEED (MANEUVER)

Your Force is extremely quick and gets an extra attack.

Prerequisite: Veteran.
Benefit: The Force can make one extra attack each round, albeit at a –4 penalty.

CALL FOR AID (MANEUVER)

Your Force receives help during the course of the battle.

Benefit: A Force can call for aid and have allied soldiers swell its ranks, increasing its hit points. A Green Force gains 1 hit point, a Trained Force gains 3, a Veteran Force 6, and a Legendary 9. If enemies surround the Force or otherwise cut them off from any allies, the Force cannot use this feat.

CHARGE (MANEUVER)

Your Force opens battle with an initial charge that has impressive results.

Benefit: On the first attack roll of a battle, the Force can Charge. It takes a –2 penalty to Armor Class, but gets a +2 bonus on its attack roll and base damage, and if it successfully hits, the opposing Force must make a DC 13 Morale check or lose its next 1d3 attacks. Multiple attacks because of a Blinding Speed or a Pronged Attack Battlefield Feats count as a single attack for this purpose.

CHARIOTS (QUALITY)

Your entire Force uses chariots.

Benefit: This Force has greater speed and mobility, and it can move at normal chariot speeds. A Chariots Force can enter battle or withdraw from the front lines without provoking an attack of opportunity or a Morale check.
Note: Forces with some chariots, but are not entirely chariot-based, move only as fast as their slowest warriors move. The chariots must crawl alongside to keep from outpacing the rest of the Force. While some units remain in their chariots during combat, others use chariots only as conveyances, riding into position before dismounting to fight on foot.

Combat Healing (Quality)

Your Force has healers available to assist wounded Captains and soldiers.

Benefit: The Force has sufficient healing magic to cure 1d8+1 points of damage done to a single Captain, as well as 1d8+1 points of damage done to normal troops each round.

Coordinated Defense (Quality)

Your Force defends itself well and has no apparent weak spots.

Prerequisite: Veteran.
Benefit: The Force is impervious to the secondary attacks of Blinding Speed and Pronged Attack maneuvers.

Deft Attack (Quality)

Your Force wields its weapons with deadly skill.

Prerequisite: Veteran.
Benefit: The Force adds +1 to all damage rolls.

Desperate (Quality)

Your Force fights better when in dire situations.

Prerequisite: Veteran.
Benefit: When fighting within 20 feet of its stronghold, or when it has lost half its hit points or more, the Force gains +2 bonus to attack rolls, damage rolls, and Morale checks, and increases its Damage Multiplier by +1.

Disquieting Yell (Special)

Your Force can shake the enemy with a great shout.

Prerequisite: Legendary
Benefit: Once per battle, the Force can shout in unison, forcing the opposing Force to make a DC 13 Morale check or flee the battle. This is a free action.

Divide and Conquer (Maneuver)

Your Force can carve an enemy Force into two smaller, weaker units.

Benefit: The Force can cut an enemy Force in half by moving through it. A square on the other side of the targeted Force must be empty. The attacking Force makes a normal attack roll. If successful they do no damage, but the targeted Force is cut in two with one-half pushed into an adjacent square (either an empty one or one occupied by their own allies). The targeted Force now suffers a –1 penalty to attack rolls, does half damage, and has –2 penalty on Morale checks. It takes two rounds for the targeted Force to regroup, provided it makes its Morale check.
Special: If the targeted Force has empty squares on two sides, the attacking Force can occupy their original square and force the two halves into those adjacent squares. This prevents the divided Force from regrouping.

Emboldening Speech (Maneuver)

Your commander knows how to inspire his Force to high morale.

Benefit: The Force gets a +2 bonus on Morale checks.

Enflamed (Quality)

Your Force fights with enthusiasm.

Benefit: The Force adds +1 to all attack rolls.

Envelop (Maneuver)

Your Force can spread out and surround an opposing Force.

Benefit: The Force can surround an opponent provided the opposing Force has at least three adjacent squares open (including the one the Force currently occupies). The Force has a +1 to attack and to damage, and the opposing Force is flat-footed until its next turn.

Faith (Quality)

Your Force believes in its Captains, its commander, and its cause.

Benefit: The Force gains a +2 bonus to all Morale checks.

Ferocious Attack (Maneuver)

By sacrificing its defense, your Force causes more enemy casualties.

Benefit: A Force uses Ferocious Attack to increase its damage against a particular opponent. For every point by which the Force decreases its Armor Class for the next round, it increases its base damage by +1 on its next attack to a maximum of –5 to AC for +5 to damage.

Fight Cautiously (Maneuver)

Through caution, your Force becomes harder to hurt in battle.

Benefit: A Force can use Fight Cautiously to increase its protection against a particular opponent. For every point by which the Force decreases its base damage on its next attack, it increases its Armor Class by +1 for the current round to a maximum of –5 to damage for +5 AC.

TABLE 7-3: BATTLEFIELD FEATS

QUALITIES

Allied Force
Battlefield Dominance
Battle-hardened
Chariots
Coordinated Defense
DeftAttack
Desperate
Enflamed
Faith
Fleet of Foot
Hardy
Heroic Might
Human Shield

Independent
Interlocking Shields
Left-Handed
Ring of Bronze
Shield Bearers
Target Captain
Unshakable
Wary
Weapons of Renown
Well-armed

MANEUVERS

Blinding Speed
Call for Aid
Charge

Divide and Conquer
Emboldening Speech
Envelop
Ferocious Attack
Fight Cautiously
Hostage
Hurl Missiles
Pronged Attack
Set Spears

SPECIAL

Disquieting Yell
Heroic Stand
Loose Formation

FLEET OF FOOT (QUALITY)

Your Force runs fast.

Prerequisite: Strength 13, Dexterity 13, cannot be wearing full panoply.

Benefit: Every fourth round, your Force can move at one-and-a-half times its normal movement rates at no additional penalty.

HARDY (QUALITY)

Your Force is comfortable in heavy armor.

Prerequisite: Strength 13, must be wearing full panoply.

Benefit: Your Force does not suffer armor penalties to its movement rate.

Special: Forces with a Strength of 15 and higher can take this and Fleet of Foot, and move at the increased rate even while wearing full panoply.

HEROIC MIGHT (QUALITY)

Your Force is stronger than average.

Prerequisite: Veteran.

Benefit: Either through improvement, training, deliberate selection of the strongest recruits, or the death of the weakest in battle, this Force has a higher than average Strength for a unit of their kind. The average Strength of most Forces is 10, but every time this feat is selected the Force's Strength improves by +2 resulting in bonuses to melee attack and damage rolls. If the Force has the Hurl Missiles feat and uses thrown weapons, it also receives Strength bonuses on missile damage.

Special: This feat can be taken multiple times.

HEROIC STAND (SPECIAL)

When badly outnumbered, your Force becomes the stuff from which legends are made.

Prerequisite: Legendary.

Benefit: When an opposing Force has more than triple the hit points of the Force with this feat, the defending Force digs in and grows determined. The Force gets a +4 bonus to Armor Class, attack, and a +4 bonus to Morale checks lasting for one battlefield round per point of its commanding Captain's Charisma bonus. The bonus remains even if that Captain dies.

The Heroic Stand may be activated as a free action. Its bonuses are cumulative with other maneuvers.

HOSTAGE (MANEUVER)

Your Force takes an enemy Captain or soldier hostage.

Benefit: The Force selects one defeated opponent and sends warriors to escort him back to their stronghold. The rest of the Force protects those envoys, preventing them from being attacked—they do not incur attacks of opportunity, even if they move past enemy Forces.

Normal: The entire Force must retreat from the field to allow the hostage to be taken back, and is subject to the usual attacks of opportunity from adjacent enemies.

HUMAN SHIELD (QUALITY)

Your Force knows how to protect its commanders.

Prerequisite: Trained.

Benefit: Captains attached to the unit (including PCs) receive a bonus to Armor Class. Trained Forces grant a +2 bonus, Veteran Forces a +4, and Legendary a +6.

HURL MISSILES (MANEUVER)

Your Force opens combat by throwing spears or firing arrows or sling stones into the enemy host.

Benefit: The Force gains an extra attack at a +2 bonus to attack and damage rolls on the first round it engages the enemy. Each time the Force leaves the battle and then returns later from a reserve position, it can make another extra attack. A Force armed only with ranged weapons has its Damage Multiplier reduced by −1 for all attacks except the extra attacks gained from this feat.

INDEPENDENT (QUALITY)

Your Force does not need a Captain.

Prerequisite: Veteran.

Benefit: A Force with Independent can perform a battlefield feat (as selected by the GM) without a Captain present, and does not need to make a Morale check when all of its Captains are killed. This force cannot target enemy Captains, however, unless it also has the Target Captain feat.

INTERLOCKING SHIELDS (QUALITY)

Your Force can knit its shields together for added protection.

Prerequisite: Veteran.
Benefit: The Force fights with shields locked together. The Force gains a +2 bonus to AC and a +1 bonus to Reflex saves. If an enemy Force routs or catches them by surprise, this Force cannot use this feat.

LEFT-HANDED (QUALITY)

All members of your Force are either left-handed or ambidextrous, naturally or by way of special training.

Prerequisite: Veteran.
Benefit: In normal combat, being left-handed has no special benefits. In mass combat, most troops are trained to face right-handed soldiers, and a unit with its weapons and shields in the "wrong" hands has a slight tactical advantage. A Left-Handed Force gains a +1 bonus on attack rolls and to Armor Class when facing a normal Force. Such a specialized unit can be assembled by selecting those soldiers who are naturally left-handed or ambidextrous or by taking right-handed troops and giving them intensive training with left-handed weapon use while their right hands are tied to their sides.

LOOSE FORMATION (SPECIAL)

Your Force minimizes damage from enemy spells and missile weapons.

Prerequisite: Veteran.
Benefit: This Force can change its formation to become more loosely packed, minimizing the effects of spells and missile attacks. The Force suffers only half damage from spell effects and has a +2 bonus on Morale checks against spells. It also gains a +2 bonus to AC against ranged weapons. All attacks made by the Force suffer a –1 penalty to its Damage Multiplier (minimum of x1). Once a Force assumed a Loose Formation, it maintains that formation in succeeding rounds as a Quality, and returns to regular formation as a battlefield action.

PRONGED ATTACK (MANEUVER)

Your Force can attack two or more Forces at once.

Prerequisite: Veteran.
Benefit: The Force can launch a second attack against an adjacent Force at a –4 penalty to the attack roll after a successful attack against a directly opposing Force. If it has opposing Forces on three sides, it can launch a third attack against the remaining adjacent Force (with a –8 penalty to the attack roll) if its second attack is successful.

RING OF BRONZE (QUALITY)

Your and your allies can surround an opposing unit and attack from all sides at once.

Prerequisite: Trained.
Benefit: If the Force and at least two allied Forces surround an enemy, it can launch a coordinated attack. Each attacker gains a +2 bonus to attack rolls and the enemy is flat-footed until its next turn.

SET SPEARS (MANEUVER)

When an opponent charges, your Force is ready for them.

Benefit: This Force gets a free attack against charging opponents, with a +2 bonus to attack rolls, in addition to the -2 AC penalty suffered by the charging attackers.

SHIELD BEARERS (QUALITY)

Assistants, whose only duty is to employ oversized shields, accompany the warriors in your Force.

Prerequisite: Veteran.
Benefit: The Force has additional troops equipped with tower shields, paired with ordinary troops to provide a +4 bonus to Armor Class. If the warriors of the Force have their own personal shields, the two AC bonuses are cumulative. The shield bearers have insignificant personal arms.

TARGET CAPTAIN (QUALITY)

Your Force knows how to target enemy leaders and champions.

Prerequisite: Veteran.
Benefit: The Force may choose to target the Captains of an opposing Force. The Force receives a +4 bonus on its attack and damage rolls against enemy Captains but its attack does not carry over to the normal troops on the Force.

UNSHAKABLE (QUALITY)

Your Force stands firm in the face of adversity.

Prerequisite: Veteran.
Benefit: In a circumstance where the Force must make a Morale check, it is allowed to make two checks, and use the better of the two rolls.

WARY (QUALITY)

Your Force is always alert for danger.

Prerequisite: Trained.
Benefit: The Force cannot be caught flat-footed, even when ambushed or surrounded.

WEAPONS OF RENOWN (QUALITY)

Your Force's weapons are better than average.

Prerequisite: Trained.
Benefit: The Force has higher quality weapons than most. This normally means masterwork weaponry. The bonuses to attack and damage rolls depend on the specifics of the Force's special weapons. For example, a force armed with masterwork weapons gains a +1 bonus to attack rolls.

WELL-ARMED (QUALITY)

Your Force is able to attack at long and close range.

Prerequisite: Hurl Missiles
Benefit: This Force is equipped with both ranged and melee weapons. After making its extra attack using ranged weapons (see **Hurl Missiles**, above), the Force switches to its melee weapon, avoiding the reduction in Damage Multiplier.

COMMON BATTLEFIELD FEAT COMBINATIONS

Battlefield feats can be used in combination to build particular unit types. Charioteers are likely to have mobility and shock-related battlefield feats; archers have skirmish-related feats and ones less related to defense and morale, and so on. The following examples illustrate how to simulate a number of unit compositions.

TROJAN CHARIOTEERS

Green: Chariots, Hurl Missiles
Trained: Chariots, Charge, Hurl Missiles, Well-armed
Veteran: Chariots, Charge, Envelop, Hurl Missiles, Unshakable, Well-armed
Legendary: Battle-Hardened, Chariots, Charge, Envelop, Hurl Missiles, Independent, Unshakable, Well-armed

ACHAEAN WARRIORS

Green: Charge, Enflamed
Trained: Charge, Enflamed, Hardy, Heroic Might

Veteran: Battle-hardened, Charge, Deft Attack, Enflamed, Hardy, Heroic Might
Legendary: Battle-hardened, Charge, Deft Attack, Enflamed, Fleet of Foot, Hardy, Heroic Might 2

PELASGIAN SPEARMEN

Green: Hurl Missiles, Well-armed
Trained: Allied Force, Coordinated Defense, Hurl Missiles, Well-armed
Veteran: Allied Force, Coordinated Defense, Hurl Missiles, Interlocking Shields, Ring of Bronze, Well-armed
Legendary: Allied Force, Coordinated Defense, Hurl Missiles, Interlocking Shields, Ring of Bronze, Target Captain, Wary, Well-armed

SAMPLE ARMY FORCES

TROJAN WARRIORS

Here are the stat-blocks for a Force composed of 100/5,000/100,000 (depending on scale) Green Trojan warriors, unarmored, equipped with throwing spear and round leather shield, commanded by a Captain with Charisma 12.

Quality: Green
Hit Points: 100 (100 x1 Green quality)
Armor Class: 12 (+1 shield)
Initiative Modifier: +2 (Captain +1 Charisma modifier, +1 no armor)
Base Attack Bonus: +0
Base Damage: 1d8 (throwing spear)
Damage Multiplier: x2 (Green quality)
Morale Modifier: −3 (−3 Green quality, Captain +1 Charisma modifier, −1 no armor)
Battlefield Feats: 2

CRETAN WARRIORS

Here are the stats for a Force composed of 100/5,000/100,000 (depending on scale) Trained Cretan warriors, equipped with throwing spear, crescent leather shield, and leather cuirass, commanded by a Captain with Charisma 14.

Quality: Trained
Hit Points: 200 (100 x2 Trained quality)
Armor Class: 14 (+1 shield, +2 cuirass)
Initiative Modifier: +2 (Captain +2 Charisma modifier)
Base Attack Bonus: +2
Base Damage: 1d8 (throwing spear)
Damage Multiplier: x3 (Trained quality)
Morale Modifier: +1 (+0 Trained quality, Captain +2 Charisma modifier)
Battlefield Feats: 4

LYCIAN WARRIORS

Here are the stats for a Force composed of 100/5,000/100,000 (depending on scale) Lycian Veterans equipped with spear, short sword, crescent leather shield, leather helmet, and leather cuirass, commanded by a Captain with Charisma 16.

Quality: Veteran
Hit Points: 500 (100 x5 Veteran quality)
Armor Class: 14 (+1 shield, +2 cuirass, +1 helmet)
Initiative Modifier: +3 (Captain +3 Charisma modifier)
Base Attack Bonus: +5
Base Damage: 1d6 (longsword) or 1d8 (throwing spear)
Damage Multiplier: x4 (Veteran quality)
Morale Modifier: +6 (+3 Veteran quality, Captain +3 Charisma modifier)
Battlefield Feats: 6

MYRMIDON WARRIORS

Here are the stats for a Force composed of 100/5,000/100,000 (depending on scale) Legendary Myrmidon warriors, armed with longsword and throwing spear, equipped with leather panoply and bronze dyplon shields, commanded by a Captain with Charisma 18.

Quality: Legendary
Hit Points: 800 (100 x8 Legendary quality)
Armor Class: 17 (+5 panoply, +2 shield)
Initiative Modifier: +3 (Captain +4 Charisma modifier, −1 full panoply)
Base Attack Bonus: +8
Base Damage: 1d8 (longsword or throwing spear)
Damage Multiplier: x5 (Legendary quality)
Morale Modifier: +11 (+6 Legendary quality, Captain +4 Charisma modifier, +1 full panoply)
Battlefield Feats: 8

CHAPTER EIGHT: RELIGION AND PIETY

Religion plays a major role in the Trojan War, but not the way people might expect. After all, when a war has religious elements it is a battle of ideologies, with one army worshipping one set of gods and their enemies worshipping another. In the Trojan War, however, both sides worshipped the same pantheon, called the Greek pantheon because Greece served as the central point from which the religion spread. Thus, the two armies involved in the war followed the same gods. Despite this, it was very much a religious battle as the Greek gods chose sides in the conflict.

The gods took a *very* active part in the war, far from just granting strength and courage to their champions. In the Trojan War, the gods actually descended and took part in the battle. This was irregular even for the Greeks, whose tales often told of gods walking among men. Homer's *Iliad* tells of no less than 10 gods who walked about the battlefield, and at least six of them engaged in direct battle against mortals and against each other!

In some ways, this element of the Trojan War merely reflects a larger truth: religion and the gods were central to Greek life. Literature, art, music, architecture, even politics and sports revolved around these deities and their whims. Additionally, the gods are meddlesome, so the GM needs to keep them ever-present in the game to capture the feel of the Homeric era.

THE GREEK PANTHEON

When talking about the gods as a whole, we usually refer to them as a pantheon. The term means "all religion," or all the related deities worshipped in an area or culture. For the Greeks, this means Zeus, his siblings, and their collective children.

The Greek gods resided on mist-shrouded Mount Olympus, the tallest mountain in Greece. From there, the gods could look out over the world and watch the activities of mortal men. And watch they did, because the Greek gods took profound interest in mortal affairs, often lending a hand to favorites or creating obstacles for those earning their enmity.

Of the various deities in mythology, the Greek gods perhaps acted the most "human" of any pantheon. Not only did they all look completely human—taller, stronger, and more attractive, though—they also exhibited a variety of human flaws, arrogance being the most common, but also carelessness, rage, and lust. The Greek gods, particularly the males but occasionally the goddesses as well, selected lovers from among the mortals, and the children produced from these unions became the foremost

heroes of the age, inheriting their mortal lifespan from their human parents but increased physical beauty and prowess from their divine blood.

The gods were by no means a harmonious family, either. They feuded amongst themselves, and humans became pawns in their arguments. A god might attack a mortal because another god favored him, while a mortal earning a god's hatred gain another god assistance just to spite the other. Zeus ruled the deities completely, and accepted no debate about his decrees, though the other gods found loopholes in his statements, or undermined his plans by attacking peripheral characters—or they simply broke his commandments when he was not looking.

Part of their behavior stemmed from their origins. Before the gods came the Titans, mammoth beings of immense power. The king of these was Chronos, who ruled with his wife Rhea. A prophecy told one of Chronos' children would best him and usurp the throne. So, Chronos swallowed all of his children to protect himself. His wife, angry at losing her children, finally tricked him by giving him a rock wrapped in

NAMES OF THE GODS

If you have read the Iliad and the Odyssey separately, you may have noticed some discrepancies in the gods' names. The Greeks developed their pantheon, and it was these gods who watched over and interfered with the lives of men such as Achilles and Hector. But the Romans later adopted the same gods, keeping most of their tales intact but changing their names to more Roman equivalents. Throughout this book, we have used the Greek names, which are the original and thus more appropriate for the Greek forces fighting in the Trojan War. Here is a list of the gods, under their Greek names, and the Roman variants, so that you can more easily identify them:

Greek	Roman
Zeus	Jupiter, Jove
Hera	Juno
Ares	Mars
Athena	Minerva
Apollo	Apollo
Aphrodite	Venus
Artemis	Diana
Hephaustus	Vulcan
Hermes	Mercury
Poseidon	Neptune
Hades	Pluto

APHRODITE

Lesser Goddess (Chaotic Neutral)

The goddess of love, Aphrodite appears as a beautiful woman with perfect skin, shining blond hair, and an ideal body. She is seductive and used to getting her way. Aphrodite was once married to Hephaestus, but he caught her having an affair with Ares, and sent her away, replacing her with a less beautiful but more amiable bride.

Aphrodite is very confident when dealing with matters of love or beauty, but she knows nothing of war or weapons. She has few favorites, but lavishes attention upon the ones she does.

Portfolio: Love, emotion, beauty, and seduction.

Domains: Chaos, Healing, and Trickery.

Holy Symbol: A seashell

Clerical Training: Aphrodite's priests arrange marriages, dispense advice to the lovelorn, train both men and women in the arts of seduction, and generally meddle in other people's personal lives. Her priests train in seduction, acting, and art, and, being hedonistic, seek pleasure at every opportunity.

Quests: Aphrodite sends her priests out into the world to find hidden beauty, taste new pleasures, and to observe scandalous affairs. They train powerful young women in the ways of love.

Prayers: Both men and women pray to Aphrodite when trying to seduce someone. Actors often pray to her as well, asking for the power to sway the audience. People enjoying luxuries or sensual pleasures offer her thanks before partaking, hoping to receive the greatest enjoyment possible.

Shrines: Aphrodite's temples and shrines are always beautifully crafted and decorated, made of expensive materials like marble and gold leaf. Silks drape across doorways, and rich rugs cover the floors making the temples feel like extravagant bedrooms. Many women keep small shrines to Aphrodite in their private chambers, so they can pray to her before bed.

Rites: The rites of Aphrodite involve sensual massages, delicately scented oils, fine silks, and flower petals. To an outsider, they seem more like a ritualized orgy, which is not far from the truth.

Herald and Allies: Doves act as messengers for this goddess, as do lovebirds. Her strongest ally is her lover Ares.

Favored Weapon: Dagger

Trojan War Attitude: Aphrodite supports the Trojans for two reasons. First, Paris awarded her the golden apple, which made him one of her favorites. Second, Aeneas, her own son, is a prince of Troy and the army's second-in-command. She is not a fighter, but frequently appears to rescue either Paris or Aeneas from danger.

APOLLO

Greater God (Chaotic Good)

The archer god Apollo (also called Phoebus Apollo) appears as a tall, well-built young man with golden curls and a golden tan.

swaddling cloths. She hid the real child, and had him was raised in secrecy. He returned as a young man to slay his father and free his brothers and sisters, who had lived all this time in the Titan's stomach. The conquering son was Zeus, and his brothers and sisters were the gods Hades, Poseidon, Hera, Demeter, and Hestia.

That was not the end of the conflict. The other Titans refused to bow to this upstart, and a war began between the two groups. Eventually the gods won, and threw most of the Titans down into a dark pit. The gods divided the world between them. Zeus, as the strongest, claimed the air, and became the overlord of the others taking Hera as his wife. Poseidon claimed sovereignty over the oceans and seas. Hades became lord of the Underworld and master of the dead.

That they had spent so many years fighting close kin may account for the gods' short tempers and their willingness to argue with each other. Once they defeated the Titans, though, their lives became much easier. In fact, their lives became too easy, and they grew bored. To amuse themselves, they toyed with the lives of mortal men, rearranging their fates at whim just to see what would happen.

Although the Greek pantheon contains many, many more than fifteen gods, only a few are powerful enough to be important enough to meddle in the afairs of mortals, and not all of them participated in the Trojan War. Alphabetical entries for each deity important to this conflict follow. Each entry provides an explanation of the god's role in the struggle and the reason for his or her involvement.

As a master archer, he can hit any target with his bow, and as a master musician, his lyre sways even the gods. Additionally, he rules over prophecy and medicine.

Apollo is swift to anger, just like his father Zeus, but also quick to forgive. He loves to laugh and sing. Apollo does not often enter battle directly; he prefers to loose arrows from high above.

Portfolio: Music, poetry, archery, prophecy, medicine, and the sun.

Domains: Chaos, Good, Healing, Knowledge, and Sun.

Holy Symbol: A golden lyre.

Clerical Training: Apollo's priests are advisors, teachers, diplomats, and healers. They prefer peaceful solutions to conflict, and mediate disputes. They train in music, and can play instruments, sing, and recite poetry. They also train with the bow, for Apollo requires them to be good hunters.

Quests: Apollo may send his priests on quests to carry prophecies to people. They also bring joy, laughter, and song to troubled regions easing the people's burdens with their music. Whenever someone claims to be a prophet, Apollo sends his priests to test him. If the person does have a genuine gift, he offers him a position within his priesthood, but if he is a false prophet, his priests denounce him publicly, and punish him for his presumption.

Prayers: Apollo receives prayers at dawn each day. Archers pray to him before every shot, and musicians and bards pray to him before each performance. Healers pray to him before working on a patient, and most prophets (though not seers) pray to him for guidance and prophetic vision.

Shrines: Apollo's temples are bright, sunny places with open courtyards and fountains. In rural areas, they stand near to small streams or natural hot springs. His temples have sickrooms for patients and a divination chamber where his priests and oracles meditate upon the future.

Rites: As the god of poetry, music, and songs, his priest always plays a lyre to accompany the god's rites. His priests perform his rituals outside in the sunlight, but the ceremonies are short, simple, and poetically worded.

Herald and Allies: The sun is Apollo's ally; it burns anyone who offends him. The phoenix is also an ally, and it sometimes carries messages for him. All songbirds answer to Apollo.

Favored Weapon: Composite longbow.

Trojan War Attitude: Apollo supports the Trojans, both because they honor him and because their military commander, Hector, is one of his favorites. Apollo often appears on the field, protecting Hector and giving him courage and strength. He also answers the prayers of several archers, not only Pandarus and Paris from the Trojans, but also Teucer of the Achaeans.

ARES

Greater God (Chaotic Evil)

The war god, famed for his red hair and hot temper, Ares is a pure fighter—bold, brash, a bit crude, and not terribly bright. He and Athena are rivals, but where she is careful and precise, he is rash and rough. Ares loves battle, and favors warriors who show strength and courage. He wanders battlefields, watching the fighters and encouraging them toward acts of reckless daring, and then wades in himself to crush entire armies with a single blow. Ares and Aphrodite are lovers.

Portfolio: War, destruction, strength.

Domains: Chaos, Destruction, Evil, Strength, and War.

Holy Symbol: A red-tipped spear.

Clerical Training: Ares' priests train extensively for combat, and are rough and blunt. They rarely train warriors, but they do encourage them to compete against each other. His priests may become commanders of the local forces, and if so, they attack their neighbors frequently. They also spend time drinking and performing feats of strength, or participating in sports like boxing and wrestling. Ares' priests attack Athena's on sight.

Quests: Ares sends his priests out to demonstrate their strength and to encourage conflict. Whenever two cities, towns, or nations think about fighting, one of his priests arrive on each side to ensure tempers flare. When a war occurs, Ares' priests flock to it, cheering on those men who show strength, daring, and recklessness. They insult anyone who hesitates in battle, and taunt those who flee.

Prayers: Ares presides over any act of brute strength or destruction and over the more violent aspects of combat. People pray to him before battle and participating in aggressive sports.

Shrines: Ares few temples look more like fortresses than they look like religious sanctuaries. Most armies have a shrine to the war god and erect trophies before it to demonstrate their strength.

Rites: Rituals for Ares are short, blunt, and filled with dark liquid, sometimes wine and sometimes blood.

Herald and Allies: Ares' major ally is his lover Aphrodite. The bull is his creature, and it obeys his commands, as do great cats.

Favored Weapon: Spear.

Trojan War Attitude: Ares promised Athena and Hera he would aid the Achaeans, but instead, he supports the Trojans. It is unclear why beyond the fact that he and Athena never get along and because his lover Aphrodite favors the Trojans. Ares enjoys wading into battle at the head of the Trojan forces scattering Achaeans everywhere.

ARTEMIS

Lesser Goddess (Lawful Neutral)

Apollo's twin sister Artemis appears as a lovely young woman, with a fit body and tanned skin of someone who spends all her time outdoors. She is shy when compared to her brother, and prefers the wilds to the company of others. Artemis is a hunter rather than a warrior—she is an expert archer, but cannot handle a sword, and is uncomfortable dealing with men in armor. Her favorites are young women, hunters, and animals.

Portfolio: Hunting, the moon, maidens, wilderness.

Domains: Animal, Healing, Law, Plant, and Protection.

Holy Symbol: A bow and arrow silhouetted against a full moon.

Clerical Training: Artemis has only priestesses who take vows of chastity and never marry. These women retreat from civilization, living in the woods where they can tend to the plants and animals. They train in hunting and animal husbandry as well as in herbalism.

Quests: Artemis sends her priestesses to protect wildlife and forested areas threatened by human hunters or supernatural creatures. She occasionally sends them to protect a young woman whose life and honor men threaten.

Prayers: Hunters pray to Artemis, as do herbalists. Young women pray to her if independent and do not want to be confined by marriage. Druids include her in their prayers, seeing Artemis as a representation of the forest itself.

Shrines: Artemis has small, simple shrines scattered throughout the wilderness. These shrines are located in sacred groves or beside pure streams. She also shares several temples with of her brother, Apollo.

Rites: Artemis does not care for elaborate rituals. Her ceremonies are short and direct, always taking place in the wild.

Herald and Allies: Woodland creatures answer Artemis' call, particularly stags, foxes, and bears. Her twin brother Apollo is her greatest ally.

Favored Weapon: Longbow.

Trojan War Attitude: Artemis sides with the Trojans mainly because her twin brother Apollo supports them; she generally follows his lead. She does not fight in the war herself, however, except when all the gods face off, and even then she is hesitant to stand against Hera.

ATHENA

Greater Goddess (Lawful Good)

Zeus' shield-maiden, Athena (also called Pallas Athene) is a tall, striking woman with strong features and a powerful physique. Her gray eyes, one of her most impressive features, shift from light to dark to reflect her mood. A warrior and master of both weapons and strategies, Athena appears on the battlefield beside her chosen warriors. Athena is bold and decisive, though fear of incurring her father's wrath keeps her in check. She shows no mercy toward those who anger her, but protects her favorites and suggests ways for them to win fame and fortune.

Portfolio: Combat, wisdom, knowledge.

Domains: Good, Knowledge, Law, and War.

Holy Symbol: A snowy owl.

Clerical Training: Athena's priests serve as teachers and judges in many communities. They learn to fight, teaching villagers enough combat to defend themselves. Most nobles learn swordplay and the use of a spear from a priest of Athena. Her priests also dabble in or support the arts, encouraging their neighbors to decorate their homes and their wares. As Athena and Ares despise one another, their priests do not get along.

Quests: Athena may send her priests on quests to discover new lands or to perfect their artistic or combat-oriented skills. A priest of Athena will aid anyone in need, even if the aid delays his quest.

Prayers: Warriors pray to Athena before battle, seeking strength and strategy. Explorers pray to her when they start a new voyage or a hike. Judges and kings pray to her before reaching a decision in a case, and orators often include her in their prayers before a debate.

Shrines: Most large towns and cities have temples to Athena. These buildings are always large, solid, and easily defended. In smaller settlements, she might have only a shrine, though carefully placed so that in case of attack, the villagers can use it for defense.

Rites: Athena does not stand on ceremony. Her rituals are short, simple, and elegant, with simple phrases and gestures.

Herald and Allies: The owls serve Athena, and carry her messages and omens. She can also request aid from any intelligent warrior. Hera is an ally as well.

Favored Weapon: Throwing spear.

Trojan War Attitude: Athena solidly supports the Achaeans. Like Hera, she hates Paris for giving the apple to Aphrodite, but she also has a strong bond with one of the Achaean heroes, Odysseus. She wants the Achaeans to win so Odysseus can win more fame and glory, all of which he dedicates to her in turn. Athena enters the war in person, found at Odysseus' side and shielding him from harm.

HADES

Greater God (Lawful Neutral)

Zeus' second brother, Hades, is a dark, brooding man with handsome but heavy features and a stern appearance. He spends most of his time in the Underworld, ruling over the ghosts and spirits, and rarely joins the other gods on Mount Olympus. Hades resents the freedom of his two brothers, who wander the world at will, but takes his duties very seriously, rarely ever leaving his kingdom.

Portfolio: Death, ghosts, the Underworld.

Domains: Death, Destruction, Earth, and Law.

Holy Symbol: A black ram.

Clerical Training: The priests of Hades study death and the dead, learning how men die and what happens to the body during the process. They also study ghosts, learning to see and speak to these unquiet spirits. His priests learn something about healing and about herbs, but focus on ending suffering quickly.

Quests: Despite what people think, priests of Hades do not deliver plagues and illnesses to communities. Rather, they visit the communities to observe the disease process and to help comfort the afflicted. Hades also sends them to stop grave desecrations.

Prayers: Hades is the first god invoked at a funeral because he claims the soul and guides it down to his kingdom. When the sick tire of fighting their illnesses, they pray to him to leave their world and pain behind.

Shrines: Hades temples lie underground or in caves. When this is not possible, temple floors are sunk below ground level. The buildings never have windows; the priests like to keep them dark and cool like the Underworld their lord rules.

Rites: Hades' priests officiate at funerals and annual rites in honor of departed ancestors. These are serious events, and treated with great respect and dignity.

Herald and Allies: Ghosts are Hades' heralds and allies. He has no great friends among the other gods, though they do respect his responsibilities.

Favored Weapon: Axe (any).

Trojan War Attitude: Of all the major gods, Hades is the only one uninvolved in the war. He does not appear on the battlefield, and takes no part in the disputes on Mount Olympus since he lives in the Underworld and rarely leaves his realm.

HECATE

Greater Goddess (Chaotic Evil)

The goddess of the Dark Moon, also called the Dread Goddess of Night, Hecate is a tall, powerful woman with long dark hair. She is beautiful and moves as gracefully as any youth, but one look in her eyes reveals centuries of wisdom, and a touch of darkness. She can also appear as a tall woman with three heads. Hecate is the patron of magic, but specifically of dark magic and of magic for profit. She encourages mortals to use magic to obtain their deepest desires, such as power or wealth. Hecate does not approve of waste, however, and takes from her followers so that the scales remain balanced. Even the other gods grow uncomfortable around Hecate, both because she knows more about magic than the rest of them and because she is so unpredictable in her moods and actions. Zeus has little control over her, and Hecate wanders wherever she wants. This is partially because Hecate is not one of Zeus' children, nor even one of his siblings—her father was Perses, whose father was the Titan Crisus, a brother to Zeus' own father Chronos.

Portfolio: Magic, the moon, abundance, and the undead.

Domains: Chaos, Evil, Knowledge, Magic, and Trickery.

Holy Symbol: The Setting Moon.

Clerical Training: Hecate does not have many priests, and the few she does have are usually witches. These witches do not preach about the goddess, or encourage others to follow her—Hecate wants only those worshippers who find her on their own. Instead, her witches spend their time perfecting their potions and unguents and spells, in order to work magic in Hecate's name. The priests who do worship Hecate love knowledge, particularly magical knowledge, and they catalog anything they learn, along with notes on how it might prove useful, and to whom. Some magicians worship Hecate, particularly if they use their magic to attain wealth and fame-other magicians dislike her, and studiously avoid her and her shrines.

Quests: Hecate encourages her followers to follow their own paths, wherever those might lead. She does not send her followers on specific quests, but encourages them to find out whatever they need for their magic, no matter where that takes them.

Prayers: Hecate presides over magic rituals. She is also invoked at feasts, in her role as the goddess of plenty. And those who walk about at night often pray to her, in the hope that Hecate will protect them, or at least not to harm them herself.

Shrines: Hecate has few temples or shrines-most of her witches gather in the nearest clearings, and have no compunctions about moving to a more advantageous location. Her priests do set up temples and shrines, but these are always dark, gloomy places, and worshippers rarely linger.

Rites: Hecate's priests preside over magical rituals, and over rites designed to bring rain or a good harvest or some other form of plenty. Her ceremonies are short, but the statements and replies are sung, and establish a slow, graceful rhythm.

Herald and Allies: Hecate uses hounds, wolves, and ravens as her messengers, and these animals plus various spirits serve as her allies. She is rarely seen without a pair of massive hounds, one at either side.

Favored Weapon: Dagger.

Trojan War Attitude: Hecate has no particular interest in the Trojan War. She does not favor either side, because neither the Achaeans nor the Trojans show reverence for magic. Hecate rarely pays attention to nations—she is more interested in individuals, particularly those who practice magic and those who loudly decry it.

HEPHAESTUS

Greater God (Lawful Neutral)

One of the only gods who can claim both Hera and Zeus as parents, Hephaestus is the master smith of Mount Olympus. He creates Zeus' thunderbolts and any other metal items the gods want. He is a tall, powerfully built man, but his features are rough, with a hunched back, and one leg twisted—he was injured when he got between Zeus and Hera during a fight; Zeus threw him from the top of Mount Olympus. Hephaestus is surprisingly calm and rational considering both his appearance and his affinity for fire. Many times, he plays the peacemaker. He is devoted to his mother, and does anything she asks of him.

Portfolio: Metalworking, fire, creation.

Domains: Fire, Law, Protection, and Strength

Holy Symbol: Hammer and anvil.

Clerical Training: Hephaestus' priests handle the forge and train village blacksmiths. They also help train warriors, and generally encourage crafts, particularly those involving stone or metal. Hephaestus' priests are trained in several crafts, and mediate disputes.

Quests: Hephaestus often requires his priests to forge their own armor and weapons from raw ore they themselves dug from the earth. He also sends his priests to carry metal goods to those who need them and to bring fire and comfort to smaller villages in times of trouble.

Prayers: Blacksmiths, stonecarvers, and other craftsmen pray to Hephaestus before beginning work on an item. Mortals offer him homage before lighting a fire, whether the fire emanates from a torch, pyre, or hearth. Some people pray to Hephaestus to settle an argument or protect them from bullies and tyrants.

Shrines: Hephaestus' stone temples are small, simple, and solidly made. A forge lies at the center of the structure, and his priests work at the forge by day, crafting weapons, armor, and other non-martial objects. His temples have sleeping areas open to anyone; beggars know they can stay at his temples for as long as they need.

Rites: Hephaestus favors direct words and actions, but he also loves beauty. His rituals involve a hammer beating against the forge, and always include fire of some sort. Small, delicately made items are sacrificed to the flames as a sign of respect.

Herald and Allies: Hephaestus is the gods' master craftsmen and he has made many wondrous items for them. Chief among these are the golden automata, life-sized golden statues with mobility and intelligence. These are his heralds, servants, and allies. Salamanders also do Hephaestus' bidding.

Favored Weapon: Hammer.

Trojan War Attitude: Hephaestus fights on the side of the Achaeans, primarily because Hera does. The fact that his former wife Aphrodite and her lover Ares champion the Trojans only makes Hephaestus more fervent in his aid to the Achaeans. Like Zeus, Hephaestus owes Thetis a great debt, and helps her son Achilles as payment. He rarely appears in battle himself, however, preferring to help by providing divine arms and armor.

HERA

Greater Goddess (Chaotic Good)

Zeus' wife-consort and the queen of the gods, Hera is a tall, well-built woman of maturity, whose handsome features have the strength and wisdom of age, while retaining the smooth skin of youth. She is a jealous wife, and hunts and kills Zeus' lovers. She also despises the children of these affairs, nursing vendettas for years. Hera, unlike the other gods, openly defies Zeus, and though she fears him, she refuses to let her unease stop her from following her own interests. She staunchly protects those she favors, but she invests her interest in cities and nations rather than individuals. Hera is not a fighter, so she rarely appears on the battlefield. She sends others as her messengers.

Portfolio: Marriage, childbirth, loyalty, revenge.

Domains: Chaos, Good, Healing, Protection, and Trickery.

Holy Symbol: A fan of peacock feathers.

Clerical Training: Hera is one of the only deities to have both priests and priestesses. As the goddess of marriage, she understands the value of both genders. Her priests live with large families while training, learning how to relate to other people. If her priests are not already married, they find a mate while in training, and married by their mentor. Hera's priests do not move often, staying in places where they know the people and can build strong ties with their neighbors and parishioners.

Quests: Hera sends priests to oversee important weddings. She also sends them to exact or witness revenge for some deed against family and old friends. Finally, when families move to a new area, Hera might send the local priest to accompany them to ensure their safe arrival.

Prayers: Hera presides over weddings, births, and naming rituals. She is also the first deity called upon when enacting revenge; she approves of deeds bringing villains to justice.

Shrines: Hera has grand temples located in major cities. In small towns and villages, her priests farm or herd sheep like everyone else, but they build small shrines to Hera in the front of their homes, spending afternoons there consulting those in need.

Rites: Hera's priests officiate weddings, naming rituals, and coronations. Her ceremonies are short and emphasize loyalty and responsibility.

Herald and Allies: Hera calls upon peacocks as messengers. She can also summon any pair of animals to serve her. Her strongest ally is her son Hephaestus.

Favored Weapon: Light mace.

Trojan War Attitude: Hera strongly supports the Achaeans, not so much because she loves them, but because she hates the Trojans and particularly Paris, who awarded the golden apple to Aphrodite instead of her. Hera rarely descends to the field herself; she lets Athena handle the direct interactions.

HERMES

Greater God (Chaotic Good)

Hermes appears as a handsome, slender, and graceful youth with smooth cheeks and a winning smile. He is a trickster, loves playing jokes on mortals and gods. These pranks are rarely dangerous, and Hermes rewards mortals who take them with good grace and good humor. He is very quick and sly, and likes to show how clever he is by thinking up complicated strategies. The other gods, particularly Zeus, often employ Hermes as a messenger or spy.

Portfolio: Travel, thieves, diplomacy, speed.

Domains: Chaos, Good, Luck, Travel, and Trickery.

Holy Symbol: The Caduceus.

Clerical Training: The priests of Hermes are travelers, messengers, and an odd combination of trickster and diplomat. They train in running and in recitation, and they learn the lineages of every noble in their nation. They also travel across the countryside, and are expert guides because they know every route in the region. His priests also learn stealth and agility, and play frequent pranks on one another while training.

Quests: Hermes sends his priests all over the lands, so they learn the region. He also sends them to carry messages from one nation to another or to play tricks on specific people—to shake up their dull lives and to remind them life should not be serious all the time.

Prayers: Runners always pray to Hermes before a competition, and messengers pray to him when they start a mission. Thieves also pray to him, as do tricksters, and travelers ask his aid in reaching their destination quickly and safely.

Shrines: Hermes has few temples, as he prefers stealth to ostentation. Instead, small shrines appear along roadways and hidden deep within cities. Often thieves use these city shrines as meeting points to discuss activities or sell off their acquisitions. Travelers and priests leave small objects from their travels at the shrines; these are not valuable, but show respect and an interest in other lands.

Rites: Hermes' rituals often involve speed, both physical and verbal. His priests employ complicated phrases and tongue twisters in their ceremonies.

Herald and Allies: Rats and raccoons, both animals known for stealth and trickery, answer to Hermes. So do ferrets and their kin. Hermes has no herald, as he *is* the herald of the gods. His strongest allies are his father Zeus and his brother Apollo, both of whom find his jokes amusing.

Favored Weapon: Dagger.

Trojan War Attitude: Hermes claims to support the Achaean army, but does not provide them any aid. His mainly runs errands for Zeus and the other gods. During the war, for instance, Zeus sends him to escort Priam safely to the Achaean camp.

IRIS

Lesser Goddess (Lawful Neutral)

Iris of the Rainbow is a lovely young woman, slender and graceful. She is the messenger of the gods, and sent to deliver commands and suggestions from Zeus to his favorites. As one of the youngest and weakest gods, she rarely intervenes on her own.

Portfolio: Speed, travel, rainbows

Domains: Air, Law, Luck, and Travel

Holy Symbol: A rainbow.

Clerical Training: Iris' priests practice running and recitation, so that they can carry messages. Like priests of Hermes, they race through the countryside, learning every possible path. Iris does not train her priests in subtlety or stealth; she teaches them performance and presentation, so their messages are always delivered with proper dramatic flair.

Quests: Iris sends her priests to take messages to various people, or to serve rulers as their private messengers.

Prayers: Runners, couriers, and actors pray to Iris. People pray to her during rainstorms and other unpleasant weather, asking her to clear the skies with a rainbow.

Shrines: Iris has small shrines along various roads and by arenas and amphitheaters. These are brightly painted and decorated with colorful flowers.

Rites: Iris enjoys spectacle, and prayers to her involve bright colors and rapid movements. Her priests race in circles while chanting her praises, performing complicated dances around her altar.

Herald and Allies: Iris is a messenger for the other gods, so she has no herald of her own. Small, brightly colored birds are her friends, as are dragonflies.

Favored Weapon: Dagger.

Trojan War Attitude: Iris has no preferences in the war, and does not get involved herself. She frequents the battlefield, however, delivering messages for Zeus and other gods.

POSEIDON

Greater God (Chaotic Neutral)

One of Zeus' two brothers, Poseidon rules the seas and is master of horses. He appears as a large, powerful man with dark green hair and a beard. He carries his great trident in one hand and either his sword or his horsewhip in the other. Poseidon resents Zeus' authority, frequently undermining his brother or simply defying his edicts. Zeus always catches on and punishes him. Poseidon is rash, particularly when angered, and once someone earns his enmity, the god holds a grudge for years.

Portfolio: Water, earth, horses

Domains: Chaos, Earth, Strength, and Water

Holy Symbol: A trident.

Clerical Training: Poseidon's priests are sailors and seamen. They learn to handle any boat, and become expert swimmers, divers, and fishermen. They craft nets, fishhooks,

and other fishing implements, and become extremely familiar with a particular coastline. Poseidon also insists his priests master horses, and many of his followers are charioteers or horsemen.

Quests: Poseidon sends his priests sailing about the world, visiting every community they can reach by sea. Most long sea voyages have one of his priests onboard. He also has his priests find and tame herds of wild horses, or dive into the sea in search of rare shells and lost ruins.

Prayers: Horsemen and charioteers always pray to Poseidon before a race, and sailors always offer him libations before a voyage. Fishermen pray to him every morning as they take their boat out onto the water, and divers pray before they search for snails, mollusks, and fish. Horse trainers also call upon his aid, as do shipwrights.

Shrines: Poseidon's temples are open structures located along coastlines, and the salt air constantly blows through them. The walls are covered in frescoes of either of the sea scenes or horses. Many of his temples have corrals in back to hold the horses his priests train and ride.

Rites: Prayers to Poseidon are slow and rhythmic, and often accompanied by a deep drumbeat. His priests sprinkle seawater about as they call upon him, and they wave whips and riding crops made from horsehair.

Herald and Allies: Tritons, merfolk, and sea nymphs carry messages for Poseidon, or they accompany him on his travels. On land, horses do his bidding for Poseidon created them.

Favored Weapon: Trident.

Poseidon favors the Achaeans. He has a long grudge against the Trojans because King Laomedon of Troy refused to pay him and Apollo for building the city's walls. Poseidon enjoys defying Zeus, and becomes more active in his aid to the Achaeans after Zeus forbids the gods to help them.

ZEUS

Greater God (Chaotic Good)

The king of the gods, Zeus is a powerful man in his prime. He has thick white hair, a beard, and piercing eyes. He can be benevolent to his followers, but his mood shifts as rapidly as a summer storm, and one minute he may seem kindly, and the next his brow furrows with rage.

A bully, Zeus lords his power over the other gods, who are all his siblings or children. He does favor boldness, however, and he admires a certain amount of arrogance. He punishes anyone who dares to compare himself to the gods, however.

Zeus also has an eye for beautiful women and chases after any beauty he sees. He rarely takes no for an answer and takes by force any woman who does not succumb to his advances. Many divine offspring have resulted from his insatiable libido. Zeus never personally takes part in battle, but sends his children and siblings to carry out his wishes, or hurls his thunderbolts from Mount Olympus.

Portfolio: Air, weather, knowledge, justice

Domains: Air, Chaos, Good, Knowledge, and Protection.

Holy Symbol: A fist holding a thunderbolt.

Clerical Training: Zeus likes his priests to understand politics and diplomacy. He encourages them to mediate disputes and observe kings holding court, to get a feel for negotiations and a sense of justice. Zeus' priests often consider themselves more important than priests of other gods—after all, their deity is the king of the gods—and they visit other temples frequently. During such visits, they inspect the temple and its priests, criticize its shortcomings, and suggest improvements.

Quests: Zeus sends his priests to gather knowledge about new lands and new people, and teach the people they encounter about the gods. He also sends his priests to places where tyrants rule. In such places, his priests organize rebellions to overthrow the ruler and install someone more just.

Prayers: Zeus controls oratory and debate, and at the start of court and before any formal debates, the participants give a prayer. As the king of the gods, he is also the first prayed to in any general prayer, followed by the worshipper's chosen god.

Shrines: Zeus has temples in every settlement where the Olympians are worshipped, and these structures are the grandest buildings in the settlement. Even small villages have a large, well-built hut set aside for his shrine.

Rites: Zeus prefers gifts of wine, blood, and fresh meat, though grain and gold are also acceptable. His ceremonies are short but grand, and priests deliver prayers to him in a loud voice.

Herald and Allies: Zeus uses giant eagles as omens and as messengers. An eagle remains at his side or nearby.

Favored Weapon: Javelin.

Trojan War Attitude: Zeus has no preference in the war. He values both Agamemnon and Priam, as both have offered him sacrifices and have always shown respect for the gods. Zeus's interest in the war lies in observing the outcome and in watching the other gods spar. He never enters the fray directly. He does lend his support to the Trojans for a time when Thetis begs him to teach the Achaeans a lesson for insulting her son Achilles.

WHEN GODS WAR

Bitter rivalries exist among the gods, and arguments often occur on Mount Olympus. Unfortunately for mortals, since Zeus forbids actual warfare among gods, the gods use humans as tools to settle their differences.

Many of the bitterest arguments occur between Zeus and his wife Hera over his roving eye and perpetual infidelity. Hera does her best to kill or ruin as many of his lovers as possible, tormenting the bastard children he fathers. Zeus, in turn, defends his children, making Hera hate them even more, forcing her to find subtler ways of attacking them. As a result, she has become a master of subterfuge. Hephaestus often finds himself in the middle of their conflicts, since he always takes his mother's side.

Ares and Athena also feud constantly. They both claim dominion over war, but they handle very different aspects of it. Ares specializes in brute strength, raw rage, and mindless destruction; Athena specializes in wise tactics and graceful, intelligent combat. Ares is also jealous of Athena's favored position with their father Zeus. Ares does his best to attack Athena's favorites when possible, but he is not terribly bright, so Athena always gets the better of him.

Ares has earned the enmity of another god as well. Hephaestus was once married to Aphrodite, the goddess of love, but she and Ares became lovers behind his back. When Hephaestus found out, he trapped the two of them in a net, and invited all the other gods to witness them caught in bed before sending Aphrodite away and selecting a new wife. Ares never forgave him for that insult, while Hephaestus has never forgiven Ares for seducing his wife. The two have a second reason to hate one another: both consider fire part of their domain. Ares uses fire to destroy, burning everything to ash; Hephaestus, the blacksmith, uses fire to purify, strengthen, and to create, rather than destroy.

Poseidon and Hades both hold grudges against Zeus because he claimed the largest domain, the heavens, and became king of the gods, even though they are both older. Hades never defies Zeus openly but he makes trouble for Zeus' favorites when possible. Poseidon is more direct, opposing Zeus' plans including attacking his champions.

Of course, the gods find it demeaning to attack humans directly. Most gods stay on Mount Olympus to demonstrate their superiority to mortals and to keep an eye on their rivals. So the gods send messengers instead, usually in the form of their own mortal champions—and such favored men often find themselves challenged by the favorites of other deities. The gods also use natural disasters as weapons, sending earthquakes, floods, and devastating thunderstorms to destroy ships, crush homes, and kill men who displease them.

Most men think it a blessing to have one of the gods look upon them with favor. Yet those who have experienced it know this is rarely true. The favor of a god is wonderful, truly, but that attention makes them a target for other gods, who attack them and destroy their lives just to annoy the god favoring them. Sadly, there is no easy way out of the dilemma. Losing the favor of the first god may make him an enemy as well, and is no guarantee the others will cease their attacks. Appealing to the other gods may also anger the first god, since it suggests he is not strong enough to combat them. And no mortal can mediate between feuding deities—claiming ability to do is a death sentence. The best a man can hope for, if he does gain the favor of a god, is for it to pass quickly, and the gods soon forget him. In the meantime, he need make offerings not only to his chosen god, but to that god's rivals to appease them and soften their rage. He must make certain the first offering is larger and grander, demonstrating his own god is still the foremost in his heart and thoughts.

OFFERINGS

The Greek gods demand constant attention and frequent proof of devotion in the form of libations, sacrifices, and other offerings. Priests or nobles generally proffer these offerings.

LIBATIONS

A libation consists of the mortal pouring wine out onto the ground in the gods' name. It symbolizes offering the god the first taste of wine (spilled because the gods do not physically arrive to accept it), which is a great honor. A full libation spills wine to each of the gods in turn, starting with Zeus, and then the mortal's favored god, and then to each of the others in order of age or rank. Libations are simple matters, and performed quickly, hence they are the most common of sacrifices. They do not cost a great deal—only half a cup of wine is spilled in the ritual. Yet it pleases the gods because it shows proper respect.

In some cases, a libation is made only to the individual's favored god. This usually occurs when someone else already offers libations to each god in turn, or when that god has clear dominance for the situation. For example, a blacksmith at work might pause to make libations only to Hephaestus, since he rules supreme in matters of the forge. When eating dinner,

however, the blacksmith would offer libations to each of the gods, starting with Zeus, then Hephaestus, and then the rest.

The quality of the wine does not matter for a libation, but it must be the same wine drunk by the hosts and guests. Offering a lesser wine to the gods insults them, just as offering a lesser wine to the guests insults to them.

If wine is not available, the individual should offer libations of whatever he is drinking. Milk and honey are good substitutes. Even water is acceptable, if offered humbly.

MEAT

After wine, the most common offering is meat. Offerings of meat are made to the gods before meals, giving them the first taste of meat just as the libation presents them with the first taste of wine. Just as with libations, these offerings do not have to be large. The most common technique is to take slices of thigh meat from the animal being cooked (usually a hog, a steer, or a sheep), fold them within layers of fat, and toss each wrapped morsel into the fire. If the flames consume the meat, the gods have accepted the offering and the meal can begin. As with libations, this offering is expected at every meal and should be the same meat as the host and guests eat.

SACRIFICES

For larger events, and to win more favor from the gods, a mortal may sacrifice an entire animal. The method is similar to the one used above, but the entire carcass is tossed into the fire to show respect, including the animal's skin and bones. Sheep and goats are most often used. Larger animals, like oxen and hogs, serve as well, but more often when those creatures are offered, the worshippers sacrifice only the thigh meat to the flames, and the worshippers eat the rest.

For truly massive undertakings, like the sailing of a fleet or the launching of an army, hecatombs are offered. These are sacrifices of 100 sheep or oxen—in Greek it is written "hekatombe," from "hekaton," or "one hundred" and "bous," which means "oxen." Hecatombs are reserved for the most momentous events, however, as when Odysseus offered them to the gods after his return to Ithaca to appease Poseidon's rage and make amends for killing the suitors in his own home.

Nor are animals the only beasts sacrificed. For extreme insults, human lives are also spent. Agamemnon sacrificed his own daughter Iphigenia to satisfy Athena and convince her to let the fleet leave the harbor and begin its trip to Troy. Achilles captured a dozen Trojan youths and sacrificed them over Patrocleus' grave to honor his fallen kinsman and to demonstrate the high regard he had earned among the Achaean army. Human blood is potent, and should not be spilled in offering unless the life and death of thousands lies in the balance; the gods can be insulted if the offering overshadows the request it accompanies.

OTHER OFFERINGS

In other cases, neither blood nor meat nor wine is required. Some sacrifices, particularly those made to the goddesses and those requesting love and happiness rather than power and success in battle, involve other materials. Hecuba, Priam's wife and the Queen of Troy, selected her most expensive robe and laid it upon Athena's altar, hoping the goddess would find the gift suitable to spare Troy. Grain also serves, either as part of an offering or as the offering itself; it was gathered while still in long stalks, and then tossed into the flames.

Purity was an important part of an offering. Heifers never having calves, sheep never shorn, and lambs not yet with horns were all considered better than their older, more experienced counterparts, because by sacrificing these animals, who had not yet reached their prime, the worshipper gave up the animal as well as its potential. Item sacrifice is the same way. A costly robe never worn was better than one that had, just as grain that had not been cut was offered instead of grain that had already been threshed.

Of course, not every offering was tangible. Warriors often dedicated victories to a particular god, just as bards might offer songs. Anything of value to the worshipper could be used to show respect to the gods. And if the gods considered the offering attractive and valuable, they might smile upon the worshipper, granting him gifts in return, such as victory, wealth, or happiness.

RELIGIOUS SERVICES

Although the Greeks were very religious, they did not have numerous large temples, nor did they gather often for services. Religion remained a private matter rather than a social one, and most prayers and offerings were conducted at home with only the family present.

This does not mean the Greeks lacked temples—some of the most famous structures in the world are ruins of these majestic buildings. Temples, however, honored the gods and provided a place where people could go and worship to be closer to them, and not to hold large gatherings.

A typical Greek family in the Homeric era offered libations to the gods in the morning before breaking their fast. Then they would offer one at the noonday meal and another at dusk before supper. Thigh meat would accompany the libations every time they butchered a hog, ox, or steer for their meal. They made additional offerings just before a harvest or a hunt and before every major family event, such as weddings, births, and so on.

What, then, did the priests do in this setting? They offered guidance for the commoners, both in prayer and in daily life. Priests officiated at weddings and funerals, attended births and blessed the newborn in the name of the gods, and served as witnesses and advisors during important business transactions. More importantly, priests tended the temples and shrines, counseling those seeking them out. People experiencing troubling dreams or seeing strange sights came to the priests, asking them to interpret these signs. Those who suffered a string of bad luck asked if they had angered a particular god, and if so, what they could do to make amends. And those who had experienced good fortune donated money and goods for the priest to offer to the gods in their name, thanking them for their divine favor.

Priests were a central part of life, particularly in smaller communities. They were the voice of the gods, but also the voice of experience, reason, and wisdom. Sometimes they were the only source of objective history in the area, keeping track of each family line and remembering who owned what land, how much they had purchased it for, and they memorized dowry amounts. Priests knew everyone, and served as mediators and judges. They owned no land, even their temples and shrines belonged to the community, and so they remained objective during disputes over property. They also had no interest in fame or wealth, the two other things that made men act irrationally. And, of course, they spoke for the gods, giving them considerable authority. When a farmer said it was going to storm soon, his neighbors demanded to know why he thought so. When a priest said the same thing, everyone began took their clothing off the drying lines and made sure their roofs were tight.

During a war, religious services were more common and much larger. Priests held prayers before each major battle, and performed funeral rites for the dead afterward. The bodies were often collected and buried or cremated en masse, and the entire army attended the services together, noble and commoner alike. During these events, the army commander often assisted the priest, showing both that he was also religious and that he recognized the priests' superior authority in these spiritual matters. Priests could also serve as mediators and ambassadors between the warring sides, since they had no interest beyond the wishes of the gods and the well being of all mankind. Priests were ideal wartime envoys for another reason: no one in their right mind attacked a priest for doing so invited the wrath of their god.

PIETY

In the *Trojan War* setting, the gods influence every aspect of life. They expect their people to honor them and to abide by their commandments. The people also have to follow the codes of their society. This obedience and respect is Piety.

All *Trojan War* characters have a Piety score, reflecting how well they have honored the tenets of their religion and culture. A pious person can perform miracles or request favors from his god, while an impious person threatens himself and possibly his community.

The Piety mechanic first appeared in *Testament*. The Piety rules presented therein have been altered here to suit the Homeric world, which has different values and different religious demands than the Biblical setting.

PIETY POINTS AND PIETY MODIFIERS

Every human is born with a Piety score of 0, and newly created PCs also have this score. Divine offspring are born with higher Piety scores, the value of which depends upon their rank; major divine offspring have an initial Piety score of 3, medium divine offspring have a Piety of 2, and minor divine offspring have a Piety of 1. A person's maximum piety equals his Wisdom +1 point per character level + his divine offspring Piety (if any).

A Piety score can drop below 0. Negative Piety has numerous consequences including the risk of divine displeasure. One-half a person's current Piety score is his Piety modifier; a positive modifier is a bonus, and a negative one is a penalty.

PIETY BOONS

If a character has a positive Piety score, once per game session, he can ask for a divine favor from his deity. This boon may be granted, or it may not, depending upon the character's current Piety score and the god's momentary interests (see **Divine Favor** in **Chapter Fourteen**, page 141 for more details). If the god grants the boon, the character's Piety Modifier is halved for 24 hours. Possible boons include any of the following.

Increased Hit Points: A character can receive a pool of temporary hit points equal to his Piety score. These temporary hit points last for one minute per level. Like other temporary hit points, these hit points are lost first.

Heal: The character heals an amount of damage up to his Piety score.

Smite: A character can make a smite attack with one normal melee attack. He receives a bonus on his attack roll equal to his Piety modifier (maximum +10) and a bonus on damage rolls equal to his class level. A character cannot use this boon to smite followers of the character's same god.

Boost Saving Throws: A character can get a +1 bonus on a saving throw per point of his Piety modifier to a maximum of +10. If the save is against mind-affecting magic forcing him into sin, the bonus to the appropriate save doubles to a maximum of +20. This boon cannot be employed against divine spells cast by clerics of the character's religion or holy creatures of his god's pantheon. A holy creature is defined as any creature that has sacred bonus to its Armor Class or one that inflicts holy damage with its normal attacks.

Boost Skill Checks: A character can spend Piety points to get a bonus when rolling for the results of a Craft or Profession skill check. He adds +1 to the skill check per point of his Piety modifier to a maximum bonus of +10.

Seeking Divinations: A character can visit a temple or other appropriate holy place and receive the benefits of a divination spell, either as cast by the god's priests or in the form of a dream or other portent. The level of spell cast depends on the supplicant's Piety score, as shown on **Table 8–1: Divination as a Piety Boon**.

TABLE 8-1: DIVINATION AS A PIETY BOON

Piety	Maximum Spell Level
1	0
4	1st
8	2nd
12	3rd
16	4th
20	5th*

*The highest level divination that can be achieved from a Piety boon.

The GM should also award bonus Piety points during play if the player character does something that seems particularly respectful and socially conscious, even if the action does not appear on **Table 8-2: Homeric Observances**. An example would be protecting a defenseless person from an attack by an armed warrior, or treating a guest well even if the guest has just insulted the character.

GAINING AND LOSING PIETY

A person gains Piety by observing religious requirements during the course of daily life, by doing great deeds dedicated to the gods, and through special sacrifices. He loses Piety by sinning against the laws of the gods and breaking the laws and social mores of his society.

OBSERVANCE

A *Trojan War* character determines how quickly his Piety score increases (if at all) by observing religious strictures and obeying the wishes of his favored god or goddess. In the *Trojan War* setting, observance cannot be assumed. Characters must maintain their observances. The gods are extremely fickle, and even if someone normally offers all of the appropriate forms, failing even once to show the proper respect can cause him to be cursed until he makes amends. Because of this, characters need to roleplay their observances and keep track of their Piety points. **Table 8-2: Homeric Observances** provides a sample list of actions earning characters Piety points. Many of these actions can be performed only once per day, while others can be done multiple times. The GM should also keep track of each character's Piety points to make sure each player's records are accurate.

At the GM's discretion, the same observance earns more Piety if performed for *every* god rather than just for the character's favored god, and other times it is worth less. This depends on the nature of the observance. Libations should be offered to every god, because that shows respect for the entire pantheon. Dedicating a military victory to all the gods is too general; dedicating the conquest to your favored god is more specific and means more because you are showing that your devotions focus upon that deity.

PIETY AWARDS FOR ADVENTURERS

Adventurers undertaking missions for the good of their nation or quests at the command of their deity receive 1 Piety point each time they complete a mission/quest and each time they gain a level.

SINS

Sins reduce a person's Piety total. **Table 8-3: Homeric Sins** provides a list of activities considered sinful in the Homeric setting. Some entries may seem strange to modern sensibilities. A GM can ignore or modify them if they seem too odd, although it is good to keep them, if only to remind the players that they *are not* playing in a modern milieu.

The list also includes the Piety loss connected to the sin and the maximum punishment a sinner receives for sins that are also crimes. Public lashing is a public display where the character is whipped across the back. Fine and recompense means the sinner must not only replace the goods stolen or damaged, but must pay an extra amount depending on the severity of the crime. The other punishments are detailed in the sections following this one.

Defending oneself or those unable to defend themselves incurs no Piety penalties, nor does killing someone in a time of war, nor any act committed at the direct behest of a deity. The only exception to this is killing a divine offspring—even during war, the gods dislike seeing their children die and the act earns a minor penalty along with the displeasure of the dead character's divine parent.

The Greek gods are demanding, and insist every character maintain his observances, no matter where he is or what occurs. Failing to offer libations is a sin, even if the character is a guest in a home where the spilling of wine is a major offense. It is possible to be forced to sin, because no matter what the character does, it will offend someone. The gods use these situations as tests of the characters' devotion, and insist the sin be against a mortal rather than against them.

CONTEMPT

Certain sins, while having no actual punishment, earn contempt for the character. Neighbors, friends, and even family disapprove of the character's actions, and find him lacking in honor and courage. This expresses itself as a –2 penalty to Charisma checks when dealing with anyone who knows the character or recognizes his name. Strangers who make an Appraise check to denote status have either heard about this person and his actions or simply sense that he has done something inappropriate, and the Charisma penalty applies. Once the character's Piety score reaches 0 again, the Charisma penalty drops to –1. When the character has earned a Piety score of 4 or more, the penalty vanishes; he has now made amends to the gods, and demonstrated improved social behavior.

Severe contempt works the same way as contempt, except that the penalty is –4, dropping to –2 when the character's Piety

TABLE 8-2: HOMERIC OBSERVANCES

Observance	Piety Points Earned	Observance	Piety Points Earned
Pouring libations to the character's favored god	1	Building a temple to each of the gods	8
Pouring libations to all the gods	2	Building/dedicating a boat to a favored god	10
Sacrificing a heifer to a favored god	3	Building/dedicating a boat to all the gods	8
Sacrificing heifers to all the gods	6	Building/dedicating a city to a favored god	15
Sacrificing a hecatomb to a favored god	4	Building/dedicating a city to all the gods	10
Sacrificing a hecatomb to each of the gods	8	Burning barley as an offering to a favored god	2
Offering thighmeat to a god before a meal	2	Burning barley as an offering to all the gods	4
Offering thighmeat to each of the gods before a meal	4	Treating a guest well	4
Sacrificing a maiden to a favored god	10	Treating a stranger well	2
Sacrificing a youth to a favored god	10	Treating a beggar well	3
Dedicating a military victory to a favored god	15	Giving rich gifts to a guest	1
Dedicating a military victory to all the gods	5	Showing mercy to a foe	1
Dedicating an individual combat to a favored god	10	Showing respect to a priest	2
Building a shrine to a favored god	10	Showing respect to a commander or king	1
Building a shrine to all the gods	5	Obeying a priest	2
Building a temple for a favored god	12	Offering a priest protection	4
		Observing a god's holy day	1
		Attacking a god's enemies	2
		Sparing a creature or plant sacred to a god	3

points reach 0 again, −1 when his Piety reaches 3, and 0 when he reaches a Piety of 6 or higher.

OSTRACISM

Some sins, like killing a guest, are so extreme and so dishonorable, mere contempt is not enough. The character is ostracized instead. No one who knows the character speaks to him or acknowledges him in any way; they will not sell items to him, and they will not stand aside to let him pass. It is as if the character had become a ghost, moving soundlessly through the world. Anyone meeting the character must make an Appraise check to denotes status. If the check succeeds, the person realizes the character has been ostracized, and they should ignore him. Anyone who recognizes this but acknowledges the character anyway receives contempt from everyone else who knows the character's status.

Ostracism does not simply fade. Even after a character's Piety score returns to 0 or above, everyone still ignores him. The only way to overcome this and become a viable member of society again is to perform a major deed (something worth 5 or more Piety points), go on a quest, or accept exile (see below for details on these actions). The character gains no Piety points from these activities, but has paid his debt to society, and can interact again.

Someone who, in the space of a week, commits three or more sins requiring ostracism is permanently ostracized. He can no longer live in the same kingdom because his name and deeds have spread everywhere. No act of Piety will restore him to acceptable social status. His only option is to seek out another land where no one has heard of him, and hope that no one recognizes him and tells his new neighbors of his ill deeds.

DIVINE DISPLEASURE

Often, characters commit sins or crimes and receive no penalty from friends, family, and neighbors, but these actions may still displeasure the gods. When a character displeases one or more gods, the god or gods strike the character with a string of bad luck. This can range from minor misfortunes to utter disasters to the ruin of an entire nation (see **Divine Displeasure**, **Chapter Fourteen: Running the Game**, page 143 for more details).

When someone's Piety drops to −10, he must make a DC 10 Piety check or receive divine displeasure from his god even if his specific sins do not list divine displeasure as a punishment. At every increment at −10, a new Piety check must be made. Divine displeasure accumulates until the character performs deeds to demonstrate his repentance. The gods instantly kill any character whose Piety score reaches −40, as the character's very existence offends the gods.

REDUCING SIN

Characters can reduce their sins in three ways: they can perform deeds to earn positive Piety points, they can go into exile, and they can accept quests. No *one* action can raise them to 0 and give them a positive Piety score, however. If the action earned them

PIETY AND CONVENTIONAL ALIGNMENT

Most references to Piety scores in Trojan War include alternative rules for those using only the conventional d20 alignment system. When an alternative isn't provided, assume that a good alignment equals a score of +5 or above, an evil alignment is a score of -5 or below, and a neutral alignment is -4 to +4, with the GM deciding exactly where in the range an individual character rests.

TABLE 8-3: HOMERIC SINS

Sinful Offense	Piety	Punishment
Insulting a guest	-6	Severe contempt
Insulting a beggar	-2	Contempt
Insulting your host	-4	Severe contempt
Insulting a priest	-5	Contempt, Divine displeasure
Insulting a priest of your favored god	-8	Contempt, Divine displeasure
Killling a priest	-15	Ostracism, Divine displeasure
Killing a guest	-10	Ostracism
Killing a stranger for no reason	-10	Ostracism
Killing a beggar	-8	Public lashing, severe contempt
Breaking your word	-8	Severe contempt
Offering libations to all the gods, but missing one	-4	Divine displeasure
Offering sacrifices to all the gods, but missing one	-6	Divine displeasure
Offering barley to all the gods, but missing one	-2	Divine displeasure
Comparing yourself to a god	-5	Divine displeasure
Claiming you are better than a god	-10	Divine displeasure
Claiming you are better than a god at that god's best feature or ability	-15	Divine displeasure
Turning away a beggar	-2	Contempt
Not performing proper rites for the dead	-4	Contempt
Killing a divine offspring	-1	Divine displeasure
Murder	-5	Ostracism
Murder of king	-10	Death
Theft	-3	Fine and recompense, contempt
Theft from a temple or shrine	-10	Fine and recompense, severe contempt, divine displeasure
Vandalizing a temple or shrine	-15	Ostracism, divine displeasure
Lying	-1	Contempt
Military desertion	-3	Public lashing, severe contempt
Failing to wash hands before making an offering	-1	Contempt
Failing to bathe before performing a religious rite	-2	Contempt

enough points to receive a positive score, the score raises to 0, and the remaining points are lost. For example, if someone with −2 Piety dedicates a temple to a god, which is normally worth 12 Piety points, his Piety rise to 0, but no higher, and the rest of those Piety points disappear. Once the person's Piety reaches 0 again, he can perform other deeds to regain a positive Piety score.

EXILE

A character can voluntarily leave his home and family to wander the world in demonstration of his regret for past misdeeds. For every month the character voluntary goes into exile, his negative Piety reduces by 1. The character may take one or two kinsmen or friends with them, but no more. Going off to war does not count as voluntary exile.

QUESTS

A character can accept a quest from a god or from a priest of that god to remove his sin. If the character sinned against a particular god, the quest must be from that god—if his sins are more general, then he can accept a quest from his chosen god instead. The quest must be something the character would not do otherwise (hunting down people who insulted his family is not a religious quest, but hunting down people who insulted the god is). The quest cannot earn the character any personal rewards—any money earned must be donated to the temple, and any victories

must be dedicated to the god. A character who completes a quest successfully, upon offering it with a libation to the god in question, has his negative Piety reduced by 1 for each week of the quest's duration (minimum of 1 week). If a priest assigned the quest, the character must return to offer libations before that particular priest, and hand over any material gains from the quest before considered completed. Going to war can count as a quest if the character would not otherwise have participated.

OATHS

In a world where the power of the gods is real, speaking an oath binds a person to a deed. Once sworn, the oath must be adhered to in every respect. If the oath involves a deed with a CR equal to that of the speaker and his party, he gains 1 to 3 Piety points upon fulfillment of the oath. Failure to fulfill the oath within a reasonable time (GM's discretion) costs the character −1 to −3 Piety. If he continues to renege on the oath, he suffers further Piety penalties periodically. If a character later regrets an oath he swore, he may go to a priest of the god in whose name he swore the oath and be absolved of it at a cost of 50 XP per character level.

CHAPTER NINE: THE HOMERIC WORLD

The Homeric setting is both specific *and* difficult to pin down. The area is an easy; the epics occur in the Mediterranean, specifically the Greek islands, Crete, and Asia Minor. The time, however, is less clear. Some scholars suggest the Trojan War began in 1218 BCE, but others cite 1194 BCE as the starting date. Homer, as many authors do, blurs the lines between his own time and the time of his stories, mixing his culture and theirs to create a new one for the tales. So, while the exact time is uncertain, the *Trojan War* setting can safely focus on two of the major regions involved in the most famous war in all history.

ACHAEA

The Achaeans—sometimes called Danaans, Minoans, Hellenes, or Argives—dominated culture in the Mediterranean during this time. Achaea consisted of a collection of islands and peninsulas, each with its own king, all united under a single overlord. The Achaeans specialized in two things: sea travel and war. They assembled fleets and sailed about the region, invading and conquering other nations, absorbing each into their realm. Every Achaean kingdom began as an independent realm, but fell to the invaders, forced to swear fealty to their conquerors.

Given their warlike nature, Achaean cities and large towns were heavily fortified. Fights erupted between neighbors, though the overlord always intervened to prevent all-out war. Young Achaean men led raids upon nearby kingdoms, carrying off livestock, women, and other valuables. Most of these men were nobles hoping to earn status through their military prowess. Commoners tended to livestock and handled the crafts. They trusted their lords to protect them from harm.

GEOGRAPHY

As a collection of smaller kingdoms, Achaea's geography is highly varied. Some of the islands, like Ithaca, were too rocky for horses or cattle—Ithaca had many sheep and goats and large olive groves, but no pastures and few farmlands. Other kingdoms, like Mycenae, were much larger and gentler, with rolling meadows where vast herds of cattle and horses roamed. The one uniting feature was the sea. Every Achaean kingdom had a coast for at least one border, and every nation had its own boats. All citizens, both noble and common, knew how swim, having learned as small children, and most owned small fishing or sailing boats.

HISTORY

The city of Mycenae in Argolis served as the center of Achaean culture. The hero Perseus, son of Zeus, founded Mycenae. Zeus had visited the princess Danae as a stream of gold, and impregnated her. Her father, King Acrisius of Argos, feared this unborn grandchild because prophecy warned the child would kill him. After Perseus' birth, Acrisius put the boy and his mother in a chest, and cast them into the sea. Zeus protected them, however, and they washed up on the shore of Seriphus. When Perseus grew older, Polydectes, the king of that island, sent him to retrieve the head of Medusa, hoping the young man would never return. Hermes and Athena aided the youth, however, and he succeeded in his quest. On his way back to Seriphus, Perseus saved Andromeda, the princess of Ethiopia, from a sea monster. The two married and they returned to Seriphus. There, Perseus killed his Polydectes, and then returned to Argos, where he accidentally killed his grandfather, Acrisius. Perseus inherited the kingdom, but shame prevented him from ruling a land whose king he had killed. Instead, he exchanged kingdoms with Megapenthes of Tiryns. Megapenthes became king of Argos, and Perseus ruled Tiryns. In Tiryns, he established the city of Mycenae, whose name means "cap," and some legends say Perseus named it thus because his cap fell to the ground there, which he took as an omen.

Perseus' descendents ruled Mycenae for many years, but Eurystheus, Perseus' grandson, hated his cousin Heracles, and so he imposed the twelve labors upon him. Though Heracles did complete the labors, he later died, and Eurystheus waged war upon Heracles' children, the Heraclid or Heracleidae. Heracles' children proved victorious, killing Eurystheus and his children. Eurystheus had left the brothers Atreus and Thyestes—the sons of Pelops, who ruled the Peloponnesus—in charge of Mycenae during his absence, and after his death, they claimed the throne. They quarreled over Mycenae and over Atreus' wife, Aerope. Finally, Atreus defeated his brother, and claimed the kingdom for himself, killing all of Thyestes' sons in the process. Thyestes had one last son, a boy named Aegisthus, though. whom Atreus had raised. Aegisthus killed Atreus in turn. Atreus had two sons, Agamemnon and Menelaus, called the Atreidae or Atreides. Agamemnon, the older of the brothers, inherited the kingdom, and ruled Mycenae and all of the Peloponnesus during the Trojan War.

POLITICS

Agamemnon ruled all Achaea, but beneath him, kings ruled each separate kingdom comprising Achaea. Menelaus, his brother, was king of Sparta and one of Agamemnon's chief vassals. In each kingdom, the king's noble family members handled many of the bureaucratic functions for their royal relatives. Cities and towns each had their own local government, which answered to the king in turn.

The king was known as a "wanax." Beneath him was the lawagetas, or military commanders, and then the telestai, or ruling nobles. After them were the basileus, or minor officials,

Most houses were made of mud bricks, though palaces could be stone blocks below and mud brick and timber above. The walls were often corbelled—each new row of blocks was set in just a little to create an arched effect. Blocks ranged from massive irregular stones to neat square blocks (called ashlars) to polygonal shapes carefully fitted together. Cisterns or wells were also common, particularly in larger towns and cities. Buildings were painted, usually with geometric patterns or warlike frescoes with a geometric border. Similar designs adorned their pottery.

The larger Achaean homes had an open porch supported by columns, leading into a main room called the megaron. This square room had a round hearth in the center and four large wooden columns around it. The columns supported a chimney and a raised roof. One side of the room held the family's chairs—or the throne, if a palace. Storerooms, open-air courtyards, kitchens, and pantries took up the rest of the first floor, while the second floor held the women's quarters and the master bedroom. Furniture consisted of benches, chairs, footstools, tables, and a variety of rugs and furs that could be piled into beds and seats. Writing did exist during this period, though it was not common. Some Achaeans could write well enough to inventory goods, and most writing was simple lists and catalogs. They made marks using stone or wood styluses, carving the symbols into wax or clay tablets. Clay tablets, once filled with information, could be fired to make them permanent, and palaces often had archive rooms containing racks of these thin slabs.

ECONOMY

Achaea earned money through trade and gained other goods through conquest. Its fleet ranged up and down the coast, attacking small towns and trading with larger ones. Their wares included olive oil, grain, ceramics, and woolens. The Achaeans were not sharp traders, but other nations feared their wrath, and few merchants dared to cheat them. Smaller towns hoped to avoid Achaean notice by hiding any local treasures or wares, and they carried their goods to larger cities where they could trade safely.

Within each kingdom, the Achaeans lived by farming or raising livestock, or by practicing various crafts. Nobles and kings taxed their people annually, leaving the commoners enough to survive, but gathered enough treasure to keep themselves in luxury. Most nobles owned their own lands, where slaves or servants farmed in return for food and shelter.

RELIGION

The Achaeans all worshipped the Greek pantheon (see **Chapter Eight: Religion and Piety**). Shrines were more common than temples, particularly in smaller communities, and families had small shrines in their own homes. The town lacked any central place of worship. Larger cities did have grand temples, one devoted to their chosen god and one to the rest of the pantheon. Religion formed a central part of Achaean life, and people performed small ceremonies of respect throughout the day, particularly before each meal. Special occasions, like weddings and funerals, involved elaborate ceremonies and public offerings to the gods.

According to Homer, the Achaeans practiced ritual cremation for their dead, at least for those who died in battle. They placed

the korete (local governors), their porokorete (deputies), and finally the demos (landholders).

CULTURE

Despite their love for battle, the Achaeans kept excellent records of produce and taxes, and enjoyed a thriving trade with other nations. Their boats carried wares throughout the Mediterranean, particularly goods like woolens, pottery, and grains, returning with copper and tin. Many of the larger kingdoms had established roads, though rural areas might only have beaten paths. Slavery was a common, accepted practice. Most slaves were women, though some were male prisoners taken from previous wars.

Thick walls surrounded the major cities, transforming them into citadels when necessary. All men were trained with the spear and the shield, and most had at least a throwing spear and a dagger at home for defending their families and their lands. Men wore loincloths and short kilts and short, sleeveless tunics when working. Formal tunics had short sleeves and fuller skirts. The men only covered their legs when hunting or going to war, and then usually with linen or metal greaves. Women wore loose skirts and robes. White, yellow, and blue were the most popular colors.

Achaeans ate a variety of foods, including all manner of meats (lamb, goat, pork, beef, and wild animals), seafood (shellfish, octopus, and murex sea snails), vegetables (peas, lentils, vetches, beans), fruits (figs and plums), grains (wheat and barley), cheese, and milk. Olives were a major food for the area, and olive oil was a source of wealth.

the bodies on pyres, surrounded with several trophies (though not their armor, which went to the dead man's heir). They lit the pyre and allowed it to burn throughout the night, the fire reducing the body to bone and ash. They then gathered the bones and ash with great care keeping the remains separate from any other materials or other bodies, placing them in a large urn. They sealed the urn with hot wax and placed them within a stone cairn, preferably upon a high spot overlooking the sea.

For non-warriors dying at home, they dug 10-foot-deep grave shafts instead, and placed the body intact within the tomb. The shafts had a layer of pebbles at the bottom and rubble lined the sides, with ledges set near the top. Once the body was interred, they added a low wooden roof, which rested upon the ledges. The Achaeans covered the tomb with earth, and placed a stone slab near its head to mark the spot.

Important individuals had single graves, while other graves might contain an entire family. The Achaeans buried the bodies in their finest clothes, and for nobles, placed metal masks over their faces to preserve their image in the afterlife. Royal graves sometimes had an aboveground beehive structure—known as Tholos tombs—and were elaborately shaped and carved with stone walls and high arches. The bodies within were sealed inside large painted jars, or placed on a bier with their funeral offerings. In several places, the middle class used chamber tombs instead of the grave shafts. These were chambers carved into rocky hillsides, and entire families could be placed on ledges within—the tomb would be sealed after each burial, and then reopened whenever another family member was interred. The Achaeans did not place much stock in corpses once funeral rites were over, however. They believed the soul had then gone on to the afterlife, and the bones could be tossed aside with impunity. This did not mean that they dug up their old comrades during the war, but in chamber tombs, they might shove aside an earlier body to make way for the recently deceased.

TROY

The city-state of Troy, the center of the Trojan nation and the strongest non-Achaean presence on the Mediterranean, stood in Dardania on the northwest coast of Asia Minor.

GEOGRAPHY

Troy was set in a narrow valley facing the Mediterranean. Hills rose on both sides and behind it, effectively protecting it from attack on three sides, but also limiting trade roads or escape routes. A single plain stretched before the city, narrowing as it passed through the hills, before widening into a peninsula jutting out into the sea, providing a perfect stretch of beach for landing boats.

Troy was a large, heavily walled city, whose front gates faced the open plain. Smaller gates along the side faced the hills, and on the north side, lay the Xanthus River. Broad streets, wide courtyards, public squares, deep wells, and large palaces rested within the walls. Most of the buildings were made of stone, though poorer quarters had upper stores made of mud brick. The royal palace sat near the square at the city's center, facing toward the front gates. This massive building housed the king, queen, and most of their many children—the palace had 50 bedrooms for Priam's sons and their wives, and on the opposite side of the courtyard had 12 more rooms for his daughters and their husbands. Those children who had their own homes, such as Hector and Paris, lived nearby, in smaller, but equally sumptuous, dwellings.

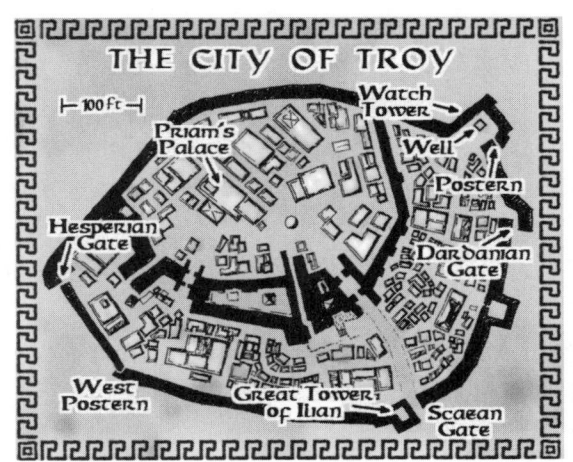

THE CITY OF TROY

├ 100 ft ┤

Priam's Palace · Watch Tower · Well · Postern · Hesperian Gate · Dardanian Gate · West Postern · Great Tower of Ilian · Scaean Gate

Small towns dotted the nearby hills, filled with shepherds, farmers, and simple craftsmen. These settlements had no outer walls and no major defenses. The people retreated into Troy to avoid attack.

The entire region around Troy was often referred to as the Troad. The name Troy referred to the city or the entire nation. The city had also been called Ilium, Ilion, or Ilios.

HISTORY

The region originally belonged to the Teucrians, ruled by King Teucer, son of the river god Scamander and the nymph Idaea. Dardanus, a son of Zeus and Electra who lived in Samothrace, fled his homeland after Zeus killed his brother, Iasion, and settled on the opposite mainland, naming it Phrygia. Teucer welcomed Dardanus, and married his own daughter, Batia, to the stranger. Dardanus then founded a city of his own. After Teucer's death, he became king, and named the land Dardania after himself. When Dardanus died, his son Erichthonius became king, and his son Tros inherited the land after him, renaming it the Troad and its people the Trojans.

Tros had a son, Ilus, who went to Phrygia and won a wrestling contest held by the king. As his prize, he received 50 youths, 50 maidens, and a cow. The king, obeying the words of an oracle, asked the young man to found a city wherever the cow should lie down. Ilus agreed, and when the cow rested on the hill of Ate, he built his city there, and he named it Ilium. Zeus sent the Palladium falling to earth to prove it was the proper site for the city, and it became a major artifact of Troy. Ilus became king of Ilium, or Troy, but his brother Assaracus remained king of the Dardanians.

The next king of Troy was Laomedon, whom the gods tested. Apollo and Poseidon disguised themselves as mortal men—some say of their own free will, while others say as a punishment from Zeus—and offered to fortify Troy if properly paid. Laomedon agreed, and the two gods built the city's high stone walls, which no mortal could overwhelm. However, when after a full year's work they had finished, the king refused to pay them for their labor. In revenge, Poseidon sent a sea monster to devour the people, and Apollo

CULTURE

The Trojans' culture mimicked the Achaeans', for they shared certain common ancestors. Their clothing style was similar, as was their architecture. The Achaeans favored elaborate designs in their clothing and in their artwork, however. They were also great horsemen—Trojans were often referred to as horse-tamers—and the mighty steeds were central to their culture. Horse and chariot races were common, and commoners had horses of their own, whereas for the Achaeans, owning horses was a sign of wealth, and only nobles could afford them. Herds of horses roamed the hills—these and sheep were the nation's main livestock. The Trojans enjoyed most sports, particularly boxing and sprinting. They also enjoyed hunting, and left their cities to wander the hills, bows in hand. Women had more respect in Troy than in Achaea, and could hold positions of authority in larger towns.

During times of peace, people entered the cities freely. The great gates and lesser gates remained open, and hunting parties wandered out for a day or a week, while women carried their washing to the river and sat by its bank to sing, sew, and bathe. Horsemen thundered across the plain, racing to the ocean and back, and travelers walked across the same plain to pay their respects at the city. Smaller communities throughout the hills grew crops, raised animals, or produced useful items of cloth, wood, stone, or clay.

In times of war, everyone retreated into the city, and the gates were closed tight, shielding the people from harm but trapping them within high stone walls and cold stone streets. Large warehouses near the edges of the city served as bunkhouses, and families huddled within them, clutching whatever belongings they brought with them. The cities had wells and could provide sufficient water for their people, and had large food stores set aside in case of a siege, but the Trojans were accustomed to open fields, and they grumbled mightily if held within the walls for too long.

Trojans were not aggressive by nature, but every man trained in the use of spear and shield, and stood ready to defend his home and his land if necessary. The Trojan nobles were expert charioteers, and their horses gave them an advantage over most opponents. Many of them also perfected their hunting skill with a bow, and could devastate enemy's force by killing their captains from the safety of their own walls.

ECONOMY

The Trojans earned most of their money from their horses, which were widely prized throughout the region. They also taxed ships passing through the Hellespont, the narrow strait separating Europe from Asia Minor—Troy sat along this strait, and it could easily blockade it. The hills around the region were covered with copses, and the Trojans sold wood to many people, particularly for shipbuilding.

RELIGION

The Trojans had the same religious beliefs as the Achaeans, worshipped the same pantheon, and followed the same rituals. The city of Troy had a temple dedicated to Athena, another to Apollo, and a third to Zeus. The other gods were worshipped at smaller shrines within individual homes. The Trojans cremated their dead, and they placed the urns within cairns or family tombs.

struck them with a plague. To appease them, the king set his daughter, Hesione, upon the rocks for the sea monster to devour. Heracles saw her there, and he offered to rescue her in exchange for the horses of Tros, which Zeus had given Laomedon as payment for his affair with Ganymede. Laomedon agreed, but after his daughter was safe, he refused to pay the hero. Heracles stormed the city in response, leading 18 ships against it. Despite their small force, Heracles and his allies breached the walls, and killed Laomedon and all his sons save young Priam, who became the next king of Troy. Hesione was given to one of Heracles' companions, Telamon—their son, Teucer, returned to attack the city years later with his half-brother Aias.

Priam was still the king of Troy during the Trojan War, though he was an old man. He had 100 sons, the greatest of whom was Hector.

POLITICS

King Priam ruled Troy alone. He was not only master of the city, but overlord of the Trojan nation, which included Dardania and several other kingdoms. As with Achaea, each of these kings handled the daily affairs of his own lands, but answered to Priam and helped defend the nation against invasion. When not at war with outsiders, the kingdoms often fought amongst themselves, and Priam frequently stepped in to settle disputes between his vassals.

Towns and villages may have had a village elder, who settled disputes and tallied goods. These elders reported to the nobles of their area, who reported to their kings, who answered to Priam. Other walled cities existed in the Troad, and these were the homes of the kings or their noble relatives, who served as local governors and as commanders of the militia. The villagers paid taxes to the local lords, but in return, they received protection from invaders, and could request food and other goods during lean periods.

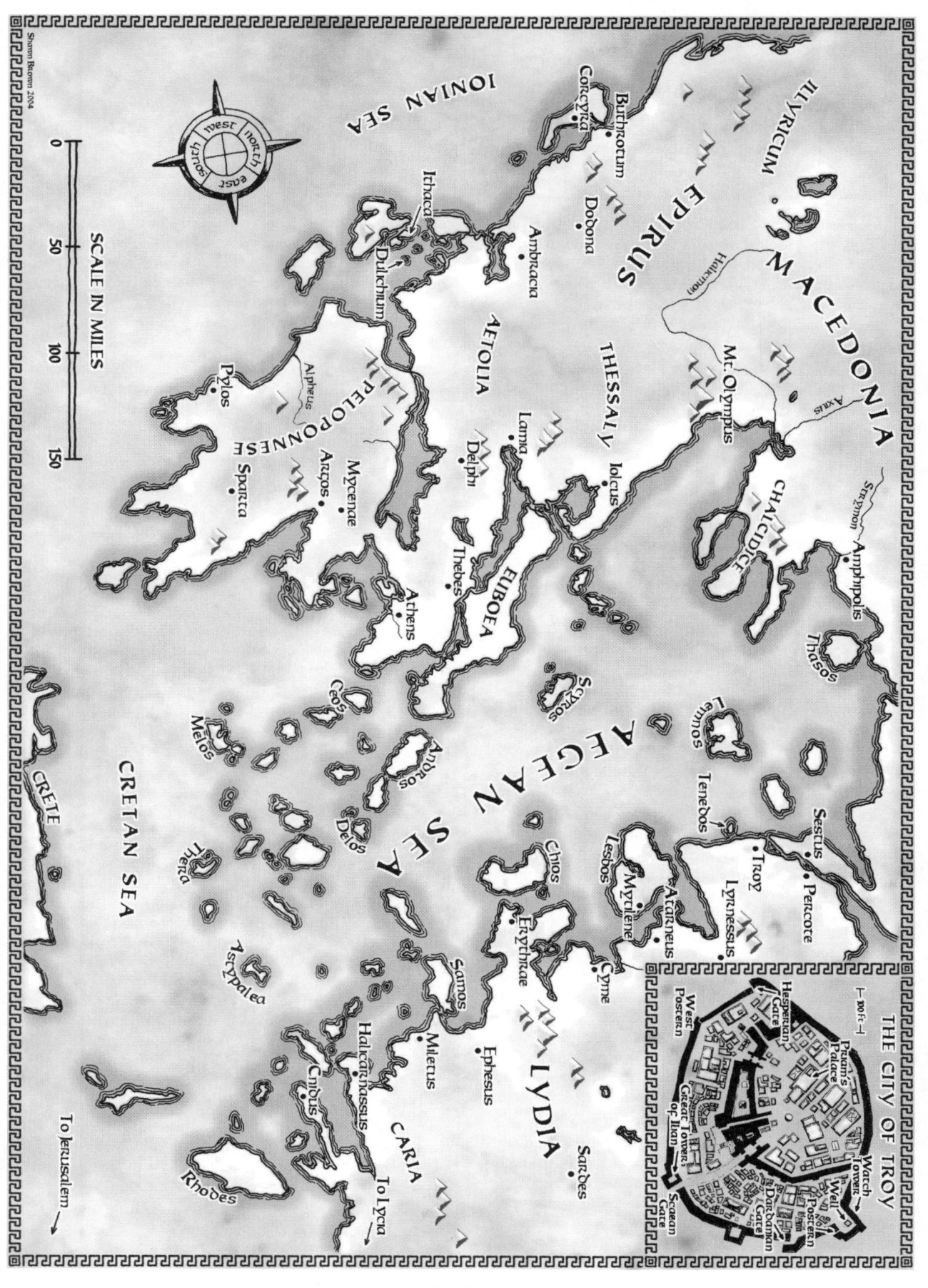

CHAPTER TEN: CAPTAINS OF LEGEND

Achilles. Hector. Odysseus. These and many others are what made the Trojan War both so great and so awful—so great because it was an epic battle against magnificent warriors, and so awful because so many of the age's mightiest men lost their lives during the struggle. It is sad to think if either side had not had such powerful fighters, the war might have ended much more quickly and with fewer casualties. But, just as the gods themselves took a hand in the conflict, so too did the greatest men of the region also clamor to participate, each fighting either for home or for country, striving for personal glory. The heroes on both sides, as much as the location and era, are what make this setting so powerful and so unique. Few other stories can boast a band or team with such powerful members, and none has such impressive rosters on both sides of the battle.

Below are descriptions of the major figures from both armies, and their stats as characters. This allows you to play those characters or to use them as NPCs. Each character is described as he stands at the start of the Iliad. Additional notes are provided for those few who change gear during the battle. For details on class abilities, consult **Chapter Three: Character Classes** in this book and **Chapter Three: Classes** in the *PHB*. Feats marked with a "*" are detailed in **Chapter Four: Skills and Feats**.

ACHAEAN CAPTAINS

The invaders from Greece and its surrounding islands, the Achaeans fought for the honor of their country, and the oath each king had sworn when wooing Helen. The Achaeans as a whole were expert sailors and skillful warriors, but their leaders rose above them and challenged even the gods for personal strength and martial prowess.

ACHILLES

Achilles is a large, muscular young man with handsome features. His skin is bronzed and his hair is long and sun-bleached blond. His features are rugged, with a heavy brow and a strong jaw. His eyes are a deep blue, and turn almost black when he is angry.

Achilles is the prince of Thessaly and the leader of the Myrmidons. His father is Peleus, King of Thessaly, and his mother is the water-nymph Thetis. Even though she was only a lesser goddess, Fate decreed that Thetis would bear a son even greater than was the father. Both Zeus and Poseidon coveted her, but because of this prophecy, they gave her to mortal Peleus instead. It is this prophecy that makes Achilles a major divine offspring, despite his lesser parentage.

When he was an infant, Thetis took her son to the river Styx and dipped him in its waters. The magical stream transformed his skin, making it rougher and extremely tough. The only place not protected was his heel, where she had held him when she dipped him. Thetis grew angry with her husband shortly after that and left him, and so the centaur Chiron raised him, teaching the young man to run, hunt, and fight.

Thetis knew her son would win great glory if he ever went to war, but she also knew he would not survive the conflict. When the Atreides summoned men to attack Troy, she took Achilles and hid him the court of Lycomedes, disguised as a girl. Odysseus discovered him by offering the girls gifts and mixing a sword and spear in with the jewelry and clothing—when he instantly went for the weapons, Achilles revealed his identity.

Achilles is confident in his own skills and physical prowess. He is the strongest warrior on the battlefield, and knows it. He is also very volatile, and inclined to loud boasts, quick laughter, and black depression. His mood can shift in an instant, sometimes without warning or reason. His closest friends are Patroclus, Aias Telamonian, Nestor, and Odysseus. Achilles dislikes Agamemnon because the older man orders him around—he obeys, though, because he knows his honor and the honor of his father depends upon proper respect to the Achaean overlord.

Achilles has two immortal horse, Balius and Xanthus, the children of the wind-god Zephyr and the harpy Podarges. Poseidon gave them to Peleus as part of his wedding present, and he gave them to Achilles.

ACHILLES

Male major divine offspring Charioteer 10/Runner 10; CR 22; Medium-size outsider (native); HD 10d10+40 plus 10d10+40; hp 190; Init +7; Spd 50 ft.; AC 36, touch 14, flat-footed 33; Base Atk +20; Grp +24; Atk +29 melee (1d6+9/17-20, *Sword of Peleus*) or +27 ranged (1d8+12/19-20, *Spear of Peleus*); Full Atk +29/+29/+24/+19/+14 melee (1d6+9/17-20, *Sword of Peleus*) or +27 ranged (1d8+12/19-20, *Spear of Peleus*); SA agile runner, extended attack, fast entry, lightning strike, momentum, sideswipe, skilled charge, skillful maneuvering; SQ capture, chariot expertise, damage reduction 10/magic, difficult target, evasion, gauge skill, quick defense, skilled horseman, steady, trained steed, voice command, +4 to saving throws against divine spells; AL CN; Piety 4; SV Fort +10, Ref +17, Will +7; Str 19, Dex 16, Con 19, Int 10, Wis 12, Cha 17.

Skills and Feats: Climb +6, Drive +16, Intimidate +7, Jump +6, Knowledge (tactics) +13, Spot +14, Swim −2; Chariot Attack*B, Cleave, Drive-By Attack*B, Endurance, Lion in the Field*, Noble*, Power Attack, Run, Stunning*.

Possessions: *Armor of Achilles*, *Shield of Peleus*, *Spear of Peleus*, *Sword of Peleus*, *Golden Chariot* drawn by Balius and Xanthus. For details on the named artifacts, see **Chapter Twelve: Treasures**.

BALIUS AND XANTHUS

CR 6; Large Magical beasts (extraplanar); HD 8d10+48; hp 103; Init +3; Spd 60 ft.; AC 19, touch 19, flat-footed 16; Base Atk +8; Grp +20; Atk +15 melee (1d6+8, hoof); Full Atk +15 melee (1d6+8, 2 hooves), +13 melee (1d4+4, bite); Space/Reach 10 ft./5 ft.; SQ damage reduction 10/magic, darkvision 60 ft., low-light vision, scent, spell resistance 17; AL CN; SV Fort +12, Ref +9, Will +6; Str 26, Dex 17, Con 22, Int 11, Wis 18, Cha 13.

Skills and Feats: Listen +15, Spot +15; Multiattack, Power Attack, Run.

AIAS

Aias (or Ajax) is the king of Salamis, and the largest and strongest man in the Achaean army. He is its greatest fighter after Achilles. Aias is tall and handsome with curly brown hair and brown eyes. He has a massive build and heavy features.

Aias is arrogant about his size and strength, and wades into battle when he should not; he trusts his own might to protect him. He is not bright, but is content to follow the lead of the other kings. He is straightforward, however, and does not like clever stratagems, preferring to attack head-on. Aias is closest to his cousin Teucer, who often stands behind his shield and fires arrows into the enemy forces. Aias is also good friends with Aias the Runner (sometimes known as Lesser Aias), with Achilles, and with Patroclus. He is one of the few who dislikes Odysseus, since he disapproves of the smaller man's constant need for cleverness.

ACHILLES

AIAS

male human Fighter 19; CR 19; Medium humanoid; HD 19d10+76; hp 180; Init +7; Spd 20 ft.; AC 40, touch 11, flat-footed 39; Base Atk +19; Grp +23; Atk +26 melee (2d6+11/17-20, *+1 bronze greatsword*) or +21 ranged (1d8+5, *+1 throwing spear*); Full Atk +26/+21/+16/+11 melee (2d6+11/17-20, *+1 bronze greatsword*) or +21 ranged (1d8+5, *+1 throwing spear*); AL CG; Piety 1; SV Fort +15, Ref +7, Will +6; Str 18, Dex 13, Con 18, Int 10, Wis 10, Cha 14.

Skills and Feats: Boat +4, Climb +10, Decipher Omen +1, Diplomacy +4 (+6 against commoners), Drive +7, Handle Animal +6, Intimidate +18 (+22 against commoners), Jump +14, Knowledge (tactics) +6, Ride +5, Spot +2, Swim +4; Cleave, Distinctive*, Diehard, Dodge, Endurance, Great Cleave, Greater Weapon Focus (greatsword), Greater Weapon Specialization (greatsword), Improved Critical (greatsword), Improved Initiative, Improved Sunder, Lion of the Field*, Mobility, Noble*, Power Attack, Shield Swing*, Thick Skin*, Weapon Focus (greatsword), Weapon Specialization (greatsword).

Possessions: +1 bronze panoply, Shield of Ajax, +1 bronze greatsword, +1 throwing spear. For details on the *Shield of Ajax*, see **Chapter Twelve: Treasures**.

AGAMEMNON

Agamemnon is a handsome, powerfully built man just past his prime. He has strong, craggy features and a full beard, dressing in simple but handsome clothing or in glittering armor. He is the king of Mycenae and overlord of Achaea.

A strong king and a good ruler who considers the welfare of his people, his flaw is his greed. He uses his position to claim the best prizes for himself after a military conquest. He gets angry when anyone contests his authority, and dislikes Achilles because he knows they need the younger man's strength.

Agamemnon is closest to his brother Menelaus, and to Odysseus and Nestor.

AGAMEMNON

male human Fighter 10/Orator 4; CR 14; HD 10d10+30 plus 4d6+12; hp 115; Init +3; Spd 25 ft.; AC 32, touch 11, flat-footed 31; Base Atk +12; Grp +15; Atk +23 melee (1d8+9, Scepter of the Atreides) or +14 ranged (1d8+4, *+1 throwing spear*); Full Atk +23/+18/+13 melee (1d8+9, Scepter of the Atreides) or +16/+11/+6 melee (1d6+4/19-20, *+1 short sword*) or +14 ranged (1d8+4, *+1 throwing spear*); SA suggest, taunt; SQ captive audience, charmer, glib; AL LG; Piety 5; SV Fort +11, Ref +5, Will +9; Str 16, Dex 12, Con 16, Int 14, Wis 14, Cha 20.

Skills and Feats: Appraise +6, Bluff +14 (+18 audience, +22 audiences of commoners), Diplomacy +14 (+18 audience, +22 audiences of commoners), Disguise +5 (+7 acting), Gather Information +9, Intimidate +25 (+29 audience, +33 audiences of commoners), Knowledge (tactics) +10, Perform (oratory) +15 (+19 audience, +23 audience of commoners), Sense Motive +8; Cleave, Combat Expertise, Distinctive*, Endurance, Greater Weapon Focus (heavy mace), Noble*, Persuasive, Power Attack, Quick Draw, Skill Focus (Perform: oratory), Weapon Focus (heavy mace), Weapon Specialization (heavy mace).

Possessions: Agamemnon's armor, *+2 chased round bronze shield*, scepter of Atreus, *+1 throwing spear*, *+1 bronze short sword*. For details on Agamemnon's armor and the scepter of Atreus, see **Chapter Twelve: Treasures**.

CALCHAS

Calchas is the Achaean's seer. His skills provided insight as to how long the war would last, by correctly translating the omen of the serpent and the sparrows. When the Trojans could not depart from Aulis because of unfavorable winds, Calchas divined that the fairest of Agamemnon's daughters would have to be sacrificed, unwittingly spelling Agamemnon's doom at the hands of his grieving wife.

Calchas offers a constant voice of support and wisdom to the Achaean lords. However, he is prideful and jealous. He believes his intellect and acumen to be higher than any other mortal, and is easily threatened when another voices a differing opinion. In fact, his opinion of his skills is so great that when a rival outwits him Calchas dies of grief.

CALCHAS

Male human Bard 8/Seer 10; CR 18; Medium humanoid; HD 8d6–8 plus 10d6–10; hp 45; Init +1; Spd 30 ft.; AC 11, touch 11, flat-footed 10; Base Atk +11; Grp +1; Atk +12 melee (1d4/19-20, masterwork dagger); Full Atk +12/+7 melee (1d4/19-20, masterwork dagger); SA bardic music (12/day—countersong, inspire competence, inspire courage +2, *fascinate*, inspire greatness, *song of freedom*, *suggestion* (DC 19)); SQ accurate sight, bardic knowledge +13, deathly sight, deathly speech, divine assessment, divine clarity, divine scrutiny, divine understanding, divine vision, future glimpse, future sight, pious sight; AL N; Piety: 3; SV Fort +4, Ref +14, Will +17; Str 10, Dex 12, Con 8, Int 16, Wis 19, Cha 15.

Skills and Feats: Appraise +24 (+26 denote status), Concentration +20, Decipher Omen +31, Diplomacy +14, Heal +16, Knowledge (arcana) +14, Knowledge (history) +14, Knowledge (nobility and royalty) +24, Knowledge (religion) +14, Listen +17, Search +13, Sense Motive +19, Spellcraft +15, Spot +23, Survival +16 (+18 following tracks); Alertness, Divine Sight*B, Extra Music*, Iron Will, Negotiator, Self-Sufficient, Silent Spell, Skill Focus (Decipher Omen), Track.

*See **Chapter Four: Skills and Feats** for details;

Bard Spells Known (*Cast per Day* 4/4/4/1; save DC 12 + spell level): 0—*daze*, *detect magic*, *know direction*, *lullaby*, *read magic*, *resistance*; 1st—*comprehend languages*, *detect secret doors*, *identify*, *lesser confusion*; 2nd—*detect thoughts*, *enthrall*, *suggestion*, *tongues*; 3rd—*charm monster*, *glibness*, *good hope*.

Possessions: masterwork dagger

DIOMEDES

Diomedes, son of Tydeus, is the king of the city-state of Argos. His father was one of the "Seven against Thebes," a group of warriors who attacked that powerful city but failed to defeat it and died instead. As a young man Diomedes and the other children of the Seven completed what their fathers started, and conquered the city. Diomedes won fame for his

skill in battle, and after returning home became the king of Argos. He is a large, powerfully built man with brown hair and brown eyes, and is not particularly good-looking but not ugly either. Diomedes is one of the more intelligent fighters in the Achaean army, and that, plus his even temperament and good nature, have made him well liked off the battlefield, while his sense of strategy and his fighting prowess earned him respect in combat. He is closest with Odysseus, and the two often scout the Trojan forces together.

Late in the war, Diomedes and Glaucus met on the battlefield. Upon exchanging names and lineages, they realize their fathers were friends, and so they vow not to fight one another as long as other foes remain. To prove their friendship, they exchanged armor—Diomedes gives Glaucus his *+1 layered bronze panoply*, and receives Glaucus' *+2 burnished layered bronze panoply* in return.

DIOMEDES

DIOMEDES

Male human Charioteer 10/Runner 8; CR 18; Medium humanoid; HD 10d10+30 plus 8d10+24; hp 153; Init +10; Spd 40 ft.; AC 27, touch 13, flat-footed 24; Base Atk +18; Grp +21; Atk +22 melee (1d8+4/19-20, *+1 bronze longsword*) or +20 ranged (1d8+4, *+1 throwing spear*); Full Atk +22/+17/+12/+7 melee (1d8+4/19-20, *+1 bronze longsword*) or +20 ranged (1d8+4, *+1 throwing spear*); SA extended attack, momentum, sideswipe; SQ agile runner, capture, chariot expertise, difficult target, evasion, fast entry, gauge skill, quick defense, skilled charge, skilled horseman, skillful maneuvering, steady, trained steeds, voice command; AL NG; Piety 3; SV Fort +8, Ref +15, Will +6; Str 17, Dex 15, Con 16, Int 14, Wis 13, Cha 10.

Skills and Feats: Balance +9, Climb +11, Concentration +9, Drive +15, Handle Animal +7, Intimidate +14, Jump +17, Knowledge (tactics) +17, Listen +9, Ride +10, Spot +8; Chariot Attack*B, Chariot Shield*, Cleave, Drive-By Attack*B, Endurance, Improved Initiative, Lion of the Field*, Noble*, Power Attack, Run.

Possessions: +1 layered bronze panoply, +1 bronze round shield, +1 bronze longsword, +1 throwing spear

MENELAUS

Menelaus is Agamemnon's younger brother and king of Sparta. He is also Helen's husband, and it is to avenge himself that the war began. Menelaus is a large, powerfully built man with red-gold hair and beard and handsome features. He is hot-tempered, and loves to fight, but he can also be kind and considerate when not in battle. His closest allies are his brother, Odysseus, and Diomedes.

MENELAUS

Male human Fighter 15; CR 15; Medium humanoid; HD 15d10+45; hp 127; Init +3; Spd 25 ft.; AC 26, touch 13, flat-footed 23; Base Atk +15; Grp +19; Atk +21 melee (1d6+7/17-20, *+1 keen bronze short sword*) or +19 ranged (1d8+5, *+1 throwing spear*); Full Atk +21/+16/+11 melee (1d6+7/17-20, *+1 keen bronze short sword*) or +19 ranged (1d8+5, *+1 throwing spear*); AL LG; Piety 2; SV Fort +9, Ref +6, Will +5; Str 18, Dex 17, Con 16, Int 13, Wis 12, Cha 15.

Skills and Feats: Appraise +5, Boat +7, Climb +5, Decipher Omen +5, Diplomacy +4 (+6 against commoners), Drive +8, Handle Animal +3, Intimidate +11 (+15 against commoners), Jump +4, Knowledge (tactics) +5, Ride +9, Spot +5, Swim +0; Cleave, Combat Expertise, Distinctive*, Favored*, Fierce*, Great Cleave, Improved Trip, Noble*, Point Blank Shot, Power Attack, Quick Release*, Shield Swing*, Step-Back*, Weapon Focus (short sword), Weapon Specialization (short sword).

Possessions: +1 bronze panoply, +2 round bronze shield, +1 keen bronze short sword, +1 throwing spear.

NESTOR

Nestor is the king of Pylos, and the oldest combatant in the Trojan War. In his prime, he was one of the mightiest warriors in Achaea, and he is still respected for those skills, but now he is better known for his wisdom and his talent at oration. Nestor is the finest speaker in the Achaean army, even better than Odysseus, and he mediates disputes among the other kings, using his age and his words to calm them. He is a tall, handsome older man, no longer as muscular but still fit, with snow-white hair and beard. His closest allies are Odysseus, Diomedes, and Agamemnon, though everyone likes Nestor and admires him. His son Antilochus is the second-in-command of their charioteers, and a powerful warrior in his own right.

NESTOR

male human Charioteer 5/Orator 9; CR 14; Medium humanoid; HD 5d10+5 plus 9d6+9; hp 73; Init +1; Spd 25 ft.; AC 30, touch 11, flat-footed 30; Base Atk +9; Grp +10; Atk +11 melee (1d6+2/19-20, *+1 short sword*) or +10 ranged (1d8+1, throwing spear); Full Atk +11/+6 melee (1d6+2/19-20, *+1 short sword*) or +10 ranged (1d8+1, throwing spear); SA awe, lull, sideswipe, suggest, taunt; SQ assess audience, beast tongue, captive audience, chariot expertise, charmer, gauge skill, glib, improved charmer, skilled horseman, trained steeds; AL LG; Piety 4; SV Fort +5, Ref +8, Will +10; Str 12, Dex 13, Con 12, Int 15, Wis 17, Cha 14.

Skills and Feats: Appraise +7, Bluff +19 (+28 against an audience, +32 against commoners), Diplomacy +19 (+28

against an audience, +32 against commoners), Disguise +2 (+4 acting), Drive +7, Handle Animal +11, Intimidate +23 (+32 against and audience, +36 against commoners), Perform (oratory) +14 (+21 against an audience, +25 against commoners), Sense Motive +16, Spot +18; Chariot Attack*B, Chariot Shield*, Distinctive*, Drive-By Attack^B, Negotiator, Noble*, Persuasive, Skill Focus (Perform: oratory).

Possessions: Bronze panoply, *Gold Shield of Nestor, +1 bronze short sword*, throwing spear. For details on the *Shield of Ajax*, see **Chapter Twelve: Treasures**.

ODYSSEUS

Odysseus (known to the Romans as Ulysses) is one of the greatest figures of the Trojan War, and a major strength for the Achaeans. He is a mighty warrior, but more than that, he is a powerful orator and the cleverest strategist in either army. Odysseus is a short man, standing almost a head shorter than the other kings, but with broad shoulders and a powerful build. His features are handsome and he looks extremely wise, so much so men stop to listen when he starts to speak. His real power rests in his voice, however, which can charm the listener to a standstill, and in his mind, which examines every situation and looks for the advantage. Odysseus' one weakness is his pride, which insists that he get credit for his stratagems and tricks, and which takes umbrage when anyone claims to be smarter than him. Odysseus is the king of Ithaca, and tried to avoid the war be pretending to be insane, but once the other kings saw through his ruse Odysseus agreed to fight and became one of Agamemnon's greatest allies. Nearly everyone likes him. Odysseus himself is closest to Diomedes and Nestor.

NESTOR

ODYSSEUS

Male human Rog 2/Dedicated Warrior (Athena) 10/Orator 6; CR 18; Medium humanoid; HD 2d6+8 plus 10d10+40 plus 6d6+24; hp 155; Init +2; Spd 35 ft.; AC 26, touch 12, flat-footed 24; Base Atk +14; Grp +18; Atk +19 melee (1d6+5/19-20, *+1 bronze short sword*) or +17 ranged (1d8+5/19-20, *+1 keen throwing spear*); Full Atk +19/+14/+9 melee (1d6+5/19-20, *+1 bronze short sword*) or +17 ranged (1d8+5/19-20, *+1 keen throwing spear*); AL NG; Piety 4; SA sneak attack +1d6, lull, suggest, taunt; SQ captive audience, charmer, damage reduction 1/–, divine celerity, divine shield (2/day), divine strength (3/day), evasion, glib, improved charmer, improved strength, trapfinding, trap sense +2; SV Fort +13, Ref +10, Will +11; Str 18, Dex 14, Con 18, Int 17, Wis 13, Cha 14.

Skills and Feats: Appraise +9, Bluff +15 (+21 against an audience, +25 against audience of commoners), Boat +9, Concentration +11, Decipher Omen +6, Diplomacy +21 (+27 before an audience, +31 against audience of commoners), Disguise +7 (+9 acting, +15 before an audience, +19 against audience of commoners), Drive +12, Gather Information +8, Handle Animal +12, Heal +6, Intimidate +19 (+25 audience, +29 against audience of commoners), Jump +7, Knowledge (nobility and royalty) +8, Knowledge (tactics) +8, Listen +6, Perform (oratory) +13 (+17 against commoners), Profession (sailor) +8, Ride +4, Sense Motive +14, Spot +6, Swim +5; Distinctive*, Divine Sight*, Favored*, Iron Will, Noble*, Persuasive, Step-Back*, Unfazed*.

Possessions: +1 bronze panoply, +1 bronze dyplon shield, +1 bronze short sword, +1 keen throwing spear.

PATROCLUS

Patroclus is Achilles' best friend and chariot driver, and the second-in-command of the Myrmidons. He is a handsome man several years older than Achilles, and looks similar to him but not as muscular and with darker hair (light brown instead of blond). Patroclus is more even-tempered than Achilles, in part because he has lesser fighting skills and so less arrogant. He tries to temper his younger friend's arrogance and console him during his dark moods. He rarely battles on his own, preferring to handle Achilles' chariot so Achilles can be free to fight. Everyone likes Patroclus, but he is particularly close with Aias, Nestor, Odysseus, and Diomedes.

PATROCLUS

male human Charioteer 12; CR 12; Medium humanoid; HD 12d10+24; hp 90; Init +5; Spd 25 ft.; AC 26, touch 13, flat-footed 23; Base Atk +12; Grp +15; Atk +15 melee (1d6+3/17-20, bronze short sword) or +16 ranged (1d8+4, +1 throwing spear); Full Atk +15 melee (1d6+3/17-20, bronze short sword) or +16 ranged (1d8+4, +1 throwing spear); SA sideswipe, wheeled attack; SQ capture, chariot expertise, gauge skill, skilled horseman, skillful maneuvering, trained steeds, voice command; AL LG; Piety 2; SV Fort +6, Ref +11, Will +6; Str 16, Dex 16, Con 14, Int 11, Wis 14, Cha 16.

Skills and Feats: Balance +2, Boat +4, Concentration +5, Drive +12, Handle Animal +8, Intimidate +8 (+12 against commoners), Jump +3, Knowledge (tactics) +9, Ride +7, Swim –6; Chariot Attack*B, Chariot Shield*, Chariot Specialization*, Drive-By Attack*B, Improved Critical (short sword), Noble*, Pious*, Point Blank Shot.

Possessions: Bronze panoply, +1 round bronze shield, bronze short sword, +1 throwing spear.

Note Patroclus does not have his own chariot at Troy, but is Achilles' charioteer and can treat the *Golden Chariot* drawn by Balius and Xanthus as his own.

PHILOCTETES

Former Argonaut, suitor of Helen, and now leader among the Achaeans, Philoctetes kills Paris with Heracles' bow and arrows. Philoctetes also joins Odysseus and hides inside the Trojan Horse to end the war. The lord of Olizon, Meliboea and other locales throughout Thessaly, he is bound by the Oath of Tyndareus, like many other Achaean lords. When the Greeks raise the war cry, Philoctetes answers.

Unfortunately, he does not immediately join the war. While making the journey to Troy, Achilles kills King Tenes despite warnings from his mother Thetis. To assuage the anger of the gods, Achilles makes an offering to Apollo, but a water snake emerges from the altar and bites Philoctetes, incapacitating him with a wound leaking a terrible stench. Unable to bring the injured lord along for the stink of the injury, the Achaeans leave Philoctetes on the isle of Lemnos to recover. There, Philoctetes survives by shooting birds from the sky. Eventually, the seer Calchas (see page 101) prophesized the city could only be taken if the Achaeans had the bow and arrows of Heracles. And so Odysseus and Diomedes return to Lemnos to retrieve the great archer and his weapons. Healed by a son of Asclepius, Philoctetes rejoins the war and slays Paris with a poisoned arrow.

ODYSSEUS

PHILOCTETES

male human Fighter 8/Ranger 6/Assassin 2; CR 16; Medium humanoid; HD 8d10+16 plus 6d8+12 plus 2d6+4; hp 93; Init +5; Spd 25 ft.; AC 26, touch 15, flat-footed 26; Base Atk +15; Grp +19; Atk +20 melee (1d6+5/19-20, +1 short sword) or +28 ranged (1d8+12/x3 and poison, +5 composite (+4) longbow of distance); Full Atk +20/+15/+10 melee (1d6+5/19-20, +1 short sword) or +26/+26/+21/+16 ranged (1d8+12/x3 and poison, +5 composite (+4) longbow of distance); SA combat style (archery), death attack, favored enemies (humans) +4, improved combat style (archery), poison use, sneak attack +1d6; SQ animal companion, poison save +1, uncanny dodge, wild empathy +7; AL NE; Piety: 1; SV Fort +15, Ref +15, Will +5; Str 18, Dex 20, Con 14, Int 11, Wis 12, Cha 8.

Skills and Feats: Climb +5, Disguise +3, Handle Animal +8, Hide +17, Jump +5, Knowledge (nature) +8, Listen +11, Move Silently +15, Ride +9, Spot +11, Survival +7 (+9 aboveground natural environments); Alertness, Diehard, Dodge, EnduranceB, Far Shot, Greater Weapon Focus (composite longbow), Great Fortitude, ManyshotB, Mobility, Point Blank, Precise Shot, Rapid ShotB, Shot on the Run, TrackB, Weapon Focus (composite longbow), Weapon Specialization (composite longbow).

Assassin Spells Prepared (Cast per Day 1; save DC 10 + spell level): 1st—*detect poison, cat's grace, true strike.*

Possessions: +1 bronze panoply, bronze round shield, +1 short sword, +5 composite (+4) longbow of distance, 20 arrows, 8 doses of poison (as deathblade, Injury DC 20; 1d6 Con/2d6 Con)

OSPREY

Animal companion; CR —; Tiny animal; HD 3d8; hp 13; Init +4; Spd 10 ft., fly 60 ft. (average); AC 20, touch 16, flat-footed 16; Base Atk +2; Grp –8; Atk +8 melee (1d4–2, talons); Full Atk +8 melee (1d4–2, talons); SA —; SQ evasion, low-light vision, share spells, tricks (fighting, hunting); AL N; SV Fort +3, Ref +6, Will +3; Str 7, Dex 18, Con 10, Int 2, Wis 14, Cha 6.

Skills and Feats: Listen +2, Spot +14; Weapon Finesse.

SINON

Sinon is famous for two things. First, he lights the beacon alerting the Achaeans to attack Troy for the final time. Second, he is history's greatest liar.

With the Wooden Horse secured in the city, the Trojans capture wily Sinon, putting him to the question. Claiming he would not lie, Sinon tells a tale of his persecution at the hands of Odysseus, stemming from Sinon's former service as squire to Palamedes. As Sinon nursed vengeance in his heart, Odysseus thought, according to the tale, to offer up Sinon as a sacrifice to allow the Achaeans to leave the battlefield. Fearing for his life, Sinon quit the Achaean force and snuck into the city. Sinon is a naturally gifted liar and the Trojans believed him. Sinon went on to say that the Achaeans erected the wooden horse to appease Athena, who was angered by the theft of the Palladium, but built it so large, they believed the Trojans could not bring it into the city.

Through Sinon's convincing lies, King Priam was duped. Sinon threw open the hatch and let the Achaeans free to wreak havoc in the city. And when he waved the brand by the tomb of Achilles, he summoned the waiting Achaeans outside the walls to invade, thus ending the war.

SINON

Male human Rogue 8/Fighter 4; CR 12; Medium humanoid; HD 8d6+8 plus 4d10+4; hp 62; Init +6; Spd 30 ft.; AC 17, touch 12, flat-footed 17; Base Atk +10; Grp +11; Atk +12 melee (1d6+1/19-20, masterwork short sword) or +12 ranged (1d8+1, throwing spear); Full Atk +12/+7/+2 melee (1d6+1/19-20, masterwork short sword) or +12 ranged (1d8+1, throwing spear); SA sneak attack +4d6; SQ evasion, improved uncanny dodge, trapfinding, trap sense +2, uncanny dodge; AL CN; Piety: 1; SV Fort +7, Ref +9, Will +3; Str 12, Dex 14, Con 12, Int 13, Wis 11, Cha 16.

PATROCLUS

Skills and Feats: Appraise +12, Bluff +21, Climb +4, Diplomacy +20, Disguise +14 (+16 acting), Hide +14, Intimidate +7, Jump +4, Listen +11, Move Silently +14, Search +12, Sense Motive +13, Spot +11, Survival +0 (+2 follow tracks), Use Rope +4; Dodge, Improved Initiative, Mobility, Negotiator, Persuasive, Piteous*, Run, Skill Focus (Bluff), Stealthy.

*See **Chapter Four: Skills and Feats** for details.

Possessions: masterwork leather cuirass, leather helmet, leather peturgis, masterwork leather dyplon shield, masterwork short sword, throwing spear

THERSITES

Thersites is repulsive, both morally and physically. He is greedy and a coward. He is also a grotesquely twisted hunchback with a lame foot and bandy legs. He has a few wispy hairs on his bald head.

Thersites joins the Trojan War because he does not want to miss any opportunities for plunder and glory, like many other soldiers. However, Thersites is a coward at heart and a braggart to boot. When Agamemnon tests his troops, suggesting a withdrawal from the war, Thersites argues the wisdom of a retreat, making him despised by the Achaeans' greatest warriors.

Soon after Hector dies, Achilles faces Penthesilia, the Queen of the Amazons. Achilles defeats and slays her, but feels remorse for destroying such a lovely woman. In an act of foolishness, Thersites mocks the champion's grief. Achilles responds and kills this irritating man.

THERSITES

**Male human Rogue 5/Fighter 2/Orator 2; CR 9; Medium humanoid; HD 5d6+5 plus 2d10+2 plus 2d6+2; hp 44; Init +0; Spd 25 ft.; AC 20, touch 10, flat-footed 20; Base Atk +6; Grp +8; Atk +10 melee (1d8+2/19-20, masterwork longsword) or +6 ranged (1d4+2/19-20, dagger); Full Atk +10/+5 melee (1d8+2/19-20, masterwork longsword) or +6/+1 ranged (1d4+2/19-20, dagger); SA sneak attack +3d6; SQ captive audience, charmer, evasion, glib, trapfinding, trap sense +1, uncanny dodge; AL NE; Piety: 0; SV Fort +5, Ref +4, Will +3; Str 14, Dex 10, Con 12, Int 14, Wis 8, Cha 16.

Skills and Feats: Appraise +4, Bluff +15 (+17 against audiences), Diplomacy +17 (+19 against audiences), Disguise +3 (+5 acting), Drive +2, Forgery +10, Gather Information +9, Handle Animal +5, Hide +8, Intimidate +19 (+21 against audiences), Knowledge (local) +10, Knowledge (tactics) +6, Listen +7, Move Silently +8, Perform (oratory) +18, Ride +2, Search +4, Sense Motive +7, Spot +7; Distinctive*, Investigator, Iron Will, Persuasive, Quick Draw, Skill Focus (Perform: oratory), Weapon Focus (longsword).

*See **Chapter Four: Skills and Feats** for details.

Possessions: Masterwork bronze panoply, masterwork bronze round shield, masterwork longsword, 3 daggers.

TROJAN CAPTAINS

The Trojans have fewer numbers than the Achaeans, but fight with more fervor because they are defending their homes and families. Most Trojans are expert horsemen, and prefer fighting from chariots to fighting on foot.

AENEAS

Aeneas is a large, well-built man with blond hair and extremely handsome features. He is the son of Aphrodite and the Trojan prince Anchises, and the leader of the Dardanian forces. Aeneas is also second-in-command of the Trojan forces, and considered their greatest military leader after Hector. Aeneas is a warrior, and like Hector, he favors direct speech and action. He is less blunt than Hector, however, and uses his words and his looks to good effect. Aeneas' closest ally is his mother Aphrodite, who constantly watches over him.

AENEAS

Male major divine offspring Charioteer 14/Orator 2; CR 18; Medium humanoid; HD 14d10+42 plus 2d6+6; hp 132; Init +4; Spd 35 ft.; AC 32, touch 14, flat-footed 28; Base Atk +15; Grp +18; Atk +19 melee (1d6+4/19-20, *+1 short sword of speed*) or +19 ranged (1d8+4, throwing spear); Full Atk +19/+19/+14/+9 melee (1d6+4/19-20, *+1 short sword of speed*) or +19 ranged (1d8+4, throwing spear); SA sideswipe, wheeled attack; SQ beyond limits, captive audience, capture, chariot expertise, charmer, glib, gauge skill, improved voice command, skilled horseman, skillful maneuvering, trained steeds, voice command, +4 bonus to saves against divine spells; AL LG; Piety 3; SV Fort +7, Ref +13, Will +9; Str 16, Dex 18, Con 16, Int 12, Wis 14, Cha 18.

Skills and Feats: Bluff +10 (+12 against audiences, +16 against commoners), Diplomacy +8 (+10 against audiences, +14 against commoners), Drive +11, Gather Information +6, Handle Animal +11, Intimidate +14 (+16 against audiences, +20 against commoners), Knowledge (tactics) +8, Listen +4, Perform (oratory) +8 (+10 against audiences, +14 against commoners), Ride +6, Sense Motive +6; Chariot Attack*B, Distinctive*, Drive-By Attack*B, Favored*, Noble*, Pampered*, Persuasive, Stunning*.

Possessions: *+1 burnished layered bronze panoply*, *+1 layered round bronze shield*, *+1 short sword of speed*, throwing spears, metal chariot drawn by the Horses of Tros, heavy warhorses granted by Zeus to King Tros in payment for his abduction of Ganymede. They are faster than any mortal horse (+10 land speed), and have damage reduction 10/magic.

AENEAS

GLAUCUS

Glaucus is a grandson of Bellerophon, and a cousin to Sarpedon—he is a prince of Lycia, and their second-in-command. Glaucus is a tall, well-built man with open, attractive features. He is easy-going and friendly, and well liked by everyone—in the Trojan War he serves the same role for Sarpedon as Patroclus does for Achilles, offering calm counsel to sooth the other's hot temper. Glaucus is a powerful warrior in his own right, and during combat, he focuses fully upon the battle, but he prefers drinking and talking with friends to fighting.

GLAUCUS

male human Fighter 10/Runner 6; CR 16; Medium humanoid; HD 10d10+30 plus 6d10+18; hp 136; Init +2; Spd 45 ft.; AC 24, touch 12, flatfooted 22; Base Atk +16; Grp +19; Atk +20 melee (1d6+6/19-20, *+1 bronze short sword*) or +18 ranged (1d8+3, throwing spear); Full Atk +20/+15/+10/+5 melee (1d6+6/19-20, *+1 bronze short sword*) or +18 ranged (1d8+3, throwing spear); SA extended attack, fast entry, momentum; SQ agile runner, evasion, +4 bonus to saves against divine spells, skilled charge, steady; AL NG; Piety 2; Fort +9, Ref +8, Will +5; Str 16, Dex 15, Con 16, Int 10, Wis 14, Cha 12.

Skills and Feats: Balance +6, Climb +3, Jump +6, Knowledge (tactics) +13, Spot +8, Swim −4; Cleave, Endurance, Great Cleave, Noble*, Power Attack, Quick Release*, Run, Shield Swing*, Step Back*, Weapon Focus (short sword), Weapon Specialization (short sword).

Possessions: *+2 burnished layered bronze panoply* with an outer layer of gold, bronze dyplon shield, *+1 bronze short sword*, throwing spear.

Near the end of the war, Glaucus and Diomedes exchange armor. Glaucus after this point has Diomedes' *+1 layered bronze panoply* instead of his own golden armor.

HECTOR

Hector is the eldest son King Priam, and the leading prince of Troy. He is also their most able warrior, and the commander of their army. Hector is a tall, handsome man with black hair and dark eyes. He is direct and honest, almost rude, but generous with his friends and gentle with his family. The people of Troy admire him a great deal, and consider him their hero and their one chance of winning the war. Hector is an excellent leader, though his pride sometimes causes him to make bad strategic decisions. When all else fails, he relies upon his own strength and the favor of Apollo. His closest allies are Aeneas, Sarpedon, and Glaucus. Hector dislikes his brother Paris, blaming him for the war and disapproving of his brother's cowardice.

HECTOR

Male human Dedicated Warrior 10/Charioteer 10; CR 20; Medium humanoid; HD 10d10+30 plus 10d10+30; hp 170; Init +10; Spd 30 ft.; AC 35, touch 14, flat-footed 31; Base Atk +20; Grp +23; Atk +24 melee (1d6+4/17-20, *+1 keen bronze short sword*) or +25 ranged (1d8+5/19-20, *+1 keen throwing spear*); Full Atk +24/+19/+14/+9 melee (1d6+4/17-20, *+1 keen bronze short sword*) or +25 ranged (1d8+5/19-20, *+1 keen throwing spear*); SA sideswipe; SQ capture, damage reduction 1/–, divine celerity, divine shield (2/day), divine strength (3/day), gauge skill, improved strength, skilled horseman, skillful maneuvering, trained steeds, trap sense +2, voice command; AL LG; Piety 6; SV Fort +13, Ref +14, Will +8; Str 16, Dex 18, Con 17, Int 11, Wis 10, Cha 15.

Skills and Feats: Balance +6, Concentration +7, Decipher Omen +5, Diplomacy +9 (+13 against commoners), Drive +10, Handle Animal +7, Heal +5, Intimidate +10 (+14 against commoners), Jump +5, Knowledge (religion) +5, Knowledge (tactics) +5, Ride +11, Spot +6; Chariot Attack*B, Distinctive*, Drive-By Attack*B, Favored*, Improved Initiative, Lion of the Field*, Noble*, Quick Release*, Step-Back*, Thick Skin*.

Possessions: *+2 layered bronze cuirass*, *+1 layered tin greaves*, leather-strip peturgis, *+2 layered round bronze shield*, Silver Helmet, *+1 keen bronze short sword*, *+1 keen throwing spear*, metal chariot drawn by the most excellent steeds in Troy, Xanthus and Podarges. For details on the *Hector's Silver Helmet*, see **Chapter Twelve: Treasures**.

HELEN

Helen is the most beautiful woman in the world, tall and shapely with long golden hair and lovely blue eyes. She is the daughter of Zeus and Leda and the wife of Menelaus of Sparta. Paris seduced her and convinced her to run away to Troy with him, where she lives as his wife. Her departure was the cause of the Trojan War.

Helen is very soft-spoken and very tenderhearted. She feels a great deal of guilt for her part in the war, and constantly berates herself for giving in to Paris' entreaties. Helen does her best to stay out of the way of the other Trojan women, who despise her for what she has caused. Her only real allies are Priam and Hector, who are both kind to her, and of course, Paris himself.

HELEN

Female major divine offspring Bard 4; CR 6; Medium-size humanoid; HD 4d6+4; hp 18; Init +3; Spd 35 ft.; AC 16, touch 13, flat-footed 13; Base Atk +3; Grp +3; Atk +3 melee (1d4, dagger); Full Atk +3 melee (1d4, dagger); SA spells; SQ bardic knowledge, bardic music, countersong, fascinate, inspire competence, inspire courage +1, +4 to saving throws against divine spells; AL CN; Piety 3; SV Fort +2, Ref +5, Will +6; Str 11, Dex 16, Con 12, Int 10, Wis 14, Cha 21.

Skills and Feats: Appraise +7 (+9 woven goods), Craft (weaving) +7, Diplomacy +14, Intimidate +7, Knowledge (nobility and royalty) +7, Perform (sing) +12, Sense Motive +9; Distinctive*, Stunning*.

Possessions: elegant robes and girdle, beaded sandals, ivory-handled dagger.

HELEN

MEMNON

Summoned by King Priam, Memnon, the King of the Ethiopians and son of the goddess Eos, leads his armies from the Ethiopia conquering all in his path. When he arrives, Memnon fills the gap left by the now dead Hector.

Memnon kills many Achaeans, but when Nestor asks Achilles to return the armor of his dead son, Achilles and Memnon face each other in single combat. Though Achilles wins, it is important to note Memnon manages to injure the Achaean champion, no small feat indeed.

MEMNON

Medium male divine offspring Divine Champion of Eos 20; CR 21; Medium outsider (native); HD 20d10+80; hp 190; Init +4; Spd 35 ft.; AC 29, touch 12, flat-footed 27; Base Atk +20; Grp +24; Atk +27 melee (1d8+7/19-20, *+3 longsword*) or +23 ranged (1d8+5, *+1 throwing spear*); Full Atk +27/+22/+18/+13 melee (1d8+7/19-20, *+3 longsword*) or +23 ranged (1d8+5, *+1 throwing spear*); SA divine strength 6/day; SQ damage reduction 3/–, divine blessing, divine celerity, divine shield 5/day, trap sense +2, +4 to saving throws against divine spells; AL LN; Piety: 4; SV Fort +16, Ref +8, Will +6; Str 18, Dex 15, Con 18, Int 11, Wis 10, Cha 18.

Skills and Feats: Climb +6, Diplomacy +12, Drive +6, Handle Animal +10, Intimidate +6, Jump +6, Knowledge (nobility and royalty) +6, Knowledge (religion) +6, Knowledge (tactics) +10, Ride +8, Swim +6; Battlefield Seasoned*, Cleave, Distinctive*, Leadership, Lion of the Field*, Power Attack, Stunning*.

*See **Chapter Four: Skills and Feats** for details.

Possessions: *+3 bronze panoply*, *+2 bronze round shield*, *+3 longsword*, 2 *+1 throwing spears*, and a masterwork metal cab chariot.

PARIS

Paris is a prince of Troy, and Hector's brother. He is extremely handsome, with dark curls and large dark eyes, and he can be very charming. In battle gear, Paris looks like an excellent warrior, but he has no real skill at warfare, and is a coward, preferring to hide behind his brother and the other warriors. Paris is an excellent archer, however. He is at least partially to blame for the Trojan War, since his abduction of Helen was the initial cause of the conflict, and his refusal to return her prevented a peaceful solution. The women of Troy admire Paris, but most of the men dislike. His only real allies are his mother Hecuba and the goddess Aphrodite.

PARIS

Male human Bard 6/Orator 6; CR 12; Medium humanoid; HD 6d6+6 plus 6d6+6; hp 54; Init +4; Spd 25 ft.; AC 27, touch 14, flat-footed 23; Base Atk +7; Grp +8; Atk +8 melee (1d8+1, throwing spear) or +13 ranged (1d8+3/x3, *+2 composite [+1] longbow*); Full Atk +8/+3 melee (1d8+1, throwing spear) or +11/+11/+6 ranged (1d8+3/x3, *+2 composite [+1] longbow*); SA lull, spells, suggest, *suggestion*, taunt; SQ bardic music, bardic knowledge, captive audience, charmer, countersong, fascinate, glib, improved charmer, inspire competence, inspire courage +1; AL CN; Piety 1; SV Fort +4, Ref +7, Will +10; Str 13, Dex 18, Con 12, Int 12, Wis 10, Cha 18.

Skills and Feats: Appraise +16, Bluff +19 (+23 against an audience, +27 against commoners), Decipher Omen +15, Diplomacy +25 (+29 against an audience, +33 against commoners), Disguise +4 (+6 acting, +10 against an audience, +14 against commoners), Drive +13, Intimidate +19 (+23 against an audience, +27 against commoners), Perform (oratory) +19 (+23 against an audience, +27 against commoners), Sense Motive +15; Distinctive*, Noble*, Pampered*, Persuasive, Point Blank Shot, Rapid Shot.

Bardic Spells Known (*Cast per Day* 3/4/3; save DC 14 + spell level): 0—*daze, know direction, lullaby, mage hand, message, summon instrument*; 1st—*charm person, disguise self, hypnotism, sleep*; 2nd—*animal messenger, calm emotions, eagle's splendor*.

Possessions: Masterwork burnished layered bronze cuirass, burnished layered tin greaves, burnished layered bronze helmet, burnished layered round bronze shield, *+2 composite [+1] longbow*, 20 arrows, 3 throwing spears.

PENTHESILIA

The daughter of Ares and Otrera (the matron and ancestress of the Amazons), Penthesilia accidentally slew her sister Hippolyte, who had the magical girdle Heracles took for one of his Twelve Labors. When Penthesilia joins the Trojans, King Priam purifies her, absolving her of her past misdeeds. Leading the Amazons to fight alongside the Trojans, she dies at Achilles hands, but her beauty is so great her death breaks her killer's heart.

PENTHESILIA

Medium female divine offspring Barbarian 16; CR 17; Medium outsider (native); HD 16d12+32; hp 136; Init +2; Spd 45 ft.; AC 21, touch 12, flat-footed 19; Base Atk +16; Grp +20; Atk +21 melee (2d6+7/19-20, *+1 greatsword*) or +19 ranged (1d8+4/x3, masterwork composite (+4) longbow); Full Atk +21/+16/+11/+6 melee (2d6+7/19-20, *+1 greatsword*) or +19/+14/+9/+4 ranged (1d8+4/x3, masterwork composite (+4) longbow);; SA greater rage, rage 5/day; SQ damage reduction 4/–, fast movement, illiteracy, improved uncanny dodge, indomitable will, trap sense +5, uncanny dodge, +4 to saves against divine spells; AL CN; Piety: 3; SV Fort +12, Ref +7, Will +5; Str 18, Dex 14, Con 14, Int 8, Wis 10, Cha 16.

Skills and Feats: Bluff +3 (+7 against commoners), Climb +12, Decipher Omen +6, Diplomacy +5 (+9 against commoners), Handle Animal +9, Intimidate +11 (+15 against commoners), Jump +12, Listen +6, Ride +8, Survival +9, Swim +12; Battlefield Seasoned*, Distinctive*, Lion of the Field*, Power Attack, Noble*, Stunning*, Track.

*See **Chapter Four: Skills and Feats** for details.

Enraged: When Penthesilia is in a rage, use the following statistics. HD 16d12+80; hp 184; AC 19, touch 10, flat-footed 17; Atk +24 melee (2d6+7/19-20, *+1 greatsword*); Full Atk +24/+19/+14/+9 melee (2d6+7/19-20, *+1 greatsword*); Fort +15, Will +7; Str 24, Con 20.

Possessions: Masterwork layered leather cuirass, leather greaves, bronze helmet, leather peturgis, *+1 greatsword*, masterwork composite (+4) longbow, 20 arrows

PRIAM

Priam is the king of Troy, and has been for many years. He is a tall, slender old man with snow-white hair and deep blue eyes. In his prime he was an able charioteer, but now he is too old to fight, and stays within the city walls. He is a wise man, and a gentle one, who loves his people and his city dearly and would do anything to save them. Priam is a talented orator, and uses his words to soothe conflicts among his people and their allies. He relies upon his sons for military support.

Priam, male human Charioteer 5/Orator 5; CR 10; Medium humanoid; HD 4d10 plus 5d6; hp 39; Init +0; Spd 30 ft.; AC 10, touch 10, flat-footed 10; Base Atk +7; Grp +7; Atk +8 melee (1d8+1, *+1 heavy mace*); Full Atk +8/+3 melee (1d8+1, *+1 heavy*

mace); SA lull, sideswipe, suggest, taunt; SQ captive audience, chariot expertise, charmer, gauge skill, glib, skilled horseman; AL LG; Piety 4; SV Fort +3, Ref +6, Will +8; Str 10, Dex 11, Con 10, Int 12, Wis 17, Cha 16.

Skills and Feats: Appraise +6, Bluff +9 (+14 against an audience, +18 against commoners), Concentration +5, Diplomacy +9 (+11 against an audience, +15 against commoners), Drive +5, Intimidate +13 (+18 against an audience, +22 against commoners), Knowledge (nobility and royalty) +6, Perform (oratory) +12 (+16 against an audience, +20 against commoners), Sense Motive +7; Chariot Attack*B, Distinctive*, Drive-By Attack*B, Favored*, Noble*, Persuasive.

Possessions: royal robes, crown, sandals, *+1 heavy mace* (scepter).

SARPEDON

Sarpedon is one of the mightiest warriors in the Trojan army. He is the king of Lycia, and his father was Zeus himself—his mother was Laodameia, the daughter of the hero Bellerophon. Sarpedon is a large, powerfully built man with handsome features. He is every inch a warrior, and lives for battle.

Sarpedon is confident to the point of arrogance, and charges into every fray, trusting his strength and his father's protection to bring him victory.

SARPEDON

Male major divine offspring Fighter 10/Runner 6; CR 18; Medium outsider (native); HD 10d10+40 plus 6d10+24 (runner); hp 152; Init +4; Spd 50 ft.; AC 32, touch 12, flat-footed 30; Base Atk +16; Grp +20; Atk +21 melee (1d8+5/19-20) or +19 ranged (1d8+5, *+1 throwing spear*); Full Atk +21/+16/+11/+6 melee (1d8+5/19-20) or +19 ranged (1d8+5, *+1 throwing spear*); SA extended attack, fast entry, momentum; SQ agile runner, evasion, +4 bonus to saves against divine spells, skilled charge, steady; AL CG; Piety 3; SV Fort +13, Ref +10, Will +6; Str 18, Dex 14, Con 18, Int 10, Wis 12, Cha 16.

Skills and Feats: Balance +6, Climb +6, Jump +9, Knowledge (tactics) +13, Spot +7, Swim −1; Cleave, Endurance, Favored*, Great Cleave, Lion of the Field*, Noble*, Power Attack, Quick Release*, Run, Shield Swing*, Stunning*, Thick Skin*.

Possessions: +2 layered bronze panoply, +1 layered bronze crescent shield, +1 bronze longsword, +1 throwing spear.

PLAYING THE LEGENDS

Whenever you have a game set in a known setting with established characters, you run into the same question—should you let the players use those known characters or make them create their own?

The advantage to playing an established character is you already know something about him. We know what Achilles and Odysseus are like, and how Hector acts, and what armor Diomedes wears. If the players have read the *Iliad*, they may already have a sense of the personality, so they can slide into that character quickly.

The disadvantage is playing an established character can be constraining for them. Hector cannot flee a battle, even if he loses—it is just not in his character. Ajax Telamonian cannot come up with brilliant battle plans—he is not that bright. The players have to restrict themselves to what has already been written about these heroes, meaning they cannot make the roles their own. Playing an existing character is very much like being an understudy—you are supposed to follow the main actor's lead, not rewrite the role to suit yourself.

The other drawback is letting them play these characters can muck with the history. What if someone plays Menelaus and accepts Paris' challenge as happens in the books, but overwhelms him quickly, killing Paris before Aphrodite can save him? What if the players take the Trojan characters and Paris kills Menelaus instead? That will rewrite the entire war, really, plus the arcs of those characters. Do you allow the players to do that, or do you tell them "No, if you're playing these guys you have to follow the events established in the books, and that's not how it happens."

You should never tell the players "no, that's not how it happens." Remember this is their game as much as it is yours, and you all create the story together. You use the gods and the NPCs to influence events—Athena or Hera could save Menelaus, just as Aphrodite traditionally saves Paris—if you need a certain outcome. You could also just let the characters affect the story and see where it goes. What does happen to the Trojan War if Menelaus, the original offended party, is killed? Will the Achaeans decide they no longer have a reason to fight? Will the Oath of Tyndareus no longer hold the former suitors? Or will they all demand revenge for his death, and fight even harder?

If you do let the players use existing major characters, make it clear that this is an alternate version of the story. Just because someone plays Odysseus, and he survives the war, does not mean his Odysseus will automatically survive. By playing these major roles, the players are rewriting the story and anything can happen.

The other option is to shift the focus away from the characters Homer discusses. We know what Achilles and Hector do throughout the war, but we have less idea about Diomedes and Sarpedon, each a major warrior for their sides. Players could take those roles and have a lot more freedom without changing the Iliad's storyline. Since this is an alternate version, perhaps Diomedes and Sarpedon decide the outcome of the conflict. Maybe Aias the Runner plays a larger role, or any of the other secondary characters for that matter. You should not remove Agamemnon and Hector and Odysseus, but the war lasted for nine years and involved two powerful nations—surely a few other heroes appeared on the field during this time, and Homer was simply too busy with his story to notice them.

COMMON FOES

As the Trojan War setting lacks the common types of monsters encountered in other fantasy settings, such as goblins, orcs, and bugbears, the PCs are likely to face off against the soldiers on the battlefields instead. The following opponents mirror the experience and training level of the common troops as examples. Given that both sides employed soldiers similarly armed and equipped there is no distinction here between Achaean and Trojan. Also included are sample Amazons to show a possible variation for creating unique soldiers on the battlefield. Use the Amazon example as a guideline for how to create other legendary forces like the Memnon's Ethiopian army for your own campaign.

GREEN SOLDIERS

These soldiers are untrained and untested.

GREEN SOLDIER

Male human Warrior 1; CR 1/2; Medium humanoids; HD 1d8+1; hp 5; Init +0; Spd 30 ft.; AC 14, touch 10, flat-footed 14; Base Atk +1; Grp +2; Atk +2 melee (1d6+1/19-20, short sword) or +2 ranged (1d8+1, throwing spear); Full Atk +2 melee (1d6+1/19-20, short sword) or +2 ranged (1d8+1, throwing spear); AL any; Piety: 0; SV Fort +3, Ref +0, Will +0; Str 13, Dex 11, Con 12, Int 9, Wis 10, Cha 8.

Skills and Feats: Climb +1, Intimidate +1, Jump +1, Swim −1; Power Attack, Weapon Focus (short spear).

Possessions: linen cuirass, linen peturgis, cap, leather crescent shield, short sword, throwing spear.

TRAINED SOLDIERS

Trained soldiers have fought in a few skirmishes and battles, which makes them more reliable than green soldiers.

TRAINED SOLDIER

Male human Warrior 2; CR 1; Medium humanoids; HD 2d8+2; hp 11; Init +0; Spd 30 ft.; AC 16, touch 10, flat-footed 16; Base Atk +2; Grp +3; Atk +3 melee (1d6+1/19-20, short sword) or +3 ranged (1d8+1, throwing spear); Full Atk +3 melee (1d6+1/19-20, short sword) or +3 ranged (1d8+1, throwing spear); AL any; Piety: 0; SV Fort +4, Ref +0, Will +0; Str 13, Dex 11, Con 12, Int 9, Wis 10, Cha 8.

Skills and Feats: Climb +1, Intimidate +1, Jump +1, Swim −3; Power Attack, Weapon Focus (short spear).

Possessions: leather cuirass, leather greaves, leather helmet, leather peturgis, leather dyplon shield, short sword, 2 throwing spears.

VETERAN SOLDIERS

Veteran soldiers have fought in several consecutive campaigns. They know the ways of battle and never shrink from a fight.

TRAINED SOLDIER

Male human Warrior 5; CR 4; Medium humanoids; HD 5d8+10; hp 32; Init +1; Spd 25 ft.; AC 20, touch 11, flat-footed 19; Base Atk +5; Grp +8; Atk +9 melee (1d6+3/19-20, masterwork short sword) or +7 ranged (1d8+3, throwing spear); Full Atk +9 melee (1d6+3/19-20, masterwork short sword) or +7 ranged (1d8+3, throwing spear); AL any; Piety: 1; SV Fort +6, Ref +2, Will +1; Str 16, Dex 13, Con 14, Int 10, Wis 12, Cha 8.

Skills and Feats: Climb +4, Intimidate +5, Jump +4, Swim −1; Cleave, Power Attack, Weapon Focus (short spear).

Possessions: masterwork leather cuirass, tin greaves, bronze helmet, leather strips peturgis, bronze round shield, masterwork short sword, 2 throwing spears.

LEGENDARY SOLDIERS

These soldiers are far above other soldiers in terms of skill and discipline. Legendary soldiers are rare and usually unique. The below example is an Amazon warrior.

AMAZON WARRIOR

Female human Warrior 8; CR 7; Medium humanoids; HD 8d8+16; hp 52; Init +2; Spd 30 ft.; AC 19, touch 12, flat-footed 17; Base Atk +8; Grp +11; Atk +12 melee (1d8+3/19-20, masterwork longsword) or +11 ranged (1d8+3/x3, masterwork composite (+3) longbow); Full Atk +12/+7 melee (1d6+3/19-20, masterwork longsword) or +11/+6 ranged (1d8+3/x3, masterwork composite (+3) longbow); AL any Lawful; Piety: 2; SV Fort +8, Ref +3, Will +2; Str 16, Dex 14, Con 14, Int 10, Wis 12, Cha 8.

Skills and Feats: Climb +11, Intimidate +8, Jump +11, Swim +11; Cleave, Great Cleave, Power Attack, Weapon Focus (composite longbow).

Possessions: masterwork leather cuirass, tin greaves, bronze helmet, leather strips peturgis, masterwork longsword, masterwork composite (+3) longbow, 20 arrows.

SARPEDON

CHAPTER ELEVEN: HOMERIC BESTIARY

The Trojan War involved horses, humans, divine offspring, and gods. No other races took part in the battle or posed a threat in any way. Great boars and other creatures are mentioned, however. In the *Odyssey*, there are actual monsters, including the Cyclopes, Scylla, and Charybdis. Clearly, then, monsters should exist in the setting, and if, at any time, you want to set your game outside the battlefield, it helps to know the type of creatures the heroes could encounter.

HOMERIC MONSTERS

The creatures of Homer's epics and Greek myths are now staple creatures in most fantasy games. Of course, many were modified during the translation into game format.

In Greek myths, monsters are either individuals or clustered into small families. Gorgons are not a race; they are three sisters. Medusa is one of those sisters, and she is the only one of her kind. Her two sisters have the same power to turn people to stone, but they are immortal whereas Medusa is mortal. The Minotaur in these stories is an unfortunate creature, the son of Zeus and Io (Zeus slept with her while in the form of a bull, which is why the Minotaur has the head of a bull). It makes sense to generalize these creatures as races in generic fantasy settings, but that does not suit the Homeric setting.

Most Homeric monsters have one of two origins: either they are the offspring of gods, gods and humans, or humans and animals; or they were once human but the gods cursed them. The Minotaur is an example of the former type: the child of a bull (or a god masquerading as a bull) and a human. Medusa was once a beautiful human, but Athena cursed her for comparing herself to the goddess, so her origins are of the second type.

Every monster has a story, and it is usually a sad one. Though the monsters may be hideous, and they kill and destroy recklessly, warranting them no sympathy, the story of their origins can wring pity from even the most callous hero. Destroying these monsters is very much a mercy killing, allowing the pitiful creatures to move onto the afterlife, a place where they can finally gain acceptance and peace.

The other result of their origins is that most monsters are intelligent, at least smart enough to converse with heroes and to pursue crafts and other interests. The Cyclopes, for instance, one of the few actual races, lived on their own island. Odysseus met Polyphemus and talked with him. Polyphemus captured Odysseus and his men, and devoured several of them, but he also tended a flock of sheep, for which he built pens in his cave home. He was interested in the wine Odysseus offered, and he was smart enough to make a joke about eating Odysseus. This is very different from the usual notion of a cyclops as a mere brute that can only hurl rocks and nothing more.

Since most monsters are unique creatures in this setting, does that mean you cannot use any that have already been mentioned? For example, we know that Perseus chopped off Medusa's head long before the Trojan War. Does that mean you cannot have Medusa make an appearance in your campaign? Of course not. This is a game, after all, so you can do whatever you want. If players

question her appearance, you have several ways to explain the discrepancy. The gods have restored her to life afterward—they are capricious enough to do such. Perhaps she is immortal, after all, and her head grew back a year later, just like the Hydra's heads grew back when they were severed. Maybe this is one of her two sisters, who took on Medusa's appearance after she had died. Greek myths have people who died but were restored, and creatures that re-grew missing portions, and various other ways to allow a long-dead monster to resurface.

The fact that most monsters come from the gods gives any monster encounter more depth, as well. Poseidon cursed Odysseus for blinding his son Polyphemus. Perseus only managed to kill Medusa because Athena, who still bore a grudge, helped him. Whenever you bring in a monster, think about how it relates to the gods. Is it the child of a god? If so, which god, and does that god watch over his monstrous child and protect it from harm? The characters could be risking the hatred of a god by attacking the creature. Was the monster once human, cursed by one of the gods? If so, the characters might earn Piety points for killing the creature. However, what does all this say about the god? The fact that the gods so callously destroyed people's lives, and usually for petty reasons like insulting them or comparing themselves to the gods, should give some characters pause. It does show how powerful the pantheon is, but also how uncaring they actually are about people in general. It may become hard to worship a god who would do such a thing, and then send heroes to kill the monster and hide the evidence of that lapse in judgment.

KNOWN MONSTERS

First, recall the *Trojan War* campaign setting primarily deals with the struggle for victory between two equal armies. Introducing monsters into your game, while consistent with much of classical mythology, diverts attention from the battle for Troy. Great heroes like Achilles and Menelaus pale before the might of an enormous red dragon, or a horde of trolls, or any other monster from the MM. Instead of the usual foes, monsters in the *Trojan War* are manifestations of divine experimentation or justice. Most monsters are unique, and each has its own story.

The following monsters exist in the Homeric setting. This is not an exhaustive list, only some of the creatures you will find mentioned in *The Iliad*, *The Odyssey*, and other prominent Greek works. Many of these monsters appear in the *MM*, a few in

MONSTERS FROM OTHER SOURCES

BOOK OF FIENDS

Even though the Homeric world lacks the cosmological structure of the *Book of Fiends*, it does have varied layers in the Underworld, including Tarterus, the prison of the titans, and other places certainly evil enough to house the terrors like daemons, devils, and demons. Recall, most characters in the Trojan War setting lack in magic weapons, and so may not have the tools to adequately combat these evil outsiders. So use them carefully. The following monsters from the Book of Fiends are appropriate for the Homeric World.

Demons: Abyssal Dragon, Alrune, Eurynomus, Herensugue, Inmai, Jilaiya, Orusula, Schir, Stygian Interloper.

Daemons: Any of the daemons are suitable, though the cosmology must necessarily change to fit within the Homeric world. Daemon comes from the Greek daimon, a guardian spirit, neither good, nor evil. You could use the daemons as spirits sent by the gods to test or punish mortals.

Devils: Bulugon, Dagon, Darksphinx, Hellwarden, Herlekin, Ice Stalker, Kere, Knocker, Oubliette, Phl'taurian, Phlogiston Monitor, Soulsniffer

TESTAMENT

Most of the monsters presented in Testament can be adapted for use in the Trojan War. Of them all, perhaps the phoenix is the most appropriate.

Green Ronin's *Book of Fiends* and *Testament*, the Epic rules, and other official and unofficial sources. The list below is an index of ideas. In most cases, these monsters reflect an advanced version of an existing monster, or a monster blending the characteristics of two or more creatures. Recommendations, or references to other sources, are included for each creature.

ARANEA

These creatures could be the descendants of Arachne, a woman of Lydia who became the finest weaver in the land. The hubris of her boasts compelled Athena to transform her into a spider. Aranea could easily be her children.

BOAR, CALYDONIAN

A boar of phenomenal size and strength. To derive the statistics for this monster, advance a dire boar to 21 HD, making it a huge creature. Note changing a monsters Hit Dice also increase other factors such as base attack bonus, saving throws, skill points, and feats.

BULLS, HEPHAESTAN

Brass-footed bulls that puff fire from their mouth. Hephaestus created them, and gave them to Aeetes, the king of Colchis, as a gift. Use statistics for a gorgon in the MM, but replace its breath weapon with 30-foot cone of fire.

CENTAURS

These creatures are one of the only races not created by the gods. They have human torsos, arms, and heads. From the waist down, they are horses. Most centaurs are rowdy drunkards, but a few, like Chiron, are wise and gentle. Use statistics for centaurs found in the MM.

The Cyprian centaurs, or horned centaurs, look like standard centaurs, but they have rougher coats, larger teeth, longer ears, and they have bull's horns sprouting from their temples.

Some say Zeus created them when he spilled his seed upon the ground, while others say they came from the Lamusides nymphs. There are 12 in all, named Aesacus, Amphithemis, Ceteus, Eurybius, Gleneus, Nomion, Orthaon, Petraeus, Phanes, Phaunus, Riphonus, and Spargeus. Use statistics found in the MM, but give them 1d6 levels of barbarian and a gore attack as a secondary weapon. Their gore attack deals 1d8 points of damage on a successful hit.

CHIMERA

A creature with the head of a lion, the body of a goat, and the tail of a serpent. It breathes fire and lives in the mountains around Lycia. In classical mythology, there was only one chimera. The chimera's in the MM refer to the lesser breeds, perhaps the children of the primogenitor chimera.

Though destroyed by Bellerophon, the chimera could have returned. To derive its statistics, advance the base to 27 HD, changing its size to Huge. Note changing a monster's Hit Dice also increase other factors such as base attack bonus, saving throws, skill points, and feats.

CYCLOPS

This one-eyed race of giants lives on their own island in homes carved into the hills. They worship Poseidon, who fathered their leader Polyphemus, and they herd sheep and goats. They also enjoy devouring travelers. To derive statistics for stone giants, simply use the stone giant in the MM.

DRAGON

Several dragons appear in the Homeric world. One guards the Spring of Ares; in the myths, Cadmus stole its teeth, which were transformed into the Spartans. Another dragon guards the Golden Fleece, while a third has been known to devastate Thespiae. Also, two dragons born of the titans' blood draw Medea's chariot. Python, another dragon, guards Themis' oracle at Delphi.

The traditional dragons as found in the MM are (not surprisingly) not present in the Trojan War. Dragons may be of any color, and have any breath weapon. Most dragons are more serpentine than they are in the MM, though statistically they are unchanged.

GIANTS

These creatures look like humans except for their monstrous size. Several different giants appear in the world, and each has a different origin. Most giants use statistics presented for giants in the MM.

There are several instances of truly horrific giants. Campe, one of the jailors of Tarterus, the prison of the titans, is a massive abomination, with poisonous serpents for hair and covered in thick scales from the chest down. Instead of hands, she has curved claws and a scorpion tail protrudes from her back. Such a monster obviously has no counterpart in the MM, but you could still create monsters like Campe through liberal modifications of templates. In her case, simply take the stone giant and add the half-dragon template, but instead of a breath weapon attack, she gains a wyvern's sting attack.

GORGONS

These three sisters, Stheno, Euryale, and Medusa, have poisonous serpents for hair. Their faces are so hideous anyone who sees them turns to stone. Athena cursed the youngest, Medusa, who was once beautiful. She is also the only mortal of the three.

Though Medusa is dead by the time of the Trojan War, there is not reason for her or similar creatures to exist. For Medusa's statistics, simply give her ten or more levels of ranger, aristocrat, or even fighter to depict this powerful creature of legend. Otherwise, for minor versions of the gorgons, use the medusa stats as presented in the MM.

GRAEAE

These three old women are sisters of the gorgons, and they were born old. They have only one eye and one tooth between them, and they share them to see and to eat. Their names are Dino, Enyo, and Pephredo. Use any of the hags in the MM for these terrors.

GRIFFIN

Although more Eastern in origin, griffins do appear in Greek myths, and often pull the gods' chariots. They have the body of a lion but the beak and wings of an eagle. The griffon is unchanged from the MM.

HARPIES

These four sisters have the bodies of birds and the faces of young girls. They are fierce hunters, and often prey upon careless travelers. The harpies are Aello, Celaeno, Ocypete, and Podarge. Because these harpies are presumably unique creatures, to depict them accurately, you should advance these creatures by adding at least six levels of ranger.

HECATONCHEIRES

These three monsters—Briareus, Cottus, and Gyes—have 100 hands each. They are children of the Titans, making them cousins to the gods, fought with the gods against their parents. But Zeus did not trust the 100-handed, so he consigned them to life in Hades after his victory. This monster is presented in the official Epic rules.

HYDRA, LERNAEAN

A serpent-like monster with nine heads, one of which is immortal. Its other eight heads can be harmed, but whenever one is cut off, two heads grow to replace the lost one. This monster is one of the offspring of Typhon and Echidna. Use the lernean hydra as presented in the MM for this creature.

MINOTAUR

A bull-headed man, the child of Pasiphae the queen of Crete and the Cretan Bull (some claim the bull was actually Zeus in disguise), the Minotaur was a terror unmatched, feasting on those trapped in the labyrinth of Minos. There is only one Minotaur in the Homeric world, though, presumably, he could have spawned children. The Minotaur of this setting is a 12th-level minotaur fighter.

MYRMIDONS

The Myrmidons were originally worker ants. Aeacus, the king of Aegina, was the son of Zeus and Aegina, the daughter of the god Aesopos, and named the island in his mother's honor. This made him a target of Hera, and she cast a plague upon their island. Aeacus and his mother were the only survivors on the island. Aeacus saw ants that were unaffected from the pestilence, and prayed to his father, explaining that if he and his mother were to survive on the island, he needed to repopulate it. Aeacus asked that the new people be as hardy as the worker ants. Zeus answered his son's prayer by transforming the ants into humans. These ants became the Myrmidons. The Myrmidons were also fierce warriors, as well as loyal subjects. When Aeacus exiled his two sons, Peleus and Telamon, for murdering their half-brother, Phocis, Peleus went to Phthia. A group of Myrmidons followed Peleus to Thessaly. When the Greeks fought in the Trojan War, Peleus' son, Achilles, brought the Myrmidons to Troy. These Myrmidon warriors wore black armor and shields. Myrmidons use normal human statistics, except they are all immune to disease.

PEGASUS

This is a beautiful winged horse. Though its parents are Poseidon and Medusa, legends claim that it sprang from the neck of its mother when Perseus removed her head. Like so many creatures of the Homeric world, Pegasus is a unique creature. To accurately depict Pegasus in the Trojan War, advance the pegasus in the MM to 8 HD, and apply the half-celestial template. Note changing a monster's Hit Dice also increase other factors such as base attack bonus, saving throws, skill points, and feats.

SATYR

These woodland creatures have the upper body of a man and the legs of a fawn. They accompany Dionysus, the god of wine and revelry, and are often seen gamboling in the woods. Satyrs avoid men, but chase any woman they meet. Use normal MM statistics for satyrs.

SPHINX

This monster has the head and chest of a woman, the body and legs of a lion, and the wings of an eagle. The sphinx can usually be found on the road west of Thebes. It sits there, blocking the road, and asking its riddle to anyone it meets. If the traveler cannot guess the answer, the sphinx eats him. Use statistics for the gynosphinx in the MM, but advance it to 24 HD. Note changing a monster's Hit Dice also increase other factors such as base attack bonus, saving throws, skill points, and feats.

TITANS

These massive, powerful humanoids originally ruled the world. Their king, Chronos, fathered the gods, who usurped him and then defeated all the Titans, casting them into Hades. The Titans look like large, handsome humans, and they are intelligent but a bit crude. Use the greater titan from the Epic rules for these creatures. Likely, some or all titans have class levels in addition to their racial Hit Dice.

TRITONS

The creatures are the children of the original Triton, the son of Poseidon and Amphitrite. They have human torsos and heads, but fine scales cover their bodies, and they have gills along their neck. Below the waist, they have a curving fishtail. Some tritons can transform into a fully human form. Use the statistics for the triton in the MM.

LEGENDARY ANIMALS

Throughout classical mythology, there are references to fantastic animals, endowed with unusual characteristics such as fantastic size, or bizarre abilities, such as the ability to walk on water, fly, or blow flames from their mouths. Examples include Laelaps, the magical hound Zeus gave to Europa, the swiftest hound in the world, who always catches his prey, or the Nemean Lion, whom Heracles killed with his bare hands because weapons would not work against it, or even the Mares of Diomedes, horses that ate the flesh of men. The Legendary Animal template applies to all of these and more; it allows the GM to create any possible creature, bound only by the limits of his creativity.

CREATING A LEGENDARY ANIMAL

Legendary Animal is an inherited template that can be added to any animal (referred to hereafter as the base creature).

A template uses all the base creature's statistics and special abilities except as noted here.

Size and Type: The creature's size and type are unchanged.

Hit Dice: The base creature gains additional Hit Dice. The amount of extra Hit Dice depends on the Hit Dice of the base creature. Recalculate base attack bonus, saving throws, skill points and any other feature of the base creature whose abilities depend on Hit Dice.

HIT DICE

Old Hit Dice	New Hit Dice
1–3	+2
4–7	+4
8–11	+6
12–15	+8
16 or more	+10

Speed: Increase the base creature's land speed by +10 feet.

Armor Class: Natural armor improves by +4.

Attack: The base creature retains all of its natural attacks, though the base attack bonus increases because of the increase to Hit Dice.

LEGENDARY ANIMAL: MARES OF DIOMEDES

Legendary Heavy Warhorse, Large Animal

Hit Dice: 8d8+48 (84 hp)
Initiative: +3
Speed: 60 ft. (12 squares)
Armor Class: 20 (–1 size, +3 Dex, +8 natural), touch 12, flat-footed 17
Base Attack/Grapple: +6/+17
Attack: Hoof +12 melee (1d8+7)
Full Attack: 2 hooves +12 melee (1d6) and bite +10 melee (1d6+3)
Space/Reach: 10 ft./5 ft.
Special Attack: —
Special Qualities: Low-light vision, scent
Saves: Fort +12, Ref +9, Will +5
Abilities: Str 24, Dex 17, Con 23, Int 2, Wis 17, Cha 6
Skills: Listen +8, Spot +9
Feats: Endurance, Multiattack, Run

Environment: Temperate plains
Organization: Domesticated or herd (6–30)
Challenge Rating: 4
Alignment: Always neutral
Advancement: 9-16 HD (Large), 17-24 HD (Huge)
Level Adjustment: —

This massive steed has a shiny coat and bright intelligent eyes, clearly an excellent specimen of its kind. However, there is something sinister about this steed, for all its beauty.

This example uses a heavy warhorse as the base creature.

These animals appear to the casual viewer as a normal heavy warhorse. However, these steeds are far more powerful, and have a terrible appetite for the flesh of men.

COMBAT

Riders suffer a –4 circumstance penalty to all Ride checks when riding these creatures. The Mare can fight while carrying a rider, but the rider cannot also attack unless he or she succeeds on a Ride check.

Carrying Capacity: A light load for a Mare of Diomedes is up to 700 pounds; a medium load, 701–1,400 pounds; a heavy load, 1,401–2,100 pounds.

Damage: Increase the damage dice for the base creature's natural attack by one step, as if the animal had increased in size. Use the following to determine new damage for natural attacks.

characteristics, increasing the CR as indicated. Sum the CR modifiers and ignore any leftover fractions. Add this to the CR of the base creature.

DAMAGE

Old Damage	New Damage
1d2	1d3
1d3	1d4
1d4	1d6
1d6	1d8
1d8	2d6
2d4	2d6
1d10	2d8
2d6	3d8
2d8	3d8

SPECIAL QUALITIES

Quality	CR
Armored	+.5 per additional +2 of natural armor bonus
Blindsense	+.5
Blindsight	+.5
Fast	+.5 per additional 10 feet of speed
Frightful presence	+1
Scent	+.5
Tremorsense	+.5
Unusual Movement	
Burrowing	+.5 per 20 feet of speed
Climb	+.5 per 20 feet of speed
Fly	+1 per 20 feet of speed (always clumsy maneuverability)
Swim	+.5 per 20 feet of speed

Special Qualities: Normally the base creature gains no new attacks. However, depending on the nature of the change, especially when a god is involved, the animal may gain a special characteristic, in the form of an extraordinary ability. A legendary animal may gain any of the following

NEMEAN LION

Large Magical Beast

Hit Dice: 14d10+84 (161 hp)
Initiative: +4
Speed: 50 ft. (10 squares)
Armor Class: 19 (–1 size, +2 Dex, +8 natural), touch 11, flat-footed 17
Base Attack/Grapple: +14/+28
Attack: Claw +24 melee (1d8+10)
Full Attack: 2 claws +24 melee (1d8+10) and bite +18 melee (2d6+5/19–20)
Space/Reach: 10 ft./5 ft.
Special Attacks: Improved grab, pounce, rake 1d8+5
Special Qualities: Damage reduction 20/adamantine and bludgeoning, low-light vision, scent
Saves: Fort +15, Ref +12, Will +7
Abilities: Str 31, Dex 19, Con 23, Int 2, Wis 16, Cha 10
Skills: Hide +5*, Listen +7, Move Silently +8, Spot +7
Feats: Alertness, Improved Critical (bite), Power Attack, Run, Weapon Focus (claw)

Environment: Warm plains
Organization: Solitary
Challenge Rating: 9
Treasure: None
Alignment: Neutral
Advancement: 15–30 HD (Large), 31–45 HD (Huge)
Level Adjustment: —

This enormous lion appears like any other lion, except for its size, and the faint metallic sheen to its hide.

This example uses a dire lion as the base creature.

The Nemean lion is a patient hunter, but strikes against large prey fearlessly. With its magical ability to withstand attacks, it has nothing to fear from other creatures. The Nemean Lion is 15 feet long and weighs 3,700 pounds.

COMBAT

The Nemean lion attacks by running at prey, leaping, and clawing and biting as it rakes with its rear claws. It does not hesitate to jump on large opponents. For the purpose of overcoming damage reduction, the Nemean lion's natural attacks count as magical.

Improved Grab (Ex): To use this ability, a Nemean lion must hit with its bite attack. It can then attempt to start a grapple as a free action without provoking an attack of opportunity. If it wins the grapple check, it establishes a hold and can rake.

Pounce (Ex): If a Nemean lion charges, it can make a full attack, including two rake attacks.

Rake (Ex): Attack bonus +23 melee, damage 1d8+5.

Skills: Nemean lions have a +4 racial bonus on Hide and Move Silently checks.

*In areas of tall grass or heavy undergrowth, the Hide bonus improves to +8.

Saves: Modify saving throws based on new Hit Dice.

Abilities: Increase from the base creature as follows: Str +6, Dex +4, Con +6, Wis +4.

Skills: A legendary animal gains skill points as an animal and has skill points equal to (2 + Int modifier) x (HD + 3). Treat skills from the base creature's list as class skills, and other skills as cross-class.

Feats: Increase feats based on the adjusted Hit Dice.

Challenge Rating: +2 plus any modifiers based on additional special qualities.

Advancement: A legendary animal advances as follows. It may advance up to double its new Hit Dice and remain the same size, and up to triple its new Hit Dice as one size larger than normal.

CERBERUS, THE GUARDIAN OF HADES

Gargantuan Magical beast (Extraplanar, Evil)

Hit Dice: 30d10+300 (465 hp)
Initiative: +2
Speed: 60 ft. (12 squares)
Armor Class: 41 (–4 size, +2 Dex, +43 natural), touch 8, flat-footed 39
Base Attack/Grapple: +30/+57
Attack: Bite +41 melee (2d8+22 plus poison spittle)
Full Attack: Bite +41 melee (2d8+15 plus poison spittle), 2 bites +39 melee (2d8+7), tail snakes +39 melee (2d6+7 and poison)
Space/Reach: 20 ft./ 20 ft.
Special Attack: Petrification gaze, poison, poison spittle, trip
Special Qualities: Damage reduction 15/epic, frightful presence, immune to cold, disease, fire, poison, regeneration 15, resistance to acid 20 and electricity 20, scent, spell resistance 39
Saves: Fort +27, Ref +19, Will +11
Abilities: Str 40, Dex 15, Con 30, Int 11, Wis 14, Cha 13
Skills: Listen +28, Search +15, Spot +28, Survival +13
Feats: Awesome Blow, Cleave, Combat Reflexes, Great Cleave, Improved Bull Rush, Improved Initiative, Improved Sunder, Lightning Reflexes, Multiattack, Power Attack, Track

Environment: The Underworld
Organization: Solitary (unique)
Challenge Rating: 28
Treasure: None
Alignment: Neutral evil
Advancement: —
Level Adjustment: —

Before the gates of the Underworld stands a massive hound with three slavering heads and baleful red eyes. The end of its tail separates into a nest of writhing serpents. It appears watchful and alert, scenting the air for intruders.

Cerberus is the mythical guardian who guards the entrance to the Underworld. Those seeking entry into the land of the dead without the consent of Hades, or his consort Persephone, must face this creature. For a time, Heracles, whole stole the monster to complete his Twelve Labors, kidnapped it. Since, Cerberus returned to Hades' realm and maintains its vigilant watch for those seeking to break in or out of the mist shrouded forlorn realm of death.

Cerberus understands, but does not speak, all mortal tongues.

COMBAT

Cerberus is a vicious opponent. It opens combat by using its paralysis gaze on the obvious spellcasters, before launching in with its bite attacks. When fighting in melee combat, it opens with its central head attack, and if the poison from its spittle does not kill the foe, Cerberus makes a trip attack to drag the unfortunate victim to the ground before worrying it with its two extra head attacks, and the nest of serpents serving as its tail. For the purpose of overcoming damage reduction, Cerberus' melee attacks all count as magical, evil, and epic.

Petrification gaze (Su): As a full round action, Cerberus can turn a single opponent within 30 feet who fails a DC 26 Fortitude save to stone. The save DC is Charisma-based.

Poison (Ex): Snake tail, Fortitude DC 35, initial damage 1d6 Str, secondary damage 2d6. The save DC is Constitution-based.

Poison spittle (Ex): Bite, Fortitude DC 35, initial damage 3d6 Con, secondary damage death. The save DC is Constitution-based.

Trip (Ex): If Cerberus hits with a bite attack, it can attempt to trip the opponent (+27 modifier) as a free action without making a touch attack or provoking an attack of opportunity. If the attempt fails, the opponent cannot react to trip Cerberus.

Frightful Presence (Ex): Cerberus is unsettling simply by being in its presence. Whenever Cerberus attacks, charges, or bays, all living creatures with 60 feet must succeed a DC 26 Will save or suffer one of the following effects based on their Hit Dice. Creatures with 4 HD or less that fail their Will save become panicked for 4d6 rounds, those with 5 or more HD become shaken for 4d6 rounds. Major divine offspring and the gods are immune to Cerberus's frightful presence. The save DC is Charisma-based.

Regeneration (Ex): Damage from holy or sacred sources deal normal damage to Cerberus. If Cerberus loses a head, another regrows in 3d6 minutes.

Skills: Cerberus's extra two heads give it a +4 racial bonus on Listen, Search, and Spot checks.

MAGICAL LEGENDARY ANIMALS

The Legendary Animal template allows GMs to create unusually fine specimens of animals to show the best of the species. However, there are several instances in the Homeric World of bizarre animals with spell-like or supernatural abilities. For example, what about the Cretan Bull, a massive, snow-white animal capable of walking on water? Some times these creatures serve as omens or as warped span of idle gods. Where legendary animals represent extraordinary breeds of animals, magical legendary animals are perversions.

To make a magical legendary animal, use the legendary animal temple in this chapter, but change the creature's type to magical beast. Refigure hit points and base attack bonus. Apply all of the other modifiers granted by the template.

The magical legendary animal likely has a special property to make it magical. In theory, this creature could have the ability to cast any spell in this book or the *PHB*, some supernatural augmentation, breath weapon or some other unusual continuous effect, like the ability to walk on water at will, or the ability to spew acid, or damage reduction, spell resistance, or something minor like allowing the monster to see perfectly in darkness. Whatever it is, a magical legendary animal has one special feature to make it unique. If the spell-like or supernatural attack or quality improves the monster's combat effectiveness in a minor way, increase the CR by +1. Such increases could include be the ability to change shape, constriction, disease, improved grab, minor poison, a spell-like ability replicating a spell 2nd level or lower, and so on. If the special attack or quality significantly improves its combat effectiveness, such as a continuous spell effect of 3rd level or higher, the ability to summon other monsters, pounce, sonic attacks, breath weapons and so, increase the CR by +2 or higher, depending on the monster.

NEW MONSTERS

You should also feel free to create entirely new monsters for your game. Remember the two possible origins for any monster. Is this new creature the child of a human and god or a human and an animal? If so, what god? What animal? What elements of that animal parent did the child inherit?

The naga, from East Indian mythology, are depicted as either creatures with human heads but snake bodies or creatures that are human above the waist and snake below. They could easily become part of this setting if they were born of a god and a snake, or of a human and a god in snake-form. Monsters born of the gods usually look at least half-human, whereas those cursed by the gods range from mostly human to completely inhuman in appearance.

If you create a cursed monster, then think about the identity of the original person, for he or she should have a history. Which god cursed him or her, and why? The gods curse people for disobedience, sins, or boasting about being better than the gods at something. The curse usually fits the crime. Someone who always blurted out other people's secrets might be cursed with the head of a donkey, braying all the time. Someone who claimed to be a faster runner than Hermes might gain legs of stone or four short, stubby legs that make him walk in circles.

The gods also like giving people multiple body parts, so a monster could have two heads or four arms or three mouths or anything of that sort. This is a more general punishment, so most monsters like this are guilty of general sins, disobedience, and lack of respect, rather than a specific crime against the gods.

These monsters can still have human intelligence. They could wear armor, carry weapons, and lay ambushes. If you want to make them slightly more sympathetic, they could tend cattle, raise crops, and live in nice, quiet homes when they are not out slaughtering innocent people. The juxtaposition of normal and bizarre makes for some very creepy scenes. Imagine a boar-headed monster with tusks and thick bristles everywhere who kills people, but then carves them like a roast and serves them to guests in a handsomely prepared dish.

Ultimately, when creating a new monster in the Homeric setting, make them clearly not human. Even if they have the right number of limbs and are the right height for a human, something about them shows their monstrous nature, as with Medusa's snake hair and her hideous face. Monsters in this world can never pass for normal people, for the gods have marked them, whether deliberately or not. Some of these creatures might not be evil. They might simply be lonely, frustrated, or angry at being shunned from society; but such is their fate. The gods have decreed, however, monsters shall not mingle with men, and they often send heroes to slaughter them.

SPIRITS

While not technically monsters, one cannot talk about supernatural creatures in the Homeric world without mentioning ghosts. When people die, their spirits descend to the Underworld to the kingdom of Hades. Not all spirits go right away, and some do not stay there peacefully. If the individual died before completing some task, or if the fate of his family remains at risk, he may wander the world as a ghost. These spirits rarely appear to mortals directly, but often steal into someone's dreams and communicate with them in that manner.

Ghosts are invisible to most people, though seers and certain spellcasters can detect them, and they pass right through solid objects. The ghosts are not dangerous since they cannot touch anything physical, but they can be unnerving—usually, however, they provide valuable information and timely warnings. Ghosts can be vengeful though, particularly if they were murdered and received no funeral rites. Such ghosts haunt their murderers, appearing in their dreams and preventing them from resting properly. The ghosts may be able to affect a person's luck as well, bringing misfortune to their enemies and providence to their friends and kin.

Ghosts know a great deal about the world, and always know if someone has died. They can be bribed for information with fresh blood, with libations of wine and of milk and honey, and by placing offerings upon their graves or promising to do so.

According to those ghosts who have returned from the Underworld, Hades is a cold, unforgiving place, with bare stone walls and dim lights. Those who are forgotten by their families shudder in dark corners, while those who are properly remembered have the warmth of family affection to shield them from the chill.

CHAPTER TWELVE: TREASURE

Two forces drive many of the men fighting the Trojan War: fame and fortune. Fortune means not only good luck but also material wealth: treasure. For the nobles, this could be a chance to add to their existing riches, as most of the leaders are kings in their own right, having palaces filled with valuables in their homelands. For lesser nobles, though, and the common soldiers, war offered an opportunity to earn far more than they ever could through farming, herding, or hunting. A poor man who showed skill with a blade could become part of his king's army, and as a soldier, he could bring home silver and sometimes even gold to support his family. If gone for years, or never making it back, at least his wife and children would receive his share of the spoils, providing enough to comfortably survive.

Homer's epics feature detail the treasures won on the battlefield. Other Greek tales tell of treasures in dark caves and ancient palaces, as well. Fearsome monsters often guard these troves, only making claiming them more rewarding. So if the characters have reached a position where you feel they should be rewarded, what can you give them?

MUNDANE ITEMS

Though magic exists in this world, most treasures in this setting should be of the mundane variety. Bronze, silver, and gold, whether as coins or talents, are highly prized. Often metals are kept unrefined until needed, so heroes can discover lumps of raw copper, silver, gold, or even foreign tin, imported to create bronze. Iron can also be found here—though it is used for tools rather than jewelry or weapons, it is still valuable. During the funeral games for Patrocleus, Achilles gives a large chunk of raw iron as one of the prizes, saying the winner will not need to buy iron to keep his people in tools and equipment for several years. Talents are too large and valuable for anyone but the richest nobles to possess and coins were rare because they took too much time and effort to make. Most people had small lumps of metal, which they kept in belt pouches.

Jewelry is popular among both the rich and the poor. For the poor, jewelry consists of amber beads, seashells, and copper wire, while the rich had precious gems and gold or silver. Jewelry also makes good currency because it is small and easily carried, and because an expert jeweler can take a lump of gold and craft a ring or necklace worth far more than the original material alone. Unset gems are also valuable and useable as currency—amber and pearls are native to the region, but other gems have made their way here through trade.

General household items have value, particularly if crafted from fine materials. Chairs, stools, and tables can be made of gold, silver, or rare wood with precious metal inlays. Cauldrons and tripods are not only useful but also ceremonial, and can be cast from copper, bronze, or even gold. Bolts of cloth, particularly dyed cloth, are extremely portable, and handsome clothes have value. Wine and olive oil are sources of wealth in many kingdoms, and quantities of either, particularly if the liquid is of high quality, can be worth their weight in gold.

Livestock is another mundane form of treasure. Possession of horses, cattle, sheep, hogs, and goats indicates wealth, so they can also count as treasure. A fast, well-trained horse is worth quite a bit of money, and can aid its new owner in winning yet more fame and fortune. The other animals provide food, leather or hide, and other useful materials.

The most valuable living treasures, however, are women. Soldiers claim attractive women as prizes, who become their mistresses or servants—or both. These women usually resign themselves to their fate, being well treated and having more luxury than they did before, all in exchange for their freedom. A warrior who mistreats such a woman is dishonorable, so men make an effort to show kindness to their women. Still, they treat them as objects rather than as people.

ITEM VALUE

It is difficult to attach exact monetary values to these treasures, particularly since they can vary depending upon the location. In a land filled with cattle, a heifer has less value. Fast horses are always expensive, however, and beautiful women skilled at needlework or singing or other decorative skills always have value.

Of course, the type of treasure available depends upon the situation. If the characters defeat a troop of enemy soldiers on the battlefield, they will not find women, sheep, and casks of wine lying nearby. Instead, they acquire some money and possibly some jewelry, but most of the wealth consists of the fallen soldiers' weapons and armor. Armor and weaponry has more than monetary value; it also gives the victor prestige by showing the caliber of man he defeated. Warriors are quick to strip their victims of arms and armor, and keep such trophies in their own tents. If they survive through the war, they carry these items home to display on their walls. The quality of the armor varies, depending on the wealth and martial prowess of the victims, and the better the items, the more value they have.

A weapon or piece of armor can have value in three different ways: its materials, its craftsmanship, and its history. An item made from good materials has value because of its composition. A gold-handled bronze sword is worth more than a silver-handled bronze sword, which is worth more than a wood-handled or leather-wrapped bronze sword. Craftsmanship is about how well the materials are used, which can be the effectiveness of the item or the artistic quality of it. A bronze cuirass with delicate gold traceries on it is no more effective in battle than a regular bronze cuirass, but it appears more impressive, and so it is worth more.

On the other hand, a layered bronze cuirass might look the same as a regular bronze cuirass, but it is more valuable because its layers offer more protection. The item's history derives from its origin, its previous owners, and its current owner. The armor of Agamemnon is handsome, well made, and layered, but its real value lies in the fact that it belonged to the King of Cyprus, who sent it to Agamemnon as a gift. Such armor, worn by two kings in succession, is a royal prize to anyone who can claim it.

MAGIC ITEMS

Magic items exist in the Homeric world, but they are not common. To create a magic item, the crafter must channel the power of the gods or his personal inner power. Not many people can do either, and so use their gifts sparingly. Magic items should be rare in this setting.

In **Chapter Ten: Captains of Legend**, the major figures of the war carry at least one magic weapon or piece of armor. They have access to these items because they are the greatest warriors and leaders of their two nations, and some of them are directly descended from the gods. A lesser noble might have one enchanted item, a simple *+1 short sword* or *+1 round shield*, but no more. Common soldiers have no magic at all. Finding even a *+1 short sword* is a rare and marvelous thing, and the weapon is likely the handsomest of gifts any footman or lesser charioteer has ever seen.

Items with specific powers are even more rare. Crafting these items requires more power, more concentration, and a higher level of skill. Most magic items in the Homeric world are unique items, hand-crafted by some magician or priest for a specific individual and a particular purpose. No one creates *extending shields* or *universal wands* by the dozens, or manufactures them to sell at a bazaar; they make one item, and offer it as a gift for their king or to some hero who perhaps saved their life.

Does that mean only one *extending shield* exists in the world? No, because the idea of that particular item is simple enough for anyone to think of and create. Each *extending shield*, *universal wand*, or any other magic item has its own story. When you include a magic item in the treasure haul, you should know its history before the characters find it. Who fashioned the item? Where were they from? Who was the item for? What happened to that person? Did the item have other owners since then?

The characters probably will not know any of these details right away, unless a bard is in company, but with the right spells or the right skill checks, they can discover this information and learn the item's history. This history makes the item even more valuable. Finding a *+1 ring of protection* is one thing, but finding a ring that the magician Themius fashioned for the king of Crete, whose wife then stole it to ensure his death at the hands of her lover, is far more exciting. The item has more value because it touched such illustrious hands and because it figures into such a prominent story.

Mundane treasures can also have stories, and valuable items, whether mundane or magical, should have a history, but the GM should create stories for *all* magical items. In this world, finding a magic item is not simply a question of acquiring treasure; it is also a way of taking part in the legends of the past and shaping the legends of the future.

The only exceptions to the idea that magic items are unique are organic items like *moly* or items that gain power from their material or their creator, like the *purple silk* (see **Wondrous Items**, page 121 for both). The nymphs make bales of this silk, and it is all enchanted because they are magical creatures themselves, and by working the cloth, they grant it some magic.

The silk is rare, since constructing it is a slow process, but even so, it is worth less than most of the other items listed below. *Moly*, on the other hand, is a plant properly harvested and prepared. Anyone could find the plant and carve off pieces from it, but without the proper knowledge and skill, they would have nothing more than some nonmagical leaves or roots. Thus, *moly* is very valuable because few people know how to prepare it.

Most of the existing magic item types can be used in this setting without alteration. Weapons and armor are very popular items to enchant, though obviously, only the types of armor and weaponry found in this region—no one would make a suit of magical full plate, but most kings have an enchanted cuirass.

Wands are popular, since magicians require them to cast magic—a magical wand might let the magician use a particular spell more often than normal, or give him access to spells he does not have.

Kings, both as a symbol of office and as a weapon, often carry rods. Travelers, herdsmen, and old men often use staffs for support or defense. Both men and women wear jewelry, and it provides decoration and an easy means for carrying wealth.

Potions are perhaps the least common type of magical treasure in the Homeric world; more often a wine is enchanted instead. To convert existing potions to this style, simply make them into wine that has been given certain spell-like properties. This also helps mask the flavor of any magical ingredients. Wondrous items, while not common, do appear in many stories, and often form the principle treasure in a tale.

NEW MAGIC ITEMS

The following magic items expand those found in the *DMG*. The prices below assume the standard pricing as found in the core rulebooks. Adjust their value based on the currency system you employ. See **Chapter Six: Equipment** for details.

ARMS AND ARMOR

EXTENDING SHIELD

This shield is a sturdy *+2 bronze round shield*. On speaking the command, however, a circle of bronze and one of leather slide downward, transforming it into a *+2 bronze dyplon shield*. Upon saying the command word again, those two lower layers slide back up, making the shield smaller and easier to carry once more.

Faint abjuration; CL 4th; Craft Magic Arms and Armor, *adjust*; Price 5,250 gp; Cost 2,500 gp + 200 XP.

SINGING SWORD

This *+1 keen bronze short sword* sings on command. It has a lovely female voice, and any male hearing its song, except the wielder, must make a Will save (DC 15) or be affected as if by hypnotism for 2d4 rounds.

Faint enchantment; CL 5th; Craft Magic Arms and Armor, *hypnotism*; Price 17,310 gp; Cost 8,500 gp + 680 XP.

SYMPATHETIC SPEAR

The bronze head of this *+1 throwing spear* has been enchanted to resonate with any bronze it encounters. The head passes through bronze armor or shields as if they did not exist, as if under the effects of the *sheer* spell.

Faint transmutation; CL 3rd; Craft Magic Arms and Armor, *shear*; Price 26,300 gp; Cost 13,000 gp + 1,040 XP.

STABBING SPEAR

The haft of thus *+1 throwing spear* can extend to become a footman's spear on command.

Faint transmutation; CL 5th; Craft Magic Arms and Armor, *adjust*; Price 12,300 gp; Cost 6,000 gp + 480 XP.

WONDROUS ITEMS

BAND OF TRUTH

This heavy gold ring allows rulers to know whether their subjects speak the truth. Anyone who kisses the ring must succeed a DC 13 Will save or be unable to lie for the next 2 minutes.

Faint enchantment; CL 3rd; Craft Wondrous Item, *zone of truth*; Price 12,000 gp

BEGGING BOWL

This simple but well-crafted wooden bowl is highly prized among beggars because its magic encourages people toward charity. On command, the bowl forces a target within 10 feet to succeed a DC 14 Will save or feel compelled to give the beggar something, as if under the effect of *suggestion*. The gift must have real value—food and drink are acceptable, but trash or old bones are not.

Faint enchantment; CL 5th; Craft Wondrous Item, *suggestion*; Price 27,000 gp; Weight 1 lb.

CAP OF NIGHT

A master scout crafted this close-fitting leather cap to make his nighttime forays even easier. The wearer gains a +5 bonus to Hide and Move Silently checks. In addition, he gains the benefit of *darkvision*, as the spell, for as long as he wears the cap.

Faint transmutation; CL 3rd; Craft Wondrous Item, *darkvision*; Price 29,000 gp; Weight 1 lb.

GROWING TRIPOD

This rather strange but undeniably useful device looks like a thick bronze circle with three large studs placed evenly around its sides. Once per day, upon speaking the command word, the studs suddenly start to grow, becoming sturdy bronze legs and transforming the ring into a very solid tripod. Speaking the command word again causes the legs to shrink back into simple studs.

Faint transmutation; CL 5th; Craft Wondrous Item, *stone shape*; Price 750 gp; Weight 2 lb.

HIDDEN CHAINS

These chains are patterned after the invisible chains of Hephaestus. Though not as impressive, these sturdy iron chains are still difficult to see—anyone looking for them must make a Spot check (DC 16) or think the chains are simply shadows. The chains are otherwise normal iron links and manacles.

Faint illusion; CL 3rd; Craft Wondrous Item, *silent image*; Price 1,500 gp; Weight 10 lb.

LIBATION CUP

These wine cups are always handsomely made, and made either of silver with gold trim or of pure gold. A priest blesses each cup as soon as it is finished, and from then on, it is reserved for libations to the gods. Double Piety points earned from libations made with this cup. If anyone but a god ever drinks from the cup, it instantly loses this power.

Moderate evocation; CL 7th; Craft Wondrous Item, divine power; Price 10,800 gp; Weight 3 lb.

LOTUS, DRIED

These dried and preserved lotus flowers come from the Land of the Lotus Eaters. Anyone who eats one must make a DC 15 Will save (DC 15) or instantly forget everything. The effect fades 1d4 hours after consumption of the last flower.

Moderate enchantment; CL 10th; Craft Wondrous Item, *modify memory*; Price 1,000 gp; Weight —.

MOLY

This herb has magical properties if collected and prepared in a particular fashion. Those touching *moly* with their bare skin gain spell resistance 21 for 9 minutes. *Moly* remains potent for 2d4 hours after it is cut and prepared. It can be wrapped in grape leaves to retain its magic longer, in which case, after unwrapping it, it has only 1d4 hours of magic.

Moderate abjuration; CL 9th; Craft Wondrous Item, Craft (alchemy) 12 ranks, *spell resistance*; Price 2,250 gp; Weight —.

PURPLE SILK

The nymphs of Ithaca create this thin purple silk in their hidden cave by the sea. It is valued its color, smooth texture, and strength. *Purple silk* can be used to create armor or shields, which have the same strength as comparable items made of leather but weight a quarter less. Anyone trying to craft armor or shields from this fabric needs at least 5 ranks in each of the following skills: Craft (armorsmithing), Craft (weaving), and Profession (tailor). Armor fashioned from purple silk has no armor check penalty and no chance for arcane spell failure. Light armor made of purple silk costs 5,000 gp more than normal, Medium armor 10,000 gp more than normal. Note only armor normally made from organic materials can be made of purple silk. Purple silk armor may be enchanted as normal.

RUNNER'S SANDALS

These handsome ox-hide sandals have straps that lace around and up the calves. Anyone wearing both sandals, once per day on command, can increase their base land speed by 30 feet, counting as an enhancement bonus, for 1 hour.

Faint transmutation; CL 3rd; Craft Wondrous Item, Extend Spell, *expeditious retreat*; Price 2,400 gp; Weight 1 lb.

STYGIAN SALVE

Collected from the river Styx, this rare salve can be used to coat the body. It thickens to form a horny protective coating, increasing the user's AC by +4 but reducing his Charisma by –2. The salve dries and flakes off after 1d4 hours. A single 10-oz. jar contains enough salve for one Medium creature.

Faint transmutation; CL 3rd; Craft Wondrous Item, *stygian armor*; Price 300 gp; Weight 1/2 lb.

TRAVEL MAT

This handy item looks like a small scrap of cloth when folded, barely large enough for a napkin. When unfolded, it becomes a thick rug fully eight feet long and eight feet wide. This can be used as a sleeping mat—the owner can fold it over and then sleep on top of it on warm nights, or sleep between the two halves in cooler weather. As it is folded back up, it becomes smaller and thinner and lighter, until it is fully folded and back to its scrap appearance.

Moderate conjuration; CL 7th; Craft Wondrous Item, *secure shelter*; Price 11,200 gp; Weight 1/4 lb.

WIND BAG

This lesser version of *Aeolus' bag of wind* (see below) is popular among sailors. The large leather bag holds enough wind for 1d4 strong gusts (treat as 1d4 *gust of wind* spells). It can also be used to capture wind and store it until needed. To capture the wind, the wielder must open the bag and succeed a DC 18 Reflex save. Capturing wind can only be performed when the bag is already empty. Once captured, the wind bag stores 1d4 more uses of *gust of wind*.

Faint evocation; CL 3rd; Craft Wondrous Item, *gust of wind*; Price 12,000 gp; Weight 1 lb.

STAFF AND SPECIAL WAND

WATER STAFF

Many believe Poseidon blessed these staffs. Crafted from coral and capped with mother-of-pearl, this staff allows the following spells:

- water breathing (1 charge)
- water walk (1 charge)
- glass wave (1 charge)

Moderate transmutation; CL 9th; Craft Staff, water breathing, water walk, glass wave; Price 29,530 gp.

UNIVERSAL WAND

These handsomely made wands, crafted of polished rosewood and capped in silver, are the preferred treasure of magicians everywhere. Normally, a magician must craft his own wand to prepare it for his spells. These wands, created by master magicians, are already prepared. Any magician, upon finding one of these wands, can spend an hour meditating over it and, with a successful DC 15 Intelligence check makes the wand his own. In doing so, he erases any previous spells or charges in the wand. He can attempt to read the wand first (see the **Magician** in **Chapter 3: Character Class**) to learn any new spells it contains. The other advantage to a universal wand is that it has been enchanted for strength, and is more durable than normal wands (30 hp, hardness 25).

The only drawback to a universal wand is that another magician can steal it and claim it for himself just as easily, so most magicians who find one use the spell *treasured possession* to keep it close by.

Strong universal; CL 12th; Craft Wand; Price 6,500 gp + any spells it contains; Weight 1 lb.

ARTIFACTS

Some items in the Homeric setting can be considered artifacts. These are items of major legend. They are not simply owned by an important hero or king, but are instrumental in some major event, like the recovery of a lost city, the rescue of a beautiful maiden, or the death of a hideous monster. The gods have blessed these items for their participation in such important stories, and so the items now carry a holy aura, even if a mortal smith originally created them. Many artifacts, in fact, originally held no magic at all until after the event, when the god's blessing gave them magical abilities. Only the gods can create artifacts. Every artifact radiates an overwhelming divine aura, and they should be considered holy items.

MINOR ARTIFACTS

Either men originally these items and bestowed them onto the gods for blessings, or the gods created the objects themselves. Great heroes and kings own most of these minor artifacts.

AEOLUS' BAG OF WIND

This large sack contains the four winds. If the bag is opened, one or more of the winds can escape. Each is the equivalent of the spell *gust of wind* as cast by a 15th-level magician, except the wind lasts for 1d6 minutes. Once per day, if it is windy, the bag's owner can try to capture another wind (if the bag has three or less left at the time). Capturing the wind requires a DC 10 Reflex save. Failure indicates the wind was not captured.

Strong evocation; CL 18th; Weight 3 lb.

AGAMEMNON'S ARMOR

This *+6 chased burnished layered bronze panoply* includes a handsome pair of greaves with silver ankle clips and a four-layered plumed helmet. The most stunning piece, however, is the cuirass, which King Cinyras of Crete gave to Agamemnon. The cuirass has two layers of bronze, but atop the outer layer are enameled strips: 10 of dark blue enamel, 12 of gold, and 20 of tin. Six iridescent enameled snakes, which rise up three on each side, encircle the neck of the cuirass. This cuirass protects Agamemnon from any poison of any kind. Finally, anyone seeing this cuirass must make a DC 15 Will save or become panicked.

Strong enchantment; CL 20th; Weight 25 lb.

ARMOR OF ACHILLES

Hephaestus fashioned this *+8 layered tempered burnished chased bronze panoply* for Achilles after Hector claimed the armor of Peleus. The armor is decorated with elaborate scenes of combat, and it strikes fear into the heart of opponents, as per the *cause fear* spell as cast by a 20th level magician. In addition, the wearer gains immunity to all fear spells and effects.

Strong enchantment; CL 21st; Weight 20 lb.

GOLD SHIELD OF NESTOR

This *+6 burnished layered round shield* has an inner layer of bronze but an outer layer of gold. Its wielder can calm any horse within a 60-ft. radius as per the *calm animals* spell cast by a 20th level caster.

Moderate enchantment; CL 12th; Weight 15 lb.

GOLDEN CHARIOT

The golden chariot was part of Poseidon's wedding present to Peleus, who then gave it to Achilles. The chariot is made of bronze with gold inlays, and gives its driver +5 competence bonus to Drive checks and +2 bonus to all Strength or Dexterity checks or skill checks related to driving and to controlling the horses.

Strong transmutation; CL 23rd.

HECTOR'S SILVER HELMET

This *+2 burnished silver helmet* was a present from Apollo himself. It provides its wearer with a +2 bonus to Will saves and +4 bonus against light-based attacks or spells.

Strong abjuration; CL 21st; Weight 5 lb.

HERACLES' CLOAK

Heracles' cloak is the skin of the Nemean lion, a beast invulnerable to weapons. The cloak grants its wearer a +6 deflection bonus AC, and has grants its wearer damage reduction 20/bludgeoning.

Strong abjuration; CL 20th; Weight 10 lb.

INOS' SCARF

This delicate sea-green silk scarf, when wound about the waist, shields the wearer from any damage dealt by a water source. If the wearer is submerged, he immediately floats to the surface again at will. However, he can breathe underwater as if under the effects of the *water breathing* spell. To use this minor artifact, the user cannot wear any other clothing or armor.

Strong transmutation; CL 18th.

IRON MACE OF AREITHOUS

King Areithous was known as the Mace man because his favored weapon was this *+2 heavy mace of speed*. In addition to its normal effects, its wielder gains the benefits of Great Cleave and the Lion in the Field feats while wielding it as his primary weapon.

Strong transmutation; CL 20th; Weight 8 lb.

ODYSSEUS' BOW

This *+7 composite [+8] longbow* originally belonged to Eurytus, the archer King of Oechalia, who had taught Heracles how to use the bow. Iphitus, Eurytus's son and an old ally of Laertes presented the bow to young Odysseus as a mark of their friendship. It cannot be strung by anyone with a Strength less than 18 or fired by anyone with a base attack bonus of less than +10. Odysseus left the bow in Ithaca before leaving for the Trojan War.

Strong transmutation; CL 36th; Weight 3 lb.

ORION'S BRONZE MACE

Orion wielded this *+4 heavy mace* in battle, and when he transformed into a constellation, his weapon remained in the world of mortals. The wielder of Orion's Bronze Mace gains a +2 to bonus to their Strength and Constitution, and may cast *heroism* once per day as a free action cast by a 20th level spellcaster.

Strong enchantment and transmutation; CL 20th; Weight 8 lb.

SCEPTER OF ATREUS

Hephaestus crafted this studded golden scepter for Zeus, who gave it to Hermes, who then gave it to Pelops. When Pelops left his kingdom in the hands of Atreus and Thyestes, he gave them the scepter as the sign of rulership. Atreus eventually passed it to his son, Agamemnon. The scepter functions as a *+6 heavy mace* and grants the wielder a +4 bonus to his Charisma score.

Strong transmutation; CL 18th; Weight 8 lb.

SHIELD OF PELEUS

Hephaestus fashioned this *+2 burnished five-layered round bronze shield* for Achilles, and it matches his armor. The shield is decorated in fabulous designs of constellations, cities, fields, and men. Any foe who faces the man carrying this shield must succeed a DC 20 Will save become panicked.

Strong enchantment; CL 20th; Weight 40 lb.

SHIELD OF AJAX

This huge *+8 tower shield* has seven layers of ox-hide and one of bronze. It is so large that it requires a 16 Strength bonus to carry. It is built specifically for Ajax and is large enough to cover two individuals.

Strong transmutation; CL 30th; Weight 85 lb.

SICKLE OF ADAMANTE

Gaea gave this unbreakable *+6 keen vorpal sickle* to her son, the Titan Chronos, to castrate his father Uranus. Zeus later used it to fight the monster Typhon, and Hermes used it against Argus Panoptes. The last known use of the sickle was when Perseus borrowed it from Hermes to sever Medusa's head. It has since vanished.

Strong transmutation; CL 36th; Weight 2 lb.

SPEAR OF PELEUS

This impressive *+8 keen throwing spear* has an ash wood shaft (from an ash tree on Mount Pelion) and a long bronze head.

Chiron the centaur crafted it and gave it to Peleus as a wedding present. Peleus gave it to Achilles for the war.

Strong transmutation; CL 20th; Weight 4 lb.

SWORD OF PELEUS

This *+5 keen bronze longsword of speed* was given to Peleus as a wedding present. He gave it to Achilles when he went off to the war.

Strong transmutation; CL 18th; Weight 4 lb.

MAJOR ARTIFACTS

These items belong to the gods themselves. They jealously guard them, so few mortals have ever seen a major artifact. Anyone who dares to steal one earns the displeasure of the item's true owner.

AEGIS

The aegis can be either a *+4 layered round bronze shield* or a *+4 layered bronze cuirass* with tassels around the edges. It belongs to Zeus, but his daughter Athena normally carries it in his stead. At its center, in place of a boss is the head of a woman with snakes for hair. This is Medusa the Gorgon, and one glance at her turns anyone who fails a DC 30 Will save to stone as *flesh to stone* cast by a 30th level wizard.. The Aegis also grants an additional +2 deflection bonus to AC rays and touch attacks. In addition, the aegis grants its wielder a +2 bonus all to saving throws against spells and spell-like effects. Finally, the inside of the shield is mirror-bright. As long as the wielder carries the shield, he cannot be flanked.

Strong transmutation; CL 28th; Weight 10 lb.

CADUCEUS

This shepherd's staff first belonged to Apollo but he gave it to Hermes in exchange for the lyre. The Caduceus has two snowy wings on either side near the top and two serpents intertwined around it. While holding it Hermes always retains his Dexterity bonus to his Armor Class, and cannot be flanked as if he had both Uncanny Dodge and Improved Uncanny Dodge. Three times each day, the rod gives him the power to fly as per the *overland flight*

spell, for up to one hour at a time. The serpents grant Hermes the power to *speak with animals* at will and to *charm animals* three times each day as per the spell. The rod also gives him a +10 bonus to Disable Device, Hide, Move Silently, and Sleight of Hand checks. When used by someone other than Hermes or someone he has chosen, however, the two serpents come to life and bite the wielder, +20 attack bonus, dealing 2d8 points of damage and poison. The poison has a DC 23 Fortitude save, initial and secondary drain 2d4 Str. Each day after the first, the venom strikes again, forcing the subject of the attack to succeed a new save or takes the Strength drain again. Once poisoned, the subject can only be healed by Hermes or one of his priests.

Strong enchantment and transmutation; CL 30th; Weight 4 lb.

CESTUS

The magic girdle of Aphrodite contains the power of love and inspiration. Anyone wearing the cestus gains +4 bonus to Charisma and can cast a modified version of *charm person*, at will. Anyone targeted by the charm person effect and failing a DC 23 Will save becomes a Fanatic instead of Friendly.

Any NPC whose attitude is fanatic gains a +2 morale bonus to Strength and Constitution scores, a +1 morale bonus on Will saves, and a −1 penalty to AC whenever fighting for the character or his or her cause. This attitude will remains for one day plus one day per point of the character's Charisma bonus (minimum 1 day), at which point the NPC's attitude will revert to its original attitude (or indifferent, if no attitude is specified).

Treat the fanatic attitude as a mind-affecting enchantment effect for purposes of immunity, save bonuses, or detection by the Sense Motive skill. A fanatic will give his life to serve the wearer of the cestus, such as fighting to the death against overwhelming odds, or throwing himself in from of a giant to let cestus-wearer escape.

Strong enchantment; CL 36th.

HELM OF DARKNESS

The *helm of darkness* belongs to Hades. The Cyclops made it during the war against the Titans. Perseus borrowed the Helm during his quest against Medusa. This jet-black helm completely covers Hades' head, and has no eye slits or breathing holes. Once worn, it turns the wearer invisible, as if under the effects of *greater invisibility*, and proof against detection, as if under the effects of an *amulet of proof against detection and location*. The helmet also bestows darkvision out to 120 feet, *water breathing*, as the spell, and immunity to mundane or magical inhaled poisons. The cap can be used for three hours each day, after which it must recharge.

Strong transmutation; CL 36th; Weight 10 lb.

INVISIBLE CHAINS

Hephaestus created these heavy iron chains and used them to capture his wife Aphrodite and her lover Ares. They are invisible except to Hephaestus himself. Each chain, and the manacles attached to them, has a Hardness of 40 and 200 hp. They cannot be opened without a the key, and require a DC 120 Escape Artist check to escape them.

Strong illusion; CL 30th; Weight 40 lb.

PETASUS

Hermes wears this winged cap. When donned, the wearer can assume the appearance of any person he likes, as if under the effect of the *shapechange* spell, except he can perfectly assume the form of any creature, even individuals. The cap also provides the wearer with the benefit of see invisibility and darkvision out to 120 feet.

Strong transmutation; CL 24th; Weight 8 lb.

POSEIDON'S SWORD

The god of the ocean carries this *+4 keen vorpal longsword of speed* into battle. Its blade looks like a frozen wave of water, and can pass through the gaps in any armor as if it had *shear* upon it, but the sword does full damage with each strike.

Strong transmutation; CL 36th; Weight 4 lb.

POSEIDON'S TRIDENT

The Cyclops made this *+4 keen trident* for Poseidon to use in the war against the Titans. Whenever the wielder successful hits a target with the trident, and if a body of water is nearby, the weapon casts *vengeful wave* as a free action, targeting the subject of the attack. If the trident scores a critical hit, it affects the target with horrid wilting as if cast by a 20th-level spellcaster.

Strong transmutation; CL 20th; Weight 4 lb.

SILVER BOWS

There are two silver bows, one for Apollo and the other for his twin sister Artemis. Each bow counts a *+5 composite [+8] longbow*. The bow's range increment, however, is 1,000 feet, and arrows shot from the bow count as *keen* arrows. Arrows fired from *silver bows* are never at risk from miss chances derived from concealment, *invisibility*, or the incorporeal subtype. Finally, the bows are under the effects of the *treasured possession* spell, and so are never far from the gods' reach.

If used by anyone other than Apollo or Artemis, the bow deals 4d8 points of damage each round to the wielder, and the bow imposes a −10 circumstances to all attack rolls. Apollo and Artemis can suppress this aspect of the bow's defenses if they grant permission to the mortal to wield it.

Strong transmutation; CL 38th; Weight 3 lb.

TALARIA

These winged sandals grant a wearer a 120-foot fly speed, with excellent maneuverability, and no more concentration than walking. The sandals can maintain this for four hours each day. When not actively flying, the sandals actually hover just above the ground, allowing the wearer to ignore earthquakes and any other instabilities of the ground, and to move across any surface at full movement rate.

Strong transmutation; CL 28th.

THUNDERBOLTS OF ZEUS

The Cyclops made the thunderbolt for Zeus for the war against the Titans. They have since become the sky god's symbol and favored weapon. Each thunderbolt appears to be a *+3 throwing spear* with a lightning bolt etched along the haft. Once thrown, however, the spear transforms into a 20d6 lightning bolt, as per the *lightning bolt* spell, but with unlimited range. The weapon is consumed when thrown.

Strong evocation; CL 30th; Weight 4 lb.

CHAPTER THIRTEEN: NINE LONG YEARS

Wars can last for years, and each war is comprised of many battles, usually over key locations. Winning a single battle does not mean winning the war, but winning enough battles provides you with a far stronger position.

As a war, the Trojan War is a bit unusual. Not because it lasted so long—modern wars have dragged on for years, as well, but the entire Trojan War occurred on a single battlefield. Taking either of the two key locations involved meant winning not only a battle but also the entire war. In fact, if not for its duration, the conflict would certainly have been labeled a battle instead of a war. Since it lasted for more than nine years (roughly nine and a half, so some call it a decade-long war) and it involved two nations with dozens of kingdoms on each side, it most definitely constitutes a full-scale war.

THE BATTLEFIELD

The Trojan War unfolded before the city of Troy, hence its name. The Achaeans arrived in a fleet of boats, beached them upon the shore, and then marched over the plain toward the city. The Trojans and their allies issued forth from the city, meeting the invaders halfway across that plain. Then the battle began.

Reading the *Iliad*, you discover an interesting fact about the battlefield. On its strongest days, the Achaeans could fight all the way up to the walls of Troy, and on their strongest days, the Trojans could push the Achaeans all the way back to their ships. Each night, however, when the sun went down, battle ceased. Both sides stopped and returned to their strongholds. The Achaeans' stronghold consisted of their camp on the beach around their ships; for the Trojans, it was the city of Troy itself.

Every morning, the Achaeans came from their camp and the Trojans from their city, and met in the middle of the plain to battle. The entire battlefield, from end to end, could be crossed in a single day! On some days, the Achaeans pushed to the walls of Troy, and then the Trojans would repulse them, or the Trojans would get to the Achaean camp, but they would be turned back; so, they could actually cover the field in half a day if the way remained unobstructed. Given that a man can walk about three miles in a single hour, and that Troy probably had 12 hours of daylight (around six A.M. to about six P.M.), the entire field could not have been more than 20 miles long. That is a large plain, of course, but a small place to hold a war.

Of course, the field was not perfectly flat and empty, either. Near Troy lay several streams and rivers, which flowed down from the mountains. Achilles pursued some Trojan warriors into the Xanthus River once, and was almost overwhelmed by its current, which did more damage to him than any Trojan had managed. The banks of these waters formed one boundary of the battlefield, and just beyond them stood the mountains. In quieter times, the Trojan women often carried their wash to these streams, though during the war, they did not dare to leave the city.

No much is known about what lay on the other side, but it may have been hilly, too irregular for chariots and too difficult even for armored men to cross. Homer does mention grassy meadows where the Trojans grazed their sheep, though, and these may have been along this side.

At one end of the field stood the city of Troy, with its high stone walls. The ground sloped up slightly at this end, giving the city an excellent vantage over the area.

At the other end, the field narrowed, with hills rising up on either side to form a bottleneck. Past this point, the land widened again, becoming sandier as it reached the sea. This area past the bottleneck actually formed a small peninsula of its own, and made the ideal landing place for boats approaching the city.

Upon their arrival, the Achaeans beached their fleet all along the peninsula, forming a row of black boats stretching from end to end. Ajax Telamonian had the ship at the southern edge, closest to the passage leading onto the plain. At the opposite end were Achilles and his Myrmidons, whose boats were perched on the far edge of the peninsula, easily launched to attack other cities along the coast. Agamemnon, as the commander of the army, had placed his boat at the very center of the line, and his camp, set before it, served as the meeting place for the senior commanders. Right in front of that sat an even larger tent with benches placed all around for the general assembly of the troops.

For the first nine years, the Achaeans did nothing to fortify their position, trusting their strength to keep the Trojans at bay. When Achilles announced he would no longer fight, though, the other commanders realized they might need better defenses. They built a sturdy wall across the bottleneck, with high battlements and a stout palisade, and then dug a wide ditch before it. They set ramps across the ditch so their troops could cross easily, but these could be drawn back to prevent Trojan soldiers and chariots from crossing. A wide set of double gates stood at the center, with thick wooden beams securing it at night. The Achaeans posted sentries along the wall at night to watch the battlefield and the lights of Troy across it.

The Trojans, for their part, did not bother with additional fortifications. Poseidon himself built their outer walls, and they could withstand any attack. Likewise, their strong gates could repel most forces. High towers provided a good vantage to watch the enemy, and Troy's narrow streets confounded any stranger trying to race through them.

Because the field was so small, and so clearly bordered by obstacles, certain military strategies could not be used.

Sneaking up on the Trojans at night proved impossible because they hid within their walled city. Sneaking up on the Achaeans was also impossible because they controlled the only land entry to their peninsula, and the Trojans had no way to get boats around the plain and into the ocean behind them. The hills and rivers along the side prevented armies from circling around and attacking from behind—smaller forces could circle around by skirting the edge of the battlefield, but the enemy could see them approaching and guess their intent. Both sides had a solid wall behind them, and could retreat behind it if necessary, so the only way to surround a force was to overwhelm both sides of the army and force everyone into a smaller area in the center of the field. Both sides had forces waiting behind their respective walls, and they could charge onto the field as reinforcements at a moment's notice. This is why the war raged back and forth in waves, as first the Achaeans and then the Trojans dominated the field, forcing the enemy back before being repulsed again and retreating themselves. Ultimately, guile rather than sheer force that won the war, for without the Trojan Horse the battle could have continued for another decade as neither side had the strength needed to break down the walls and crush their opponents.

DECADE-LONG CONFLICT

If we use the most commonly held date, the Achaeans arrived on the Trojan shores in 1218 BCE. They finally conquered the city, torched it, and left in 1209 or 1208 about 10 years later. The war lasted a full nine years, and finally ended in the tenth year.

What does it mean to spend an entire decade fighting? First, the Achaeans had not seen their homes or their families in 10 years. Odysseus left a wife and a young son—too young to really remember him—back in Ithaca, and it took him another 10 years after the war to return home. By then, his son, Telemachus, was a grown man. Agamemnon and Diomedes' wives turned to lovers in their 10-year absence—but Odysseus' wife Penelope remained faithful the entire time. Many people the warriors had once known, including close family members, were dead and gone when the warriors finally returned home. Children had grown to adulthood and they often had children of their own. Achilles fathered a son, Neoptolemus, in Scyrus shortly before the war, and in the war's final year, Odysseus retrieved the boy, who then fought in his father's place. Of course, Achilles was already dead by then, but if Neoptolemus was old enough to fight, he must have been at least 12, and was probably closer to 14. Those who left behind had 10 long years to nurse grudges, as Clytemnestra did—she never forgave her husband Agamemnon for sacrificing Iphiginia, their daughter, to gain favorable winds on the way to Troy; she spent the 10 years planning her revenge.

The 10-year absence had other consequences for the Achaeans. Most of the Achaean commanders ruled their own kingdoms, and they had taken all of their best fighters with them to the war, thus their kingdoms had no leader and no real defense for an entire decade. Some kingdoms survived intact, but others were conquered easily, and their kings eventually returned to find strangers sitting on their thrones. Business also suffered, since the Achaean leaders were not home to encourage trade, to receive merchants, or to arrange sales of their nation's wares. Furthermore, with so many men gone, many local industries suffered. And each nation brought enormous amounts of food (sheep, oxen, and cattle) with them to weather them through the conflict, leaving their people at home with less to eat.

Nor were the Achaeans the only ones suffering. In some ways, the Trojans had an easier time during the war because they could return home every night to their families. Hector's son, Astyanax, was still so young in the last year of the war that his father's helmet frightened him so he must have been less than nine years old, which means he was born after the war began. Troy also had the home field advantage. Their warriors knew the area, but more than that, they had allies in the neighboring territories that could send reinforcements.

Despite this, the Trojans suffered. They could no longer safely leave their city. Their women used to wash clothes in the nearby river, but the war made that unsafe so they remained imprisoned within the city walls for the full 10 years. Shepherds and herdsmen ran the risk of attack by Achaean raiding parties, and each such attack cost them the animals they herded. In addition, Troy was a major seaport, with the peninsula across the plain providing an easy landing spot for travelers and traders. Since the Achaeans had taken that peninsula as their camp, they effectively landlocked the Trojans. The Trojans, therefore, had no more sea trade, and no access to other lands except over the mountains to either side. Reinforcements sent from neighbors had to scale those hills and cliffs to reach them, and they probably only arrived in small bands. Food would also have been difficult to bring in. The Achaeans could launch attacks at other cities along the coast, taking food supplies from them, but

the Trojans were limited to what they had stored in the city and whatever they dared to farm or herd along the nearby hills.

Of course, the men did not fight nonstop for the full 10 years. Truces occurred several times, during which both sides buried their dead, performed funeral rites, and possibly met together to discuss ending the war. Some of these truces ended in duels, such as the one where Paris fought Menelaus. Others involved Achaean envoys going to Troy and asking for the return of Helen and money to compensate the army for its losses. The truces never lasted, and none of the meetings resulted in a final agreement, but they did allow both armies a chance to rest and recover. Some scholars claim that, when taken all together, the truces totaled almost three years, which meant the armies only fought for a little over six years, not a full nine or more.

Both armies also respected the military conventions of the day, the most important being that they did not fight at night. Every evening, as dusk approached, the armies returned to their respective strongholds to cleanse themselves and offer libations to the gods before dinner. Every morning, at dawn, both armies gathered and issued forth onto the plain to continue the battle. Ceasing in the evenings allowed the warriors to eat supper each night and get a good night's sleep—both sides kept sentries upon their walls, but this was almost a formality since neither side attacked in the dark.

The armies were also so large and the battlefield so small that neither army could field all of its men at once. Groups hung back, watching the conflict from the far edges of the field or even relaxing behind the walls, but they joined the fight when called. Thus, each army could bring in reinforcements during the day, letting the first wave of troops retreat to eat, bind wounds, and rest before returning again. Even when an army committed all of its forces, troops along the edges had to wait and watch until opponents could reach them.

Of course, the daily fighting took its toll. Men on both sides grew tired of battle. The Achaeans felt righteous indignation the

first year, and the Trojans responded with fierce pride and strong defense. Eventually the war fatigued them both, and the fighting never seeming to end made them weary. The Achaeans could advance all the way to the city walls, but they could not breach the gates. The Trojans could fight through the bottleneck and reach the boats, but they could not set them ablaze. Neither side could claim a certain victory, nor could either see an end to the hostilities. The war had become an accepted part of life for both armies, as if it had always been there and always would be.

Not every warrior had given up. Some became so desperate to succeed, they took bigger risks to gain victory. The leaders on both sides, men of skill and renown, pushed their troops harder to get them to fight, but they also fought harder themselves. Both sides grew frustrated as the enemy refused to quit, surrender, or simply fall, and this hatred kept them fighting.

In the midst of this, allies quarreled. A disagreement flared between Achilles and Agamemnon—partly over the girl Briseis, but that was really just the spark. Their frustration over the continuing war and their inability to defeat the Trojans really fueled the argument. Achilles grew angry that Agamemnon, the army's commander, could not find a way to defeat the Trojan army. Agamemnon, on the other hand, blamed Achilles, his mightiest warrior, for not being able to break the enemy's forces. If the subject of Briseis had come up a few years earlier, it might have been settled more peacefully, but both men were already on edge, and they allowed their frustration to boil over. The other commanders tried to mediate, but many of them felt the same bitterness and fatigue, and they all just wanted the war to end.

What does all this mean for roleplaying? It means, if taken seriously, the Trojan War was not fun and games. It was a long, protracted struggle between two powerful nations, and one neither side would willingly lose. For the Achaeans, the war was a point of pride, proof of their supremacy in the Mediterranean. For the Trojans, it was simple survival

RUNNING PART OF THE WAR

Since the war lasted almost a decade, you do not have to set your game in the final stretch of it. You can select any point throughout the war, from beginning to end, to start your campaign. Be aware, however, that each portion of the war offers different roleplaying possibilities, so you should select the period that best reflects the goal of your game.

ACHAEAN ARRIVAL

Your game could start when the Achaeans first reach the Trojan shore. They have not yet seen Troy itself, or the Trojan army, and have no idea what awaits them. The Trojans, for their part, know the Achaeans are coming—lookouts have warned of the fleet's approach—but they do not realize how large a force they are bringing or how determined they are.

When the Achaeans first land, they send Menelaus and Odysseus to Troy as emissaries to beg Troy to return Helen to avoid war. The Trojans treat the two men well during their stay, and some Trojans even want to acquiesce to their requests, but Paris refuses to surrender her. Thus, two men return to their boats to prepare the army for battle.

This time makes an excellent starting point for a game, especially if the players are not familiar with the *Iliad*. They

can arrive with the rest of the army and discover the plain and the city for themselves. Alternatively, if Trojan, they can meet Menelaus and Odysseus in the assembly, and watch with horror as Paris' stubbornness dooms the entire city to war. Since the fighting has not started yet, the characters can even try to stop it, whether by reasoning with Paris, begging the Achaeans to change their minds, or even stealing Helen to return her to the Achaeans themselves.

CONSCRIPTIONS

For that matter, the game could start before the Achaeans ever land. It took several years for Agamemnon and Menelaus to gather all of the other leaders and troops. Many young nobles were eager for the chance to fight and win glory, not realizing they would be gone ten years. Others were not so enthusiastic, and some even tried to avoid the summons, by hiding or by claiming a disability (as with Odysseus, who pretended madness). This is an exciting time for characters to play. The entire Achaean is buzzing with the news that the kings are going to war. Every young man who can carry a spear hopes to go to war to win money and fame.

Nor were the Trojans idle during this time. Paris, the king's son, returned home with a beautiful woman named Helen.

The people learned she was married to Menelaus, the king of Sparta, and Paris had abducted her (even though she went willingly—since she was already married, it counted as an abduction). Most of the Trojans grew furious with him, his brother Hector most of all. Some knew Menelaus would come for her with an army.

The abduction has already occurred, and Trojans are in turmoil during this period. Some beg Paris to return Helen, others look for ways to appease Menelaus and his brother, and others still prepare for war.

SAILING TO TROY

It took the Achaean fleet some time to reach Troy because they stopped along the way to acquire fresh food and drink, to make repairs, and to pirate. Pirating gave the men a chance to practice with their weapons, to earn some renown, and to gain booty. The Achaeans did not just stop to visit or to trade; they attacked almost every city they encountered along the way. In other words, for at least a year, the Achaeans raided coastal towns and looted small kingdoms.

Using this period as a starting point allows you to run a *Trojan War* game filled with battle and danger away from Troy. Characters can be members of the fleet, putting in at various ports to attack the locals and loot their homes. While some cities make easy targets, others fight back. The Achaeans always win, but some victories are hard-fought ones.

The Trojans during this time are in a state of heightened alarm. They hear reports of the approaching Achaean fleet destroying towns all along the coast. With the Achaeans en route, they know it is too late to send Helen back. They might be searching for ways to appease them, however. Just in case, the Trojans start preparing for war, and begin sending messengers to their allies with requests for aid.

Characters can play messengers or Trojan nobles sent over the mountains to neighboring kingdoms, carrying news of approaching war as they try to win promises of support from these other lands.

EARLY CONFLICT

The early conflict consists of the first two years of the war. During this period, both armies are still learning about their foes, taking their measure, finding out who the leaders are, and getting a sense of who is the most dangerous.

The Achaeans are still learning the terrain, as well, and getting used to living out of tents rather than their own homes. The Achaean forces may try climbing the hills and mountains, hoping to find ways to flank Troy. For the Trojans, they slowly realize they are isolated from the rest of the world, particularly by sea. The Trojans may be roaming the mountains in search of escape routes or ways to obtain supplies from other lands.

The Trojans are still using the surrounding fields for their livestock, and the Achaeans start to launch raids against them as they learn the lay of the land.

Characters may play explorers, making new discoveries about the terrain to aid the war, or they might offer tactics on how to fight the war.

MIDDLE CONFLICT

The next seven years count as the middle conflict. Both armies settle on tactics. The Achaeans are firmly entrenched on the peninsula, while the Trojans pull everyone into the city proper, including the livestock. Both sides realize they cannot attack from behind, and so the only route remains across the battlefield. The war wages back and forth, with occasional truces.

This is probably the least exciting time for a game. The battles continue, with both sides resigned to the conflict. Everyone realizes that this will not be a quick, easy victory, and many young men begin losing their taste for battle. They know now, even if they win fame and fortune, it will take years before anyone learns of it. The army commanders have given up on finding a quick solution or a sudden hole in their enemy's forces, and they now resign themselves to winning through sheer force and stubbornness. This does not mean that this period has nothing going on, but it has all become routine.

Characters in this period are probably soldiers slugging it out on the front line.

SIDE BATTLES

The Trojans are pinned down within their walls throughout the war, unable to do more than fight on their doorstep and send small parties into the mountains for information, materials, or aid. This is not true of the Achaeans. With the sea at their back, they can easily pull their boats into the water and set sail. The Achaeans make frequent trips to towns and villages along the coast, sacking them just as they did when first approaching Troy.

These side battles serve three purposes. First, it prevents nearby nations from gathering forces to aid the Trojans, and it prevents them from sailing in and attacking the Achaeans from behind. Second, it keeps the troops active, giving them something to do during truces. It also provides some easy victories to bolster morale. Finally, attacking these other towns provides fresh booty: food, drink, and actual treasure. This is how the Achaeans keep themselves supplied; when supplies run low, they send out ships to restock through force.

Of course, these activities do not always go as planned. Some of those coastal towns have strong defenses, and some can repulse the Achaean invaders. When that happens, the Achaeans simply send a larger force—they do not need many men to protect the bottleneck, and during a truce, they only need a few sentries to make their camp look occupied.

The Achaeans earn many enemies from these side trips, of course, but it does not concern them much. They are the single strongest force on the coast, and everyone knows it. They are already fighting the only people strong enough to stand up to them. With Troy occupied, the smaller kingdoms are defenseless.

These small forays make excellent adventures. Characters can man an Achaean warship, launching attacks up and down the coastline, capturing whatever they can store. Some of these adventures last longer than others, and the characters can easily wind up staying in a village or small city for a week or two, making sure it has been properly defeated and finding any treasure they might have missed along the way.

PLAGUE

Near the middle of the ninth year, the priest Chryses finally reaches the Achaeans. He begs them to return his daughter, Chryseis, and he has brings a great deal of treasure with him to trade for her safe return. The Achaeans call an assembly to discuss the matter. Most of them are in favor of the trade—the wealth he offers is more than enough to compensate for her, and he is a priest (of Apollo), which means he should be respected. However, Agamemnon, who claimed Chryseis for himself, refuses to give her up, and he insults the priest and sends him away. As revenge, Chryses begs Apollo to punish the Achaeans, and the archer god sends a plague upon them. The warriors sicken and die, and the army thins drastically. Everyone is horrified—losing friends in battle is one thing, but having them sicken and die in camp is another, and clearly this is a sign of a deity's displeasure. Moreover, the remaining Achaeans have to fight even harder to keep the Trojans from overrunning them.

This is an interesting period for a game, and it is the closest to horror you will find in this setting. The plague literally descends from nowhere—men are healthy one day, coughing the next, and dead the following morning. Moreover, it can hit anyone, though it seems to bypass the army's leaders, striking the regular soldiers instead. Hundreds, possibly thousands, die from it, and funeral pyres light up the peninsula. The Achaeans believe strongly in the gods, and this is obviously not a natural illness, so they all know the god punish them. The quick decimation terrifies them.

HECTOR

For the Achaean leaders, this time is even worse. Though they are not sick, their men die all around them, and they cannot do anything to stop it. Some realize Agamemnon caused the plague by insulting Chryses and refusing to return his daughter, and this is even more frightening than the plague. Agamemnon is their leader, the overlord of the Achaean nation, and if he has become so selfish and unreasoning, putting everyone at risk, then his every order is questionable. Many leaders, even if they do not connect his behavior to the plague, are horrified that he refuses to give Chryseis back. It is reminiscent of Paris refusing to return Helen, and the similarity makes them wonder: if the first event led to this war, what will this more recent parallel bring? Whatever it is, the results cannot be good.

Some of the Trojans take heart from the Achaeans' suffering, seeing their army growing smaller, and hoping to finally drive them back to the sea. However, others are not so comfortable. After all, illness can strike anyone of any nation. They worry the plague may spread to their own. Still, other Trojans recognize the hand of the gods, and worry, if the gods pay such close attention to the war, then maybe they could be next to earn a god's displeasure.

This time is excellent for gaming because it is filled with suspense, danger, indecision, and mistrust.

THE ILIAD

The most famous portion of the Trojan War is the end of the ninth year and start of the tenth. The *Iliad* details this period. Beginning with Calchas, the Achaean seer, who revealed Apollo sent the plague as punishment because Agamemnon would not return Chryseis. This leads to the argument between Agamemnon and Achilles, and Achilles declares he will no longer fight the Trojans. With him and his Myrmidons out of the picture and the Achaeans already diminished by the plague, the Trojans have their best chance at defeating the invaders for good. The battle becomes fierce again. The Trojans fill with hope, while the Achaeans fill with desperation; several notable leaders fall on both sides. The Achaeans build a wall before their camp, but the Trojans overrun it and almost manage to set the boats aflame. Finally, Achilles allows his friend Patrocleus to wear his armor and drive the Trojans back from the boats. When Patrocleus pursues the Trojans onto the field, Hector kills him, enraging Achilles. Achilles makes amends with Agamemnon, and returns to the battle, filling the Achaeans with hope and the Trojans with dread. Achilles destroys several Trojan leaders, and finally kills Hector, the Trojan commander. He drags Hector's body behind him all the way across the field. The Achaeans hold funeral games to honor Patrocleus, and King Priam comes to Achilles to beg for the return of his son's body. Achilles finally agrees, and Priam returns to Troy with Hector's corpse to prepare it for burial.

This is the obvious choice for a game because it is the most exciting time in the war. Things change rapidly throughout this period. When Achilles steps aside, the Trojans think they have finally won, and they almost do. Then, when he returns, the Achaeans think they can finally take Troy, and they come close to succeeding. Several major figures die on both sides, and everyone senses the war will soon end.

CLOSING CONFLICT

The last few weeks of the Trojan War are just as tumultuous. Paris shoots Achilles with an arrow, killing him, not long after Hector's death. Paris is killed in turn, leaving very few Trojan princes left, and the Trojans begin to despair. The Achaeans finally turn to prophesy for help, and they bring Achilles' son, Neoptolemus, into the battle, along with the bow of Heracles. Finally, they tire of fighting openly, and Odysseus suggests a clever ruse involving a large wooden horse. The plan works, and a group of Achaeans sneak into the city at night, killing its leaders, and then throwing open the gates for the rest of the army to enter. They overtake Troy, and the war ends.

This period is the last hurrah of the war for both sides. The Achaeans feel they can finally win the conflict, while the Trojans begin to realize their doom. Characters may play Trojan forces

desperately seeking some way to stave off disaster, or they can be Achaeans looking for stratagems to overtake the city. The Achaeans also send several groups to retrieve the people and items mentioned in the prophecies, which provides a good opportunity for adventures. Characters can be part of the mission to find Neoptolemus, and they can bring him back to fight the Trojans. Alternatively, they can be a part of the group that searches for Philoctetes in the wilderness of Lemnos, bringing him back, along with the bow and arrows of Heracles. Several Achaeans also sneak into Troy to steal the sacred icon known as the Palladium, and this can be an exciting adventure for the characters, as well.

On the Trojans' part, they are hunting for a way to save their city and themselves. They send envoys to new lands in search of military support, and others petition the gods for divine protection. Characters can be part of these groups, or they can come up with their own plan to protect the city. Some characters may even approach the Achaeans and beg for mercy.

AFTER THE WAR

Of course, after the war ends, the Achaeans still have to get home. So do the Trojan allies. Though many died during the sack, some may have escaped the carnage. For more about this period, see the **Aftermath** on page 136 for details.

Ultimately, pick any time during the Trojan War for the start of your game. The key is finding the portion of the conflict with the feel you want, whether that is initial enthusiasm, quiet resolve, or burgeoning panic. In addition, you should consider how long your game will last. If you run a *Trojan War* campaign for the next several years, it might be a good idea to start with the beginning of the war, so you do not run out of material before your campaign ends.

CHOOSING SIDES

Do your players want to be the Achaeans or the Trojans? This is the first question you should ask before starting your *Trojan War* game.

Both sides were powerful forces, as shown by their ability to maintain the war for nine plus years. Both sides had impressive leaders and several gods on their side. Both sides had a great deal to lose if defeated.

ACHAEANS

The Achaeans were strong, fast, and deadly in battle. They had an impressive fleet of ships, dangerous charioteers, and wave after wave of determined footmen. Why play them?

To start, the Achaeans are the invading force. That means they do not know the territory, the neighboring kingdoms, or even the animals prowling the hills. Everything is new, offering opportunities for the characters to discover things both useful and deadly. They can also freely explore the area, as most Trojans are contained within their city effectively giving the Achaean forces run of the area.

The Achaeans also have right on their side: Paris was wrong to steal Helen, and Menelaus is completely within his rights to show up with an army to demand her return. The Achaeans even sent emissaries to ask for her peaceful return, preventing war altogether. Nevertheless, the Trojans are proud and stubborn, and they refused to admit their mistake, so they deserve to be taught a lesson.

Achaea is a large nation comprised of smaller kingdoms, so a wide variety of men and women serve within its army. Characters can be from any of these kingdoms, so they can pick their appearance, origins, former occupation, and other details with very little restriction. Most of the Achaeans serve as foot soldiers, but charioteers do ride across the battlefield, and priests also accompany the troops. Magicians and rogues may also be here, disguised as regular fighters and a few bards might arrive, so characters can play any of the available classes.

Playing an Achaean gives characters freedom of movement. It gives them the chance to deal with military politics, since each kingdom has its own troops and leaders, and each is now thrown together in the camp. Warriors answer to their own king, but they have to live with and fight alongside men from other nations, and everyone tests each other to discover which neighbors are weak enough to dominate and which are strong enough to demand respect.

For the army commanders, the Achaean force also offers a chance to play with military strategy. The leaders gather most evenings in Agamemnon's tent to discuss tactics and suggest new plans. Some of those ideas are rejected outright, but others might be tried even if the chance for success is slim.

Then, as mentioned above, the Achaeans are also experienced sea raiders. They take their boats and roam along the coast, attacking everyone they find. Therefore, characters are not restricted to serving in the land battle. They can play members of a boat crew instead, searching for loot and information from coastal settlements.

TROJANS

The Trojans are the defenders. This is their land, their kingdom, and their home. The war takes place right on their doorstep. If the Achaeans lose, they can flee in whatever ships remain, and return home. If the Trojans lose, their entire city will be destroyed, along with everyone in it. They fight for their lives and the lives of their families.

Although the Trojans know every inch of the surrounding land, they cannot use this knowledge well, for they are all trapped inside the city. Troy is large and strong, but it has far too many warriors inside, including every ally who sent men to their aid. The streets are cramped, and every house overflows, except for the royal family's home, which houses the royal family and their guests and kin only.

Since the Trojans have many allies here, characters can also choose from a variety of races and cultures, including the Amazons, who sent a troop of fierce female warriors. Within the city, the Trojans have more bards and rogues than the Achaeans, as befits an urban setting. They also have more priests, and the priests have permanent temples and shrines rather than the makeshift altars of the Achaean camp.

Since all the Trojan people are here, Trojan characters can interact with nonmilitary members, including women and children. They also have to deal with the council of elders. Priam and his councilors run the city. Hector leads the army, but he still answers to his father, and the army has no say over nonmilitary matters. This means characters can deal with more politicking than they could as Achaeans. Trojan councilors spend the days arguing about how to run the city and how to remove the Achaeans, and often search for ways to overpower political opponents. A Trojan who is not a soldier will most likely find himself trapped in these social contests, and may even use them to improve his own standing.

Another major conflict within Troy stems from the cause of the war. Paris is one of the princes of the city, but his selfish actions led the entire nation into a decade-long conflict. True, Helen is lovely, but is she really worth all the deaths her betrayal has caused? Many Trojans feel Paris is to blame for everything and Helen should be sent back to the Achaeans—some even argue Paris should be sent with her, for Menelaus to punish as he sees fit. Others agree taking Helen was a mistake, but claim the damage is already done, and nothing except defeat will stop the Achaeans now. Some of them claim the Achaeans, thirsty for territory and riches, would have invaded some day regardless, and Paris' actions only hastened their arrival. The city is divided in its attitude toward the prince and his new consort, and men who fight back-to-back outside the walls are at each others' throats once inside.

The allies have their own political games as well. All of them came at Priam's behest, and they answer to him and to Hector, but many fight for the right to call themselves the second strongest force or Troy's favorite ally. These games range from bribing councilors for favors to challenging other captains to duels to poisoning public opinion against rivals. In many ways, the Achaeans are a more unified force because everyone there owes fealty to Agamemnon. In the Trojan army, however, many of the men are there only as a favor to a neighbor, and they could walk away at any time.

The Trojans are also looking for a way out. They seek escape routes, military strategies, or peaceful ways to end the war and save their city.

Keep in mind, as well, the historical Troy had at least seven incarnations, the seventh being the home of Priam, Hector, and Paris. That means the ruins of six previous cities lie beneath it. Thus, Troy offers excellent opportunities for dungeon crawls, as characters search through the ruins for treasure, artifacts of possible aid to the army, and tunnels perhaps allowing the women and children to escape to safety.

CHANGING OUTCOMES

The one disadvantage to playing games set in a historical event is we already know the outcome. After all, the Achaeans ultimately win, and Troy is destroyed, right?

Not necessarily. This is *your* game, after all. You are using the classical setting, but that does not mean you have to follow it to the letter. If you did, neither you nor the players would have any fun; you would be recounting the *Iliad* rather than creating a story of your own.

So how much can you change? Quite a lot, really. Here a few suggestions.

HELEN

Paris, prince of Troy, abducted Helen, the wife of Menelaus, and carried her back to his homeland. This event caused the war. What if he had not abducted her? What if Helen had refused his advances, or he had not been interested in her, or had been intercepted before he could get back home? What if Helen did not even exist?

This is the most drastic change possible because it could prevent the entire war from occurring. If the war does happen, it might occur for different reasons, and the armies might be seen in a different light. In the *Iliad*, the Achaeans attack Troy to reclaim Helen, which is extreme but ultimately the correct path. The Trojans defend themselves but know the abduction was wrong—they admit their mistake, but cannot remedy it.

What if Helen hadn't been taken? What if the Achaeans had invaded Troy simply because they wanted its lands? Now suddenly the Achaeans are the villains and the Trojans are in the right, changing the entire nature of the conflict.

While we're not recommending you change things this drastically, you could make minor alterations to Helen's story and retain the essence of the tale. For example, Helen is the daughter of Leda and Zeus. She has one sister, Clytemnestra, who is her fraternal twin, and two brothers, the twin warriors Castor and Pollux. What if she had a few more siblings? The

characters could play Helen's brothers and sisters, determined to rescue her at any cost. Especially if, instead of running away with Paris willingly, Helen really had been abducted, taken from home against her will and carried off to Troy as a prisoner.

Another possibility is to change Helen's marital status. Most of the Achaean nobles sought her hand in marriage, and her father Tyndareus (or, rather, her mother's husband, who raised her as his own daughter) selected Menelaus. What if Helen was abducted before her marriage, or before her hand had been promised to anyone? Now Paris is a little less of a fiend, seducing a single woman instead of abducting someone else's wife. Now every Achaean commander has even more reason to attack Troy: in addition to fame and fortune, each of them hopes to win Helen for himself.

OATH OF TYNDAREUS

As so many nobles sought Helen's hand, King Tyndareus feared picking one among them, as the rest might turn on the winning suitor, waging war against his kingdom as revenge. To avoid this, Odysseus suggested that every man there swear an oath, the Oath of Tyndareus, to defend Helen's husband and marriage against any attack. This oath forced the other kings to accompany Agamemnon and Menelaus to Troy and to participate in the war.

What if that oath did not exist? Then all the kings who joined the Achaean army would need another reason to participate. Fealty is not enough, since the army is invading a land far away, one posing no threat to them. Agamemnon and his brother would have to convince each of the kings in turn, promising them something for their trouble. This makes an interesting game if the players each played kings or at least captains of various kingdoms. Now it becomes a very political situation, maneuvering to gain the best advantage from the Atreides and taking as little risk as possible. It also means, throughout the war, Agamemnon would need to placate them, or they might simply take their forces and leave.

In the war, when Achilles argues with Agamemnon, he takes himself and his men out of the battle, but he does not sail for home; he does not leave because the oath (through his father, Peleus) binds him to the war. If the oath did not exist, Achilles could leave, and then the Achaeans would have no one to turn to in their extremity—except for the player characters.

LEADERSHIP

Homer tells us who ruled each of the major kingdoms and who led each of their forces. Agamemnon controlled the Achaeans, and Priam ruled the Trojans but his son Hector led the armies. But what if different men took charge? Though proud and greedy, Agamemnon proved an able commander. His brother Menelaus was more of a hothead, though braver in battle. What if their positions had been reversed and Menelaus had been in charge? Would the Achaean army have been bolder and more aggressive, or would it have used worse tactics? And what if Hector, calm and arrogant, had not commanded the Trojans? His second-in-command, his cousin Aeneas, was more thoughtful and less aggressive—what if he had been the army's leader instead? Would the Trojans have held back more, or shown more subterfuge? Changing the army leadership changes how the army fights, which could change the outcome of the war.

Another option is to change the command of individual forces rather than the whole army. For example, Diomedes leads the Argosian forces, and is one of the strongest and bravest warriors in the Achaean army. At one point, he routs the entire Trojan army single-handedly. However, what if he was never there? What if, for example, the player characters led the Argosian force? Not only would this change the outcome of certain battles, but it would also give the characters a place as senior commanders.

Of course, many Achaean kingdoms have kings and commanders who do not play a major role in the war, such as Thoas of the Aetolians and Meges of Dulichium. Player characters could easily replace these figures without altering any of the major characters from Homer's epic. The same is true on the Trojan side. For example, Asius commands the men from Percote and Practius, while Hippothous leads the tribes of Pelasgian spearmen.

ACHILLES

One variant of the *Iliad* removes Achilles entirely, leaving Aias as the mightiest hero in the Achaean army. This is similar to Arthurian tales that have Gawain as the finest knight alive, not Lancelot, who is never mentioned. What would happen if Achilles had not been present? The Myrmidons might be there under a different commander, or they might not have attacked Troy at all. Other commanders would vie for the title of the mightiest warrior of the Acheans, and the Trojans might not focus all their dread upon a single captain of the enemy. The war might still go the same way—even in that variant, Troy falls—and, after all, Achilles had died before the war ended. But without his presence, certain events might have gone differently, and some of the Trojan commanders might live to see the final defense of their beloved city. This gives characters the opportunity to become the most famous warriors on the Achaean side, or gives them a better chance of defending Troy against the invaders.

THE FIELD OF BATTLE

The battlefield is extremely limited in space and in variety of terrain, but what if it was not? What if, for example, Troy lay right by the water's edge? Then the Achaeans would not be able to land and sweep across that plain; they would have to land somewhere else and march toward the city, possibly over hills and through valleys. Troy would not be as isolated, and the city could launch its own boats, both to seek out new allies and to attack the Achaeans from behind. More of the battle could be at sea, and the conflict probably would have ended much sooner, for once a fleet loses all of its boats, the battle is over.

Perhaps Troy sat on a tall hill and the terrain stretching between it and the sea was rough and uneven. Then chariots would have a harder time and might not have been used at all. The armies would have used different tactics, sending out smaller units to take each hill in turn, rather than covering the plain in broad waves. Warriors could ambush troops from the hills, attacking quickly and then retreating to cover. More Trojans would be rangers instead of warriors, trained in wilderness lore, stealth, and archery, and the Achaeans might be unprepared for this combat style.

Another possibility involves moving the Xanthus River slightly, so it flows right before the walls of Troy. Drawbridges lead over the river and into the city, and the city can draw these up in times of war. The Achaeans can no longer charge right to the city walls; they can only get as close as the riverbank. Without siege engines, they can never take Troy by storm, meaning they need some other way to win the war. Perhaps single combat will work, challenging the Trojan commander for the last time. Perhaps they need more subterfuge, damming the river so that they can walk across its bed.

By changing the terrain and shifting the city's location slightly, you create new challenges for the player characters. This gives them more opportunity to be creative, and changes the war from a straight battle across an open plain into something more complicated and more interesting.

TRUCES

Truces occurred several times during the war, though they rarely lasted more than a day or two. However, what would happen if they had been more frequent and had lasted longer? What if the Trojans had sent emissaries to the Achaean camp or Achaean emissaries had gone into the Trojan city? What if both had happened, each side sending a handful of trusted men to speak with the opposing leaders?

This makes the game much more political. You could set your campaign during one of these truces, making the player characters the envoys entering the home of their enemies. Now they have to present their case and convince the leaders to end the war. How much can they promise? Can they guarantee their own leaders' agreement to the negotiated terms? What about the various factions within each army, some of which do not want a peaceful solution?

Another option is to create a neutral territory, somewhere near the battlefield but not on it where envoys from both sides can meet. This would be a temporary settlement, made of tents, prohibiting weapons. Here both sides could peacefully discuss a solution to the war. This creates both political opportunities as people manipulate each other, but also possibilities for espionage. For example, if the Achaeans send the characters to assassinate the Trojan commanders, the characters have to infiltrate the area where the leaders meet, kill someone in a place that does not allow weapons, and then escape alive. Depending upon their orders, they might need to make the murder look like a natural death or point blame at someone else. If the Trojans send the characters to kill Priam, ordering them to make it look as if the Achaeans killed him, Hector would become king, and vow to exterminate the Achaeans utterly, making some of his allies very happy indeed.

Another type of truce happens every night, when both armies stop fighting and return to their camps. Why do they do this? For one, it is a matter of honor, but it is also because no one can see very well at night. Things change, however, if one side does not abide by this convention. Odysseus and Diomedes sneak out one night to investigate Trojan activity, and kill one of the Trojan scouts in the process. Maybe they then led a band of warriors, attack the Trojans during the night, and kill many of their best men. What if the Trojans scaled the Achaean walls at night and set fire to their ships? What if neither side cared about dusk, and attacks occurred at any time, day or night? Both armies would be more cautious and more paranoid. They would both have commando troops, small units of men trained for stealth, speed, and night fighting. The war would be even more brutal and vicious than it was, but it also might end faster too.

DEATHS

Many of the major figures in the *Iliad* die during the Trojan War—Patrocleus, Achilles, Sarpedon, and Hector, to name a few. But what if those deaths did not occur? How would the Trojan War have gone differently if Patrocleus had survived? Achilles might not have ended his feud with Agamemnon and returned to battle, and Hector might have survived as well, giving the Trojans more hope and military strength toward the end. Changing any major death in the war could affect the outcome. The biggest advantage to this is if the players have read the *Iliad*, they no longer know what to expect. It makes the adventure more exciting because now anything can happen, and those players will be just as confused and excited as players who have never read the epic and do not know its ending.

TROJAN HORSE

When the Achaeans finally realize they cannot take Troy by force, they resort to subterfuge. Odysseus comes up with a plan to build a large wooden horse and leave it in their camp. They then take their ships and sail out of sight. The horse is hollow and Odysseus hides inside with a group of handpicked warriors. The Trojans, finding the horse, drag it back to the city, and that night the Achaeans sneak out and open the city's gates from the inside, allowing the rest of their army to into the city, whereupon they slaughter Troy's inhabitants.

How would things have changed if they had not? What would Odysseus have done if Agamemnon had refused the horse stratagem? Maybe the Trojans, sensing deception, burned the horse and the men inside it. What if they had not dragged it back into the city at all? What if guards had resisted the Achaean intruders and had raised the alarm?

Even without the Horse, the Achaeans might have won the war, but their victory would not have been as certain, as sudden, or as ruthless. Removing the Trojan Horse allows the player characters to come up with something of their own, some new and clever plan to gain access to the city or to break the Trojans' will. From the Trojan side, it also makes the outcome less certain—anyone who read the *Iliad*, upon hearing the horse described, knows exactly what is happening, but if the horse never appears, those players will be left guessing, and will be just as surprised by events as everyone else.

FINAL VICTORY

The final question, of course, is which side wins. In the *Iliad*, and in history, the Achaeans prove victorious. They do not have to be. Maybe the Trojans won instead, and pushed the Achaeans back into the ocean—or burned all their boats, stranding the warriors in enemy territory. Maybe some third force appeared and conquered both weary armies. For example, what if the Egyptians suddenly showed up and took over? The Achaeans and the Trojans could wind up fighting on the same side, at least long enough to drive back this new enemy.

As with the discussion about Helen, this is a drastic change, though not as severe a change as removing the major impetus for the war in the first place. If war occurs, someone must ultimately win. Sometimes history gets the facts wrong. For example, if the Trojans win the war, their city could still be destroyed in the process, forcing them, maybe even using the Achaean boats? Anyone watching would think the Achaeans

had won because Troy was burning and the black boats were sailing away. It would be an easy mistake to make.

Ultimately, you should not feel constrained by history or legend. Yes, you are running a game set in the Trojan War, but it is *your* game. If changing the battlefield a bit, shifting Troy closer to the water, or removing Achilles from the war makes the setting more interesting, do it. Once the game has started, let the characters' actions affect events. If they convince Agamemnon that the Trojan Horse is a stupid idea, that is fine; let him veto the plan. If they play Trojans and come up with a way to beat the Achaeans, let them.

Let the outcome reflect the game's events, and if the outcome does not match history, who cares? You are telling a new version of the Trojan War, with new characters and new scenes—which means, as long as your setting matches the flavor of the original and everyone has fun, it does not matter if all the details stay the same.

After all, no one even agrees on the exact date of the Trojan War, and it took centuries before scholars even agreed about the city's location, let alone its very existence. Who is to say they didn't get other details of this ancient conflict wrong?

AFTERMATH

If your campaign runs to the end of the war, or starts with the end of the war, what happens next? That's it, right? The Achaeans turn around and head for home, leaving nothing but a burning ruin behind them.

Not quite.

The situation is a lot more complicated than that. First, the Achaeans do not simply go home. They have to sail back to their various kingdoms, which takes a while. They stop and raid along the way, to stay in practice and to re-supply. Further, some of the Achaean kings do not have a nice easy journey; they have offended the gods, and are punished with delays, tragedies, even death.

Second, Troy has been destroyed, but that does not guarantee everyone is dead. Aeneas survives, along with his father, Anchises, and his son, Ascanius. They escape the city with several servants. Antenor and his family also survive, spared by the Achaeans because of their earlier efforts to end the war and return Helen to Menelaus. Other Trojans might have escaped death, as well. Though the city is destroyed, it can be rebuilt.

GLAUCUS

Then we have allies. The Achaeans are all technically one nation composed of many smaller kingdoms, so they count as a single unit. At least, they did during the war. Once Troy falls and Helen rescued, the war ends and the Oath of Tyndareus no longer binds anyone together. The kings are now independent allies again, as some of them demonstrate when they leave without the rest of the fleet. On the way to Troy, the fleet united. Now, it fragments into several smaller forces, and some of them do not get along, particularly if one king envies another's accomplishments or treasure. Many of the forces have different leaders than when they arrived, as their captains died during the war—for example, Aias Telamonian is dead, and so his Salamites follow a different man home. Many also resent Odysseus, who partially caused Aias' death. Now the various Achaeans end up fighting one another, either before leaving Troy, or on the open sea, or even when they get back to their respective kingdoms.

The Trojan allies are even worse. Many of them were simply neighbors of Troy who sent troops to Priam out of old friendship. Now Priam is dead, and Troy gone, which means all of the Trojan lands are ripe for the taking. The Trojan allies had much looser ties to one another than the Achaeans, and they do not have any treasure to show for their troubles. The best they can get now is to claim Troy as their own, attach it to their kingdom, and rebuild the city as part of their own territory. Several ugly fights might occur before a final victor appears.

What of those who escaped? If Antenor chose, he could gather forces and return to Troy, reclaim it, and rebuild it. So could Aeneas—he is actually a prince of the realm and Priam's nephew, making him the closest heir to the throne.

The other concern is the surrounding area. Troy was the major power of this region, but now that power is gone, who keeps the peace among all these coastal kingdoms? Many of them stand in smoldering ruin, sacked by the Achaeans. Anyone with a decent fleet of ships could sail in and take control of the entire region with little effort, creating a strong kingdom from the ashes of several. Troy itself would be the logical place for a new capital, being centrally located and easily defended.

Clearly, the end of the war is not the end of the story—or at least it does not have to be. When two major nations clash and one destroyed, everyone with ties to either nation is affected. Those effects ripple outward, influencing world events for years to come.

Of course, the gods also have a role. Several of them championed the Achaeans and are thrilled by their victory, but others supported the Trojans, and may take out their anger upon the victors. This is why several Achaean kings do not survive the voyage home, and why others take years in the process. The gods might have their own plans for the land that was Troy, including encouraging someone to rebuild it and establish a new kingdom there. And for those who oppose the gods, war might be the least of their troubles.

CHAPTER FOURTEEN: RUNNING THE GAME

The Trojan War. The most famous battle in human history. Gods and heroes faced off for almost a decade. Everyone has heard of it, even if few have actually read the *Iliad*. Who wouldn't want to play a character fighting in this epic war alongside Achilles or Hector?

When you sit down to actually read the *Iliad*, though, you discover something you never realized before: it's (to be charitable) a bit dry. Large portions of the poem recount people's parentage, describe something in excruciating detail, or repeat the same message over and over again. The fight scenes move ponderously slow—not the fights themselves, but the descriptions. Every other paragraph, it seems, details someone's lineage, and the phrasing for each combat attack reads very similarly—you can only read "and night descended on his eyes" so many times before frustration sets in.

So, why would anyone want to play a game set during the Trojan War? Well, the *Iliad* is Homer's epic account of that legendary battle, just as the *Lord of the Rings* is Tolkien's tale of the War of the Ring. The *Iliad* follows the conventions of its time, meaning it uses lots of stock phrases, repetition, and side treks into personal histories. And the tale itself still captivates. Two nations war for a decade over a woman! Even the gods themselves take part in the struggle. Their children fighting alongside mortal men and often die themselves! The Homeric era is perfect for gaming. The trick is to running your game to match the era, not copying the poems.

EPIC CONVENTIONS

Homer wrote epics. The *Iliad* and the *Odyssey* are epic poems. Any tale told during the Trojan War should be epic as well. So what does *epic* mean, exactly?

It means on a grand scale. Epics relate enormous events that shake the world. One man attacking another is dramatic, but one nation fighting another is epic. Two armies clashing for a day is impressive; a war lasting nine years is epic.

Does that mean your campaign has to last nine years? No, of course not. It should run as long as you and your players decide it should run. However long you run your campaign, you should make your version of the Trojan War reverberate as the significant event it was. The war's outcome should affect more than just a few people. Changing the lives of a boat and its crew or a small town will not do; the outcome must affect whole nations. Since you are telling the story of the Trojan War, the story must affect the Achaeans and the Trojans, the two forces fighting the war.

Think of it this way: Achilles' killing Hector ultimately tells of two men in single combat. Yet one of those men, Achilles, is the son of a god and the mightiest warrior in the Achaean army. The other, Hector, leads the Trojan army and is the Trojans' strongest fighter. The outcome of their combat affects both armies profoundly. That's what makes it epic.

Another element of the epic is lineage. As mentioned above, Achilles is the son of a god. Hector is the son of the Trojan king. Both have distinguished parentage, which helps make theirs an epic tale. If the tale merely told of two common men fighting, the conflict would be less impressive. This is why Homer's major characters recite their lineage in battle; they remind the listener (reader) that they come from long, distinguished bloodlines, which makes them more important.

In your game, how many of your players have selected the Noble feat or the divine offspring race? Selecting the Noble feat implies they are nobility in some kingdom, so sit down with them and figure out which one and how they fit into the royal family. It's not necessary for each Noble character to be the only son of a king, but noble characters should be the king's children, siblings, first cousins, or nephews. In other words, they should have clear ties to the throne. As for divine offspring, work with the player to select the character's divine parent—unless you would rather surprise the player. The gods target nobles as their lovers, so most divine offspring should also be noble, and you can pick which kingdom they're from and how close they are to the throne, as well. Encourage your players to create family histories for their characters; when in battle, they should rattle off this created ancestry. Award experience to players who create interesting stories and those who really get into the whole "my family is more illustrious than yours" mentality. That's very epic indeed.

Epics also tend to toward the extreme. Odysseus does not just have a tough journey home; he loses all of his crew, every boat, every bit of treasure, and stranded for 10 years. When he finally does return to Ithaca, he has even more treasure than he did before he left Troy. Bad breaks in an epic should be catastrophic, like the shattering of a favorite weapon or the loss of an entire warship to a tidal wave. Good luck should be just as extreme, like finding the long-lost sword of a demigod, discovering a secret pass through impassable mountains, or meeting the *one* person who can show you the way home. That does not mean characters cannot have small things happen to them, but most events should be large and almost absurd in their extremity.

Honor is also important in the epic. True epic heroes maintain their honor, and refuse to do anything inappropriate, like insulting a priest, ravaging a woman, or desecrating a temple. These men always keep their word and honor their oaths. Some epic villains follow the same rules, while others cannot be trusted and lie, cheat, and steal whenever possible. Since the player characters are presumably heroes, they should act honorably at all times, meaning they should keep their word and show respect to their elders and to the gods. They should also follow the rules of combat, requiring them to announce themselves before attacking a noble foe and to abstain from fighting between the hours of dusk and dawn. In particular, they must obey the customs and rules of their society—even though they make little sense and put the characters at a disadvantage (like throwing away their armor to face an unarmored foe on equal terms)—as this is very epic.

Epics overflow with passion and high emotion. Epic characters rarely keep calm and collected. When happy, they dance, sing, and shout. When sad, they moan, weep, and throw themselves upon the ground. When angry, they gnash their teeth, stamp about, and often hurl things. Epic characters feel everything to the extreme. They may curse the gods and bemoan ever being born one minute, but the next minute, they proclaim themselves the luckiest creatures alive. Epic characters live in the moment.

GAMING VS. EPIC STORYTELLING

So, now you know what epic means. Not every epic convention works in a roleplaying game. For example, the Homeric epics are filled with repetitions. Zeus tells Iris to carry a message to Agamemnon, and Iris flies down and repeats the message—which is fine, except that you wind up reading the same message twice in the space of two pages. If you did that to your players, repeating everything that everyone said verbatim, you'd not only have a phenomenal memory, you'd have really bored players.

Thus, some of the conventions fit and others don't. The key is to keep the ones that make the game more fun, and lose the ones that you and your players don't find interesting.

Look at the bit above about increased emotions. Do your players enjoy hamming it up? Great, then they shouldn't have any problem playing that aspect of the epic. If they can weep, moan, gnash, dance, or sing as the occasion demands, that's wonderful for your game. Some players, however, don't enjoy that sort of thing. They're more comfortable playing characters who keep their emotions under control. And that's fine, too. It's not really epic, but that doesn't matter—what matters is that making the characters have to weep and gnash is going to make the players uncomfortable, which means they won't enjoy the game as much. If you have players of the latter type, then downplay this aspect in favor of another epic element.

Another element is the intense detail found in the Homer's epics. Homer spends four pages describing the detailed work on Achilles' shield, four pages… about a shield. Scholars have been able to create images of the shield that match perfectly because the description is so detailed. That's okay for an epic poem, where the audience wants to know every little intricacy, but do your players? Find out. When they first encounter a suit of fine armor or an elaborately carved door or something else of great workmanship, describe it in full Homeric detail. If they start looking bored, cut things short, and give more abbreviated descriptions in the future. If they lap up the details and want more, then you know they'll love every full-page description you write for the items they encounter.

If the players don't enjoy hearing such long descriptions, you can try other ways to provide details. Pictures work well, so show

MENELAUS

them an illustration of Achilles' sword and save yourself four pages of recitation. Maybe draw a simple diagram, and then describe each portion in some detail—but by using a picture as a framework, you can cut down on what you have to tell them and make the description move more quickly. You could even try writing up full-page descriptions of items and emailing them to everyone after the game. This way, they can read the full details if they want, or ignore them if they were satisfied with what you've already told them about the items.

Stock phrases are another epic convention. Read the *Iliad* and you'll find a lot of "and he died where he fell" and "long-shadowed spear" and "night descended upon his eyes." Characters are often referred to with phrases attached to their names, like Menelaus of the mighty war cry, Hector of the flashing helmet, and Diomedes tamer of horses. This reminded Homer's listeners which characters were which, and it created stronger mental images of the characters for them. Should you use these techniques in your game? Again, see what the players like and don't like. If you start calling one of their characters "Iolus of the mighty hands" or "man-rending Jason" and they take pride in the title, keep using it. If you create such phrases for your characters and your players don't react favorably—or at all—to them, quit using it. The same thing goes for stock phrases. If every time a player character kills a rival warrior, you say "and the night descended upon his eyes," and they all cheer, keep doing it. If they roll their eyes and mutter, then return to using casual dialogue. You can also create your stock phrases—if you've been playing with the same people for a while, chances are you already have a few. So what if "Boo-yah!" isn't appropriate for the period? If that's what the players (and you) like to shout on critical hits, go for it.

Just don't wrest control of the game from your players. This can be particularly tempting in an epic campaign. After all, what if a player character decides not to accept Hector's challenge to a duel? You can already see the scene in your head, and you have all the fancy Homeric phrases flowing for it, so you overrule the player and tell him exactly what happens during the duel.

Not good.

While this *is* your campaign, keep in mind that it really belongs to all of you; without players, you wouldn't have a campaign, so you don't want to lose their interest.

So, yes, epics can create grand scenes, and as the GM, you probably have some of those scenes plotted out in your head, but some of them will have to stay there. Let the players determine the course for their own characters. If they aren't interested in accepting that duel or charging that army, so be it. They'll come up with something else to do, and you can run with that, giving it the appropriate epic feel. They want to climb the hill and look for mountain passes? Fine—the hill becomes a mountain of its own, and they encounter a band of Trojan scouts as they reach the top. Or they find a river just beyond the hill, but must appease its god before they can cross. Don't force the player

characters to act in epic ways, just describe what they do in epic tones, and build the epic around them. Doing so will make the game far more exciting for everyone.

Another potential problem is the grandiose nature of the epic. Sometimes the characters just want to sit and think about things, talk quietly together, or take a look around without being jumped by charioteers or halted by gods. Even the *Iliad* has its quiet moments. Achilles sits brooding for long periods, Odysseus occasionally stops to watch the battle, and even Hector takes time off to go home to visit his wife and son. Let them have their downtime. When they do act, then you can bring in the epic elements. But if they want to do something quieter, that's fine—those lulls will make the grand action scenes even more impressive by comparison.

FAME AND FORTUNE

Why did so many warriors agree to travel to Troy? Some of them went out of loyalty, certainly, whether to their own lords or to Agamemnon. Outrage drove others—a foreigner had stolen an Achaean woman from her husband, and that disrespect needed to be answered by a show of force. But most of the war's participants were young men who go for two reasons: fame and fortune.

The Achaean kingdoms were filled with young nobles. Each small country had its own king, plus all of his children, relatives, distant kin, and all those related to him by marriage, as well. So, lots of nobles lounged around the palaces, many of them with little more than their names, their swords, and their lineages. These young men hoped to better themselves, improve their name, and to earn respect. Basically, they joined the military to kill Trojan heroes, win notoriety for their deeds, and to gain their victims' armor as trophies to display upon their walls. And, since war killed so many, some of these men even hoped that the fighting would thin the ranks of their own relatives, leaving them with family estates and more titles—perhaps even the crown itself. Even if their more highly ranked relatives survived, demonstrating bravery and skill in the war may have earned these young nobles an honored place at the royal table and perhaps a position as captain of the king's guard or chief counselor to the throne.

The second hope, of course, was to gain fortune. The Achaeans sacked towns on their way to Troy, and eventually sacked Troy itself. Every fighter in the army received some share of the spoils, and how much depended on their rank and their involvement in the specific battle. A common footman earned several silver pieces during the course of the war—and, since the army fed and clothed him during the war, he could bring back those coins to his wife and children. That was more than those men would normally earn in years of hard labor, enough

AIAS

to keep them and their families comfortable through any lean years to come. For nobles, who were usually squad leaders or charioteers, the rewards were even greater: they received gold instead of silver. Moreover, when a man killed a foe, he could strip the fallen man's armor and weapons to keep as trophies. A bronze panoply was worth far more than a few gold coins, both for the armor's actual value and for the warrior's reputation—nobles and captains called out their names and recounted their lineages when challenging an opponent. So, when Tlepolemus and Sarpedon faced each other and called out their names and lineages, they were not only issuing a challenge and demonstrating their own noble blood, but they were are also laying claim to their opponent's arms. If some other Trojan warrior turned up with Tlepolemus' armor after that confrontation, everyone would know that he had stolen the gear that it rightfully belonged to Sarpedon.

The Achaeans had more opportunity for fortune than the Trojans, since they also sacked towns along the coast. The Trojans only gained whatever arms and armor they stripped from their fallen foes. But both sides earned fame and glory, but for the Trojans, fortune was not as important; they were protecting their families and property from invaders.

Warriors from both sides could hope to win one other benefit, as well: if they fought bravely and with skill, they would earn the blessing of a god, which made them even stronger in battle. This was a double-edged sword, however, because being touched by a god, however briefly, made that warrior a target for men favored by other gods, and some of those were warriors had long-standing relationships with their deities and had martial prowess no other man could match. Staying well clear of Achilles, Hector, Diomedes, or Sarpedon was the best way to stay alive. Fame and fortune meant little to ghosts, after all.

DEUS EX MACHINA

The gods could and did bless warriors who impressed them, but they did a good deal more than that during the Trojan War. Throughout Greek myths and legends, the gods appeared to their favorites and took a direct hand in events, but most of the gods participated in the war, and they even walked the battlefield themselves. At one point, the gods even faced each other across the field, and fought one another directly, which had not happened since the gods and the Titans battled for mastery of the world.

So how do you deal with this in your game? First, you need to decide whether you really want the gods to appear at all.

While the *Iliad* mentions the gods' appearance, some scholars argue that this is metaphorical rather than literal. When Athena lent strength to a man, or helped him ignore his wounds, according to these scholars, the text actually meant the man in question found his second wind or overcame his pain. You could assume this stance in your game. Tell the players that the Greek gods are representations rather than individuals. Then when you say Ares fights alongside a warrior, you really mean that the fighter is using his rage to add to his strength. When you say Athena lends courage to a man, you then mean the man's own combat experience reminds him he can succeed. If you use this method, you can still mention the gods by name, but they become similes—"You move as though Hermes had leant wings to your feet," you might say to a player. This would actually explain why the gods often took the form of men in the armies: the gods did not really appear; the men on the field just spoke such notable things that they appeared to have been divinely inspired.

Admittedly, that route feels cheap. After all, this is the Homeric world, a land of epic adventure. Why shouldn't the gods exist? Actually, in a world where men can single-handedly route armies and foretell events accurately, where sacrilege can cause earthquakes and tidal waves, and where magicians can transform sailors into swine, how could the gods not be real? Also, if the Greek gods are merely metaphors, then praying to them becomes a bit foolish and a significant waste of time—all those hours Odysseus spent praying to Athena for help, he could have used to focus on his own talents and been home more quickly.

If you decide to let the gods be real figures, you still have a choice: keep them on the sidelines, or let them walk the field.

With the sideline option, the gods are real, and they do answer men's prayers. They just don't come down from Mount Olympus to participate directly. Athena would breathe strength into a man or suggest a plan of attack to Odysseus, but she wouldn't descend to earth personally. She wouldn't need to as she could work her will through her champions. This route gives the gods a certain amount of control, but it also makes them aloof and mysterious. Mortal men do their bidding without knowing exactly what the gods intend, and they accept these divine gifts as the result of prayer and dedication. The other advantage to sidelining the gods is they can see events more clearly from on high, and they can interfere with more events because they can watch everything at once. The drawback, of course, is the gods do not actually appear on the battlefield. When they offer suggestions to mortal men, as when Apollo tells Diomedes to step back and not fight against the gods, they are merely speaking into the listener's mind rather than aloud. It makes the gods more powerful in some ways, and they become more unapproachable and a little less human.

The most traditional method, of course, is to have the gods actually appear, just as they did in the *Iliad*. Aphrodite shields her son Aeneas with her own body, and is actually chased and wounded by Diomedes for her trouble. Hermes disguises himself as a mortal youth to escort Priam to Achilles' tent. Ares wreaks havoc on the Achaeans. The gods walk among men and influence the events of the war, and no major event occurs during the nine years that one god or another does not affect in some way.

The advantage to this method is it is epic, and it keeps perfectly with Homer's work. It also makes the gods much more human and more fallible. After all, when they stand on the field in mortal form, they can only see as far as a mortal, so something occurring on the other side of the field can easily escape their notice. Having the gods appear in person also strengthens the faith of their warriors, who can now see the gods do exist and pay attention to prayers and petitions.

The disadvantage is having gods in the game can become unbalancing. Who can possibly stand against Ares in battle? What mortal would be foolish enough to block Athena's path? Why, if the gods are taking part in the War, haven't Athena, Hera, and the other Achaean supporters simply torn down the walls of Troy already?

One of the reasons is Zeus. As the king of the gods, Zeus tries to maintain neutrality in divine conflicts. He lets the other gods pick sides in the war, but stays on Mount Olympus himself, watching everything. If he feels a god has gone too far, he sends Iris to tell him so, and orders him or her to cease efforts immediately. When Zeus does take a hand in the war, he does so not because he favors one side but because Thetis has requested his support. He also decrees Patrocleus, then Hector, and then Achilles will die because it is their destinies.

AGAMEMNON

Once Zeus makes such a decree, he forbids the other gods from interfering. Athena and Hera must watch as the Trojans sweep the Achaeans back to their ships because Zeus has declared it will happen. It is only when he allows them to enter the fray again the gods all descend to face each other in battle.

Another reason the gods do not simply overwhelm everything is because they do not want to. To them, humans are chess pieces—even favorites are kings and queens, and nothing more. Shoving the chessboard aside and punching each other is immediate but less satisfying because it requires less skill and takes up less time. One of the fundamental truths about the Greek gods is they are bored. In truth, they seek mortal lovers and take such interest in their champions because it amuses them. Ending the conflict themselves is too quick and too easy, so the gods force themselves not to get too involved, only providing encouragement here and there to move the pieces about the board.

Also, the gods might also be weaker than most people suppose. Certainly, when walking the earth, any god is a match for any warrior, but Ares descends to earth and Diomedes actually wounds him enough to send the war god running home again. True, Athena helped land the blow, but even so, a mortal wounded a god, and one of the strongest gods at that. This suggests the gods are not as invincible as they claim they are. It also may be the gods, when they take physical form, cannot access all of their powers. Thus, while on Mount Olympus Ares is the supreme god of war. When he walks behind Hector, he is still incredibly powerful, but less so. When Ares fights Diomedes in the flesh, by assuming flesh he reduces his power still further. Why, then, would he ever take on flesh? Again, boredom is the answer. Ares loves to fight, and the most satisfying method is fighting in the flesh. If that means limiting his powers, Ares is confident he can still

best mortals while in that form. All the gods are this arrogant, in fact, which explains why they take mortal form so often. They assume no one can harm them, and interfering in person is much more satisfying than manipulating from afar.

The gods also delight in tricking or testing mortal men. Often they appear in disguise before their favorites, to see if the men can see through their disguises. This need to test them is also part of the reason the gods do not take Troy themselves; the gods want to see how men handle the challenge and particularly how their favorites perform under pressure. Odysseus is Athena's favorite above all other men, and yet often she sits back to watch how he handles a situation, only interfering when he needs her help or when he calls upon her directly.

One of the dangers of having the gods appear in your game is characters can grow too dependent on their aid. Why fight alone when you can summon Athena or Apollo to stand by your side? Why solve a puzzle when you can ask Hera to solve it for you? This can make characters very lazy, and it can get boring for everyone. It is easy to fix, however. Look at the *Iliad*. The gods do not always answer men's calls. In fact, if men call upon them too often or too arrogantly, not only will the gods not answer, but also they may become annoyed and punish the offending person for taking them for granted. Once players see the gods can be cruel as well as kind and do not like to be bothered for foolishness, they will restrict their prayers to utter emergencies. And when the gods bestow gifts without warning or request, it's a good time for characters to start looking around and worrying about what's about to happen next. You should always remember that the characters are merely chess pieces to the gods, so let the players realize this for themselves. It will make their characters more humble and more hesitant to ask for divine aid.

PRIAM

DIVINE FAVOR

In **Chapter 8: Religion and Piety**, we talked about earning Piety points and gaining divine aid for having a positive Piety score. The list of boons a character can ask for is slim in that chapter. That table provides basic possibilities. The Greek gods, after all, are the supreme powers of the Homeric setting. They can do almost anything they like. They can transform people into animals or trees, create people from stones and ants, turn boats into mountains, cover the lands in darkness, and so on. It makes sense that a god can do a lot more than just heal a character's wounds or improve his saving throws.

What exactly can a god do, and what are the criteria for deciding what he does? Well, although the gods can do almost anything, they won't do certain things. It is considered rude for a god to interfere in another god's realm. For example, Athena will not halt a wave or summon a flood because water

is Poseidon's realm, not hers. She can do anything involving wisdom or combat and anything not belonging to another god's realm, but she will not impose her will upon another god's spheres, though she might petition another god for a favor from his realm, like asking Poseidon to summon a wave for her.

When deciding whether a god will honor someone's request, you must determine whether it lies within the particular god's sphere of influence. If the answer is yes, then you must decide if the god cares enough to grant the request. The gods are capricious, after all. They enjoy watching mortals, manipulating them, and helping their favorites. They also get easily distracted, bored, or irritable. Asking a god for help when he is upset is never a good idea because he might take out his frustrations on you, even if you are one of his favorites.

You can gauge the god's mood yourself, of course, by considering what is going on in the world and what, if anything, might have his interest at the time. For example, Apollo is the god of music, so if someone is playing a lute very badly, the music might irritate him. The easiest option, however, is to roll on **Table 14-1: Divine Mood**. Apply the modifiers to the Piety roll when determining whether a god answers a request.

The god's response to a request also depends upon the severity of the request. Something minor may not be granted simply because it is not worth the god's time and effort. On the other hand, something extreme, like sinking a boat or destroying an army may be either beyond a god's power or simply more than he is willing to do for the mortal at that time. You can use the **Table 14-2** to determine how the severity will affect the god's response.

Roll 1d20 and apply the modifiers from mood and severity. Then add the character's Piety points and consult **Table 14-3** to decide whether the god actually honors the character's request

Thus, when Chryses prayed to Apollo for a plague upon the Achaeans, he found the god in a content mood (+1) and asked for a major boon (+0). Chryses is a priest, and probably had a Piety of at least 4, which means he rolled a 14 or higher because Apollo happily granted his request. Notice Apollo was outraged when he heard how Agamemnon had treated his priest, but his anger did not extend to Chryses himself—rather the anger was on the priest's behalf, and it made Apollo more inclined to grant the old man's request for revenge.

TABLE 14-1: DIVINE MOOD

Roll	Mood	Modifier
1	Enraged	–3
2	Angry	–2
3-5	Irritable	–1
6-10	Bored	0
11-15	Calm	0
16-18	Content	+1
19	Cheerful	+2
20	Jubilant	+3

Of course, you can simply decide for yourself how the god reacts, but the Tables gives you a basic guideline. The best method is to roll on the chart and then modify the result as you see fit.

Another thing to remember is that bored gods are particularly dangerous gods. A cheerful god grants his follower's request, but a bored god might not only grant it, but he might add some extra results just to make things more interesting.

Additionally, you must consider the god's intentions when deciding outcomes. Agamemnon offered Zeus wine and flesh, praying the god would grant him victory over the Trojans. Zeus had already decided the Achaeans would suffer for a while, since Thetis begged him to make them regret insulting Achilles. Even if Agamemnon had rolled well enough, Zeus still wouldn't grant the request because it did not match his own agenda.

Players want to know what the god does, of course. Do not feel constrained to tell them. The gods are mysterious, and they do not answer to mortals. Even if a god does accede to a request, he may send subtle help rather than intervene directly. If he decides not to help, he will not bother to explain himself. If a god grants the request, you have to decide how the aid appears (if it does), and if the player demands to know why the god didn't help or where the help is, just shrug and say, "Who can fathom the ways of the gods? They are beyond mortal ken." Then smile, and leave it at that. If the player pushes, remind him the gods are short-tempered, and they do not like being questioned—a character who takes offense because his request was refused may find himself earning divine displeasure instead, and will soon regret not keeping his anger to himself.

TABLE 14-2: BOON REQUEST SEVERITY

Severity	Modifier
Negligible (provide wine, remove rain, etc.)	–3
Minor (provide better food, aid, sleep)	–2
Useful (send animals for the men to hunt or show a path through wilderness)	+0
Important (provide food for a starving character, reveal the way out of a maze)	+0
Emergency (save the character from immediate attack)	+1
Major (save a ship's crew from drowning, shield a man from enemy troops)	+0
Severe (sink a ship, drown a family, destroy several warriors)	–2
Extreme (sink a fleet, drown a town, destroy an army)	–3

TABLE 14-3: BOON REQUEST RESULT

Roll	Result
1	The god is infuriated, and he strikes the character with divine displeasure
2	The god is displeased, and he drops the character's Piety score to -1
3-5	The god is annoyed, and he drops character's Piety score to 0
6-10	The god grudgingly grants the request; subtract 2 from the character's next roll on the Boon Request table
11-15	The god grants the request without thought to the requestor
16-18	The god pleasantly grants the request; add 2 to the character's next roll on the Boon Request table
19	The god happily grants the request and allows the character to retain half his current Piety points
20	The god is thrilled to grant the request and allows the character retains all his current Piety points

DIVINE DISPLEASURE

The Greek gods feel everything strongly. When they love, they pour all their desire into the object of their affections. When they admire, their respect bathes the subject in a golden glow. But when they anger, their wrath consumes all in a vast dark cloud. To make matters worse, the gods are fickle in their reactions. They can adore a human one minute, and then despise him the next simply because he carelessly commented about another person or let the god's adoration go to his head. While the gods forget quickly how much they admired a person, they nurse their grudges for years, sometimes even for generations. This is divine displeasure, and it destroyed many a life and laid low many a nation.

The first measure of a god's displeasure is negative Piety points. These indicate the person does not honor and respect the gods, and that always irritates them. A character can overcome this, and as his Piety score rises, the gods' anger will fade because they see the character genuinely repents his sins.

Characters can also gain divine displeasure by demanding a boon that is beneath the god's ability, outside of the god's realm, or one that is simply inappropriate.

Additionally, the character may earn divine displeasure by committing a sin against a god, against his priests, or against his children. The gods fiercely protect their chosen people, and immediately dislikes anyone who so much as insults one of their priests. Apollo struck the entire Achaean army with a plague because Agamemnon insulted his priest and refused to surrender the priest's daughter.

Another way to earn a god's enmity is to upset his plans. Unfortunately, humans cannot tell what a god's plans are unless they have been specifically told, and so often a person will marry a woman the god had fated for someone else, or kill a man the god intended to honor later, or do something else to upset the god. This is why people sometimes suffer from divine displeasure when they seem to have done nothing wrong. Priests and seers can usually divine what action the person committed offending the god, and then they can advise the person how to make amends—usually by offering sacrifices and libations until the god is satisfied.

If the character does something to attract a god's ire, consult **Table 14-4** and add up the character's total transgression modifier to see how badly he offended the deity.

Now roll 1d4 and add the result to the total. You can skip this part if you prefer, but it allows for that element of chance. After all, sometimes the gods punish people disproportionately to their crimes, while other times the culprit receives only an insignificant punishment for the crime. Whether you use the 1d4 or not, compare the character's Divine Displeasure total to **Table 14–5: Divine Displeasure Results** to see how long the god expresses displeasure and over how many people.

For most forms of divine displeasure, the duration is finite. The god eventually relents. During the period of divine displeasure, however, the target suffers a −2 penalty to all rolls (attacks, saves, and even skill checks) because the god is constantly interfering and making life worse for him. The character also receives only half the normal Piety points for any good deeds done during this period, as the god deliberately withholds his favor. Priests, if they offend their own god, cannot petition for spells during this time, and dedicated warriors cannot call upon supernatural abilities. Priests of the offended god will not cast spells on the character's behalf, either, and divine spells that fall within the angered god's domain will not work when the character is present.

The most severe forms of divine displeasure are far worse. If a character has a Piety of −40 or below, the god instantly strikes him dead. If his Piety is below −50, his immediate family also dies, even if they are nowhere near one another geographically. Severe displeasure means that the entire family line is destroyed, or the immediate family dies, and everyone else suffers a −4 to all rolls (attacks, saves, and skill checks). Any illness or threat entering the area targets that family automatically. Intense displeasure means the same thing but for an entire town—in addition to illnesses, natural disasters target the town, and within a year, that settlement lies in ruin. Extreme displeasure destroys an entire nation. Enemies attack from all sides, earthquakes tear the ground apart and swallow whole cities, tidal waves drown coastal towns, etc. The gods make examples of these nations, reminding everyone else to respect them properly. They also remind their priests to counsel people in danger of displeasure; it is far better for a man to go into exile than for his entire kingdom to perish.

TABLE 14-4: DIVINE DISPLEASURE MODIFIERS

Situation	Modifier
Negative Piety points	Piety modifier (half Piety score)
Dedicated a victory to the god and lost	−3
Promised to dedicate a town, but failed to build it	−4
Promised the god a temple, but did not deliver	−5
Insulted a priest	−1
Insulted a priest of his own god	−2
Killed a priest	−4
Killed a priest of his own god	−8
Broke his word	−1
Stole from the god's shrine	−5
Defiled the god's shrine	−10
Asked for too small a boon	−2
Asked for too great a boon	−1
Forgot to offer the god libations	−1
Forgot the god when offering libations	−2
Forgot the god when offering barley	−1
Forgot to offer the god a sacrifice	−2
Forgot the god when offering sacrifices	−4
Killed one of the god's children	−2
Approached the god when irritable	−1
Approached the god when angry	−2
Approached the god while enraged	−3

TABLE 14-5: DIVINE DISPLEASURE RESULTS

Total	Degree of Displeasure	Target	Duration
1-2	Negligible	Individual	one month
3-4	Mild	Immediate family	one month
5-6	Slight	Extended family	one month
7-8	Minor	Town or city	one month
9-10	Noticeable	Nation	one month
11-12	Targeted	Individual	one year
13-14	Lasting	Immediate family	one year
15-16	Focused	Extended family	one year
17-18	Moderate	Town or city	one year
19-20	Widespread	Nation	one year
21-25	Powerful	Individual	one decade
26-29	Notable	Immediate family	one decade
30	Sincere	Extended family	one decade
31-35	Strong	Town or city	one decade
36-39	Serious	Nation	one decade
40	Lethal	Individual	death
41-45	Grave	Immediate family	death
46-49	Severe	Extended family	destruction
50-54	Intense	Town or city	ruin
55+	Extreme	Nation	obliteration

It is possible to overcome divine displeasure and at least mollify the god's hatred. This usually requires a major quest on the god's behalf. As with reducing sins, the character gains no personal wealth or fame from this endeavor, but if he succeeds, he reduces his Divine Displeasure total by half. This means that a character can still have divine displeasure yet have a positive Piety total again, but until he has won the god's grudging acceptance (by reducing the Divine Displeasure total to 0), he can only receive half the normal Piety points for each action.

Some characters have been beloved by one deity but hated by another. Odysseus is the prime example; he was Athena's favorite, but he angered Poseidon by blinding his son. Diomedes was well liked by Athena, but both Ares and Aphrodite hated him for wounding them during the war. Unfortunately, the gods usually step aside and let their peers attack humans who offend them, even their own favorites. Thus, Athena did nothing to stop Poseidon from destroying Odysseus' crew and stranding him for 10 years. She only came to his aid after Poseidon agreed to let the man return home.

When a character earns divine displeasure, think about the circumstances behind the displeasure and the god involved. Did the character do something he knew would anger the gods? If so, you can make their anger obvious: the skies darken overhead, the temperature plummets, the seas churn, and so on. If the character does not know what he did, keep him in suspense for a while. Keep the signs of divine displeasure subtle and too general to point toward any one deity. If the seas swamp a boat, that is Poseidon. If the sky rains blood, that is Zeus. If the animals balk, the firewood is too damp to light, or the food turns, any of the gods could be behind the bad luck. Make the character figure out what he did. He can figure it out on his own, or he can seek help from a priest or seer.

Remember, the gods like to see mortals beg. They wait until someone is utterly desperate for relief before admitting they happen to have a quest in mind for him. Even after the character paid off his debt, the god may remind him to be more careful; someone who angers Poseidon may never have smooth sailing again, just because the god does not want anyone to forget how powerful he is and how dangerous his anger can be.

OMENS

The gods cannot leave well enough alone. They watch everything, and they cannot resist interfering. Often, rather than leaping into the fray themselves or even addressing someone directly, they send a vague message. They do this because it amuses them to be mysterious and because they like to challenge people. If the recipient can figure out the message, he earns the right to have that extra information or reassurance. If not, he should work harder to understand the will of the gods. These messages, which can be private or public, dream or reality, are collectively termed omens.

An omen is, simply put, a hint of what will come. Omens do not show information about the present; they reveal tantalizing details

about the future. The most famous omen in the Trojan War is the snake and the birds. The Achaeans, on their way to Troy, see a strange sight: a mother sparrow is sittings upon her branch with her eight babies, when a red-banded snake slides from the bushes and attacks. It swallows one chick after another, and then it swallows the mother. Afterwards, the snake turns to stone. The Achaeans take this as a sign; after all, snakes do not normally petrify. They decide it is an omen from Zeus, warning them how long the war will last. There were nine birds in all, so the war would last nine full years, but in the tenth year, it would end. They were right.

Of course, they could have interpreted that event to mean that nine men would die on their voyage, or they would kill one Trojan for every nine Achaeans. That is the problem with omens; they have to be interpreted correctly. Omens can be tricky to use, but no Homeric game is complete without them.

ORIGIN

The first question with any omen is who sent it. Omens are messages from the gods, but each god has his own agenda and his own information. Gods may send false omens, as when Zeus lets Agamemnon think the Achaeans will win the day, even though he intends to award that victory to the Trojans. If you know which god sent the sign, you can determine how reliable it is.

One way to tell this is to study the elements of the omen itself. Anything water-based comes from Poseidon, for water is his realm and none of the other gods would dare infringe upon his domain. Fire usually indicates Hephaestus, though it could mean Ares. Anything with the sun is from Apollo, as is anything musical. Zeus controls the sky, so most weather-based omens are his, as are most omens that involve birds. The gods do like to be clever, though, and they may deliberately disguise their hand. Thus, a snake is not tied to any one god, but if it has wave patterns in its scales, it may be from Poseidon; if it has gray eyes, Athena probably sent it.

Consider which gods are likely to watch the characters. Athena always watches Odysseus, and Apollo always keeps an eye on Hector, just as Aphrodite looks after both Aeneas and Hector. Other gods can send omens to these people, but those gods are the most likely to do so, so they should be the first ones considered. Does any god have a grudge against a character? If so, he might send a false omen.

Consider the events. Which gods are invested in the outcome? Zeus had plans for the war itself and for many of its major combatants, so he often sent omens to keep the armies doing what he wanted. Apollo was the Trojans' strongest supporter, and he sent them omens to keep up their morale. If a god does not care about the war or about a particular battle and has no attachment to the people involved, he has no reason to send an omen. The gods never send omens for no reason; they may have malicious intent, but they always have something to gain from the effort.

CONTENT

The second issue with omens is their content. What information does the message contain?

The gods never send omens without a reason, and they never bother sending them if the content is obvious or meaningless. Letting a mortal know he will die someday is foolish—all mortals die. Telling him he will die before the war ends, however, is important. Revealing one of the armies fighting over Troy will be defeated is so obvious it is silly, but revealing which army will suffer defeat is vital information.

The gods rarely give such clear indications, however. This may be because they cannot guarantee the outcome, or because they want men to work for the result, or because they like to make men suffer from not knowing, or all three. Both armies want to know if they will win the war, yet the best they ever get are signs indicating whether the day is theirs. Such signs do not guarantee the outcome—they don't even ensure the army won't take heavy losses. All they indicate is which side the gods favor at that moment.

One of the only clear, long-term omens is the snake and the sparrows. But the meaning was not clear to everyone initially, and it was so far in advance it did not give men much additional help. Nor did it specify when the war would end, only it would last nine full years.

Omens can also be conditional. "If you would win, you must retrieve the bow and arrows of Heracles" is a good example. The omen does not say the Achaeans will win; it only tells them that they cannot win without that bow and those arrows. The gods used these omens to make men do their bidding and to encourage them to follow a particular course of action.

Think about the god sending the omen, and the intended recipient. Is this a message for the entire army or for one particular commander? Is the god helping the recipient, misleading him, or just giving him more information in general? Again, gods never do anything without a reason—it may be a selfish, petty reason, but they always have something in mind. Iris tells Hector not to attack until he sees Agamemnon wounded and fleeing in his chariot. Her message is not an omen—it is too clear—but Agamemnon's retreat is, and she tells him because Zeus wants Hector to attack at the proper time. Zeus sends an eagle winging across the sky to reassure Priam he will not be harmed on his way to Achilles' tent. You decide what the god is trying to say, and to whom, and then make the message just clear enough to offer hope or a possible course of action, but vague enough the PCs can easily misinterpret it.

FORM

The third question with an omen is its form. Omens come in three varieties: dreams, signs, and events.

TABLE 14-6: OMEN RECOGNITION MODIFIERS

Feature	Modifier
Only normal creatures	−2
Creatures with unnatural coloring	+1
Supernatural creatures	+2
Only normal events or weather	−2
Weather that does not fit the area	+1
Unnatural weather (blood rain, etc.)	+2
Drastic change in conditions (clear skies to storm clouds)	+1
Localized change in weather or light	+1
Divine magic (snakes turn to stone, etc.)	+3
The omen is invisible to everyone else	+3
A dead or absent friend appears	+2

Dreams are exactly that. They occur when a character is sleeping, and anything can happen in them. The sleeping character either speaks to someone else, who tells them something important, or they see a sign or event. When they wake up, they remember the dream perfectly. This is the easiest way to know when a dream is really an omen, as most people can normally only remember bits of their dreams. Gods often appear to people in dreams, either in their own form or in the guise of someone the dreamer knows and trusts. Dreams are always private—a god might appear to each member of a group in dreams, but each dream will be different with the god saying different things to each dreamer.

Signs are static images. A tree shattered by lightning and now standing split is a sign—it is not active, but its very appearance means something important. Signs can be as small as a chipped tooth or a torn hem and as large as a perfectly flat sea or a cloudless sky. They are technically public, since anyone can see them, but often the intended recipient will notice it. Signs can also be mundane in appearance, again like the split tree, or clearly supernatural, like the sea becoming still from horizon to horizon.

Events are active. Lightning striking a tree is an event because the tree is not the whole message—the fact it was struck is the real omen. An eagle attacking a dove is an event, as was the snake devouring the sparrows. Events are always public, and several people usually see them. Some events are unnatural, but most involve natural elements and could mean very little— eagles attack doves whenever possible, and birds are a favorite food of most carnivorous snakes.

Some gods favor dreams for their messages. Others prefer signs, while others like events. Each god is different. Zeus favors events, for example—he is too domineering to use static messages, and enjoys showing his power by making the lightning flash and the clouds roll across the sky. Athena is more subtle, preferring her messages reach only their intended recipient. Hera is a master of deception and diplomacy; she frequently uses dreams. Ares is too blunt to try anything but violent events. In other words, the form of an omen should fit the god's personality and his spheres of influence.

RECOGNITION

Once an omen appears, will people recognize it? Some omens are clearly signs for the gods—the clouds do not normally rain blood upon the field. Others, like a choppy sea or a lone eagle, could be normal events. How do the characters tell whether something is an omen?

Honestly, they cannot. They can make a good guess, but without a god standing nearby or a clear supernatural element to the event, they could always be mistaken. That is the beauty of omens; they are subtle things, and people who look for them too actively will find them everywhere, while those who do not look will never see them at all.

Have characters attempt a Decipher Omen check, or if they lack that skill a Wisdom check, when an omen appears. If they succeed, they recognize it as an omen. If they fail, they think it merely a normal event. Consult **Table 14-6** for modifiers:

Keep in mind noticing an omen is not the same thing as reading it. When the sky turns blood red and rains blood, everyone in both armies knows this is a sign from Zeus. Most of them have no idea what it means.

READERS

Who can read omens? Seers are expert omen readers; they receive divine guidance from the entire pantheon and can find concrete information in even the vaguest sign. Oracles answer only to Apollo, the god of prophecy, and can interpret his or Zeus' omens with ease, but have trouble translating signs from other gods. Priests are also experts at interpretation, though their knowledge is more general. They can pinpoint the omen's creator more easily, but may only get a general idea of its meaning. Nobles also have some gift for interpretation, as do dedicated warriors and divine offspring. Anyone with any connection to the gods can see the signs and try to interpret them. When an omen appears in public, everyone who can read it usually does, so conflicting translations often occur.

One thing to remember about omens, too, is that they may apply to many events. If nine men did die on the trip to Troy, someone could claim that the snake and the sparrows had presaged that, and the evidence would support the statement.

If characters need omens interpreted, their best source would be a seer. If a seer cannot be located, a priest of the particular god may be of assistance. Dedicated warriors of that god are next in line, followed by priests, and then any character with ranks in the Decipher Omen skill. Individuals dedicated to a god whose rival sent the omen should not be asked, for their own god may deliberately give them a false interpretation just to foil their rival's plans.

Only people who have the Decipher Omen skill can interpret an omen. Others can guess, of course, but they have no real knowledge of the gods' will. Interpretation is difficult, and even experienced seers can be wrong if they miss some aspect of the omen, mistake its creator, or misjudge the god's mood.

USING OMENS

You should create a list of possible omens from each god involved in the war. If Ares never appears in your game, don't worry about omens from him. If he does take an interest, even if he just watches from Mount Olympus, you should have omens for him. Think about what the god might want to reveal to people. Ares, for example, might point out pivotal warriors in each army, encouraging other fighters to attack those men. He might also remind men of natural formations they could use for defense, or hint at weapons they could use to attack more efficiently. Then think about how he would convey these messages. Ares would use events, violent ones. His spheres are war, strength, and fire, so he might have flames licking over a field, or dogs attacking a deer, or stone outcroppings splitting as if struck by a heavy blade. Write down the omens you have for him, and keep the list handy. Then, whenever you think Ares might send someone information, you can use one of those omens. Never use the same omen twice, but you can change it slightly or keep the general idea. Ares might have several rocks split by invisible blades, but one reveals a hidden cave, while another creates a marker pointing toward an old weapons cache. Having the list allows you to insert an omen at any time from any god involved.

When should you use omens? Obviously, you could insert them whenever the characters are at a loss and do not know what to do. After all, the gods send signs to keep their favorites focused. The gods also counter plans they do not like. If the characters are dead-set on going one way, and one of the gods wants them to fail, send them an omen suggesting they turn around. When they stop to debate what they should do, send them an omen encouraging a specific course of action.

Use omens sparingly, however. If the gods send signs every few minutes, the characters never have to think for themselves; they just have to follow these divine markers all the way home. The gods want worshippers to work for their reward, and they only send omens when they feel it necessary.

Once an omen appears, do not offer any clarification. Describe it clearly but without adjectives or adverbs because those can reveal the omen's true meaning. If you say "a black snake devours a small red bird, and turns to stone," the characters have to figure out the meaning on their own. If, instead, you say "a hideous

black snake angrily devours a small, handsome red bird, but then the monstrous viper is transformed into cold gray stone," you're revealing too much. Now the players know that the snake is evil and the bird good, and the petrification is punishment for the snake's earlier victory. They no longer have to interpret the omen, as you have given them most of the information already. Instead, leave it open for them. The snake could be heroic and sacrificing itself by removing the villainous bird. It could be saving other nearby birds by accepting the stone onto itself, so only one bird has to die at all. By only relaying the bare details, you give the players more room to maneuver and their characters less obvious clues. Do not answer any questions about the omen, either. If the players ask you if the snake seemed evil, just shrug or tell them that the ways of the gods are mysterious to mortal men. Let them figure things out for themselves. This also means they have more room for error, but in the Homeric world people often misinterpret omens.

BUILDING A HOMERIC ADVENTURE

The easiest way to create an adventure during the Trojan War is to set it up as part of the war itself. Though the armies fought for nine years, we only see a few days of the conflict. That leaves a lot of room to maneuver.

Remember, too, the battlefield does not have to be the entire setting for your game. The city of Troy is large and strong, and we catch only a glimpse of it in the *Iliad*. You can set a variety of stories in there and never touch the fighting occurring outside. We see the Achaean camp only when the commanders are back for the evening, but secondary forces could be resting there during the day, and political stories could easily occur between various

kingdoms and their leaders. The area around the battlefield is also open for use. Hills could hold scouting or raiding parties for either side, or for both, approaching allies, and Trojan villagers who refuse to leave their homes. All manner of monsters or other creatures could also hide in the mountains, beings the Trojans know not to disturb but the Achaeans have never encountered. While the war should play a major role in your story, it does not have to be the focus. It could be the backdrop instead, providing the reason for the characters to be in the area.

The gods, however, always play a role in the story. Previous sections described the levels of divine involvement you can

of finding a passage that leads into the hills. What really lurks beneath the walls of Ilium? What destroyed that original city?

STRIKE FROM THE SEA

The characters sail a Trojan bireme and spent their time trading with other nations. They return to find their city under attack and the Achaeans occupying the peninsula. Now they have to decide what to do. Should they leave, gather allies, and return with a fleet that can attack the Achaeans from behind? Should they attack on their own, in the hopes of destroying the Achaean boats? Should they look for some other place to beach their own boat and find a way to sneak into the city to join their family and friends?

HILL BLOCKADE

The Achaeans pin the Trojans within their city, but they have allies in the kingdoms on either side, and those allies try to send in reinforcements. The Achaeans need to cut them off, so the leaders send the characters into the hills to prevent the allies from reaching Troy. Can they really stop an approaching army all by themselves?

DELPHIC ORACLE

The war has dragged on for years, showing no sign of an end. The Achaean commanders start to wonder if they have offended the gods. They send the characters to the Oracle at Delphi to make sure they are doing everything they can to win. It is a long, perilous journey back to Delphi, and the Achaean fleet left a lot of enemies in its wake.

SURPRISING RESISTANCE

The characters command of a group of boats, and conduct raids along the coast. Most of the settlements fall quickly, but one offers surprising resistance. How can such a small, plain-looking town withstand the might of the Achaean army? What secrets does the town hold? And can the characters use that secret to give their army an advantage against Troy?

RETRIEVING THE MAN-GOD

The gods often father divine offspring. One of these, a child of Zeus and a wood nymph, lives in the hills near Troy. The Trojans know this being only as the Man-God, and villagers offer him food and wine to appease him and to keep him from destroying their homes. What if he joined the war, fighting for the Trojans? His size and strength are legendary, and he is said to be even greater than Achilles. So the characters venture into the hills to locate this elusive being, make peace with him, to convince him to accompany them back to Troy.

CAPTURE THE PALLADIUM

According to the seers, the Achaeans cannot conquer Troy as long as the Palladium stands within its walls. Odysseus sends the characters into the city to capture the artifact and carry it back to the Achaean camp. But how are they supposed to sneak into a walled city, find this religious icon, steal it, and carry it across the plain without being noticed by Trojan guards or even normal Trojan citizens?

use. Think about which gods might be watching, why, and what they want from the characters. Has a god stashed his monstrous child in the hills? If so, will he throw obstacles at the characters if they get too close? Has he decided that his child is too great a danger, and does he send the characters to finish him?

Remember Homeric characters seek fame, fortune, or divine approval. Whatever you set up for your adventure, it should offer one of those possibilities for the characters. Just having the characters wander the hills will not work because they cannot win respect from men or gods for such minor actions, but if monsters lurk in the hills, or the Trojans have allies trying to sneak onto the field, or wealthy Trojan merchants try to escape to a neighboring nation, the characters have incentive to act. They will want to get involved because doing so gives them a chance to prove their worth and their Piety, and it gives them a chance to win acclaim and wealth in the process.

Here are a few adventure suggestions. Each is brief, but you can flesh out these ideas to create stories. You can have them running behind other events, giving the world more depth. Even if you decide not to use any of these, they should give you an idea of the possibilities for gaming in this setting.

INTO THE CATACOMBS

Priam worries about his citizens, and wants a way to get his people to safety if the Achaeans overrun Troy. He reveals to the characters that the city was built upon the ruins of an earlier city, whose origins are lost in the past. Then he sends the characters to explore those ruins deep beneath the current city, in the hopes

APPENDIX: REFERENCE TABLES

TABLE 4-1: NEW SKILLS

Skill	Bbn	Brd	Cht	Ddw	Drd	Ftr	Mag	Pri	Rgr	Rog	Sor
Boat	C	C	cc	cc	C	cc	cc	cc	C	cc	cc
Decipher Omen	C	C	cc	C	C	cc	cc	C	cc	cc	C
Drive	cc	cc	C	C	cc	C	cc	cc	cc	C	cc
Knowledge (tactics)	cc	C	C	C	cc	C	C	C	C	cc	cc

TABLE 4-2: FEATS

Feat	Prerequisites
Battlefield Seasoned	—
Chariot Attack[1]	Str 13, Dex 15, Drive 6 ranks
Chariot Shield[1]	Dex 13, Drive 4 ranks
Chariot Specialization[1]	Drive 6 ranks
Distinctive	Cha 15
Divine Sight	Wis 13, Sense Motive 2 ranks
Drive-by Attack[1]	Drive 4 ranks
Elusive	Hide 12 ranks
Favored	Must have a chosen god
Fierce	—
Lion of the Field	Base attack bonus +3
Noble	—
Pampered	Must have a chosen god
Pious	Piety 10, chosen god
Piteous	
Quick Release[1]	Dex 17, Base attack bonus +6
Shield Swing	Str 13, shield proficiency
Step back	Dex 13, Base attack bonus +4
Stunning	Divine offspring, Cha 17
Thick skin	—
Unfazed	Iron Will
Valuable	Noble
Metamagic Feat	
Battlefield Magic	—
Targeted	Ability to cast 3rd-level spells

[1] A fighter may select this feat as one of his fighter bonus feats.

TABLE 6-1: BARTER BLUFF CHECKS

Item Availability	Example	DC
Abundant	Everybody has one	30
Plentiful	All but the poorest have one	25
Common	Available in most markets	20
Uncommon	Few dealers have one	15
Scarce	Nearly impossible to find	10

TABLE 6-2: APPRAISE CHECKS

Scarcity	DC
Abundant	12
Plentiful	14
Common	16
Uncommon	18
Scarce	20

TABLE 6-3: WEAPONS

	Cost	Dmg (S)	Dmg (M)	Critical	Range Increment	Weight[1]	Type
Simple Weapons							
Unarmed Attacks							
Unarmed Strike	—	1d2[2]	1d3[2]	x2	—	—	Bludgeoning
Light Melee Weapons							
Dagger	2 gp	1d3	1d4	19–20/x2	10 ft.	1 lb.	Piercing or slashing
Mace, light	5 gp	1d4	1d6	x2	—	4 lb.	Bludgeoning
Sickle	6 gp	1d4	1d6	x2	—	2 lb.	Slashing
One-Handed Melee Weapons							
Club	—	1d4	1d6	x2	10 ft.	3 lb.	Bludgeoning
Mace, heavy	12 gp	1d6	1d8	x2	—	8 lb.	Bludgeoning
Two-Handed Melee Weapons							
Quarterstaff[3]	—	1d4/1d4	1d6/1d6	x2	—	4 lb.	Bludgeoning
Ranged Weapons							
Sling	—	1d3	1d4	x2	50 ft.	0 lb.	Bludgeoning
Bullets, sling (10)	1 sp	—	—	—	—	5 lb.	
Martial Weapons							
Light Melee Weapons							
Axe, throwing	8 gp	1d4	1d6	x2	10 ft.	2 lb.	Slashing
Shield, any	Special	1d2	1d3	x2	—	Special	Bludgeoning
Sword, short	10 gp	1d4	1d6	19–20/x2	—	2 lb.	Piercing
One-Handed Melee Weapons							
Throwing spear	2 gp	1d6	1d8	x2	40 ft.	4 lb.	Piercing
Battleaxe	10 gp	1d6	1d8	x3	—	6 lb.	Slashing
Longsword	15 gp	1d6	1d8	19–20/x2	—	4 lb.	Slashing
Trident	15 gp	1d6	1d8	x2	10 ft.	4 lb.	Piercing
Warhammer	3 sp	1d6	1d8	x3	—	5 lb.	Bludgeoning
Two-Handed Melee Weapons							
Footman's Spear[4]	5 gp	1d6	1d8	x3	20 ft.	6 lb.	Piercing
Greatsword	50 gp	1d10	2d6	19–20	—	8 lb.	Slashing
Ranged Weapons							
Longbow	75 gp	1d6	1d8	x3	100 ft.	3 lb.	Piercing
Arrows (20)	1 gp	—	—	—	—	3 lb.	
Longbow, composite	100 gp	1d6	1d8	x3	110 ft.	3 lb.	Piercing
Arrows (20)	1 gp	—	—	—	—	3 lb.	—
Shortbow	30 gp	1d4	1d6	x3	60 ft.	2 lb.	Piercing
Arrows (20)	1 gp	—	—	—	—	1 lb.	—
Shortbow, composite	15 gp	1d4	1d6	x3	70 ft.	2 lb.	Piercing
Arrows (20)	1 sp	—	—	—	—	1 lb.	

[1] Weight figures are for Medium creatures. A Small weapon weighs half as much.
[2] This weapon deals nonlethal damage [3] Double weapon [4] Reach weapon

TABLE 6-4: ARMOR AND SHIELDS

Armor	Cost	Armor/Shield Bonus	Maximum Dex Bonus	Armor Check Penalty	—Speed— (30 ft.)	(20 ft.)	Weight
Belt	2 gp	+1	—	0	30 ft.	20 ft.	1 lb.
Cuirass							
Linen	10 gp	+1	−2	0	30 ft.	20 ft.	5 lb.
Canvas	10 gp	+1	−2	0	30 ft.	20 ft.	8 lb.
Leather	20 gp	+2	−3	−1	30 ft.	20 ft.	10 lb.
Tin	100 gp	+2	−3	−1	30 ft.	20 ft.	15 lb.
Bronze	150 gp	+3	−3	−1	20 ft.	15 ft.	15 lb.
Greaves							
Linen	8 sp	+1	—	0	30 ft.	20 ft.	1 lb.
Canvas	5 sp	+1	—	0	30 ft.	20 ft.	1 lb.
Leather	1 gp	+1	—	0	30 ft.	20 ft.	3 lb.
Tin	10 gp	+2	—	0	30 ft.	20 ft.	5 lb.
Bronze	20 gp	+2	—	0	30 ft.	20 ft.	5 lb.
Helmet							
Cap	5 sp	+1	—	0	30 ft.	20 ft.	1 lb.
Leather	2 gp	+1	—	0	30 ft.	20 ft.	3 lb.
Bronze	10 gp	+2	—	0	30 ft.	20 ft.	5 lb.
Peturgis							
Linen	8 sp	+1	—	0	30 ft.	20 ft.	1 lb.
Canvas	5 sp	+1	—	0	30 ft.	20 ft.	1 lb.
Leather	1 gp	+1	—	0	30 ft.	20 ft.	3 lb.
Leather Strips	2 gp	+1	—	0	30 ft.	20 ft.	2 lb.
Crescent Shields							
Leather	7 gp	+1	—	−3	30 ft.	20 ft.	15 lb.
Bronze	20 gp	+2	—	−3	30 ft.	20 ft.	20 lb.
Dyplon Shields							
Leather	10 gp	+1	—	−2	30 ft.	20 ft.	15 lb.
Bronze	30 gp	+2	—	−3	30 ft.	20 ft.	20 lb.
Round Shields							
Leather	7 gp	+1	—	−5	25 ft.	20 ft.	10 lb.
Bronze	20 gp	+2	—	−5	25 ft.	20 ft.	15 lb.
Tower Shields							
Leather	10 gp	+2	—	−10	20 ft.	15 ft.	20 lb.
Bronze	30 gp	+3	—	−10	20 ft.	15 ft.	45 lb.

ARMOR PROPERTIES

Armor Property	Cost Modifier
Breathable	x2 total price
Burnished	+200 gp
Chased	x2 total price
Doubled	x2 total price
Fitted	x2 total price

TABLE 6-5: GOODS

Item	Cost	Weight	Item	Cost	Weight
Backpack (empty)	2 gp	2 lb.	Loincloth	1 cp	*
Barrel (empty)	2 gp	30 lb.	Mug		
Basket (empty)	4 cp	1 lb.	Leather	4 cp	1 lb.
Bedroll	1 sp	5 lb.	Wooden	2 cp	1 lb.
Blanket, winter	5 sp	3 lb.	Stone	2 cp	2 lb.
Bowl, mixing			Pitcher, clay	2 cp	5 lb.
Wood	5 cp	1 lb.	Platter		
Silver	25 gp	1 lb.	Wood	3 cp	2 lb.
Gold	250 gp	2 lb.	Silver	10 sp	4 lb.
Bucket (empty)	5 sp	2 lb.	Gold	40 gp	10 lb.
Candle	1 cp	*	Pot, iron	5 sp	10 lb.
Canvas (sq. yd.)	1 sp	1 lb.	Pouch, belt	1 sp	3 lb.
Cauldron			Robe		
Copper	1 gp	10 lb.	Simple	1 sp	10 lb.
Bronze	10 gp	10 lb.	Formal	5 sp	10 lb.
Iron	5 gp	20 lb.	Expensive	15 gp	12 lb.
Chair, backless			Clasped	20 gp	14 lb.
Wooden	1 sp	4 lb.	Rope, hemp (50 ft.)	1 sp	10 lb.
Bronze	6 gp	6 lb.	Sack (empty)	1 cp	1/2 lb.
Gold	250 gp	10 lb.	Shift	1 cp	1 lb.
Chair, backed			Stool, folding	3 sp	2 lb.
Wooden	3 sp	8 lb.	Table		
Bronze	15 gp	10 lb.	Large	4 cp	40 lb.
Gold	300 gp	18 lb.	Small, plain	3 cp	10 lb.
Chest (empty)	8 sp	15 lb.	Small, fancy	9 sp	12 lb.
Fishhook	1 cp	*	Tent	1 gp	20 lb.
Fishing net, 25 sq. ft.	4 sp	5 lb.	Thread, colored	varies	*
Footstool			Torch	1 cp	1 lb.
Wood	2 cp	1 lb.	Tripod		
Stone	5 cp	4 lb.	Copper	2 sp	5 lb.
Bronze	2 gp	2 lb.	Bronze	5 gp	5 lb.
Gold	60 gp	4 lb.	Iron	3 sp	10 lb.
Goblet			Tunic		
Bronze	2 gp	2 lb.	Plain	3 cp	1 lb.
Silver	6 gp	2 lb.	Formal	2 sp	2 lb.
Gold	18 gp	3 lb.	Expensive	5 gp	3 lb.
Jug, clay	3 cp	9 lb.	Waterskin	4 cp	4 lb.
Kilt	1 cp	1 lb.	Whetstone	1 cp	1 lb.

TABLE 6-6: DYES

Dye	Source	Cost per 1 oz. vial
Black	Ground coal or burnt wood	10 gp
Light green (sap green)	Crushed parsley, grass, and leaves	10 gp
Yellow-green	Crushed seeds and grass	10 gp
Dull yellow	Iron oxide	10 gp
Brown	Peat	10 gp
Dark green	Plant sap	15 gp
Blue-green	Verdigris	25 gp
Bright yellow	Ground sulfur	25 gp
Rose red	Crushed madder root	25 gp
Rust red	Iron powder	25 gp
Carmine	Crushed insects	30 gp
Orange	Crushed red worms ("bloodworms")	35 gp
Indigo Blue	Indigo shrub	35 gp
Sky blue	Ground snails	40 gp
Bright blue (Egyptian blue)	Ground snails	50 gp
Tyrian purple	Crushed sea-snails	100 gp

TABLE 7-1: TROOP STATS

Quality	Hit Point Multiplier	Base Attack Bonus	Base Morale	Damage Multiplier	Feats
Green	x1	+0	–3	x2	2
Trained	x2	+2	+0	x3	4
Veteran	x5	+5	+3	x4	6
Legendary	x8	+8	+6	x5	8

TABLE 7-2: SPELL EFFECTS

Spell	Effect
"Mass" spell	Affects entire Force as written
Any *death* spell or *power word kill*	2 points damage/caster level
Instantaneous damage spell (*e.g., fireball*)	1/10 damage to a Force
Charm effect, 20 ft + radius	Morale check or Damage Multiplier reduced by –1
Courage effect, 20 ft.+ radius	Bonus on all Morale checks
Curse effect, 20 ft.+ radius	Penalty to Armor Class
Deafen effect, 20 ft.+ radius	Morale check or negate maneuver
Enervation/poison effect, 20 ft.+ radius	Penalty to damage roll
*Entangle/*paralysis effect, 20 ft.+ radius	Morale check or penalty to attack bonus
Fear effect, 20 ft.+ radius	Morale check or rout
Fly	+2 Armor Class bonus to target vs. ground-based opponents
Haste	+2 to Force's initiative checks
Illusion effect, 20 ft.+ radius	
Demoralizing illusion (*e.g.*, show many people dying)	Morale check or rout
Reposition Illusion (*e.g.*, enemy is somewhere they're not)	Penalty to attack bonus
Summon illusory opponent	Morale check or lose next attack
Invisibility	+2 Armor Class bonus
Invisibility, 20 ft.+ radius	bonus to Force Armor Class, bonus to base damage
Silence, 20 ft.+ radius	Morale check or negate maneuver
Sleep effect, 20 ft.+ radius	Morale check or penalty to attack bonus
Slow, 20 ft.+ radius	–2 to a Force's initiative checks
Stun effects, 20 ft.+ radius	Morale check or lose next attack
Wall of force/iron/etc.	
positioned to isolate a commander	Reflex save or Captain is isolated until barrier is gone
positioned to block charge, missile hurling	Negate maneuver
positioned as a general barrier	Penalty to Force's attack bonus

Spell Type	Morale Check Penalties
Spell is 1st-2nd level	–0 to enemy Morale check
Spell is 3rd-4th level	–2 to enemy Morale check
Spell is 5th-6th level	–4 to enemy Morale check
Spell is 7th-8th level	–6 to enemy Morale check
Spell is 9th+ level	–8 to enemy Morale check
Power word	–1 additional Morale

Bonus/Penalty: If a spell gives a bonus or penalty to one or more of a Force's statistics, a 1st-2nd-level spell gives a +/-1 bonus/penalty, 3rd-4th-level spells give +/-2, 5th-6th level spells give +/-3, 7th-8th-level spells give +/-4, and 9th (or higher) level spells give +/-5. If the effect comes from a supernatural or spell-like ability that does not have an equivalent spell, divide the caster's Hit Dice by 2 to get the equivalent spell level. If a spell affects multiple statistics, split the bonus or penalty between the statistics; *e.g.*, a 9th-level spell could adjust five statistics by +/-1 each, or one by +/-5.

Negate Maneuver: This means that no battlefield maneuver may be deployed that round.

TABLE 7-3: BATTLEFIELD FEATS

QUALITIES

Allied Force
Battlefield Dominance
Battle-hardened
Chariots
Coordinated Defense
DeftAttack
Desperate
Enflamed
Faith
Fleet of Foot
Hardy
Heroic Might
Human Shield

Independent
Interlocking Shields
Left-Handed
Ring of Bronze
Shield Bearers
Target Captain
Unshakable
Wary
Weapons of Renown
Well-armed

MANEUVERS

Blinding Speed
Call for Aid
Charge

Divide and Conquer
Emboldening Speech
Envelop
Ferocious Attack
Fight Cautiously
Hostage
Hurl Missiles
Pronged Attack
Set Spears

SPECIAL

Disquieting Yell
Heroic Stand
Loose Formation

TABLE 8-2: HOMERIC OBSERVANCES

Observance	Piety Points Earned	Observance	Piety Points Earned
Pouring libations to the character's favored god	1	Building a temple to each of the gods	8
Pouring libations to all the gods	2	Building/dedicating a boat to a favored god	10
Sacrificing a heifer to a favored god	3	Building/dedicating a boat to all the gods	8
Sacrificing heifers to all the gods	6	Building/dedicating a city to a favored god	15
Sacrificing a hecatomb to a favored god	4	Building/dedicating a city to all the gods	10
Sacrificing a hecatomb to each of the gods	8	Burning barley as an offering to a favored god	2
Offering thighmeat to a god before a meal	2	Burning barley as an offering to all the gods	4
Offering thighmeat to each of the gods before a meal	4	Treating a guest well	4
Sacrificing a maiden to a favored god	10	Treating a stranger well	2
Sacrificing a youth to a favored god	10	Treating a beggar well	3
Dedicating a military victory to a favored god	15	Giving rich gifts to a guest	1
		Showing mercy to a foe	1
Dedicating a military victory to all the gods	5	Showing respect to a priest	2
Dedicating an individual combat to a favored god	10	Showing respect to a commander or king	1
		Obeying a priest	2
Building a shrine to a favored god	10	Offering a priest protection	4
Building a shrine to all the gods	5	Observing a god's holy day	1
Building a temple for a favored god	12	Attacking a god's enemies	2
		Sparing a creature or plant sacred to a god	3

TABLE 8-1: DIVINATION AS A PIETY BOON

Piety	Maximum Spell Level
1	0
4	1st
8	2nd
12	3rd
16	4th
20	5th*

*The highest level divination that can be achieved from a Piety boon.

TABLE 8-3: HOMERIC SINS

Sinful Offense	Piety	Punishment
Insulting a guest	-6	Severe contempt
Insulting a beggar	-2	Contempt
Insulting your host	-4	Severe contempt
Insulting a priest	-5	Contempt, Divine displeasure
Insulting a priest of your favored god	-8	Contempt, Divine displeasure
Killling a priest	-15	Ostracism, Divine displeasure
Killing a guest	-10	Ostracism
Killing a stranger for no reason	-10	Ostracism
Killing a beggar	-8	Public lashing, severe contempt
Breaking your word	-8	Severe contempt
Offering libations to all the gods, but missing one	-4	Divine displeasure
Offering sacrifices to all the gods, but missing one	-6	Divine displeasure
Offering barley to all the gods, but missing one	-2	Divine displeasure
Comparing yourself to a god	-5	Divine displeasure
Claiming you are better than a god	-10	Divine displeasure
Claiming you are better than a god at that god's best feature or ability	-15	Divine displeasure
Turning away a beggar	-2	Contempt
Not performing proper rites for the dead	-4	Contempt
Killing a divine offspring	-1	Divine displeasure
Murder	-5	Ostracism
Murder of king	-10	Death
Theft	-3	Fine and recompense, contempt
Theft from a temple or shrine	-10	Fine and recompense, severe contempt, divine displeasure
Vandalizing a temple or shrine	-15	Ostracism, divine displeasure
Lying	-1	Contempt
Military desertion	-3	Public lashing, severe contempt
Failing to wash hands before making an offering	-1	Contempt
Failing to bathe before performing a religious rite	-2	Contempt

TABLE 14-2: BOON REQUEST SEVERITY

Severity	Modifier
Negligible (provide wine, remove rain, etc.)	–3
Minor (provide better food, aid, sleep)	–2
Useful (send animals for the men to hunt or show a path through wilderness)	+0
Important (provide food for a starving character, reveal the way out of a maze)	+0
Emergency (save the character from immediate attack)	+1
Major (save a ship's crew from drowning, shield a man from enemy troops)	+0
Severe (sink a ship, drown a family, destroy several warriors)	–2
Extreme (sink a fleet, drown a town, destroy an army)	–3

TABLE 14-3: BOON REQUEST RESULT

Roll	Result
1	The god is infuriated, and he strikes the character with divine displeasure
2	The god is displeased, and he drops the character's Piety score to -1
3-5	The god is annoyed, and he drops character's Piety score to 0
6-10	The god grudgingly grants the request; subtract 2 from the character's next roll on the Boon Request table
11-15	The god grants the request without thought to the requestor
16-18	The god pleasantly grants the request; add 2 to the character's next roll on the Boon Request table
19	The god happily grants the request and allows the character to retain half his current Piety points
20	The god is thrilled to grant the request and allows the character retains all his current Piety points

TABLE 14-4: DIVINE DISPLEASURE MODIFIERS

Situation	Modifier
Negative Piety points	Piety modifier (half Piety score)
Dedicated a victory to the god and lost	–3
Promised to dedicate a town, but failed to build it	–4
Promised the god a temple, but did not deliver	–5
Insulted a priest	–1
Insulted a priest of his own god	–2
Killed a priest	–4
Killed a priest of his own god	–8
Broke his word	–1
Stole from the god's shrine	–5
Defiled the god's shrine	–10
Asked for too small a boon	–2
Asked for too great a boon	–1
Forgot to offer the god libations	–1
Forgot the god when offering libations	–2
Forgot the god when offering barley	–1
Forgot to offer the god a sacrifice	–2
Forgot the god when offering sacrifices	–4
Killed one of the god's children	–2
Approached the god when irritable	–1
Approached the god when angry	–2
Approached the god while enraged	–3

TABLE 14-1: DIVINE MOOD

Roll	Mood	Modifier
1	Enraged	–3
2	Angry	–2
3-5	Irritable	–1
6-10	Bored	0
11-15	Calm	0
16-18	Content	+1
19	Cheerful	+2
20	Jubilant	+3

TABLE 14-6: OMEN RECOGNITION MODIFIERS

Feature	Modifier
Only normal creatures	–2
Creatures with unnatural coloring	+1
Supernatural creatures	+2
Only normal events or weather	–2
Weather that does not fit the area	+1
Unnatural weather (blood rain, etc.)	+2
Drastic change in conditions (clear skies to storm clouds)	+1
Localized change in weather or light	+1
Divine magic (snakes turn to stone, etc.)	+3
The omen is invisible to everyone else	+3
A dead or absent friend appears	+2

TABLE 14-5: DIVINE DISPLEASURE RESULTS

Total	Degree of Displeasure	Target	Duration
1-2	Negligible	Individual	one month
3-4	Mild	Immediate family	one month
5-6	Slight	Extended family	one month
7-8	Minor	Town or city	one month
9-10	Noticeable	Nation	one month
11-12	Targeted	Individual	one year
13-14	Lasting	Immediate family	one year
15-16	Focused	Extended family	one year
17-18	Moderate	Town or city	one year
19-20	Widespread	Nation	one year
21-25	Powerful	Individual	one decade
26-29	Notable	Immediate family	one decade
30	Sincere	Extended family	one decade
31-35	Strong	Town or city	one decade
36-39	Serious	Nation	one decade
40	Lethal	Individual	death
41-45	Grave	Immediate family	death
46-49	Severe	Extended family	destruction
50-54	Intense	Town or city	ruin
55+	Extreme	Nation	obliteration

INDEX

YOU'VE READ THE BOOK, NOW PLAY THE GAME!

There were giants in the Earth in those days, and also after that, when the sons of God came in onto the daughters of men and they bare children to them, the same became mighty men which were of old, men of renown.

—The Book of Genesis

The world of the Bible comes to life in this campaign setting for the d20 System. Play a wandering Babylonian magus, a sorcerer in the service of Pharaoh, a Canaanite maker of idols, or a prophet of the God of Israel. Walk the streets of ancient Jerusalem, stand beside King David as one of his Mighty Men, smite Philistines, ponder the mysteries of gargantuan tombs, look upon the dwellings of the gods, and battle demons, dragons, plagues, and the legendary beasts of Babylon. Testament gives you everything you need to immerse yourself in the Biblical Era, including:

- A dozen new core and prestige classes, including the Levite Priest, the Egyptian Khery-heb wizard, and the Desert Hermit.

- Over 30 new monsters, including Nephilim, Tempter Devils, and Zebub-Spawn.

- Over 50 new feats and over 100 new spells.

- Rules for barter, curses, piety.

- Guidelines for leading a small tribe through the hazards of the Bronze and Iron Age world.

- The Biblical Battlefield Resolution System, a new way to fight epic combats.

- Full cultural details on ancient Israel, Canaan, Egypt, and Mesopotamia, including history, beliefs, holy days, architecture, and more.

- Dozens of new magic items and artifacts.

Part history, part mythology, Testament is the d20 System setting that's both instantly familiar and yet unlike any game world you have ever experienced.

Testament: Roleplaying in the Biblical Era

A Mythic Vistas Campaign Setting
for the d20 System

Written by Scott Bennie

Cover by Sam Wood

240 pages, perfect bound

MSRP: $32.95

GRR1019

ISBN: 0-9726756-2-0

Dragon®

your source for the newest:
Spells & Feats,
Magic Items & Monsters,
Prestige Core Classes.

Dungeon®

your best source for:
Adventures,
Full-Color Maps,
d20 News.
The publications that give you
everything you need for the
best D&D gaming.

Undefeated™

Every issue is loaded with:
Strategies and tactics
for the miniature
games, card games, and
board games you love
to play,
Tons of product reviews,
Exclusive previews.
Undefeated™ is the only
magazine all about "games
you can win."